THE MAGICAL HISTORY OF BRITAIN

Also by Martin Wall

The Anglo-Saxon Age: The Birth of England
The Anglo-Saxons in 100 Facts
Warriors and Kings: The 1500-Year Battle for Celtic Britain

THE MAGICAL HISTORY OF BRITAIN

MARTIN WALL

AMBERLEY

For the Goddess

First published 2019

Amberley Publishing
The Hill, Stroud
Gloucestershire, GL5 4EP

www.amberley-books.com

British Library Cataloguing in Publication Data.
A catalogue record for this book is available from the British Library.

ISBN 978-1-4456-7708-8 (hardback)
ISBN 978-1-4456-7709-5 (ebook)

Origination by Amberley Publishing.
Printed in the UK.

Contents

Introduction

I think it is possible to identify an actual point in time when a sudden unbidden introjection of what the psychologist C. G. Jung called a 'hidden sub-stratum in the human consciousness' or 'synchronicity' made me unusually aware of the powerful archetypes deep in the imagination. One evening, alone in my lodgings and bored, I looked for something to read, but pretty much everything on the shelf had been read before or was of little interest. Then my eye was caught by the bulky tome *The Golden Bough: A Study in Magic and Religion* by the eminent scholar J. G. Frazer. I had dipped into this as a reference book but had never read it cover to cover. This seemed a worthwhile effort, and so I read the very first chapter that evening, entitled 'The King of the Wood'. This 'king' was the threshold guardian of the sacred grove or sanctuary of the divinity called Diana Nemorensis, 'Diana of the Wood', by the little lake of Nemi, called 'Diana's Mirror', in the Alban Hills near Rome. The setting was beautiful, but the king's task was grim. I will let Frazer continue:

> In this sacred grove there grew a certain tree round which at any time of the day, and probably far into the night, a grim figure might be seen to prowl. In his hand he carried a drawn sword, and he kept peering warily about him as if at every instant he expected to be set upon by an enemy. He was a priest and a murderer; and the man for whom he looked was sooner or later to murder him and hold the priesthood in his stead. Such was the rule in the sanctuary. A candidate for the priesthood could only succeed to the office by slaying the priest, and having slain him, he retained office till he was himself slain by a stronger or a craftier.[1]

This eerie tale drew me in, and was designed to, for Frazer chose Nemi as the place to begin his exhaustive treatise with good reason. Diana, the huntress goddess, was worshipped at Nemi in vast torchlit processions at the very hottest time of the Italian year, and indeed a perpetual fire burned at the heart of the sanctuary to which initiates and candidates flocked at the festival

---

1   J. G. Frazer, *The Golden Bough: A Study in Magic and Religion*, Dover, 2003 edn.

of Nemoralia. During her festival the hunting of wild beasts was suspended and young couples were blessed that they might have fruitful offspring. At the very heart of the grove was a round temple within which burned the everlasting vestal flame. These rituals were almost unimaginably ancient, even in Roman times. The sacred tree that the 'King of the Wood' so zealously guarded was the physical embodiment of the goddess, according to Frazer, and he was destined to remain within its shade until his inevitable doom overcame him. That he was a 'king' seems a dubious honour, but honour it was, for goddesses were also considered royal, and as her consort he had become a priest-king. (This was the common arrangement in early times, and, as I hope to show, there are powerful reasons for the peculiar resilience of monarchy in Britain, in particular.) Diana was a vengeful deity. One young suitor, Actaeon, approached her and, enchanted by her beauty, confessed that she was the loveliest thing he had ever seen. Diana transformed him into a stag and had him torn to pieces by his own hunting hounds.

The day after I read this, I was looking after two young children for the school summer holidays. I had a well-tried routine worked out, and we headed to Nottingham Museum, to be followed by a journey down Mortimer's Hole beneath the former castle. Climbing the stairs, I noticed a sign for a new exhibition I had not seen before, so I stopped the children racing ahead for ice creams and we went in. The exhibition was a reconstruction of the *original* temple of Nemi, the very heart of the sanctuary, which an English gentleman had transported from Italy to England in the nineteenth century. It was eventually donated to the museum, where it had languished among other artefacts in store ever since – until now. Somewhat bewildered, I explained to the eldest child how, incredibly, I had been reading about just this 'place' only the previous evening, powerless to convey the uncanny significance this carried for me. She was interested in the goddess, and we studied the information board to learn more. My young companion pointed out another synchronicity. The Nemoralia had been celebrated on the 13 August, and that was the very day of our visit. In itself this concatenation of events has no 'meaning', but I admit I still recall the incident with a sort of reverence, which for me is personal. These things happen, of course, but what do they mean? Are they revelations, connections with an underground stream of consciousness of some sort – as the psychologist Jung suggested, a 'collective unconscious'?

I am not alone in remarking on the potential significance of such an encounter. One day in the early twentieth century a Herefordshire gentleman called Alfred Watkins, scion of a family of brewers, was riding his horse near Bredwardine when he reined in and gazed down at the broad sweep of country beneath him to see an astonishing sight. In an instant, he perceived a vast network of glowing lines stretching for miles straight in every direction. Overlooking the criss-crossing lines, he observed that they seemed to him to converge at junctions marked by ancient megaliths and beacon hills but also, curiously, at later holy sites like parish churches. This 'vision', he claimed, had come to him in a single moment, but he was convinced that it was no trick of the light or of his mind. Watkins followed up on his vision, and his subsequent theories about ley lines are not just hokum or self-delusion; he was no mere crank. In fact, magical-religious, mystical and Gnostic ideas have permeated the cultural evolution of these islands since time immemorial, and their legacy still exerts a powerful emotional pull on the majority of the population, whether they are conscious of it or not. The present author seeks only to gently assert that despite the dominance in the academies of tradition, documentation and archaeology – the orthodox tools of the historical scholar – there exists another, more puzzling story, of a world populated by gods and goddesses, wizards and dragons, seers and sages, prophets and necromancers. They are more real to us in many ways than genuine historical figures we think we know about, and they have influenced our 'real' history in ways of which many modern people are no longer aware. The following, then, is not 'history as we know it', but a skew-wise view, an 'alternative' history, as it were, a magical history of Britain. I simply invite the reader to become 'unstuck in time', like Kurt Vonnegut's Billy Pilgrim. Any resemblance to mainstream historical scholarship is purely coincidental.

There is a strange history of this behaviour in my home region. In the thirteenth century the Anglo-Saxon clerk Layamon retired to the banks of the River Severn to write a 16,000-line poetic history of Britain, his *Brut*. In 1944, as the Second World War raged, Francis Brett Young wrote *The Island*, another long poetic history of Britain, all the way from the Bronze Age to the 'Blitz'. So, I am not merely a maverick, and this book has its value and meaning. It is meant for those whom C. G. Jung called 'those "queer folk" who no longer set much store by the uses, aims, and meaning of present-day "civilisation"'.

1

What Is Magic?

The Ancient Greeks referred to a learned class of priests called *magos,* or *magush* or *magi* in Persian, from Rhages in Iran, one of the oldest inhabited cities in the world. *Magh*, the root word, probably derives from a Proto-Indo-European word signifying 'power', 'ability' in an uncanny sense (as in magnetism) or expansiveness (as in magnify), the ability to intensify, concentrate, increase. In short, they were people who worked marvels, who could practice sorcery, by evocation and invocation, foretell future events from astrological computations, make oracular pronouncements, and communicate with the deities sacred to the people. The magi were Zoroastrians, the religion founded by Zoroaster or Zarathustra about 1,000 years before Christ. The exact origins of Zoroastrianism are obscure but it is certainly among the most ancient of the world's religions, and esoteric traditions within it may contain truly primordial material.

The main function of the priesthood was to offer libations to rivers and mountains, but another sacred duty was to tend the sacred everlasting fire. An idea was involved, more sacred than it is possible for a modern mind to imagine. A common material like wood could, if the right action was applied, combust, providing warmth and cooked meat, the essential requirements of mankind in an ice age. Matter could be transmuted into energy. Perhaps a lightning strike provided a natural example, an act of God (or the gods). But we have to contend with the fact that one day *someone* kindled the very first fire, some individual, the pioneer of magic.

The ability of this person's heirs to seemingly bring about changes through supernatural means was what defined them wherever they were encountered, whether that be by the Greeks to the west, where *mageia* became a pejorative term meaning one who engaged in unholy nocturnal practices such as bodysnatching, or the Chinese to the east, in whose lands they have been found depicted using the ancient Chinese character *myag*, which symbolizes 'shaman', 'wizard' or 'witch', and which is an exact replica of the so-called 'cross potent' or 'crutch-cross' of the West. This was the ancient symbol of the magicians, and went on to become the emblem of the Cathars, the Knights Templar and the Teutonic Knights, among others. This sinister reputation has bedevilled the term 'magic' and anathematised the magicians ever since, but divination, astrological computation, interpretation of dreams and other theurgic practices were not confined to magi.

The Zoroastrians were dualists, meaning that they saw the cosmos in terms of a great war between good, represented by Ohrmazd, the 'good' God, and evil, represented by Ahriman, a sort of proto-Devil. The universe has been created as a cosmic battlefield upon which the struggle between these two is fought out. The ultimate enemy for the devotees of Ohrmazd was the 'Lie', by which they meant the gathered forces of the fiend Ahriman. Man is enjoined to enlist in the army of the 'good' God by renouncing his adversary, whose ultimate defeat is assured. As long as he has power over humankind, Ahriman is served by a retinue of demons who enslave the unwary through their vices; meanwhile, the Ohrmazd has a company of *yazatan*, or angels, beings who assist beleaguered men and women in the fight.

Zoroastrian dualism had a profound influence far beyond Iran. The Greeks, Jews, Chinese and Indians all absorbed Zoroastrian and magical ideas, and from the Judaic religion some of them were transmitted into emergent Christianity. Some of the above ideas, particularly the 'war in heaven' scenario, will be familiar to Christians, and of course the three magi who sought out Christ's nativity. Simon Magus, a Samaritan convert to Christianity, is mentioned in the New Testament (Acts 8: 9–24) as having confronted St Peter about the sin named in his honour – 'simony', the purchase of Church offices. A strange mythology grew up around this character, and later orthodox churchmen denounced him as the 'father of all heresies', an exponent of radical Free Love, and a patron of the recondite arts such as alchemy. He was said to have made pacts with the 'principalities and powers' so that he could pursue his eternal love for Helena, a woman who reincarnates through time, including as Helen of Troy. She is the divine female principle Sophia personified. Undoubtedly many of these stories were put about to discredit Gnostic Christians, but the mud stuck. Magic had a bad name.

What lay behind this suspicion and mistrust? The answer can be given now in broadly the same terms as put forward by the groundbreaking scholar Evelyn Underhill in her classic work *Mysticism: The Nature and Development of Spiritual Consciousness*, where she is at pains to distinguish the two disciplines of magic and mysticism in basic ethical terms:

> The fundamental difference between the two is this; magic wants to get, mysticism wants to give – immortal and antagonistic attitudes, which turn up in one guise or another in every age of thought ... in magic the will unites with the intellect in an impassioned desire for supersensible knowledge ... obviously the antithesis of mysticism, though often adopting its title and style.

Magic, for Underhill, incorporates all forms of 'self-seeking transcendentalism', and as a devout Anglo-Catholic of her time she abhorred the tendency to try to reduce God to a 'thing' to be analysed and understood, famously saying that 'if He were small enough to be understood, He would not be big enough to be worshipped'. Mysticism is the way of love, the abolition of the individual, a 'movement of the heart' which depends not upon intellectual acumen or scientific knowledge but pure, selfless desire to annihilate the personality in union with the divine, henosis. At its heart mysticism relies on pure emotional yearning, while magic relies upon knowledge and applied willpower. Therefore, magic is conceived to be ethically suspect, not merely because it is condemned by holy writ but because its objective is so superficial and petty when set beside the objective of the true mystic: 'Not to *know about*, but to *Be*, is the mark of the true initiate.' The respected magician W. G. Gray agreed, stating that 'magic is about doing, mysticism about being'. Magicians have been known to be notoriously unstable. Janine Chapman says:

> In the past, many of the people who thought of themselves as magicians were extraordinary personalities, marked by a mysterious sensitivity to supernatural forces and influences. Some were spiritually sincere, dedicated to the worship of their gods and to the teaching of their knowledge. But frequently the intensity of their visions caused violent fluctuations between mania and depression. Some had emotional and interpersonal problems. Some were arrogant, cruel, selfish and petty. For some, their efforts at helping others were inappropriate, even destructive. For others, their attempts to communicate their experiences were confused or indecipherable.[2]

These profound spiritual dangers – madness, psychic possession and the personal catastrophes which can follow from experimental magic – have always clung to the reputation of the occult arts. Nevertheless, despite fundamental differences in their spiritual outlook, Underhill was a member of the same occult order, the Hermetic Order of the Golden Dawn, as the notorious Aleister Crowley. We will examine this initiatory magical order in due course.

Magic and mysticism, which seemed to Underhill irreconcilable and mutually exclusive, were, however, very often commingled, to the detriment of true mysticism, she said:

> In the youth of the Christian Church, side by side with genuine mysticism descending from the Johannine writings or brought up by the Christian Neoplatonists, we have the arrogant and disorderly transcendentalism of the Gnostics: their attempted fusion of the ideals of mysticism and magic. During the Middle Ages and the Renaissance there are the spurious

---

2   Chapman, J., *Quest for Dion Fortune*, Weiser, York Beach, 1993.

mysticism of the Brethren of the Free Spirit, the occult propaganda of Paracelsus, the Rosicrucians, the Christian Kabbalists and the innumerable pantheistic, Manichean, mystery-making, and Quietist heresies which made war on Catholic tradition.

So, magic was not only doctrinally proscribed, but potentially dangerous, not just to the individuals engaged in magical work but to the entire Church apparatus. Some traditions, apparently, are to be approved, and Underhill's study concentrates upon such luminaries of 'true' mysticism as Lady Julian of Norwich or the anonymous author of *The Cloud of Unknowing*. But clearly, from the perspective of an English Christian lady of the early twentieth century, there was a danger of interpenetration of magical and mystical ideas within Gnostic tradition through the influence of 'occult schools'. We will return to these matters in due course, but suffice to say there is and has always been suspicion and intolerance of magic and its various practitioners, whose occult practices were necessarily hidden and secret, and whose societies were exclusive, their members bound by fearsome oaths.

The magi, though, were by no means unique in practising theurgic operations. Something akin to magic exists in every human society, and anthropologists or scholars of comparative religion have shown that for all the differences of climate, locale, culture and social organisation that pertain throughout the world, notions of magic seem to arise from similar primordial beliefs, and to share broadly similar characteristics.

These beliefs, which used to be called 'primitive', and the crude rationale behind them should not make modern people smug about their comparative sophistication. In the grand scheme of things 13,000 years is not a very long time, and we should remember that only so recently as this mankind consisted of a tiny number of wandering clans desperately tracking large game for food, clothing and shelter during an extended ice age. Their technology was limited, and the hunt became a sacred act, the successful outcome of which determined life or death for the entire clan. Almost certainly the senses of such folk were infinitely keener than those of any modern human, and we might reasonably suppose that the grim exigencies of such a harsh existence may have conferred supersensible abilities which have since atrophied, or at least that some special representative of the clan, known to display such extraordinary abilities as clairvoyance or clairaudience, or who seemed to 'dream true' in matters relating to the hunt, may have been consulted beforehand. Over generations such abilities may have 'passed-down' through the bloodlines of particular families who were known for their skill in these affairs.

The basic principles of this most arcane magic have been preserved, though very precariously now, among certain aboriginal tribes of the Australian outback, or among the Bushmen or Saan people of southern Africa. The first principle is that 'like attracts like', so-called sympathetic magic. If some object resembled something else, then it took on the qualities of that thing. The second principle is that once one has been in contact with an object an indissoluble link exists between the two thereafter. It may very well be, though this cannot be definitively proven, that the cave paintings of ancient man discovered at Lascaux in the Dordogne and similar places depicting men engaged in the hunt were not 'art' as we know it, but actually magical prefigurations of the forthcoming venture. It follows from this principle that if animal quarry could be remotely influenced, and the death of mammoths and similar large beasts compassed by these means, then the death of tribal enemies or despised individuals could also be devised, by the simple expedient of fashioning effigies of them, and harming these images. By procuring possession of some object with which such a person was once in contact a similar outcome could be obtained. It will be objected, perhaps, that such notions are ridiculous superstitions, but for the people involved in these operations their absolute faith in the inviolable laws of nature, and the reputed and experiential efficacy of the procedures, left them in no doubt. Magic was a real and potent force, to be respected and feared.

For the peoples of high antiquity, the world around them was infused by elemental energies and nature spirits which they sought to propitiate lest they do harm to individual humans or the community as a whole. This begged the natural question as to whether these spirits, elementals or deities were conscious beings who could be induced in some way to alter their action upon the material world, or, alternatively, unconscious and aloof, their range of action fixed and unalterable. The inchoate religions assumed that the former case was true, and consequently their proto-priesthoods emphasised conciliation of the unseen powers, seeking to induce their gods to grant favours in accord with the needs of the community, such as to bring rain during a drought, for example. The magicians, however, adopted a different approach, one much more in sympathy with our modern, rational/scientific minds. They presumed that the universe operated within inflexible, invariable and immutable laws. That the elementals, spirits and gods existed they did not deny, but the magician arrogated to himself the power to control and manipulate these beings to do his bidding – to force the hand of chance. In *The Golden Bough*, J. G. Frazer comments:

> This radical conflict of principle between magic and religion sufficiently explains the relentless hostility with which in history the priest has often pursued the magician. The haughty self-sufficiency of the magician, his arrogant demeanour towards the higher powers, and his unabashed claim to exercise a sway like theirs could not but revolt the priest, to whom, with his awful sense of the divine majesty, and his humble prostration in the presence of it, such claims and such a demeanour must have appeared an impious and blasphemous usurpation of prerogatives which belonged to God alone.

This bifurcation, however, was a relatively recent development, for in earlier times magic and religion were one, and especially in ancient Egypt, the land of *Khem*, 'the black land', the priests of the great temples were also thaumaturgists and magicians of the highest rank. The aeons-old civilisation which had developed along the Nile was the epitome of the magicians' powers, and the marvellous and awe-inspiring temple ruins, pyramids and gigantic effigies of pharaohs still stand as monolithic testimony to a magical theocracy which presided continuously there for many millennia. The faultless construction techniques, and the advanced geometrical and mathematical calculations utilised in their construction were revealed to initiates during sacred rites in 'mystery schools'. They were so called because the profane population were completely excluded; only candidates for initiation were allowed to partake in the ceremonies, and it was strictly forbidden to disclose the hidden knowledge. This knowledge was believed to have been revealed by Thoth, the god of magic, who was also god of music and writing. The aim of initiation was to bring oneself into rapport with the universal consciousness which the god represented.

These priests were a class apart, almost divinities themselves. They claimed the ability to heal sicknesses and to make crops grow fruitfully. Their petitioners, whether the pharaohs or those of the humbler classes, reverenced them and feared their wrath, for those who could threaten the gods with destruction no man dare offend. Egypt was the spiritual hub of Western magic, and the craft endured there far into the Christian era, especially in Alexandria, the intellectual capital of the ancient Western world, where the 'mystery schools' exercised a profound influence upon Gnostic, Alchemical, Hermetic and Neoplatonic thought. The consequences of this melange of magical thought were to be very far reaching for subsequent Western civilisation.

By what means did these magicians develop their extraordinary powers? The notorious English magician Aleister Crowley explicated the matter admirably in his treatise entitled *Magick*:

> The methods advised by all these people have a startling resemblance to one another. They recommend 'virtue' (of various kinds), solitude, absence of excitement, moderation in diet, and finally a practice which some call prayer and some call meditation. (The former four may turn out on examination to be merely conditions favourable to the last). On investigating what is meant by these two things, we find that they are only one. For what is a state of prayer or meditation? It is the restraining of the mind to a single act, state, or thought.[3]

According to Crowley, whose expertise in ceremonial magical work is beyond dispute despite his scandalous reputation, these prayerful or meditative states

---

3   Crowley, A., *Magick: In Theory and Practice*, London, 1986 edn.

culminated in a fundamental transformation, an apotheosis accomplished by the practice of controlling the mind through meditative exercises (Crowley used the method prescribed by the Buddha.) After long and arduous efforts, at last:

> Finally something happens ... this consciousness of the ego and the non-ego, the seer and the thing seen, the knower and the thing known, is blotted out. There is usually an intense light, an intense sound, and a feeling of such overwhelming bliss that the resources of language have been exhausted again and again in the attempt to describe it. It is an absolute knock-out blow to the mind. It is so vivid and tremendous that those who experience it are in the gravest danger of losing all sense of proportion. By its light all other events are as darkness.

Crowley's periodical *The Equinox* bore the motto, 'The method of science – the aim of religion', and like the Theosophists he sought to emphasise the (pseudo-)scientific approach (the 'religion' whose aim he served was, of course, his own cult of Thelema). This magical 'science' was summed up by him thus:

> We assert a secret source of energy which explains the phenomenon of Genius. We do not believe in any supernatural explanations, but insist that this source may be reached by the following out of definite rules, the degree of success depending upon the capacity of the seeker, and not upon the favour of any Divine Being. We assert that the critical phenomenon which determines success is an occurrence in the brain characterized essentially by the uniting of subject and object.

The 'haughty self-sufficiency' and 'arrogant demeanour' J. G. Frazer remarked upon as characteristics of the magical temperament reached their zenith in the personage of Crowley, the sinister 'Master Therion' or 'Great Beast'. We will encounter him again later in our story, but let the reader be in no doubt, he was one of the ablest exponents of practical magic, and one of the most learned students of occult matters in the last century. His description of the practical methods leading to illumination and the 'astral' plane of consciousness are derived from direct personal experience, and even if the preliminary practices of the ancient magicians varied slightly from his, they would have been broadly similar.

Both the mystics and the magicians described a plane or 'medium' within which the material world and all created things exist. Eliphas Levi (his 'magical name'; his real name was Alphonse Louis Constance), the nineteenth-century French occultist whom Crowley regarded as one of his previous incarnations, called this plane 'the Astral', a term he borrowed from the esoteric Christians known as the Martinists. This medium or 'agent' differs little from the 'Land of Eternal Youth' of Celtic myth, or the 'true ground' of the sixteenth-century German mystic Jacob Boehme. All things there are eternal, imperishable, like in Plato's archetypal world. The entire universal memory is contained therein, somewhat like the 'Akashic records' postulated by the Theosophists and Anthroposophists. When once the magician has entered into 'the Astral', he or she has, therefore, almost limitless access to hidden knowledge about the past, present and future, and all manner of specialist powers are conferred: telekinesis, telepathy, 'action at a distance', remote vision, clairaudience and clairvoyance, to name but a few.

Similar concepts characterise various Eastern forms of mysticism. Sri Ramakrishna, a nineteenth-century Indian devotee of the goddess Kali, said: 'It has been revealed to me that there exists an Ocean of consciousness without limit. From it come all things on the relative plane, and in it they merge again. These waves arising from the Great Ocean merge again in the Great Ocean. I have clearly perceived all these things.' But none of this can be achieved without the crucial faculty of *willpower*. Eliphas Levi stresses this point in his *Dogme et Rituel de la Haute Magie*:

> Would you govern yourself and others? Learn how to will. How may one learn how to will? This is the first secret of magical initiation; and it was to make the foundations of this secret thoroughly understood that the antique keepers of the mysteries surrounded the approach to the sanctuary with so many terrors and illusions. They did not believe in a will until it had given its proofs; and they were right. Strength cannot prove itself except by conquest. Idleness and negligence are the enemies of the will; and this is the reason why all religions have multiplied their practices and made their cults difficult and minute. The more trouble one gives oneself for an idea, the more power one acquires in regard to that idea. Hence the power of religions resides entirely in the inflexible will of those who practice them.

This emphasis on the importance of disciplined will became almost a fetish for Levi's 'reincarnation', Crowley, who defined 'Magick' as 'the science or art of causing change to occur in conformity with will'. For him, there were no dogmatic or religious constraints to consider, no ethical balances to be struck as there had been for Evelyn Underhill, for he had long ago abandoned the strict Plymouth Brethren Christianity of his parents.

The spirit of the true magician, then, as opposed to the religious or mystic, is one of exaltation in the revelation and illumination conferred by knowledge – the transformation of their inscape, just reward for arduous and painstaking efforts. For the initiates who have trained their will properly, all things are possible. Magic, for the adept, is the exemplary condition of existence, besides which all else is mere dross. In *The Goetia: The Lesser Key of Solomon the King* it is written:

Magic is the Highest, most Absolute, and most Divine Knowledge of Natural Philosophy, advanced in its works and wonderful operations by a right understanding of the inward and occult virtue of things; so that true Agents being applied to proper Patients, strange and admirable effects will thereby be produced. Whence magicians are profound and diligent searchers into Nature; they, because of their skill, know how to anticipate an effect, the which to the vulgar shall seem to be a miracle.[4]

This is a description of so-called 'High Magic' as opposed to, say, witchcraft or sorcery. As we will see, magic is ubiquitous but it has developed and evolved over the centuries. Folk magic and witchcraft are relatively unsophisticated when set beside the complex operations of the high magicians, who by the seventeenth century seriously challenged the emerging physical sciences for the domination of early modern intellectual thought. However, this is not to denigrate the pagan sorcerers or to belittle the intuitive witchcraft practised in ancient times. Both 'high' and 'low' magic are predicated on the idea of an ordered cosmos in which everything is connected by a complicated system of correspondences, the manipulation of which will bring about a desired result. The means by which these outcomes were achieved were only revealed to initiates under a strict oath of secrecy.

The 'four rules' of the magus are; 'To know, to dare, to will, and to keep silent.' Francis King gives a succinct account of the basic postulates of Western magic in his *Modern Ritual Magic: The Rise of Western Occultism*:

First comes a system of correspondences between the universe as a whole (the macrocosm) and the individual human being (the microcosm) ... Thus any principle that exists in the cosmos also exists in man ... As a corollary of this theory it is believed that the trained occultist can either 'call down' into himself a cosmic force which he desires to tap or, alternatively, 'call up' that same cosmic force from the depths of his own being.

'Calling down' this cosmic force is known as 'invocation', whereas 'calling up' the cosmic force is known as 'evocation'.

From the foregoing it will be obvious that magic was controversial and divisive, particularly after the Council of Nicaea in AD 325, presided over by Emperor Constantine I. The council condemned as heretics the Arians, who claimed that Christ was essentially a human being. Arianism emanated from the city of Alexandria, like so many other 'heresies'; once the secular authority of the emperor had been allied to the newly respectable religion, the potential for persecution of other 'suspect' Christian or pseudo-Christian beliefs was obvious. The Hellenised city of Alexandria, far from

---

4   Crowley, A. (ed.) and S. L. MacGregor Mathers (trans.), *The Goetia: The Lesser Key of Solomon the King*, Red Wheel/Weiser, Newburyport, 1996 edn.

the epicentre of the Roman imperium, continued to harbour 'schools' of an esoteric bent until the Muslim invasions, but now a distinct rift between a Catholic imperial orthodoxy and Christian Gnostics (not to mention those who, though masquerading as Christian, still cleaved to the ancient mystery traditions) had emerged.

It is true that magicians were known to employ their abilities either towards good ends, so-called 'white' magic, or for destructive or self-serving purposes, 'black' magic. From the perspective of the Church authorities, however, both were equally suspect, because of the ever-present dangers of forgetting the absolute One, and of being beguiled, deceived, or deluded by the entities called forth by their conjurations. There was a political motive too, because the idea that every individual contained a spark of the divine fire, which could be kindled by specific personal practices rather than corporate worship, was the fount of all heresy. The Protestant revolution itself sprung from such libertine advocates as the 'Brethren and Sisters of the Free Spirit' in fourteenth-century Europe, who claimed that all could become sons or daughters of God, practised 'Free Love', and spurned useful employments in favour of begging.

We live in an era (at least in England) where the Church is senescent and weak, and so it is difficult to imagine the constraints and real dangers under which these earlier magicians operated. In any case, as both religion and magic have been superseded by rationalism and science, they have become increasingly obscure and irrelevant to the majority of the populace. Yet few people are aware that many of the ideas of modern quantum physics were anticipated by the 'mother' of modern occultism, Helena Petrovna Blavatsky, for example. Crowley was percipient when he observed in his *Book of Thoth*, 'The essence of Science today is far more mysterious than the cloudiest speculations of Leibnitz, Spinoza or Hegel; the modern definition of matter reminds one irresistibly of the definitions of Spirit given by such mystics as Ruysbroek, Boehme and Molinos. The idea of the Universe in the mind of a modern mathematician is singularly reminiscent of the ravings of William Blake.' There is an aloof elitism and clubbable atmosphere to the modern scientific research institute, and the unquestioning deference accorded to these 'specialists' in our day is analogous to that accorded to the priest-magicians of ancient Egypt. These ideas are therefore both ubiquitous and resilient. Even such a respectable scholar as J. G. Frazer could not restrain himself from commenting, 'If the test of truth lay in a show of hands or a counting of heads, the system of magic might appeal, with far more reason than the Catholic Church, to the proud motto, "*Quod semper, quod ubique, quod ab omnibus* [what (is) always, what (is) everywhere, what (is) by everybody (believed)]", as the sure and certain credential of its own infallibility.'

In very ancient times, magicians' duties were ambivalent. Some of their duties were beneficent, such as making rain, curing disease, or ensuring a fruitful hunt or harvest, but others involved malevolent or destructive magic against tribal enemies, as well as defensive magic against evil spirits conjured by enemy magicians. The principal emotions evoked by such men (or women) were awe, adoration and fear.

The indwelling of magical power was regarded as an essential qualification for the tribal exercise of royal governance. The link between magic and royalty was explicit. In our so-called 'democratic' age such notions may seem quaint, but only twenty years ago Britain was convulsed by an outpouring of emotion verging on the hysterical following the tragic death of Diana, Princess of Wales. The very sincere and spontaneous (within hours) public and private demonstrations of grief reminded the author very much of what the Hermetic Order of the Golden Dawn called an 'egregor', or group thought-form, an eruption of a deep-seated archetype in the national consciousness. This concept of a 'group mind' will be of exceeding importance towards the conclusion of our story.

To occupy the position of priest-king was a dubious honour, for should the harvest fail, the rains not come, the war be lost, or famine and disease decimate the tribe, the magician-king was in deep trouble, and his death might be sought so that one more able could reign in his stead. English kings from Edward the Confessor to Charles II continued to admit into their presence vast crowds of people stricken by scrofula, a disease of the lymphatic system which could allegedly be cured by the royal touch. As royalty gradually became dynastic the notion took hold that 'royal blood' contained some sort of mysterious agent which transmitted magical or divine powers from generation to generation, and among Indo-European peoples the belief in reincarnation gave rise to the idea that gods, or the spirits of particularly exemplary kings of antiquity, could manifest themselves in human form again – and, further, that these reincarnations could be anticipated by the vaticinations of specialist magicians or priests.

This book is not a grimoire, and so we need not dwell at too much length on the details of magical procedures until they become of specific interest. I feel it important to have established in the reader's mind, however, the primordial antiquity of the magicians, their ubiquity, the immense power of the earliest priests and acolytes, their control over the sacred festivals and sacrifices which marked the passing of the year – their stellar, metaphysical and natural knowledge, and their intimate connection to royalty and therefore autocratic political hegemony.

Thus far we have discussed regions at some distance from the British Isles, but it should be quite clear that although somewhat peripheral to the epicentre of ancient civilisation – the Mediterranean, the Levant, and the Near and Far East – Britain and Ireland had their own indigenous magical traditions, and were in contact with sea traders from the great civilisations of the ancient world from very early times. That the cultures of north-western Europe possessed their own magical lore and magical priesthoods there can be no doubt. Until quite recent times there was a presumption that the great megalithic monuments of Britain, Ireland and Brittany – Stonehenge and Avebury, Newgrange and Carnac, for example – must have been influenced by a diffusion of more sophisticated knowledge emanating from the Mediterranean 'core'. But scholars such as Sir Barry Cunliffe of the University of Oxford have now suggested that the development of a monumental culture among the peoples of the Atlantic seaboard of north-western Europe may have been indigenous, a cultural response to drastic social change as a nomadic hunter-gatherer society oriented to the cycles of the Moon gave way to settled, agriculturally based, solar-oriented communities in the wake of dramatic environmental changes.

In the epoch of the last ice age, when vast herds of large game such as mammoths, wild ponies, aurochs and deer roamed, and the human population was scattered and tiny (the whole of Great Britain contained fewer than 5,000 humans), the hunt provided for all the needs of the clan. Hunting was essentially a nocturnal activity, and relied on bright moonlight for success. Therefore, it was to the 'lesser light' that these early folk offered up their most fervent devotions. Because of the intimate connections between the menstrual cycles of women and the Moon, it became synonymous with the Goddess, who contained three aspects in one: the maiden or virgin at the new moon, the matron or mother at the full moon, and finally the hag or crone as the Moon waned (the old women were the 'layers-out' of the dead). Thus the whole feminine contribution to the culture was encapsulated, although the light of the 'Great Mother' was also crucial to the success of the errant menfolk as they departed in search of the vital game.

As the ice sheets retreated, large game grew too scarce to sustain the traditional way of life. During the Neolithic or 'New' Stone Age the transition to a settled, livestock-rearing social organisation began. The new social order was dreary, routine and predicated on 'deferred gratification', as the sociologists call it. There was no instant thrill as the quarry was brought down, no joyful reunion with the women and children as the beast was slung down beside the fire, no wandering over the dangerous plains or wary backwards glances lest they find themselves the quarry of more dangerous creatures. Instead there was the laborious work of clearing woodland and scrub with stone axes, constructing weatherproof permanent shelters in small communities, and ploughing and harrowing and planting – all of which had to take place before that most precarious procedure when the harvest was finally brought home at summer's end.

This new social experiment, it has been conjectured, involved great physical and psychical stress for those involved. The luminary which fructified the grain was the Sun, which represented the male, and settlement meant property ownership. A corollary of the latter development was the need to enclose and defend, to erect boundaries and borders, and to indicate to 'outsiders' some idea of the terrible power of one's own tribe, their 'connections' in the underworld vernacular, expressed in enduring monuments of earth and stone.

So, in a sense, the Moon was spiritually 'eclipsed' (if only partially) by the Sun, and it has been postulated that the status of women markedly declined as a consequence.

One of the most important tasks of the magicians was the meticulous observation of the stars and planets – astrology. In our fallen times, when this arcane science has been appropriated by charlatans and hucksters as a means of supposed entertainment, we struggle to comprehend the importance of these matters to early man. The anticipation of malevolent or beneficent events was crucial to agricultural enterprise. Yet there was more. Whenever certain planetary configurations were observed to coincide with specific occurrences, these could thereafter be anticipated because the planets move in regular motions.

Humanity happens to live in a time when the Moon in total solar eclipse forms a disc which is of *exactly* the correct size to perfectly cover the Sun's disc. The Sun is 400 times larger than the Moon, but also exactly 400 times further from Earth, facilitating this seeming miracle. There are still many people who, despite the disagreement of mathematicians, refuse to believe that the 'astronomical' odds against this being a coincidence are evidence of design in the cosmos. For early man there was no doubt whatsoever, and over thousands of years astrological data and traditions were passed down through the initiated priesthoods. The constellation which most obsessed astrologers in the northern hemisphere was Orion, which to the ancient Egyptians represented the sacrificed god Osiris. His 'belt' of three bright stars was known as the 'three kings'. In the adjacent constellation burned the brightest star in the sky, Sirius in Canis Major, the 'dog star'. This was the sacred star of Isis, the supreme goddess of the ancient pantheon.

In fact, our sophisticated modern astronomy is the direct descendant of astrology, just as our chemistry is a descendant of alchemy. In all probability the ancient peoples, on the whole, had a more thoroughgoing appreciation of the stellar display than modern humans. For instance, few modern people grasp that our solar system is not a sphere, but is a dinner-plate or record-shaped disc, extending outward into space within one plane. The planets, which lie at intervals upon the plane, are almost invariably spaced at distances that can be mathematically anticipated, Neptune being a notable exception. For ancient man, the 'occult', or outer, planets were invisible to the naked eye. At the outer edge of this plane, or flattened disc, a thin band of stars form twelve constellations along the same plane within which the planets move – the Zodiac, from the Greek *zoidiakos*, meaning 'animal figure', since many of these resembled (at least for an imaginative mind) various mythical beasts. The choice of these creatures was no accident, for each 'animal' represented some deep archetype in the human imagination derived from millennia of 'imprinting' about the characteristics and behaviour of the ram, the bull, the crab, the lion, the scorpion or the goat. This celestial menagerie was the backdrop for the interplay of the planets, which became symbolic of particular god-forms: Venus, Mars, Jupiter, Saturn et al.

In *The Measure of Albion: The Lost Science of Prehistoric Britain*, Robin Heath and John Michell make an interesting observation on this point:

> The most obvious originator of the great survey of Britain is the Bronze age Wessex culture, centred upon Stonehenge and Avebury. It was in every sense a golden age, with all the attributes that the alchemical philosophy classifies under gold – divine kingship, the inspired law-giver, the heroic warrior and a social hierarchy, reflecting the revealed order of the heavens. In this form of society – which has been known at different times throughout the world – the people are divided into twelve tribes, in imitation of the rational order of the zodiac. In each section is located an episode in the official myth which describes the adventures of a solar hero in his yearly course round the heavens. And each section has its note in the twelve-note scale of music which perpetual choirs maintained, day and night, in the monastic colleges.

There exists a Hermetic document, the 'Emerald Tablet', said to have been authored by the shadowy 'Hermes Trismegistus' (a synthesis of the Greek god Hermes with the Egyptian god Thoth, and perhaps some anonymous adept also), the putative father of alchemy. It expressed the principle, 'That which is below is like that which is above, and that which is above is like that which is below.' Hermes was said to have preceded – or even to have initiated – Abraham, and the seven Hermetic principles which underpinned his work *Kybalion* are still utilised by high magicians (these are mentalism, correspondence, vibration, polarity, rhythm, cause and effect, and gender). There are some who believe that the monumental structures and landscape sculpturing of the ancients were nothing less than an effort to literally transpose the celestial onto the terrestrial – in effect, a project to create 'heaven on earth', in accordance with this idea of 'as above, so below'.

Documentary history of these islands begins with references by Greek writers which may possibly refer to the British Isles. Diodorus Siculus between 60 and 30 BC wrote an account of Kent and Cornwall, including parts written shortly after Caesar's expeditions of 55–54 BC. He used material from an earlier (500–400 BC) history by Hecateus which was partly mythographical. In this he said, 'Opposite the Celtic coast of Gaul there is an island in the Ocean not smaller than Sicily ... in this island there is a magnificent precinct of Apollo, and a remarkable temple of round form adorned with many consecrated gifts. There is also a city, sacred to the same god, most of the inhabitants of which are harpers, who continually play upon the harps in the temple and sing hymns to the god ... Apollo visits the island once in a course of nineteen years in which period the stars complete their revolutions.'

Another Greek, called Scymnus, had a work attributed to him (which was in fact the work of an anonymous author) written about 150 BC. He refers to a huge pillar erected on the western coast of Gaul 'at the edge of the sea' dedicated to Boreas, the god of the North Wind. Ruins have been discovered at Locmariaquer, Brittany, of a 300-tonne pillar, now collapsed and lying in several massive sections, at least one of which was inscribed, depicting the image of an axe.

In the first century AD the Greek biographer Plutarch was told by Demetrius of Tarsus (recorded in 'On the Cessation of Oracles') that he had been commissioned by the Emperor Domitian to sail to Britain to discover the secrets of the Druids. Some of the stories he told were strange. Beyond Britain to the west, he said, there were certain other islands inhabited by holy men, psychopomps who conducted the souls of the dead into the Otherworld. Further west, after five days' sailing, the god Chronos, Lord of Time, was found to be confined on another island. As we will see, although these references are extremely flimsy evidence, they are also tantalising, particularly their descriptions of what may be Stonehenge and Avebury. But there was one other Greek explorer whose account we are obliged to take more seriously: Pytheas of Massalia. Although his original account has not survived, it was referred to by subsequent historians, and it is a tale to rival Jason's quest to find the Golden Fleece for sheer adventurism. We will look more closely at this account in the next chapter, but with the advent of the maritime expeditions of the Greeks, the British Isles were very firmly on the map.

In his *The Cygnus Mystery*, Andrew Collins makes a convincing argument for an ancient cult which especially venerated the stars of the constellation Cygnus, or 'the Northern Cross', which he thinks originated with shamanic spirit-journeying. Geese and swans were considered sacred birds, and were thought to bring life into the world much like our famous stork, and also, as the embodiments of recently deceased people, they were thought to take departed souls out of this world. An ancient Irish tale, *The Children of Lir*, is about four children who are transformed into swans by an enchantress. These are faint echoes, perhaps, of some deeply concealed magical lore, something powerful and mysterious but inexplicable; something one feels at the megalithic sites on certain days, in certain moods. These places, one instinctively knows, were holy, interstitial and liminal, interface zones between the living and the dead – ultimately magical places. We can only speculate as to what these ceremonies entailed, but without doubt they had something to do with astrology and something to do with geodesy – and something to do with magic.

2

Dreaming Tracks and Dragon Paths

Around 600 BC, Phoenician sailors had developed a navigational tool called a gnomon. A triangular blade on a sundial, the gnomon could be used in a similar way to a modern sextant, allowing ships to be put far out to sea while remaining able to work out their position. *Gnomon* means 'to discern' or 'to know', and the canny Greeks soon learned to utilise their superior knowledge. Eratosthenes, a learned Greek mathematician and geographer, had calculated the circumference of the Earth in around 200 BC. It was widely known among Greek sailors that the Carthaginian navigator Hanno had been dispatched beyond the 'Pillars of Hercules' (the Strait of Gibraltar) hundreds of years earlier with a fleet of sixty ships; he did not turn north, but south, founding colonies along the coast of Morocco. Eventually he reached West Africa, perhaps in the vicinity of Gabon, where his intrepid shore parties ran into fearsome 'hairy men' they called *Gorillai*. The male *Gorillai* escaped but three of the females were taken alive. They proved so dangerous that they were put to death. Their skins were sent home as proof of the remarkable discovery.

It was not gorilla skins the Greeks were after, but a far more valuable resource – tin, which when mixed with copper formed the alloy called bronze, the ubiquitous metal of those times. As Alexander romped as far east as India, the eyes of the Greek colonists along the Mediterranean began to turn in the opposite direction. From Cyprus to the Iberian coast these colonies had blossomed, including at Massalia, modern-day Marseilles in France. The Carthaginians were enforcing a blockade at Gibraltar, but Massalia may have had an independent treaty with them, or perhaps this was enforced in a desultory manner; either way, sometime around 325 BC one Pytheas, a native of Massalia, was hired to lead an expedition past them to discover the fabled 'tin islands', particularly *Belerion*, modern Cornwall, which was already known for its trade in finished ingots of the metal.

Traders arrived at a small island off the coast called *Ictis* – almost certainly St Michael's Mount near Marazion – to take delivery of ingots which weighed

80 kilograms. But the mission was more ambitious, if Pytheas's account is to be believed. The assignment was to discover new sources of the ore, and to report on the terrain and inhabitants of these northernmost outposts of Europe. By the time Pytheas returned, some years later, he had a story to tell which must have kept him wined and dined for the rest of his days.

He set down an account called *On the Ocean*, sadly no longer extant, but several later Greek historians referred to it at length, including Strabo (who was sceptical), Diodorus Siculus, and Polybius a century later, who described how Pytheas had ventured far into the interior of Britain on foot. Was it all just a 'tall story'? The eminent historian Sir Clement Markham did not think so. His *Pytheas, the Discoverer of Britain*, written in 1893, judged the stories to be authentic, and more recent scholars, notably Sir Barry Cunliffe in his *The Extraordinary Voyage of Pytheas the Greek*, concur. Of course, Pytheas was no more the 'discoverer' of Britain than Columbus was of America; many peoples had made their way to Britain and Ireland centuries before. But no one had ever set their account down in writing before him, and if the story of the voyage is true Pytheas deserves to be ranked among the most intrepid explorers in ancient history.

Our modern culture, interpenetrated by motorways and railways, and internationally accessible by regular and cheap air travel, has almost forgotten the crucial role of sea travel in ancient times. Overland travel in 325 BC was dangerous, laborious, slow and expensive, and moreover reduced profits for traders. Some have doubted that a voyage from Marseilles to Britain (and well beyond) could have been undertaken entirely by sea, and feel that Pytheas must have followed the river route up the Gironde to the Bay of Biscay before sailing to Ireland and Britain. No one really knows, of course, but Graham Robb, in his excellent *The Ancient Paths: Discovering the Lost Map of Celtic Europe*, points out that in 1959 a gold coin minted at the Greek colony of Cyrene, exactly contemporary with Pytheas, was discovered at Lampaul-Ploudalmezeau near Finistere, Brittany, home of the Osismii, 'the tribe at the end of the world'. But Pytheas was to show that the world most definitely did not end there.

Once they had been at sea for some days, Pytheas and his men sighted the coast of *Ierne* or Ireland before eventually coming to Cornwall. Like the Spanish Armada of 1588, Pytheas sailed through the English Channel. He reached *Kantion*, or Kent, but what happened next is disputed. Some later historians alleged that he circumnavigated the entire island in his ship, but Polybius claimed (a century later) that in fact Pytheas set out inland on foot to survey the interior, perhaps with a view to discovering other sources of ore. What he said he saw along the way tallies remarkably well with what we know about the ancient British peoples from archaeological digs (and our own bitter experience). The climate was so wet and miserable most of the time that threshing of grain had to be done indoors. The food was poor and the alcoholic brew, something like mead, execrable. The folk lived in wattle-and-daub roundhouses, cosy but somewhat basic to a Mediterranean mind.

Pytheas took his latitude from the position of the Sun during midwinter, progressing through the Pennines until he reached the far north of Scotland, Sutherland. That he chose to traverse these highland zones perhaps gives us a clue, for rich veins of precious ore, not just tin and copper but lead, silver and gold, were much more likely to occur in mountains than in the lowlands. At last he came to 'Orka', perhaps the Orkneys, but the incredible journey did not end there. He sailed on for six days and reached a place called 'Thule', where the Sun never set in the summer. Some people think that he had reached the Faroes, others the Norwegian coastline; but others think he may have reached Iceland or even, incredibly, the coast of Greenland. At any rate, he described dense fogs and places where he became becalmed amidst pack ice 'on which one can neither walk nor sail'.

Pytheas, thousands of years ago, left us an important legacy. He noticed that the tribesmen either painted themselves with weird patterns, or perhaps practised a form of tattooing. He called them 'the people of the designs' or patterns, *Pretanike*, and the islands *Pretani*. This word morphed into a Celtic word, still in use in modern Welsh as *Prydain*, and this became Latinised as *Britannia*, or 'Britain'.

Somehow Pytheas rendezvoused with his shipmates and sailed into the Baltic, where he made his way down the River Dnieper to the Black Sea, and thence home to Massalia. The tales he told were so extraordinary and seemed so far-fetched that many contemporaries were understandably incredulous. But there is a great deal about the account which does seem credible, and what it may show us is that Britain and Ireland were home to a thriving civilisation with resources that were highly prized and which they exploited to the full. That a man could walk the length of Great Britain from Kent to Caithness seemingly unhindered perhaps indicates that this was not a hinterland dominated by savages, and had a pre-existing transport infrastructure of some kind – but what?

The idea that our Neolithic and Bronze Age ancestors were capable of extensive land surveys or geodesy predicated on complex mathematical calculations has been dismissed by academic orthodoxy as a phenomenon whereby 'amateur' enthusiasts simply 'see what they want to see'. These enthusiasts are depicted as at best eccentric, at worst almost psychotic. In *Roman Roads*, Richard Bagshawe assures us that no such ancient science ever existed:

There appeared in 1922 a booklet by Alfred Watkins entitled *Early British Trackways*, which was expanded in 1925 into a book, *The Old Straight Track*, that ran into many editions and is still available. His contention was that many significant prehistoric straight alignments or 'leys' existed and could be proved by anyone with good sight, a ruler and a map. All one can say about this without going into too much detail is that it is an extraordinary mixture of expert photography, mistaken etymology, ignorance of map projection and surveying, random selection of objects and features of different periods of time, wrongful attribution of riders' mounting stones, unrecorded Roman roads, odd earthworks, muddled thinking, coincidences and luck to prove a theory no serious archaeologist believes, but which has many adherents.

From such excoriating remarks we may conclude that Watkins was either deluded or a fraud, and suitably chastised we can retreat into the familiar 'comfort zone' of classical historical orthodoxy, with its depictions of a 'savage', 'barbaric' or 'underdeveloped' indigenous culture which preceded the illumination of the *Pax Romana*.

But Watkins was aware of all these objections and made no attempt to evade them:

> The framework of this book makes it imperfect. It expounds a geometric aspect of topography which in itself gives little information on historic sequence, unless there is brought in the aid of separate branches of research, such as archaeology, folk-lore, documentary record, anthropology and etymology. I have brought in such limited evidence in these branches as was within my resources. But there are many gaps, and chronology in particular, which I have dealt with in another chapter, is of necessity deplorably vague.[5]

Like many who have experienced mystical revelations, or 'showings' as they were once known, Watkins was baffled by the inconsistencies and mysteries inherent in his inchoate theory. He was the epitome of the amateur 'gentleman' enthusiast and had no need of making monies from the book. He knew that it would prove controversial and encounter violent opposition. Constrained as he was by the dearth of archaeological evidence and the complete absence of any documentary records, Watkins turned to etymology and folklore, perhaps with an intimation that these ancient expressions of popular psychology and myth could still retain a cultural memory of the achievements of the ancestors, an analeptic link, as it were, between the living and the dead generations, and it is true that this approach implies a kind of mysticism or 'magical thinking' inimical to the 'scientific' model of history. Yet this can only be adduced as evidence of poor scholarship if the theory can be demonstrated to be entirely based on illusory evidence. As John Michell, one of the foremost modern exponents of ley lines predicted, 'It will not be long before Alfred Watkins is recognised for what he was, an honest visionary who saw beyond the bounds of his time.'

For those who wish to traduce the ley line theory, the amorphous nature of its putative purpose and the eccentricity of some of its exponents supplies them with abundant ammunition. In the 1960s in particular, and no doubt

---

5 Watkins, A., *The Old Straight Track*, Abacus, London, 1976 edn.

influenced by the renewed interest in things mystical and magical, all manner of strange and bizarre claims were made. It was suggested that where the lines intersected, 'nodal points' released magical forces which emanated from within the earth, providing special healing properties or consciousness-raising effects. Devotees of 'Earth Mysteries' maintain that 'sensitives' are able to trace the lines across the landscape using dowsing rods, and even that this can be done by suspending a plumb-line over a map. Ghostly apparitions are said to be attracted to the nodal points, and at the height of the renewed speculation of the 1960s and 1970s UFOs were regularly reported hovering above junctions of the leys. In the late 1980s and early 1990s 'crop circles' became associated with ley 'energies'. Now, while all this may seem somewhat amusing to the reader, I think that the important point is that these extraordinary phenomena all seem to be attempts to explicate something which in ordinary terms is inexplicable. In subjective terms these experiences are 'real', but they have had the effect of distracting attention from the main thrust of the original conception.

For Watkins these lines essentially represented a system of routeways which had been surveyed in prehistory by a class of geodetic experts he called 'dodmen', whose task was to drive the tracks through woodland straight between fixed points (the old Anglo-Saxon word *leah* literally meant a clearing in the forest, and this became 'ley', the name he gave to the system). Large-scale forest clearance commenced during the Neolithic, but Britain would still have been much more heavily wooded than it is today, and other obstructions included extensive fens and marshes. In Ireland routeways over such bogs constructed from thousands of planks of timber have been found preserved beneath the peat. Such a system would have been workable on higher ground with good drainage and clear sight lines between beacon points and the peaks of hills and mountains, and Watkins gives abundant and extremely well-researched examples from history and from his contemporary experiences showing that just such a system was widely known.

There is nothing 'magical' or 'mysterious' involved – all that was required to survey the lines were a few staves of wood. Driving the first stake in at a point in direct line of sight to the next point on the straight line, he would then have driven in another. Then a third would have been extended from the second, and the first removed and used as a new marker, a sort of 'leap-frogging' across the landscape. The chalk figure of the 'Long Man of Wilmington' in Sussex depicts a giant man who appears to be holding two such ranging poles, one in each hand. The real difficulty any traveller had to face was the problem of losing his way in low-lying areas without sight points, and it was this problem which the dodmen tried to solve.

Once the straight track had been established it was a sure and certain path between any two points, and Watkins identified 'mark-stones' which seem to have acted somewhat like later milestones. Using etymological evidence, some of it ingenious, some spurious, he attempted to find correlations between modern place names and these mark-points – he thought that 'markets', for instance, had developed around junctions of leys at 'mark-stones'. The most obvious need for such a reliable system in the Neolithic was the facilitation of trade. There was an extensive trading system in Neolithic Britain, involving commodities which had to be obtained from areas where they occurred naturally and where they were manufactured in quantity. Salt was an absolutely essential commodity for preserving meat, for instance, and Anthony Poulton-Smith has identified a major ley line terminating at the important saltpans of Droitwich Spa, Worcestershire, in his *Ley Lines Across the Midlands*. Poulton-Smith identified many similar such 'salt' leys, but other crucial commodities which had to be transported in bulk were stone axe-heads, pots and ceramic wares, and above all flint, which, although it was literally *the* 'cutting-edge' technology of the early Neolithic, only occurs in distinct widely dispersed geographical areas where deep pits which were once flint mines have been discovered. Although these lines were originally utilitarian, Watkins speculated that over centuries they became sacred in some way. Poulton-Smith makes an interesting point:

> Although they lie outside the area covered by this book, the stone circles of Avebury and Stonehenge in Wiltshire are well-known as focal points for a number of trackways and, importantly, can be dated. These two religious sites are over 5,000 years old. Clearly they were built on leys that existed before they did, hence the leys themselves are older (and likely much older).

Stonehenge and Avebury are the most iconic of these megalithic monuments in Britain, but there are many more; about 1,000 survive in Britain, Ireland and northern France. One of the earliest surviving 'circles' (they are not actually circular as a rule) in England is the Rollright Stones on the border of Warwickshire and Oxfordshire, a complex of three separate monumental structures, with the earliest, 'the Whispering Knights', thought to be around 6,000 years old. If there is a link to the ley line system, as I believe, it will be useful to examine the monuments in more detail. First of all, why were they built? Secondly, why were they located where they were? These are recondite mysteries, and until the advent of modern archaeology we had little to guide us but old folk tales. Stonehenge, for instance, was said to have been magically transported from Ireland by the wizard 'Merlin' of Arthurian folklore. A charming but fanciful tale, we might think, until we realise that only as recently as 1923 Dr H. H. Thomas determined beyond doubt that the 'bluestones' of Stonehenge were quarried in the Preseli Mountains of South Wales nearly 150 miles away and transported all the way to Wiltshire where they were erected.

It was a retired Oxford University academic, Professor Alexander Thom, who first noticed that 'circles' was a misnomer. In fact, they are usually elliptical or egg-shaped. The equipment for plotting the shape of the layouts was just as simple and effective as that employed by the dodmen, and perhaps it was they who were responsible for their designs. Thom began to notice an even more curious phenomenon, however. It had been noted in the early twentieth century by researchers such as Lockyer and Somerville that there were definitely precise correlations between the monuments and certain heavenly bodies, but this was dismissed as chance due to the preconceptions which then dominated that traduced our ancestors as ignorant, illiterate savages. This is a salutary lesson on how hidebound and inflexible mainstream academia can be. Heath and Michell take up this theme:

> A basic objection to Lockyer was his picture of astronomer priests, collaborating over wide areas in surveying alignments of sites across the country. How could this have been done and with what possible motives? Alfred Watkins, the founder of ley-hunting and alignment theories, encountered the same objections. So did Alexander Thom ... even when the existence of Stone Age astronomy became accepted by archaeologists, they tacitly drew the line at ancient land-surveyors.

But if it can be shown that the same class of experts who plotted out and supervised the erection of the megalithic structures were indeed those who had planned the ley line system, then Watkins and his vision may yet prove correct.

Newgrange Passage Tomb on the banks of the beautiful River Boyne in Ireland has been lovingly reconstructed using the original materials. When one first encounters it in the landscape it does not give the impression of being 5,000 years old – rather it seems almost futuristic in design. It is a flat-topped barrow over 50 feet high and built from 200,000 tonnes of stones, originally capped with white quartzite pebbles which would have been dazzling on a sunny day (the pyramids of Giza in Egypt were also originally faced with dazzling white marble). At the heart of the structure was a tomb, access to which lies up an extremely narrow passage. During excavations in the 1960s a 'roofbox', or rectangular slit, was found here, with a 5-tonne quartzite stone inserted to act as a shutter of some kind. It was not an entrance or an exit, for it was too small, and it became clear that it was designed to admit light into the chamber at the end of the passage – but only on one specific time and day of the year, the sunrise on the midwinter solstice. There is a similar passageway to admit the sunlight at Maes Howe passage tomb on Orkney. The design was so effective that it is still functional today, but the extraordinary thing is that this structure was planned out well in advance from careful observations of the midwinter sunrise beforehand. A whole new science, archaeoastronomy, has revealed that Newgrange is not an isolated exemplar. For a people who cannot have been very numerous, and whose technology and economic resources were constrained, to have managed these miraculous feats of construction 5,000 years ago almost defies belief.

Why did they do it? Heath and Michell comment: 'Barely touched upon ... is the grand idea that inspired these works of surveying and geodesy. The skills and science behind them were equal to ours today ... but there is no rational explanation for the main features of these works, their esoteric symbolism and the interplay of number, measure and musical harmonies that make them so beautiful and delightful to study. This is more than science as we know it; it is a form of universal priest-craft, or high magic.' An even earlier passage tomb at nearby Knowth contains huge stone blocks which have been carved with strange spiral designs. These have been described as the earliest sculptural expressions in Europe, but there may be more to them than that. It has been suggested that at certain crucial points of the year ('thin' times, as the Irish say), selected aspirants to the mysteries were immured in the passage tombs with the ancestor spirits, and that these whirling shapes were designed to induce altered states of consciousness. In his *The Prehistoric Archaeology of Ireland*, Professor John Waddell writes, 'The decorated kerbstones around the great mound at Knowth, like some adjacent settings of stones revealed by excavation, may denote important points on a processional circuit around the site (see relevant photographs). It is also an interesting possibility that the origin of some motifs may be entopic (from the Greek *entos*: within, *optikos*: vision), sensory visual images produced in states of altered consciousness induced by hallucinatory drugs, by sensory deprivation or by some other means.' We will return to the possible implications of these ceremonies in the next chapter.

There is, then, something incongruous about prehistoric Britain and Ireland. On the one hand, we are asked to believe that the inhabitants of these islands were unsophisticated illiterate savages living in squalid timber-and-thatch huts. On the other hand, we are confronted by the monumental relics of a culture capable of gigantic construction work planned and executed by a guild of master masons with astonishing astronomical, mathematical and transcendental spiritual knowledge, who were clearly able to compel the *entire tribe* to devote very substantial and valuable time and labour to projects whose purpose we can only guess at. I believe that the most fundamental purpose which underpinned their construction was magical-religious, and I am by no means alone in this. Magicians with the power to construct Newgrange, Knowth, Avebury, Stonehenge, Callanish and Carnac were more than capable of plotting out the ley lines. This is why I think that Watkins and his intuition of the system have been dismissed too carelessly by orthodox academic historians. Graham Robb thinks so too:

Anyone who writes about Druids and mysteriously coordinated landscapes, or who claims to have located the intersections of the solar paths of Middle Earth in a particular field, street, railway station or cement quarry, must expect to be treated with suspicion. In its simplest form, the idea was reminiscent of 'ley-lines', and I was uncomfortably aware of the fact that a sarcastic trick of fate had sent me to live in a house called Leys Cottage. 'Ley lines' were discovered – some say invented – in 1921 by an amateur archaeologist, Alfred Watkins. His idea was that alignments of prehistoric and other 'old' sites are remnants of 'the Old Straight Track' followed by Neolithic traders. Watkins believed that they had actually been called 'ley lines' because the word (a commonplace name meaning 'meadow' or 'pasture') appears on so many of them ... his muddling of different eras is anathema to archaeologists and historians. Yet ninety years of increasingly sophisticated prospecting and excavating have shown his original idea to be perfectly plausible: carefully aligned, long-distance paths were well within the capabilities of Neolithic people.

It is not my intention to recapitulate Graham Robb's argument, which is essentially that something closely akin to the ley line system existed in pre-Roman mainland Europe as well as Britain. A former Oxford scholar, Robb has changed the way we look at Celtic Europe, and his book *The Ancient Paths* is meticulously researched, clearly the product of a fine mind. It has been highly praised for its innovative and incisive exposition of a lost civilisation – a palimpsest, a 'Lost Map of Celtic Europe' as the subtitle says. But here is the rub. Watkins had similar intuitions, and his exposition of the ley system was equally well researched and well written. It is true that he was an 'amateur', but he was not an idiot. Like Robb, his theory came to him in a moment of 'clear-seeing', an almost compulsive spiritual inspiration, the key to some bigger secret than mere history can hope to contain – an intimation of magic.

Old legends tell of the first road makers in Britain. In 'The Dream of Macsen Wledig', a story from the *Mabinogion*, a compendium of ancient Welsh lore, we are told of how the wife of a Spanish-born Roman (usurper) emperor based in Britain called Magnus Maximus (or 'Macsen' to the Welsh) constructed a network of durable roads 'across the island of Britain'. This lady, Elen, or Helena, became known as 'Helen of the Hosts' because of the vast numbers of labourers inspired to do the work at her instigation – 'the men of Britain would not come in hosts to do the work for anyone but her'. Elen was a native Briton herself. Stretches of roads in Wales are still named 'Sarn Elen' in her honour. Similarly, in his *Historia Regum Britanniae*, written around 1136, Geoffrey of Monmouth refers to a (mythical) 'king' called Belinus:

He summoned workmen from all over the island and ordered them to construct a road of stones and mortar which should bisect the island longitudinally from the Cornish sea to the coast of Caithness and should lead in a straight line to each of the cities on the route. He then ordered a second road to be built, running west to east across the kingdom from the town of St Davids on the Demetian sea over to Southampton and again leading directly to the cities in between. He built two more roads in a diagonal pattern across the island, to lead to the cities for which no provision had been made. Then he consecrated these highways in all honour and dignity, proclaiming it to be an integral part of his code of laws that punishment should be meted out to any person who committed an act of violence upon them.

That these roads were sacrosanct is an important point for it could explain the ease with which Pytheas was enabled to traverse the country from 'the Cornish sea to the coast of Caithness'. Belinus was no 'king' but the Celtic version of Apollo, who 'visits the island once in every nineteen years' according to Diodorus Siculus. Geoffrey tells us that another king, Molmutius, was responsible for another law code which specifically protected 'foreigners' (among others) and their right to travel peaceably and unharmed throughout the land, the so-called 'Molmutine Laws'. The historian Gildas had preserved the memories of these laws, and they were thought important enough for King Alfred the Great of Wessex to have them translated into English in the ninth century.

These are only legends, of course, but they are the *only* documentary evidence we have. The roads would anyway post-date the ley lines by many centuries. 'Macsen' was Roman, and Romans famously built roads, but the figure of 'Elen' seems strange, like something out of a more mythical time. Robin Heath and John Michell suggest that the 'Roman' road system, or at least integral parts of it, may have simply overlaid a pre-existing Celtic and pre-Celtic road network, and this is not as fanciful as we may think. The Celts used light chariots, and these could not easily manoeuvre over rough ground, requiring something more durable than mere tracks. Ultimately, however, I think there is more to the ley line mystery than just utilitarian transport. My own hunch is that both the leys and the megalithic monuments formed part of a complex magical-religious faith of extreme antiquity.

In order to engage with this mystery, we have to be prepared to participate in what William Blake called 'a Work of the Imagination'. History, archaeology, anthropology; none of these noble disciplines can guide us on the way we have to travel. We must follow the 'dreaming tracks' and the 'dragon paths' to where the ancestors willed that they would lead – a communion with the dead ancestors in 'the Land of Eternal Youth'.

In 1987, the famous English author Bruce Chatwin wrote a sensational account of the ancient 'Dreaming Tracks' of the Aboriginal inhabitants of Australia called *The Songlines*. Although it caused considerable controversy, Chatwin's book was one of the first attempts to promulgate the animist belief system of the Aborigines – how in the 'dream-time' the creator spirits had progressed across the land literally 'singing' everything into existence, and giving things their names. Thus these lines formed 'a labyrinth of invisible pathways which meander all over Australia and are known as "dreaming tracks" or "songlines"', called among the Aborigines 'footprints of the ancestors' or 'the way of the lore'. By committing these ancient songs to memory, an Aboriginal tribesman could 'sing' his way across vast distances of which he had no previous knowledge, without any need for maps or a GPS device, tens of thousands of years ago. Indeed, some can still do this.

The ancient Chinese had knowledge about similar lines, which they called *Lung Mei* or 'Dragon Paths'. Dragon energy is thought to dissipate in straight lines beneath the earth, and it is considered potentially dangerous, so much so that structures such as megaliths and pyramids were constructed many thousands of years ago to diffuse the force, or to concentrate and accumulate it. The energy builds up during the spring, and dissipates during the autumn. Bob Trubshaw, a storyteller and lecturer on these matters who lives in the village which is enclosed within the Avebury circle (it covers an incredible 28.5 acres) – is not alone in suggesting a parallel with what may have been going on in ancient Britain.

The resemblance of the 'Dragon Paths' to ancient British folklore is telling. Two of our most famous 'English' saints were both 'dragon-slayers' – St George and St Michael. In 1969, John Michell published his *The View over Atlantis*, in which he plotted out Britain's most famous ley line, the so-called 'Michael line' which runs from Land's End, Cornwall, to Hopton-on-Sea, Norfolk. The 350-mile straight line passes through many churches and other sacred sites associated with St Michael, also incorporating such iconic places as Avebury and Glastonbury Tor. As one who has experienced inexplicable 'earth energies' atop the Tor on occasions I do not need to be convinced that it is a liminal place, but for the more sceptical reader I heartily recommend a visit to some of the places along the line. Experiential 'foot archaeology', as Watkins called it, can be a most rewarding and invigorating experience.

So what are we to make of this extraordinary conundrum? Professor Michael O'Kelly of University College Cork has postulated that the passage tombs like Newgrange were manifestations of a 'cult of the dead':

> I think that the people who built Newgrange built not just a tomb but a house of the dead, a house in which the spirits of special people were going to live for a very long time. To ensure this the builders took special precautions to make sure the tomb stayed completely dry, as it is to this day. Sand was brought from the shore near the mouth of the Boyne 10 miles away, and packed into the joints of the great roof stones along with putty made from burnt soil. And to make absolutely sure that there would be no possibility of rainwater percolating through they cut grooves in the roof slabs to channel it all away. If the place was merely designed to get rid of dead bones, there would be no point in doing all this.

These ancient people wanted to build a 'spirit house' in their territory so that the spirit guardian, god or goddess would offer protection to the tribe for many generations. They thought of their world as a shared environment, not inhabited just by themselves but by the ancestor spirits and incorporeal entities which they were obliged to respect and venerate. After expending such vast effort to construct monuments like this they must surely have been the focus for huge, all-encompassing tribal ceremonies, in which all the ingenious and meticulous planning would come to fruition in a display of, simply put, magic. The archaeological finds in the 'circles' are invariably thin on the ground, and it is speculated that this was because they were sacred sites, to be treated with utmost respect, but there is evidence that the ground around them has been trampled down, as if many people had once processed or danced there in large numbers, perhaps in ecstatic or altered states of consciousness and accompanied by 'harpers', as Diodorus Siculus reported.

Mike Parker Pearson of University College London has identified a feasting centre at Durrington Walls, a site very near to Stonehenge. This centre *does* contain abundant 'litter': vast amounts of charred animal bones, the remains of huge joints of pork and beef from beasts driven to the place specifically for slaughter, and also large pots containing offerings of dairy products. At one time it was thought that the site was a 'village' for the construction workers of the great Stonehenge itself, but a new theory suggests that there was a strict demarcation between centres designed for the living, emphasising feasting and dancing and music, and the more sombre ceremonies associated with the dead ancestors at *stone* monuments. Stone, it is postulated, was synonymous with bone, indicating places of the dead.

As I write, the summer solstice is imminent, and nowadays large crowds are permitted to gather at Stonehenge, including many self-styled 'Druids' (the Druids, incidentally, post-dated the monument by many, many centuries). But as I point out in the preceding chapter, the focus for very early man was not the Sun, and solar worship, but the Moon and the Goddess. Dr Chris Knight, in his fascinating study *Blood Relations – Menstruation and the Origins of Human Culture*, points out that of all primates it is the human female which is most precisely synchronised with the lunar phases. The Romanian scholar Mircea Eliade wrote that 'the fact remains that the lunar cycle was analysed and used for practical purposes some 15,000 years before the discovery of agriculture'.

There is an etymological connection between the Proto-Indo-European words for 'stone' (*men, man, maen* etc.) and the word for 'Moon'. The lunation cycle of 29.5 days seems to be incorporated into the mound at Knowth, County Meath, and the number of Sarsen stones at Stonehenge, for example. The glory days of the Goddess, especially the huntress goddesses like Diana, with her festival at Nemi, were long gone by the Neolithic, but they were not forgotten. She was still honoured and the magical link between the Moon, menstrual blood and stone resonated deeply in the collective folk consciousness. Dr Aubrey Burl, an expert on megaliths, postulated that the Moon 'could have been the place where people thought the dead went to, or where the living came from. It could have been the giver or the taker of life.

It could have been the place from which good harvests or spirits came.' To this day, places of the dead are places of stones. The personal tombstones of the departed still lie in rows around our parish churches.

One of the great failures of our culture (at least until very recently) has been the contemptuous way in which women have been marginalised and excluded from religious life, but our ancient ancestors realised the karmic catastrophe of such a policy. Despite the diminution of her status during the Neolithic, both the individual female and her divine representative were still honoured, loved and respected. These great monuments, I believe, were an attempt to integrate both lunar and solar cycles, expressed in an enduring material, stone, which would stand for all eternity as a testimony to their attempt at *integration* of the male and female principles, much like the *yang* and the *yin* of Chinese philosophy.

By accomplishing astonishing feats of geometry, astronomical observation, surveying techniques which have only recently been superseded, and of course, beautiful and exquisite design, the Neolithic people left us a legacy which still mystifies, enmeshing us in a web of questions for which we will perhaps never have definitive answers. Maybe that was their precise intention, for there are indeed questions for which we can supply no sure answers – and one question which still haunts our imaginations as it haunted theirs, the riddle of all riddles, is the nature of death and the afterlife. In the next chapter we will examine these ancient beliefs, and fortunately we will be on much surer ground, for the folk beliefs of our ancestors, and especially the Celtic peoples, give us many clues about how they rationalised this apparent enigma through their magical-religious practices – a cult of the dead.

3

The Cult of the Dead

In 570 BC or thereabouts, a child was born on the Greek island of Samos. His name was Pythagoras, and he is celebrated to this day for his mathematical theorem and for the famous school where he taught his complex metaphysical philosophy. Students faced a thirteen-year course before the secrets of numbers and the harmonic interactions of the cosmos were revealed, five of them spent in complete silence. This philosophy was so sublime that people claimed that it could not have emanated from the mind of a mere mortal, suggesting that Pythagoras was a son of Apollo, the Greek Sun-god.

By apprehending the divine harmonies revealed through numbers, Pythagoras believed it possible to become one with the creator. One of the cornerstones of this philosophy was his doctrine of metempsychosis, the transmigration of souls; Xenophanes, one of his contemporaries, related that Pythagoras once accosted a man who was beating his dog and made him relent, because he recognised the yelping of the poor creature as the voice of a deceased friend of his who had been reborn in the animal.

The philosophy and religion of the ancient Celtic priesthood known as the Druids was so similar to his that many later Greek historians, notably Alexander Polyhistor (105 BC), attributed their belief in spiritual reincarnation to the influence of his school. It was the Alexandrian school of writers who most earnestly debated the matter of who influenced whom. Hippolytus, writing in the third century, thought a certain Zalmoxis, one of the followers of Pythagoras, had taken his philosophy to the Celts when he had taken refuge among them, but Clement of Alexandria thought that the Druidic philosophy had come to Pythagoras from *Hyperborea*, a mythical abode of giants who lived 'beyond the North Wind', a land somewhere in the extreme north, which some thought was Britain.

In fact, the belief in reincarnation of souls is a feature among all Indo-European peoples; it prevails to this day in India, for example. The Celts were a branch of the Indo-Europeans, and by the time Pytheas made his voyage to these isles both Britain and Ireland were inhabited by tribes speaking Celtic languages, using Celtic technology and worshipping Celtic god-forms. In his *Gallic War (Book 6)* Julius Caesar says of the Druids:

> The cardinal doctrine which they seek to inculcate is that souls do not die, but after death pass from one body to another and they discourse upon the stellar movements, the size of the universe, and of the measurement of the earth, the order of nature and the potency and power of the immortal gods.

The poet Lucan, in his *Pharsalia*, says that Caesar located a sanctuary of the Gauls outside Marseille where tree trunks had been formed into effigies of the gods. These he felled, but only one with supreme courage would dare to venture therein: 'Here, barbarous rites are practised in honour of the gods and the altars are sprinkled with human blood ... the people never venture to worship very near it but leave it to the gods ... the priest himself dreads to approach and fears to come upon the lord of the grove.' When Suetonius Paulinus stormed *Ynys Mon* or Anglesey with his legions, similar gory groves were destroyed.

J. G. Frazer tells us that it was a practice among the Celts to reserve the execution of condemned criminals so that they could be sacrificed at a great festival which took place on a quinquennial basis. If the number of confined criminals proved insufficient, prisoners of war were taken to make up the requisite numbers. Some were shot to death with arrows, some impaled on wooden stakes, but for others there was a grimmer fate even than this:

> Colossal images of wicker-work or wood and grass were constructed; these were filled with live men, cattle, and animals of other kinds; fire was then applied to the images, and they were burned with their living contents ... the gigantic images constructed of osiers or covered with grass in which the Druids enclosed their victims reminds us of the leafy framework in which the human representative of the tree-spirit is still so often encased.

It is true that these barbaric representations of the Druids have come down to us principally from Roman writers whose depiction of Celtic 'savages' (from the Latin *silva*, 'a wood'; the Romans thought of all forest dwellers as intemperate and cruel barbarians) was designed for their prurient native readership. But there is no reason to doubt that some such ritual sacrifices did indeed take place among them. Many bodies have been discovered preserved in peat bogs in Britain, Ireland and Denmark, such as the remains of a man affectionately dubbed 'Pete Marsh' discovered at Lindow Moss in Cheshire in 1984. He had been subjected to the so-called 'triple death': strangulation, stabbing and clubbing with blunt instruments to smash his skull.

Strabo mentions that victims were stabbed in the back and then omens were taken from their death throes. Tacitus, usually quite a reliable source, is adamant that 'they deemed it indeed a duty to cover their altars with the blood of captives and to consult their deities through human entrails'. If these tales are not merely salacious sensationalism designed to dehumanise and calumniate their Celtic adversaries but in fact represent at least a partial truth of Celtic religious practices, it is little wonder that the macabre fascination with 'the wicker-man' and other such frightfulness has endured to this day. But were the Celts really such unrepentant barbarians? What lay at the root of these brutal rituals?

There are considerable problems in giving a satisfactory answer to the above questions. The first problem, as we have seen, is that our best documentary evidence about the Celts comes from classical Roman writers whose barely concealed contempt for these 'savages' made them emphasise their 'wildness' and bloodthirstiness. There was a 'history' between the two peoples, as they say.

In 387 BC (in other accounts 390 or 393) a Celtic tribe, the Senones, under their leader Brennus confronted and wiped out a Roman army on the banks of the River Allia just outside Rome. Uttering wild chants and shouts and blowing their bronze trumpets (called *carnyx*), the Celts were indeed magically inspired. On the eve of the battle the Celtic warriors had heard a strange voice prophesying the doom of the Roman force. Utterly fearless, and considering themselves 'deathless' – literally immortal – the crazed Celtic warriors were an unstoppable force. The slaughter of the Roman army was so complete that they did not bother to pursue the miserable escapees.

The shocked inhabitants of Rome had virtually no time to prepare a defence, and so those who could took refuge in the fortifications of the Capitoline Hill, leaving the elderly undefended. As a matter of honour, the venerable Roman senators decided to share the fate of the cowering citizens, and awaited the coming of the barbarians, sitting motionless like statues in their senatorial seats. The Celts, finding the city gates open, walked calmly in. Finding the old senators, one of the Celtic warriors had the temerity to pull the beard of one Marcus Papirius to see if he were alive or dead. Papirius struck the warrior, and it was this which caused a general massacre, a period of looting and an orgy of drunkenness. Diodorus Siculus commented that 'with their excessive love of wine they drink so greedily of it that when drunk they fall into a deep sleep or fall into fits of temper'. The Senones occupied the city for seven months but failed to capture the citadel, and having looted the surrounding countryside they eventually moved off. This disaster was never forgotten by the Romans, or forgiven, so it is little wonder that they chose to pay off old scores in their depictions of the Celtic peoples in subsequent accounts.

Another problem is that the resurgence of interest in the 'Britons' and pre-Christian religions, particularly during the seventeenth, eighteenth and nineteenth centuries, as well as the Romantic fascination with 'noble savages' (much like the newly sentimentalised Native Americans of the 'New World'), led to many ill-founded presumptions, based on a transference of a Romantic worldview on to an imagined, 'magical' and idealised Britain, its mythical past conferring upon it an arcane majesty, as befitted the centre of a worldwide empire. The Roman writers, at least to some extent, had denigrated and belittled the Celts – but these imperial-era British writers, artists and antiquarians emphasised (sometimes imagined) noble virtues in the 'British race', exemplified by William Cowper's *Ode to Boadicea*. The Alexandrian writers of the third century AD had begun a process of rehabilitation of the Druids which lionised them as benign repositories of ancient universal wisdom, based to a large extent on the accounts of the first-century writer Dion Chrysostom, who lived among the Galatians, a branch of the Celts. His emphasis on their intellectual attainments and his evident respect for the Druids (whom he compared to the Brahmin caste of India) was a useful counterpoint to the negative accounts of the Roman writers – but when taken up by British romanticists this had the effect of idealising them. Our best course then, is to take the middle road, and refer to the traditions of the Celtic-speaking peoples themselves – a treasure house of sublime myth and legend unequalled anywhere on Earth.

The key to understanding the magical-religious beliefs of the insular British tribes is their *absolute faith* in a spiritual world coterminous with this earthly one, inhabited by many types of beings, and the relationship between this Otherworld and the dead. This other plane was perceived by them to be as real as the commonplace affairs of this life – perhaps even more real. To die was 'to pass over', as they still say among themselves, and it was reported by Valerius Maximus in the first century that it was an accepted practice to take out loans which were payable in the next world. Such a view of the world is alien to our rational-scientific culture, and we are accustomed to scoff at such simplistic, childlike faith; after all, who can speak with any authority about such matters when, so far as we know, no one (except for one remarkable exception) has ever returned from death? Yet from the perspective of the ancient Celts, and the modern Tibetans, *everybody* has crossed that plain before. Most people cannot remember their previous death; however, most of us cannot remember our birth either, yet none of us doubts that we were born.

In 1911 an American scholar at the University of Oxford, W. Y. Evans-Wentz, published a groundbreaking study, *The Fairy-Faith in Celtic Countries*. This was part of a movement that had begun in nineteenth-century Ireland with the mission to gather as much evidence as possible from folk tales and primary sources in Celtic-speaking areas before they were obliterated forever by modernity. In essence, Evans-Wentz postulated that the Celts divided the universe into 'two interpenetrating parts or aspects: the visible in which we are now, and the invisible which is Fairyland or the Otherworld; and a fairy is an intelligent being, either embodied as a member of the human race or else resident in the Otherworld'. The types of beings who reside in this Otherworld are many and varied. Some are gods or goddesses, or semi-divine beings such as we encounter in the Vedic scriptures of India. There exists also a category of *daemons* which are not necessarily all irredeemably evil 'demons' in the Christian sense of the term. Below these there are a host of elemental beings, among them 'pixies', 'leprechauns', 'brownies', 'knockers', 'elves' and many others known among the Celts as 'little people', whose primary aim is to cause mischief among humans. These 'little folk' had the power to beguile humans and 'take' them irretrievably into the Otherworld by means of some ruse, or by enchanting them with fairy-music. If they did return they might find that the years they had spent there had transpired in a single night – or the reverse.

One of the most important breakthroughs the young American made in his analysis was the insight that the 'Otherworld' entities were synonymous with the spirits of the dead. At this time there was huge interest in 'Spiritualism', the contacting of the deceased through Spiritualist 'mediums'. This craze had begun on 31 March 1848 when two sisters, Kate and Margaret Fox of Hydesville, New York, claimed to have contacted a spirit on the 'other side' whom they addressed as 'Mr Splitfoot' (interestingly an old pseudonym for the Devil). The movement was soon so popular that Mary Todd Lincoln, wife of President Abraham Lincoln, took to holding séances in the White House to contact her deceased son. New York at this time was a hotbed of radical reformist thought, socialism, Quakerism, Swedenborgian societies and 'churches', and many others amenable to a radical rethinking of Christian faith. The ideas of the mesmerist Phineas Quimby, called 'New Thought', also went into this mix, claiming that God was 'infinite intelligence', physical sickness was 'all in the mind', and the divine spark was within each person. These are, of course, thoughts we have encountered before – among the mystery schools of Alexandria so many centuries before. Evans-Wentz would have been familiar with all these strands of thought, and as we will see in due course, he followed them to their ultimate logical conclusion. 'New Thought' was by no means an exclusively Christian movement, and actively promoted some non-Christian religions. As Darwinism became accepted, there was a belief that consciousness was itself evolving, and that humanity was destined to unite under an inclusive worldwide religion. So, in a sense 'New Thought' was the forerunner of the 'New Age' movement of the twentieth century.

The self-proclaimed Welsh bard and neo-Druid Iolo Morganwg ('Iolo of Glamorgan'), whose real name was Edward Williams, had traversed his native country of Wales collating evidence over a century before Evans-Wentz, but unfortunately he included invented 'evidence' he had fabricated or altered. Nevertheless, this does not discredit the whole corpus, and one document, called *Barddas*, is of particular interest. It was the work of a genuine bard named Llewellyn Sion, who lived in the mid-sixteenth century, a time when the wandering bards were prohibited from travelling from place to place by the Tudor authorities for fear of their political influence among the Welsh-speaking population. Sion felt threatened personally, but also felt a duty upon him to record the most esoteric aspects of the old faith, to save them from oblivion.

Sion says that there were three interpenetrating 'circles' of existence (not unlike those engraved upon the stones at Knowth passage tomb). First there was the circle of infinity or *Ceugant*, which is infinite unmanifest space, a little like the *Ain Soph* of Judaic Kabbalism. Then there is another 'circle', called *Abred*, where death is more powerful than life, equivalent to the *bardo* plane of rebirth in Tibetan Buddhism. Finally there is the circle of *Gwynvyd*, 'the white circle', where life becomes stronger than death – this earthly life. Of the three this is the most crucial for an understanding of Druidic religion. *Gwynvyd* holds the potential for the attainment of perfection, absolute knowledge of and union with the divine, by enduring every possible aspect of the human condition, remembering them all fully, and integrating them into perfected consciousness. *Gwynvyd* then, is the attainment of the absolute truth through experiential knowledge, and is therefore 'blessedness', ultimate bliss. Like Zoroastrianism there is an implied dualism between God and *Cythrawl*, which is analogous to Ahriman, destructive energy arising from the abyss of *Annwn*, the chthonic underworld. The tribulations and vicissitudes of this life are part of a personal quest for perfection and absolution – the hazy origins of the myth of the 'Holy Grail'. For Morganwg, as for many other neo-Druids, *Gwynvyd* or 'blessedness' is the touchstone of their faith, but is inextricably intertwined with suffering, as he expressed in 'The Druid's Prayer':

> God impart thy strength,
> And in strength, power to suffer,
> And to suffer for the truth,
> And in the truth, all light,
> And in light, *Gwynvyd*,
> And in *Gwynvyd*, love,
> And in God, all goodness.

Evans-Wentz in his conclusion to *The Fairy-Faith in Celtic Countries* had clearly begun to ponder some of the implications of the pre-Christian religion of the Celts, a road which was to ultimately lead him to the high plateau of Tibet:

> This invisible power, beginning its manifestation through a microscopic bit of germ-plasm, gradually builds for itself a more and more complex physical habitation, until, after the short space of nine months, it claims membership among the ranks of men. During the many years of its

sojourn on our planet, it renews its habitation many times. Every atom it began with in childhood is discarded and replaced by a new one long before the age of manhood is reached, and yet upon reaching manhood the invisible power remembers what it did in a child's frame. This indicates that memory or consciousness as a psychical process does not depend essentially upon a material brain ... this physiological process furnishes sufficient data to allow us to postulate that there is a psychical organ of memory behind the physical sense-consciousness, and that such an organ in itself is, at least during a human-life period, unchanging in its composition.

This brilliant young student became so engrossed in his studies of Celtic after-death beliefs that he wrote,

According to the complete Celtic belief, the gods can and do enter the human world for the specific purposes of teaching men how to advance most rapidly toward the higher kingdom. In other words, all the great teachers, e.g. Jesus, Buddha, Zoroaster, and many others, in different ages and among various races, whose teachings are extant, are, according to a belief yet held by educated and mystical Celts, divine beings who in inconceivably past ages *were men but are now gods* [my italics] able at will to incarnate into our world, in order to emphasize the need which exists in nature, by virtue of the working of evolutionary laws (to which they themselves are still subject), for man to look forward, and so strive to reach divinity rather than look backward in evolution and thereby fall into mere animalism.

In 1918 and 1919 Evans-Wentz travelled extensively across India, where he met many famous Yogis and spiritual teachers, prominent among them members of the Theosophical Society Adyar, such as Annie Besant and also Krishnamurti, the putative 'World Teacher' or *Maitreya*. Following in the footsteps of founder H. P. Blavatsky, he was soon in the Indian state of Sikkim, where he commenced his translation of the so-called *Tibetan Book of the Dead*. In this way the transition from the charlatanry of the Fox sisters to the inchoate 'New Age' movement was made – by way of Celtic folklore. That there were striking similarities between the after-death *bardo* plane of Tibetan tradition and ancient Celtic perceptions of the eternal world is poignantly recalled by the Irish writer John O'Donahue:

My father used to tell us a story about a neighbour who was friendly with the local priest. There is a whole mythology in Ireland about Druids and priests having special power. But this man and the priest used to go for long walks. One day the man said to the priest, where are the dead? The priest told him not to ask questions like that. But the man persisted and finally, the priest said, 'I will show you; but you are never to tell anyone.' Needless to say, the man did not keep his word. The priest raised his right hand; the man looked out under the raised right hand, and saw the souls of the departed everywhere all around as thick as the dew on blades of grass.[6]

Over 200 years before Evans-Wentz visited the Celtic countries to complete his fieldwork, a Welshman named Edward Lhuyd had embarked on a similar mission. As keeper of the Ashmolean Museum in Oxford, Lhuyd's travels took him to Brittany, Scotland, the Isle of Man, Cornwall and every county of Wales. This culminated in his most famous work, called *Archaeologica Britannica*, published two years before his death in 1707. This became a truly seminal work, for Lhuyd's theories about the evolution of Celtic language and so-called 'waves' of Celtic settlement in the British Isles became *the* touchstone for subsequent scholars, and even today, when almost every idea is robustly contested, his theories are reproduced as if they were unimpeachable facts.

In brief, Lhuyd proposed that there were broadly two types of Celtic languages spoken in the British Isles. The oldest, he thought, had originated with the Celtiberians in modern Spain. This he called Goidelic. Its speakers sounded the letter Q as 'cu', or 'qu', so the philologists dubbed it 'Q-Celtic' speech. These people, Lhuyd surmised, had been the pioneering Celtic settlers, the Gaels who still inhabit Ireland and western Scotland. A later development was the arrival of a group he called the Brythons, who had originated among the Gauls of what is now France. They sounded the letter Q as 'p' or 'b', and thus their language became known as 'P-Celtic'. This later 'wave' of immigrants he thought to be ancestors of the Welsh, Cornish and Bretons.

This model, faithfully reproduced and subtly tweaked, is still the dominant historical explanation of Celtic settlement. The first wave seemed to have commenced between 900 and 500 BC. The second wave, the 'Brythons', arrived some centuries later, and the theory was that they had driven the earlier inhabitants into the wildernesses of the north and west. Finally, another Celtic wave, the Belgae, had crossed from north-east Gaul about fifty years before Caesar's first landing in 55 BC. However, while neat and tidy, this model may well be entirely imaginary.

Professor Barry Cunliffe of the University of Oxford has adduced strong philological and DNA evidence which challenges Lhuyd's model, and the implications for Celtic studies are nothing less than revolutionary. Firstly, DNA profiling techniques have established that there is no evidence whatever for 'waves' of settlement. The base populations of Britain and Ireland were established long before the advent of any continental

---

6 O'Donahue, J., *Anam Cara: Spiritual Wisdom from the Celtic World*, Bantam Press, London, 1997.

settlement, in the pre-Neolithic period, before the construction of the passage tombs and megalithic 'circles' were even thought of (in Ireland 88 per cent are pre-Neolithic, in Wales 81 per cent, and even in a racially diverse nation like England the figure is 68 per cent). But the truly extraordinary thing is that he thinks that the evidence is now incontestable that all these people were speaking some kind of 'Celtic' language *over 3,000 years ago.*

What Cunliffe proposes is that the diffusion of the Celtic language and culture *commenced* in Britain, Ireland and Brittany, spreading into central Europe up the great rivers. His explanation for this may well account for the preponderance of the megalithic monuments in the west of Britain, Ireland and Brittany – and their relative absence in eastern and south-eastern Britain. If Professor Cunliffe is correct (and more and more evidence is coming to light to support his model), the Atlantic littoral was a highway for trade and cultural contact in exactly the same way as the high civilisations of the Mediterranean. Language, technology, art, and crucially cosmology and magical ideas were held in common, and similar burial rites seem to have been shared.

It is no accident, then, that the thin band of Celtic-speaking areas which lie on the extreme western margins of Europe are the very same which were the original heartland of the Celtic culture. Far from being marginal, the so-called 'Celtic Fringe', they were originally the powerhouse of a culture which came to dominate much of Europe and Asia Minor. If this is the case, then it is surely arguable that such a linguistic and cultural continuity also retained a religious continuity with the ancestors who constructed the passage tombs and megalithic monuments, those who plotted the ley lines. The Druids may have had *some* connection to Stonehenge after all, the inheritors of a primordial magical system in a direct line to the shamanic wizards of the last ice age.

The quaint and charming aspects of the 'fairy-faith', and the idealised 'history as wished for' of the neo-Druidic enthusiasts, should not obscure the complex realities of ancient Celtic religion. Like its Hindu equivalent, it had an extensive pantheon for everything in nature was thought to be a repository of spiritual realities. We have already seen that there was a dark side to Celtic religion, and their superstitions about demonic entities and the discarnate spirits of the dead literally haunted their imaginations so that they were in a constant state of terror of chthonic beings. They were head-hunters. Excavations at Bredon hill fort in Worcestershire revealed a row of skulls over the gateway, and it was a common practice to embalm the heads of fallen enemies in cedar oil, which would be kept in an honoured position in the household. It was a particular honour for visitors to be proffered an alcoholic beverage in a vessel fashioned from the skull of some deceased enemy. The head contained the vital spiritual force, a force which was indestructible. It made sense to keep an enemy's head close; his spirit wasn't going anywhere if it was under the eye of the one who had separated it from its body, and thus could do no mischief.

The strange magical landscape of Celtic Britain was eerie, sinister and menacing. There are some very remote places in Britain where this type of atmosphere is still palpable. The interplay between life and death, the constant reciprocal exchange of souls between this world and the Otherworld, saturated the culture in an all-encompassing superstition. Natural forces were perceived to be signs from the gods and goddesses; Plutarch related that Demetrius of Tarsus had witnessed a very violent storm upon his arrival in Britain, which the inhabitants informed him was a sign of the passing of 'the mighty ones'.

The direction of travel for the passing souls was always to the west. When someone dies we still say that they have 'gone west', and in the Gaeltacht of Connemara the western-facing doorway of a house is associated with sunset and death to this day. The deceased souls were irresistibly drawn westwards, sometimes accompanied by avian psychopomps in the form of swans and geese. The rendezvous for these souls was a small island somewhere off the coast of Ireland, known as 'the House of Donn'. Donn was the male consort of the goddess Danu or Dana. From thence, following the setting Sun, they disappeared into a place far beyond, perhaps where Demetrius thought Chronos was confined.

That such a place existed they did not doubt, because on rare occasions the invisible world became visible. As late as summer 1908, Evans-Wentz relates, many people saw it plainly. The Irish were so convinced of the material presence of the place they called *Hy Breasail* or 'Breasal's Island' that they marked it on sailors' charts. Columbus is supposed to have visited Galway, where he may have been inspired by the legend (and the story of St Brendan), and when the Portuguese navigator Cabral reached South America in AD 1500 he thought he had found it, naming it thus: 'Brazil'. This western Otherworld went by many other names, including *Tir-na-nog*, 'the Land of Youth', for it was a place of repose and restoration until the time came to be reborn into this material world again. Just as there were 'thin' places where the boundaries between the worlds disintegrated, there were also 'thin' times, especially Samhain (pronounced 'sow-in'), on the night of 31 October. On this night the dead ancestors were permitted to conjoin with their living descendants for a while, and this survives in a bowdlerised form in the festivities which have encrusted around 'Hallowe'en'. Even in a country with such a strong Christian tradition as Ireland, it has proven impossible to eradicate these superstitions.

Cult idols were located in ritual enclosures called *nemetons*, sacred sanctuaries and hidden groves; the actual skulls of fallen enemies might be displayed, so-called 'ghost-fences', but everywhere the menacing stares of wooden or stone heads with drooping moustaches, bulging eyes and cruel thin mouths were to be seen – an intimidating presence, reminding the visitor that the spirits watched over all. In the dense woodlands the devotees of horned gods such as *Cernunnos* or Herne were honoured, and he is often depicted in the cross-legged posture still used by practitioners of yoga. In Abbots Bromley, Staffordshire, the annual 'Horn Dance' still takes place on the Monday following the first Sunday after 4 September. Staffordshire was the territory of the *Cornovii*, 'the people of the horned-god'. Horned gods like *Cernunnos* possessed magical powers over the animals, and he was their protector and benefactor, not an exploitative deity. A form of Apollo called *Cunomaglos* possessed similar magical power over hunting dogs, his name meaning 'the hound lord'.

The Druids were particularly prevalent in the forested areas, and may have worn costumes which displayed antlers or horns. It is easy to see how their later demonization by Christians came about, for the horned god was synonymous with the Devil in Christianity. Before the destruction wreaked by the Industrial Revolution, Britain was a land covered in dense woods with trees of great size, and especially oaks. The oak was the holiest tree for the Celts, and they planted oak groves in remote locations. Pliny said that they could not perform any of their religious rites without the use of oak leaves. Indeed, the very word *druid* means something like 'oak-knower' or 'oak-seer'. Oak is the tree most particularly prone to lightning strikes, marking it out as a conduit of divine power. One of our best guides to Celtic religious ceremonies is the Gundestrup Cauldron, and Graham Robb interprets the costumes depicted on it as follows: 'To all appearances, [there is] a man dressed to look like an oak. In a costume made of brown sheep's wool ... a Druid could have passed through the oak wood less noticeably than a deer.' Robb also points out that the figures are wearing woollen caps which look suspiciously like acorns. The words for 'tree' and 'true' are both derived from a common Old English word, *treow*, which meant both things. 'Truth' was the touchstone of the Druidic philosophy. Public religious ceremonies took place outdoors and the rustling of the wind in the oak leaves was the voice of the gods. Other sacred places included wells and springs, guarded by localised goddesses and their nymphs. The shrine of one such goddess, Coventina, contained a well full of thousands of offerings, bronze figurines, coins, bells, and, of course, a human skull.

The various forest animals and the birds of the air were all venerated, and magicians or Druids were said to have the power to shapeshift into these creatures at will. At Lydney Park in the Forest of Dean a Celtic temple to the god Nodens or Nudd, a god of the hunt and hunting dogs, has been excavated, and other cults became associated with the wild boar, with the goddess of horses Epona, and with the bull and the ram. Ravens were an especially sacred bird, and like swans and geese they were avian psychopomps for dead souls. But of all the cults of this type, perhaps none is more intriguing than the ancient veneration of geese and their avian relatives, swans. Jean Markale, the famous Breton scholar, says:

Both Valerius' crow and Juno's sacred Capitoline geese belong to a very widespread mythical theme amongst the Celts. They are part of the theme of the heroic man, a kind of god, who is kept safe from danger by celestial powers manifesting themselves as birds, since the bird flies in the sky and itself belongs to the Other World. One of the foremost of these is the Irish war goddess, the Morrigan (demon of the night), the daughter of Buan (the eternal) or of Ernmas (murder). The Morrigan is also known as Bodb (the crow or raven) since she appears in the form of a bird.[7]

Another author, Andrew Collins, in his extraordinary *The Cygnus Mystery*, has investigated the cult of swans (and geese) worldwide, relating them to what he believes was an ancient shamanic priesthood oriented to worship of the constellation Cygnus or 'the Northern Cross'. The entire project is far too complex and ingenious to condense here, but he gives reliable and exhaustive examples of the cult in the British Isles which cannot be lightly dismissed. The swan goddess was Brighid, sometimes called Brid or, in Ireland, Bridget. On the Isle of Man she was known as Breeshey. Her feast day was 1 February, called by the Celts *Oimelc* or *Imbolc*, meaning 'ewe's milk'. When the ewes began to lactate it was a time of hope, for the lambing was imminent, life was returning, and the darkest days of winter were over. This hope was symbolised by Bridget's eternal flame at her cult centre of Kildare, tended by nine virgins. Although Ireland was particularly attached to her, and Christianised her as a saint (just as two Irish Druids became the first Irish-born bishops), her cult was widespread. The region of the Brigantes tribe, which extended across virtually the whole of what is now northern England, derives from one of her titles, 'the High One', and a sanctuary sacred to her endured right through the Roman occupation outside the small town of *Letocetum* or Wall-by-Lichfield in Staffordshire. Collins suggests that Bridget (or her localised variants) was personified as a swan, one of the birds which acted as a 'carrier of souls' to the Otherworld:

> In Britain, for instance, it was said that 'the souls of people' were embodied in swans. Moreover the folk of Corofin in Ireland near Loch Inchiquin, Co. Clare, believed that if one of the swans on the water were to be killed then a villager would die. In Germany the swan was seen as an omen of death and the underworld. *Es schwanet mir* (literally 'it swans me') was said whenever it was felt that someone had, as we say in Britain, walked over your grave.

The author, who was brought up by parents steeped in Celtic folklore and superstitions, heard similar stories as a child, but was inculcated with the belief that swans were birds of resurrection – a theme very evident in the

---

7   Markale, J., *The Celts: Uncovering the Mythic and Historic Origins of Western Culture*, Inner Traditions, Rochester, 1993 edn.

work of the German artist Joseph Beuys, who adopted the swan as one of his personal motifs. Beuys was fascinated by Celtic mythology.

Since Celtic mythology and their spiritual worldview will dominate the next few chapters somewhat it is important to try to empathise with their cultural mindset. Jean Markale remarked that 'they appear to delight in stories with what we would call unhappy endings, in expeditions which brought no earthly rewards but spiritual enrichment. The Quest for the Grail ends in death for Galahad and Perceval who find it; only Bohort survives. The Round Table story also ends in total disaster, with Arthur and all his knights, except Bohort, being killed.'

The deep mythology of the Celtic peoples was inculcated by a class of Druids called by the Greeks *bardoi* or bards. They were an outer order of the Druids, whose function was to relate or sing long and complex poems at the crucial gatherings which marked the passing of the seasons. Caesar says the Druids studied continuously for up to twenty years to attain knowledge and skill. This tradition of study, in Welsh *Cyfarwddyd*, is still thriving today, and means 'he/she who holds the sacred knowledge'. Much of this knowledge was astrological and calendrical, as well as historical, but it was also part of a duty upon them to reinforce and promote strict ethical and legal codes.

But the Druids were not always, I think, kindly avuncular figures. There was also darkness in them, a shadow over the heart, for they were still devotees of the ancient Moon Goddess, masters of divination and interpreting auguries. As the masters of time they counted by nights and not days, and Caesar says that 'in reckoning birthdays and the new moon and new year their unit of reckoning is the night followed by the day'. The year and its turning were the same, the new year falling on 1 November as the darkness grew strongest. Diogenes Laertius, a Greek biographer, says that the Druids were full of 'riddles and dark sayings'. They sought to inculcate three principal ethical verities: worship of the gods and goddesses; the deliberate abstention from wilful evil; and courage and fortitude in battle. But they did not deny the evils of the world, or the powers of darkness. In so-called 'sorrow tales', their objective was to bring about an emotional crescendo, to 'crack the hearts' of their audience with tales of enchantment and black magic.

A typical such tale is *The Children of Lir*:

In Ireland long, long ago ... beyond, beyond beyond the mists of twice a thousand years, there lived a proud and powerful Chieftain called Lir of the tribe of the goddess Dana. He loved and married Niamh, the fairest daughter of the Chieftain of Aran, and the foster-daughter of Bodh Dearg, the mighty King of the tribe of Dana.[8]

---

8   Campbell, T., *The Three Sorrows of Irish Storytelling*, Ogham Press, Dublin, 1986.

The happy couple are blessed with the birth of twins, a girl and a boy. A year and a day later, more twins are born to them, but Niamh dies giving birth. The grieving king takes a new wife, Aoife, the proverbial wicked stepmother. On a visit to Killaloe she bids the four children rest by the shores of Lough Derravaragh. As they take off their clothes to bathe she touches each child with her wand, and they are immediately transformed into four white swans. The frantic children churn the water and try to escape their new shapes, but to no avail. Fionnuala, the girl, discovers that despite her shape she can still speak, and demands to know the meaning of this outrage as her brothers 'thresh the water to foam'. Finally, exhausted, Fionnuala asks to know how long the curse will last, and Aoife replies:

> Better for you if you had never asked, for you must spend three hundred years on this lake, Derravaragh, in your present shapes; then you must fly to the North, to the Sea of Moyle between Ireland and Alba, and there spend three hundred more cold winters; after this you must stay three hundred years in the Western Ocean. Only when you hear the bell of the Christian God tolling throughout the land, and when the South and West of Ireland are joined, will your human shapes be restored. On the island of Glora in the Western Ocean the spell will end, and my bonds be loosed from your limbs. I, Aoife, have willed it.

There is just one bittersweet compensation. The children will retain their human speech, and their voices will be 'such that your singing will be sweeter than any music yet heard in the world'.

For 900 years thus the four cursed children endured excruciating mental and physical sufferings in their bewitched form. Then, one evening, and as had been foretold:

> It was near the Island of Glora, towards the end of their long exile, one calm spring evening as they were placidly swimming in the sea, that the four swans heard the sound of the Christian bell ... the Children of Lir remembered their star and what Aoife had foretold nearly a thousand years before; they realised that their long captivity was near its end.

The Christian holy man whose bell had been tolling already knew of the curse of the Children of Lir. The holy man or *culdee* tended to the swan-children and tried to release them from their enchantment, but the King of Connacht demanded them as a present for his wife. As he tried to drag them away in their chains, suddenly the enchantment was lifted – but at a terrible cost:

> The swans' human shapes were restored ... but the years had remained with them, the holy man ran weeping towards the four feeble creatures,

who were lying on the ground with the weight of nearly a thousand years on their withered bodies. 'I did not want your return to human form to be like this,' he cried, as he stood over the aged bodies of what had once been the Children of Lir. Fionnuala raised her grey and wrinkled face; her voice was feeble, but the holy man heard every word:

'Do not weep for us. We are dying, but our people have long gone into the earth. We are so old that even our gods are dead. Give us the holy water that we may not go into the earth godless.'

It was done, and the poor creatures were baptised, minutes before drawing their last breath. Fionnuala made one final request – for all four to be buried 'standing upright with our arms stretched round each other, as we stood together against the world and its ravages through the long ages'.

4

'Beyond the Inhabited World'

We have already noted the antagonism which existed between the Celtic tribes and Rome. The Romans, of course, saw their 'Eternal City' as the *omphalos* or world centre. Surrounding them were 'barbarian' peoples – the Greeks, who coined the term, thought the gibberish languages they spoke sounded like 'bar, bar, bar'. Any non-Greek was a barbarian, including presumably the Romans, but as soon as the latter had superseded the former as the dominant Mediterranean culture, they began to apply the term to four main groups. In North Africa there were the Libyans, and on the eastern frontiers were the Persians. Away on the far frontiers to the north-east a wandering folk called the Scythians lived on the Eurasian Steppe, and in the north-west, in what is now France, Spain, Britain and Ireland, were the notorious Celts, the drunken maniacs who had once desecrated Rome itself.

The Roman revenge, when it came, was terrible. One of the greatest generals in history, Julius Caesar, annihilated a Gallic army twice the size of his own at Alesia in Burgundy in 52 BC. The Gallic leader, Vercingetorix ('Great leader of a hundred battles') gave himself up as a prisoner in order to save the lives of those besieged in the city. After over five years of imprisonment, Caesar had him paraded through the streets of Rome to be ritually strangled in public; the Celts were not alone in their 'barbarous' practices. The Gauls, and indeed the Celtic peoples in general, were very numerous but the Roman occupation changed all that. A million Gauls were massacred and another million taken away as slaves. This virtual genocide in Gaul had very serious consequences for Britain.

Celtic peoples were tribal, but the Roman assault was so ruthless and well organised that Vercingetorix had been selected as a national resistance leader or 'high-king' of the Gauls. Not all of them supported him. Some allied themselves to Caesar, including a man named Commius. For his treachery an attempt was made on his life, and so he fled overseas to Britain, taking all his wealth and his family and personal retainers with him. There was nothing particularly unusual about this, as Gallic people had traded with Britain for centuries and some tribes had territory on either side of the Channel. Commius established himself as king of one of these tribes, the Atrebates.

Because Britain was divided into a score or more tribal territories, opinion was divided about what policy to adopt with regard to Rome. To complicate matters further, a tribal chieftain could have many sons, all anxious to secure a portion of territory for themselves. Celtic society operated a complex system called 'partible inheritance' whereby the king's sons were all eligible to rule over their own estates while their father was still living, even if they were illegitimate. Young men eager to make their fame and fortune could be reckless and bellicose, and nothing spurred them to action more than a dispute over lands and territory. Young Celtic warriors, eager for glory in battle, had crossed the sea to join the Gallic resistance, and arms and supplies reached the Gauls from their British cousins.

Caesar was determined to eliminate these threats and so intervened in a dispute between two of the most powerful tribes, the Catuvellauni and the Trinovantes. As soon as Caesar began to mass his invasion fleet to further the intervention this was immediately reported to the British chieftains by cross-Channel merchants. They hurriedly assembled a delegation and crossed the Channel to plead with him to abandon his plans, but he had no intention of doing so. Despite this, he sent Commius as his envoy with a demand that every tribal leader pay homage and surrender to him. Seeing that conflict was now inevitable, the Celtic kings had Commius clapped in chains. Caesar's raid in 55 BC was a desultory affair, and all it really achieved was the release of Commius and pledges of hostages.

The next year, however, another landing took place, this time consisting of five legions and 800 ships. The British had assembled an army, but when they looked out to sea and saw this immense fleet – the largest amphibious operation until the Second World War – they quickly took cover in the nearby hills and woods. Despite this Caesar and his army experienced very hard fighting, and were particularly in fear of the British *covinus*, a light, fast, two-wheeled war chariot. Caesar needed to show a clear, unambiguous victory, so he advanced rapidly inland to confront the British overall commander, Cassivellaunus. Caesar himself wrote:

After discovering what the enemy's plans were, I led the army inland to the River Thames on the frontier of Cassivellaunus' country. There is only one point where the river can be forded and even here the crossing is a difficult one. I observed, when we reached this place, that large enemy forces were drawn up ready for battle on the opposite bank. The bank itself was fortified with sharp stakes fixed along it and, as we were informed by prisoners and deserters, other stakes of the same kind had been driven into the bed of the stream and were hidden by the water. I at once ordered the cavalry to go ahead and the legions to follow them. Our soldiers crossed with only their heads above water, but they moved so fast and showed such fighting spirit that the enemy were unable to stand up to the combined attack of our cavalry and our infantry; they abandoned their positions on the bank and fled.[9]

Cassivellaunus did not give up, however. With a force of 4,000 chariots he continually harried the Romans, but eventually his own tribal capital was stormed. There was nothing for it but a humiliating surrender. Caesar's victory was short lived, however. Gaul had been so impoverished by the Roman depredations that a severe famine encouraged rebellion there in Caesar's absence.

Having exacted promises of hostages and monetary compensation and other tribute, the Romans departed Britain. It was to be almost a century until they returned. Within a few years the British tribal leaders had forgotten about their promises, and the tribe the Romans had defeated, the Catuvellauni ('battle experts') of the area around Hertfordshire, rapidly expanded until they were overlords of the whole south-east. Having abjured their agreements with the divine Caesar, the British chieftains were seized by a species of hubris, and it was easy for them to portray themselves as mighty warriors who had bested Rome's greatest general. But the truth will out, and Caesar's campaigns were not forgotten in Rome. In the intervening decades plans to reinvade *Britannia* gestated in the minds of successive Roman emperors.

The emperor who finally achieved a successful invasion of Britain was the most unlikely candidate for martial honours: Claudius, the disabled uncle of the assassinated Caligula–his predecessor, who had been quite mad. By contrast, despite physical disabilities, lameness, a clumsy gait and a persistent stammer, Claudius had sharp political instincts. He knew that he too was doomed unless some glorious foreign conquest could save him, and so he commissioned Aulus Plautius, his best general, to draw up an invasion plan.

This is not a military history, but a brief account of the campaign will prove germane to our story. The army consisted of 40,000 crack legionaries, the shock troops of the empire. Nevertheless, according to the historian Cassius Dio they proved very reticent about crossing the sea; Aulus Plautius had great difficulty in leading his army out of Gaul. The soldiers grumbled about having to campaign (according to the historian Cassius Dio) 'beyond the inhabited world'. This delay was actually beneficial to Plautius, because the British army massing on the coast to oppose him heard news from their informants in Gaul that the Romans had called the operation off. Consequently, when the Romans did arrive, the British army had been stood down, so the legions were completely unopposed.

Cassius Dio says that the Britons 'lurked in the marshes and woods' as the Roman army marched towards a large river where the main British

---

9   Caesar, J., *War Commentaries of Caesar*, Amereon, 1989 edn.

force was concentrating under the command of two brothers, Caratacus and Togodumnus. A desperate two-day-long battle ended in a victory for the Romans, who employed specialist auxiliaries who could swim in their full equipment. These men burst on to the British-held bank of the river and cut loose the tethers of the Britons' horses, thus immobilising their vital cavalry and charioteers. Togodumnus was killed, but Caratacus escaped.

Plautius realised that it would be easy to take the tribal capital of the Catuvellauni at *Camulodunum*, modern Colchester. Although Plautius had done all the hard fighting, the emperor was immediately summoned to take titular command of the siege, and to duly accept the surrender of the defeated Britons. Claudius stayed for only sixteen days, but accepted the surrender of eleven British tribal chieftains. An inscription in Rome declared that he had 'defeated [them] without reverse'. The conquest of *Britannia* was a remarkable propaganda coup, but in fact it was very far from a *fait accompli*. Caratacus, the wiliest British commander, had escaped into the as yet unconquered western lands. The Roman zone of occupation initially only extended along a line drawn between the Exe estuary and the Welland; beyond this frontier the Britons were unsubdued, although many tribes came to terms. The famed mineral resources of the island – the gold deposits of Dolaucothi in Wales, for example – lay well outside Roman control. Also beyond their control was the spiritual capital of the Druids, *Ynys Mon* or Anglesey, and while they remained at liberty the Roman colony stood in potential jeopardy.

Repression of the Druids had already commenced in Gaul, and was part of wider effort to destroy subversive elements, especially those thought to have access to occult knowledge – the *mathematici* and the magi had been banished from Italian territory by Emperor Tiberius in AD 16. Claudius 'completely abolished the barbarous and inhuman religion of the Druids' in Gaul in AD 54. We know from Caesar's account that the religion was thought to have originated in Britain, and that those hoping to learn its most recondite doctrines travelled there to be tutored. This information perhaps supports Professor Barry Cunliffe's hypothesis of a diffusion of 'Celtic' civilisation from Britain into mainland Europe. The elimination of the Druidic faith, then, was certainly one of the objectives of the invasion of Britain. Pomponius Mela, a Roman geographer, thought that the Druids had not even been completely expurgated in Gaul, but had merely gone underground in the dense woods and caves to teach there. Because their functions were both religious and legal, the Druids had immense power over the population. They could excommunicate any person, up to the highest rank, and banish whole communities from partaking in sacrifices, thus abolishing their legal rights. But there were even harsher penalties, for the Druids could call down curses or impose a *geis* or spiritual taboo on a person, and for the superstitious Celts the prospect of being left defenceless against the chthonic entities lurking all around them was unthinkable.

For the nine years between AD 43 and AD 52, Caratacus, the celebrated British resistance fighter, continued a bitter war against the Romans as they fanned out into Britain, facing the Silures and Ordovices tribes of what in now Wales. The war exhausted the Roman commanders, and they suffered many reverses, but eventually Caratacus was betrayed to them. He was taken out of the country to Rome, and famously survived by making an impassioned plea to the Emperor Claudius himself, to spare him and his family. It is very likely that the Druids were prime movers in the resistance, and that the protection of the Druidic groves on Anglesey or *Ynys Mon* was their vital consideration. This was the 'headquarters', as it were, of the religion, and sacrosanct – easily accessible by sea for students from many lands, but shielded on the landward side by the mighty peaks of Snowdonia and moated by the Menai Strait; an island splendidly isolated. In spring AD 61 the Roman general Suetonius, long experienced in mountain warfare against the Moors of North Africa, was dispatched with a large Roman army to destroy this most holy of Celtic holy places. The Druids, male and female, assembled among the Celtic warriors drawn up to oppose the Roman landing. The Roman historian Tacitus writes:

Among them, bearing flaming torches, women ran in funereal robes, with dishevelled hair like furies, and the Druids, raising their hands to heaven and calling down the most dreadful curses. This weird spectacle temporarily unnerved the Romans, but they advanced with their standards, and cut down all who stood against them, pushing the enemy back onto their own fires. Afterwards they destroyed the sacred groves, where the Druids practised their cruel superstitions, where they dictated that altars must smoke with the blood of prisoners and the will of the gods be discovered by examining the entrails of men.

This desecration resulted in a catastrophe for Rome, for even as the Romans were still on *Ynys Mon* news came of a formidable rebellion which had begun among the Iceni tribe of modern East Anglia, led by their widowed queen, Boudicca. As we will see, there were distinctly religious and magical elements to this revolt. It is often assumed that the storming of *Ynys Mon* and the defeat of the insurrection which followed resulted in the complete extirpation of the Druidic faith within the Roman provinces of *Britannia*. My contention is that in fact, Druidism survived – and continued to exercise considerable influence on British culture for many centuries.

The conflict between the Britons and the Romans was not just military and political but spiritual. The Romans had a materialistic culture – much like our own, in fact – but the Celts were the heirs to a spiritual tradition stretching back into almost unimaginable antiquity. Professor Markale in his *Women of the Celts* says:

For the Romans the State was a monolithic structure spread over territories deliberately organised into a hierarchy. With the Druids it was a freely consented moral order with an entirely mythical central idea. The Romans based their law on private ownership of land, with property rights entirely vested in the head of the family, whereas the Druids always considered ownership collective. The Romans looked upon women as bearers of children and objects of pleasure, while the Druids included women in their political and religious life. We can thus understand how seriously the subversive thought of the Celts threatened the Roman order ...

That threat was now personified in the shape of Boudicca, our earliest 'national' heroine. She became the implacable enemy of all things Roman, literally an avenging fury. As queen-dowager of the Iceni, Boudicca and her two adolescent daughters had inherited half of the land and wealth of her deceased husband, Prasutagus, who had been heavily indebted to Roman usurers. The loans had been made as 'gifts' originally, rather like 'overseas aid', but suddenly Seneca, the crafty advisor of the Emperor Nero, redesignated his loans and called them in. Roman officials and military hirelings began to seize land and loot the territory of the Iceni. Boudicca was dragged out and publicly flogged as her daughters, little more than children, were raped in front of her, an act of defilement to dishonour their future marriages. Nobles were dispossessed of everything they owned, and their famed horses stolen.

As the stunned Iceni recovered from this blow, news arrived of the violation of the holy sanctuaries of *Ynys Mon* and the Roman depredations there. With the main Roman army over 200 miles away, it was realised that a well-armed insurgency involving every able-bodied man and woman could burn the colony behind them. Then, the Roman army must face the woman they had dishonoured – and she was no ordinary woman, but a goddess. *Boudicca* means 'the victorious one', and at the hosting of the British tribes she stood before them on a chariot. Raising her hands to heaven, she shouted, 'I give thanks Andrasta, and call upon you as woman speaking to woman, to beg you for victory and liberty ... that you may be our eternal leader!' She had concealed a hare beneath her flowing robes, and when this was released, it ran in what was considered an auspicious direction for victory. The hare has been found depicted on coins of the Iceni, and may have been the totem animal of the tribe, rather than of the goddess as was once proposed. Andrasta was the goddess of victory, and now she wreaked her terrible revenge in an orgy of blood and fire.

The first target was *Camulodunum*. Here a great temple had been erected, the most splendid building in all *Britannia*, in honour of the Emperor Claudius, he who had 'conquered' the Britons. With their allies from the Trinovantes tribe the British numbers were immense, and even if we discount the usually inflated numbers quoted by Roman historians, there can have been no chance for the tiny population of the city. Perhaps 400 old veterans, retired onto land grants given out as rewards for long-term service, were supplemented by a measly 200 troops sent from *Londinium*, or London, the largest town in the colony. As tens of thousands of native warriors stormed in these defenders were easily overwhelmed. Terrible omens had been seen well beforehand, perhaps orchestrated by the Druids. Demented women ran around tearing their robes and wailing and mewling; at the seashore the spume frothed red like blood. As the magistrates met to discuss the emergency, unearthly cries were heard echoing around them.

The vast temple of Claudius was the only refuge for the cowering townsfolk, but even that mighty structure was torn down. The entire structure was torched, and everyone inside with it. Even the Roman dead in the nearby cemetery were exhumed and their tombstones smashed. The imperial statue of Claudius was dragged down and decapitated, the head discarded in the nearby river. There could be no going back for the rebels now, and their bloodlust and religious fanaticism was subsequently underpinned by a greed for loot. All knew the next target – *Londinium*, where the hated official responsible for their woes, Catus Decianus, had his own stone-built palace. As soon as news came in of the disaster at *Camulodunum* he immediately fled the country to Gaul by ship. Perhaps 20,000 other anxious colonists were evacuated likewise. A detachment of the Ninth Legion had been dispatched to relieve *Camulodunum*, but it was caught in an ambuscade. Its commander, Petillius Cerialis, only managed to extract his cavalry before retiring to a nearby fort where he remained for the duration of the rebellion.

A victory against professional Roman troops, in open battle, however unequal the odds, demanded a sacrifice in blood. In the sacrificial groves Roman prisoners and Romano-British collaborators were put to death after iniquitous tortures. Noblewomen were hung from trees naked and their breasts cut off before being sewn onto their mouths; others were impaled through bodily orifices lengthwise on sharp wooden stakes. All this as the crazed British warriors and their demented womenfolk cavorted in sexual orgies, feasting and drinking rich wine from looted goblets in the sacred groves of Andrasta. Excesses of all kinds are pleasing to the infernal powers. Once these sacrifices were complete, the grim procession to *Londinium* began. The ultimate holocaust was about to commence.

Despite being in his sixties, Suetonius was personally energetic and had ridden all the way from *Ynys Mon* to *Londinium* with a small bodyguard, reaching the city before the rebels. His intention was to attempt a defence, but the (as then) small city had no defensive walls or artillery emplacements. He took with him those who had the means of escape, and withdrew towards *Verulamium* (modern St Albans). Within hours, mobs of incensed British warriors broke into London and began massacring any who remained. The entire city was looted and burned – effaced from the map. The mob moved on in pursuit of Suetonius, who was racing to meet his legions somewhere in the Midlands. *Verulamium* was sacked and burned, and for some days the vast British mob dithered. In this time Suetonius had rendezvoused with his main force, some 12,000 well-trained legionaries. Within a few days Boudicca's rebels, over 100,000 strong, arrived in front of his well-chosen position. Cassius Dio has Boudicca address the British force as they prepare for the fatal encounter:

> You know from bitter experience the difference between freedom and slavery. So, some of you, because you knew no better, were deceived by the alluring promises of the Romans, but now you have tried both, you know to your cost the mistake you made in preferring an imported tyranny to your own folkways, and how much better it is to be poor with no master than a wealthy slave. For what grievous and shameful treatment have they not meted out to us since they came into Britain? Have we not been plundered of all our possessions, and those the greatest, while for those that remain we pay taxes? Besides pasturing and tilling for them they expect an annual tribute on our very bodies! We had been better sold into slavery once and for all, than, possessing empty titles of freedom, to have to ransom ourselves every year! How much better to have been slain and to have perished than to go about with a tax on our heads!

Touring the battlefield on a chariot with her outraged daughters, the visible sign of their national dishonour, Boudicca reminded the warriors of the beastliness of the Roman occupiers:

> I present myself as an ordinary woman, striving to revenge my lost liberty, my lash-tortured body, and the violated honour of my daughters. Roman greed and lust know no bounds – they violate the bodies of old women and virgins, no one is left undefiled …. look at our numbers and why we fight, and be sure you must conquer or die in this battle. That is what I, a woman, intend to do – you men live as Roman slaves if you like!

The enraged Britons surged forward in a dense mass of yelling warriors, but the disciplined Roman line did not falter. Javelins were discharged into the British front line in two volleys, followed by the advance of wedge-shaped formations of legionaries who massacred the Britons with their short stabbing swords. The Britons panicked, but were crushed in their desperate attempts to retreat, or cut down by Roman cavalry. Obstructed by the carts and wagons they had formed into a makeshift grandstand so that their wives and children could witness the expected victory, there was no way out for Boudicca's army. The Romans estimated 80,000 Britons lost their lives, at a cost of only 400 Roman dead. Even a living goddess could not survive such a reverse, and Boudicca is said to have escaped, only to take her own life by ingesting poison. Her body was interred or cremated in secret, but the fate of her daughters is not known.

In conventional histories this calamity signifies the end of the first phase of Celtic resistance, and the beginning of an effective Roman authority which endured for four centuries. But is this view correct?

This eruption of resentment, indeed hatred, against Rome was a huge shock to the Roman emperor and his officials. A scapegoat was sought, and duly found: Suetonius, the very Roman general who had defeated Boudicca. He was dismissed on trumped-up charges. As part of the process of 'Romanisation', the surviving tribal aristocracies were to be incorporated into Roman institutions and learn Roman ways. In the south-east, the east, and the Midlands a Romano-British culture was gradually imposed, with large well-planned towns, markets and shops, public bathhouses and all the trappings of Roman civilisation. In the north and west of Britain things were different. The landscape was more rugged, harder to police effectively. The population, many of whom recalled the recent Roman campaigns against their tribes, were either untrustworthy or openly hostile. In these areas it proved necessary to impose military, as opposed to civil rule, and to maintain huge garrisons.

Roman religion was observed in public at the town temples and in private by offerings to the *lares*, or household gods. The father of the household acted as the priest during these ceremonies, and the whole family and any household retainers were expected to attend as offerings of salt, wine and cake were made. Local Celtic deities were co-opted and 'Romanised', but within a few years the cult of the goddess Isis had arrived in *Londinium*. A first-century wine flagon inscribed 'to the Temple of Isis in Londinium' has recently been discovered in Southwark. Other exotic gods and goddesses were to follow, as merchants and soldiers from the furthest reaches of the empire arrived in the provinces of *Britannia*. The arch druid on Anglesey had been eliminated, but those of lesser rank, especially the bards, survived in remote regions, and in general terms Rome encouraged a policy of religious toleration. It has been alleged that one of the reasons that the Romans despised the Druids was that, like the later Christians, they were monotheistic. This precluded worship of the complete pantheon of Roman gods and deified emperors, an essential prerequisite for identification with the Roman ideal. In fact, as we will see, the Druids only became truly monotheistic when they adopted Christianity some centuries later. The abhorrence of human sacrifice, as Stuart Piggott pointed out in his *The Druids*, reflected Roman self-consciousness about 'barbaric' practices they had recently condoned themselves:

Anything too that could be construed as 'magic' was also likely to be condemned, perhaps because of an uneasy belief in its sinister powers; magic, already lower class and deplored by the Greeks, and ultimately the object of repressive legislation in Rome from the beginning of the second century AD. Unfamiliar too, though perhaps hardly to be thought reprehensible in a society neither Greek nor Roman, would be the concept of a specific priestly class, and the absence of that deep-rooted Mediterranean, and ultimately Oriental, symbol, the roofed monumental temple with its representational images.

The idea that Roman sensibilities were outraged by 'human sacrifice' is, frankly, risible. This was the same culture which garrotted its enemy prisoners in public executions, coerced prisoners and slaves into fighting to the death in the arena, and encouraged the exposure of some female babies at birth. The pretended effrontery about alleged Druidic barbarism masked the real reason for Roman hostility – the challenge the Druids represented to hegemonic political control.

Peter Berresford Ellis, in *A Brief History of The Druids*, has contested Nora Chadwick's view that the Druids perished by slow strangulation from the superimposition of 'a higher culture on a lower'. He thinks that, far from being driven into the 'caves and woods' to teach their doctrines in secret, as Pomponius Mela thought, the Druids adapted to the changed culture, and managed to survive into the Christian era. If he is correct that they 'even became priests of the new religion, and continued as an intellectual class in much the same way as their forefathers had done for over a thousand years previously', then a fascinating possibility opens up. For if, as I have postulated, the Druids formed a link to the shamanic magicians who preceded them, they who had planned the megalithic monuments, and then transmuted into another form which survived the Roman occupation, it is possible that there is a link between the British imagination of 5,000 years ago and our own today. This concept is, in essence, the theme of this book.

In their authoritative study entitled *UnRoman Britain: Exposing the Great Myth of Britannia*, Miles Russell and Stuart Laycock depict a colony which was different to the rest of the empire. The imperial project, they think, was a mere overlay upon a distinctively pre-Roman culture which continued alongside an essentially alien culture, with those who bought into it constituting a quite small and wealthy elite:

> It is also possible that most Britons may never have fully seen themselves as Romans. Unlike their Gallic counterparts, there is little sign that the British elite ever got involved in mainstream imperial politics, or ever wanted to, and even in the fourth century people in mainland Europe still seem to have seen Britain as a far-off, very UnRoman place.

Some parts of it remained 'UnRoman', for the highlands of the desolate north were never conquered, and a fearsome people called the Picts in modern-day Scotland remained at liberty. Ireland was never invaded, and the Druids there continued to practice the ancient faith unhindered. Wales was subdued after savage warfare by AD 78 but could only be held down by a complex network of garrisons. For many years the Brigantes tribe of the Pennine region were independent enough for serious rebellions to flare up in the hills.

I think Russell and Laycock are correct when they assert that the tribal areas and their aristocracies were co-opted into the Roman system of local government. The *decurions*, or chief officials, of the *civitates*, or local governmental regions, were elected, and were usually retired military officers or Roman citizens, but the dearth of such men meant that a compromise was made. In the lowlands the old tribal ruling elites allowed themselves to be made into the creatures of the Romans, adopting their dress, religion, language, legal system and lifestyle. Greek tutors were hired to educate the children of the privileged few. This luxurious new lifestyle was underpinned by a vast army of slaves, those who laboured to stoke the fires which provided the underfloor heating of their sumptuous villas. It was men such as these who were responsible for collecting local taxes, and from their ranks the magistrates and judges were elected each year. Tacitus wryly comments:

> And so the Britons were gradually led on to the luxuries that make vice pleasant – arcades, baths, and splendid banquets. They spoke of such novelties as 'civilisation', when really they were only a form of enslavement.

Such people were, however, a tiny minority. Russell and Laycock emphasize the concentration of a villa economy in 'those areas of Britain where the soils are rich – rich enough to support the necessary levels of agricultural surplus production required to generate significant levels of wealth'. Villas were by no means typical, forming only 2 per cent of the known rural settlement pattern. It was in these rural areas, the *pagenses*, from which we derive the term 'pagan', that the earlier indigenous culture went on, and in really remote areas it may not have been clear to the inhabitants that they had been 'conquered'.

The country districts were miserably poor, and the way of life wretched. There was little surplus food, and malnutrition was a constant threat. In times of desperation the head of the household had the right to sell his children into slavery, and many had no choice but to do so. The slave class had no rights, and any children born to them became the property of their master. There was always a ready market for slaves. A large estate may have required 200 to 300 slaves to keep it running smoothly. In an economy so constrained, so marginal to the dominant regime, retaining its own language and with hardly any significant contact with the elites, ancient folkways died hard, as the term 'pagan' indicates. It was in these remote places, I believe, that the oral traditions of the Druids were transmitted, and which later morphed into the Arthurian myths.

This process was and is extremely mysterious. As Professor Markale says, 'The druids had quite reasonably forbidden the myths to be divulged in writing, thereby allowing them to retain their strength and to evolve naturally. The ban on writing was the *sine qua non* of the druidic religion.' Secrecy was paramount; as Levy-Bruhl says, 'If the sacred myths were to be divulged, they would be profaned and would lose their mystic qualities. Their deeper meaning and efficacy were revealed only to the initiate.' As Berresford Ellis points out, the Druids were both male and female, and there was no prohibition on them having children. Indeed, they were a hereditary caste, as Irish texts indicate. Such children were inculcated with the sacred myths and legends of the tribe from earliest infancy. In this way also the magical powers of the Druids were preserved, if only in a diminished form. The later Anglo-Saxons recognised this when they referred to any wizard or magician as a *dry* or Druid and to the magical arts as *drycraeft.*

Such pagan lore enabled astrology, the art of the seer, natural divination, tree-honour, 'well-dressing' and similar folkways to continue, but the ancient duty to worship and honour the gods, and perhaps more importantly goddesses, was the ultimate responsibility. For, to the Celts, the gods were the ancestor-spirits, and the cult of the dead we examined earlier was an ineradicable aspect of their folk reality, a 'collective representation'. It was the vexed question of the immortality of the soul which prevented their later compliance with Catholic orthodoxy. The duty of these 'wise-folk' was to preserve the magical link between the gods and goddesses and the common people, to identify incarnated divinities and communicate with them. As among the modern Tibetans, certain signs and portents would reveal reincarnated heroes or gods and goddesses to the bards, whose vaticinations were still respected by men of the highest rank. In his *Oratio,* Dion Chrysostom pointed out this key link between Celtic kings and 'seers':

> The Celts appointed Druids, who likewise were versed in the art of seers and other forms of wisdom without whom the kings were not permitted to adopt any plan or course, so that in fact it was these who ruled and the kings became their subordinates and instruments of their judgement ...

We see here, perhaps, the prototype for 'Merlin' the wizard and 'King Arthur'. We know that there were genuine magical practices derived from the Druids, such as *taghairm* or 'divination through the mediumship of demons'. A bull was slain and the seer wrapped himself in the bull-hide and meditated by a waterfall or in a cave beneath a cliff, entering the trance state the Welsh call *awenyddion,* or inspired inner-vision. The spirits then came to him and conversed, revealing all that he wanted to know. The ever-changing British clouds were studied for omens and auspices taken from the flight patterns of birds. As we will see in the following chapter, our best evidence for the survival in Britain of Druidic ideas is that a Christian theologian from Britain, Pelagius, was accused of promoting heretical ideas said to derive from them. This was right at the end of the period of Roman rule, proving that a strain of philosophy related to the old religion had outlasted four centuries of Roman occupation.

I have dealt with the complex history of Roman Britain in more depth elsewhere, but for the purposes of this book, it is its transition into an independent political entity and its ultimate decline which is of foremost significance. We have noted earlier on the curious particularism of western Britain, those heartlands of the old hill fort culture – the Atlantic-facing lands. These lands now formed a Roman province, *Britannia Prima*. The Roman occupation had created a civil zone in the south, *Britannia Superior*, and in the north a military zone based on *Eboracum*, modern York, called *Britannia Inferior*. This border zone was, in effect, under military occupation. The Roman army were virtually self-sufficient, and their only significant contact with the local people would have been the *vicus*, the small civilian settlement which served the fort with taverns and brothels and other soldiers' requirements. Agricola, the Roman governor, had attempted to conquer the highlands of *Caledonia* as early as AD 80, but ultimately the Roman conquest of Scotland failed. Two walls were constructed, the wall of Hadrian and the wall of Antoninus Pius. The latter was abandoned and Hadrian's Wall became the final limit of Roman expansion on the island. To man the wall a full complement of 30,000 men was required – a huge commitment. This frontier zone doomed the Roman project in Britain. As Russell and Laycock say:

> Overall, therefore, it has to be said that the Roman invasion of Britain was a failure. The normal Roman way was to occupy a region, suppress opposition and when the area was finally peaceful, remove the army to serve elsewhere. Rome's ultimate failure to realistically 'conquer' Scotland, given the logistical, social and political problems identified, combined with the fact that it never even seems to have seriously considered a conquest of Ireland, meant that the Roman army could never leave Britain and the province remained a frontier country, an exposed outpost surrounded on three sides by tribes beyond Rome's control.

This is a succinct statement of fact, for it was precisely on these frontiers that the Roman project foundered. As so often in history, the unravelling of Roman Britain began with a grand project. In AD 208 Emperor Septimius Severus, a Libyan by birth, attempted an invasion of Scotland with an army of 60,000 men. He massively restored Hadrian's Wall (most of the surviving structure was actually constructed on his orders). The campaign became bogged down and Severus became so ill that he had to be carried around on a litter. Eventually he was forced to withdraw, but tried again three years later. This time he became so unwell that he died after being carried to *Eboracum*.

These huge military undertakings had the effect of concentrating very large numbers of troops on the island. In the third century there were three full legions and larger numbers of auxiliary troops stationed in Britain on a permanent basis. These auxiliary troops were of some significance because they were permitted to take wives and to father children. It became a practice among those stationed along the frontier zones to recruit from among these children, who thereby inherited Roman citizenship. By the third century a large proportion of the Roman military units in Britain were 'island-bred'. For this reason they resented redeployment to other parts of the empire, and an insular mentality took hold of them which reflected Britannia's new relationship within the empire. The large military contingent in Britain was to lead to its ultimate undoing, for they became the ones who could make or break bids for power by usurper 'emperors', many of whom were based in Britain.

As the Roman power waned, a new and revolutionary faith reached Britannia's shores: Christianity. In AD 306, the Roman legions hailed the son of Emperor Constantius Chlorus, Constantine, as emperor at York. It was this emperor, whose reign began on the island, who later converted the empire to Christianity. Those islanders who were converts to the new religion would soon need their faith. For *Britannia*, twilight was about to fall.

5

Into the Night

'Brexit' is nothing new. In the year AD 284, a Roman admiral named Carausius was appointed by the Emperor Diocletian with a commission to clear the seas of Saxon and Frankish pirates. Two years later the empire was divided between two co-emperors, Maximian and Diocletian. Maximian made an allegation against Carausius to the effect that he had been colluding with, or at the very least profiteering from, the piracy he had been sent to suppress. Carausius was duly summoned to Rome but refused to comply – an act of open mutiny. Although he was not from *Britannia* – he was from northern Gaul or Belgium – Carausius was in command of the *Classis Britannica*, or British fleet, and its sailors backed him, as did the large contingents of the army in Britain. Carausius had carefully cultivated the British, depicting himself on a coin as the husband of the goddess *Britannia*. He was in a strong position to defy the legitimate imperial authorities, and he did so. Large parts of northern Gaul, Belgium, the Netherlands and Britain seceded from the empire and formed their own regional polity. Carausius may not have intended to become a 'usurper' but simply to be recognised as the equal of Diocletian and Maximian.

This uncomfortable stand-off went on for seven years. Maximian sent a fleet against the rebels but it was repulsed. Eventually, Carausius was assassinated by his treasurer, Allectus, in AD 294 and the legitimate imperial authorities were encouraged to overthrow the independent 'mini-empire'. In AD 296 Boulogne was captured, and with a safe harbour the new emperor, Constantius Chlorus, was able to construct a large fleet. Carausius and Allectus had begun the construction of nine massive stone-walled fortresses with artillery platforms along the south and east coasts of Britannia. These so-called 'Saxon Shore Forts' were originally thought to be a defence against Saxon and Frankish piracy, under the command of a Roman commander called the *Comes Litoris Saxonici* or 'Count of the Saxon Shore'. In truth, they were constructed to defend Britannia from other 'Romans'.

By the end of the third century there was a growing desire for regional autonomy and separatism, and as we have seen Britannia had always retained a strong sense of its own separate identity. But the brief interlude of independence from Rome was brought to an end when Julius Asclepiodotus, one of the emperor's commanders, made a surprise landing near the Isle of Wight. Allectus had scraped together an army of men taken from the northern wall, the legionary bases and large numbers of Frankish mercenaries, leaving Hadrian's Wall undermanned. The Roman army confronted his force outside Silchester and routed it. Allectus tried to escape, desperately tearing off his 'imperial' insignia, but was found and killed. Taking advantage of the turn of events in the south, the Picts and Caledonian tribes broke through the northern wall and sacked the empty legionary bases of Chester and York. Rebel forces fled from London, and the legitimate emperor was hailed there as a liberator. Britannia had rejoined the empire, and for over a century it remained an uneasy member. But as the devastation in the north showed, the Roman project in the island was extremely fragile. Britain's relationship with Rome would never be the same again.

As we have seen, Christianity had reached Britain during the Roman period. Quite how early is a matter of lively debate; tradition states that a follower of Christ called Joseph of Arimathea had long-standing trading links with the south-west of Britain, and that he brought the religion here shortly after the crucifixion, and even more controversially that he had brought the boy Jesus with him on his expeditions to Britain. We will examine these stories later, but my contention is that Britain was not conventionally Christianised by the end of the Roman occupation. There were Christians, of course, but the core of the new faith was drawn from the upper echelons that formed the urban elite. They were usually lawyers, and would have been diligent about compliance with the new imperial faith. But in the *pagenses*, the 'rustic' areas, pagan temples were still in use into the fourth century. Votive offerings have been discovered from the period, and as Russell and Laycock point out the British cleric and historian Gildas referred to decaying pagan idols in the countryside in the early sixth century. Many Christians were heretics of some kind, and the heresy which most strongly reflected a 'British' identity was 'home-grown' – Pelagianism.

The sense that Britannia was in some way 'different' to the rest of the empire may have encouraged these unorthodox views, and if I am correct in my view that Christian penetration in Britain was initially weak, this may account for the strange phantasmagoria which enveloped the British imagination as the Roman influence waned. The dreams which came to *Britannia* during the dark night to come remain an elemental aspect of our folk culture. If it is true that Pelagius derived important philosophical ideas from the old Druidic religion, this may explain the strange ethereal atmosphere that pervades the Arthurian legends, for example. What I believe is that Britain was in a completely unique position, in that it had retained some vestiges of its extraordinarily ancient indigenous culture despite Roman occupation.

The Roman grip was always very tenuous, and Boudicca was still remembered by her countryman Gildas five centuries years after her death. Christianity did exist, but was bitterly divided between Catholicism and various heresies such as Arianism, Pelagianism and Gnosticism. Mosaics depicting common Gnostic motifs have been excavated at villa sites all over southern England. As Britain came under relentless assaults from pagan 'barbarians' – Irish, Picts, Saxons, Jutes and others – large parts of the island fell. The myths that emerged from this descent into the abyss are so potent that they are still being reproduced in cinematic form as I write, a distillation of a vanished realm which cannot be approached via history alone, but by magic, what the poet Robert Graves called 'Analeptic Thought' – the restoration of the past based on intuitive insight, rather than inductive reasoning. Such insights are, of course, anathema to conventional historians – but in the territory we are about to enter, conventional wisdom is frustrated in any case, and all its premises rendered tentative.

We saw in the first chapter how the imperial conversion to Christianity, culminating in the Council of Nicaea in AD 325, had created an imperially endorsed orthodoxy which had the effect of condemning Gnostics, Arians and other branches of the Christian faith as heretical. Gnosticism was declared heretical in AD 380, and it had many devotees in Britain. In his *The Sea Kingdoms: The History of Celtic Britain & Ireland*, Alistair Moffat says:

> It is fruitless to try to discover a precise pattern for the conversion of Britain and Ireland since there are so few reliable records for the fifth and sixth centuries. The best that can be safely managed is a rough sequence which places some figures in a chronological order relative to each other. One of the most tantalizing and pivotal names is that of Pelagius, one of the first Celtic heretics. Roughly contemporary with Ninian, he travelled to Rome around 400, where he got his name. Pelagius is a Greek/Roman version of his Celtic name, perhaps Morgan, which meant 'Son of the Sea'. For familiar simplicity, his friends called him 'Brito', much in the same way that Scots attract the name 'Jock' in London. Perhaps a country boy with an ascetic training, Pelagius was profoundly shocked by the licentious behaviour of the clergy in the great city.

In fact, there is some dispute about his Celtic origins. Pelagius may have been British, but his sometime friend and later adversary St Jerome described him as 'a fat hound weighed down by Scotch porridge'. Some have taken this to mean that he was Irish (the tribe called the *Scotti* lived in Ireland and south-west Scotland). Wherever he originated, it was his stubborn refusal to abandon the time-honoured beliefs of his ancestors which brought him into conflict with the Catholic establishment. He was directly accused of reviving 'the Natural Philosophy of the Druids'. He asserted that there is no such thing as original sin; man was naturally good. A newborn infant came into this world without the blemish of the sin of Adam. This was spiritual dynamite, but to compound this Pelagius and his followers also propagated politically subversive ideas which were an early progenitor of socialism. Another Briton, a bishop named Fastidius, sounded almost 'Marxist' when he wrote in AD 411:

> Do you think yourself Christian if you oppress the poor ... if you enrich yourselves by making others poor, if you wring your food from others' tears? A Christian is a man who never allows a poor man to be oppressed when he is nearby, whose doors are open to all, whose table every poor man knows, whose food is offered to all.[10]

Another Pelagian activist from Sicily, known only by his sobriquet of 'the Sicilian Briton', wrote a tract called *Tractatus de Divitiis* ('a tract on wealth') which carried the simple motto *'tolle divitem et pauperem non invenies'*, or 'abolish the rich and you will have no more poverty'. We simply do not know if this man was 'British'. It could well be that many radicals called themselves 'Britons' out of solidarity with this innovative philosophy from the far frontiers of empire. Of one thing we may be sure: the Roman imperial authorities would have been no happier with these egalitarian and potentially revolutionary ideas than their capitalist counterparts are today.

So what were these enduring Celtic beliefs which Pelagius refused to relinquish? We have seen how the Druids venerated the concept of 'truth' as sacrosanct and ethical moral action as a duty upon the individual. The Irish differentiated between right action, *fas*, and wrong, *nefas*. The Druids had acted in a capacity known as the 'soul friend', guiding the individual and discouraging error, and this was facilitated in large part by female Druids. Following the persecutions of the imperial authorities a debased form of this service was still provided by people known as *gutuartri*, or 'fathers of invocation' or 'prayer fathers'. Undoubtedly such people would have been educators, and even during the English occupation of Ireland during the late Middle Ages 'hedgerow teachers' still operated a system of instructing one pupil in an isolated location while another kept watch for any intruders.

One of the key tenets which underpinned these teachings was the aspiration of the individual to *Gwynvyd*, the state of blessedness which could only be attained by submission to suffering for the sake of 'the truth'. The teaching of St Augustine of Hippo, a theologian contemporary with Pelagius, threatened to completely undermine this ancient moral order. He claimed that mankind as a whole had inherited the original sin of Adam and Eve, and that through the sexual act this was transmitted automatically – predestination. This was a serious challenge to everything the Celts held sacred, and also, Pelagius believed, dangerous because a corollary of such a philosophy is that sin is also preordained, and so, rather than resisting evil, the temptation is to

---

10 Fastidius, *De Vita Christiana.*

indulge it, for one has no choice in the matter. Rather like the later Martin Luther, Pelagius looked about him in Rome and saw churchmen of the highest rank indulging themselves in acts of gross licentiousness which would have appalled the simple folk of his own country. St Paul himself had written: 'Shall we go on sinning so that grace may increase? By no means!'[11] Pelagius skilfully argued against Augustine's doctrine, and for some time he had the upper hand in the debate.

It is unclear what status Pelagius held within the Church hierarchy. Professor Markale thought he was a monk for a time in Rome but elsewhere he is described as a *veluti monarchus*, one who had received a monastic education and adhered strictly to its rules while not being an actual member. This was exactly the relationship to the wider monastic movement the later *Culdees* adopted. The very notion of absolute good implied that individuals should aspire to that state of 'blessedness', as he said, 'If I ought, I can.' Essentially the conflict between orthodox doctrine and Pelagianism came down to a philosophical debate between the sovereignty of God and human freedom, as so often subsequently. The denial of the concept of original sin, although it was a cultural outgrowth of Druidism, was a fundamental stumbling block, for the touchstone of the Christian faith is that humankind *is* inherently sinful. The Pelagian ideas, though, were to profoundly influence the mythology of the sub-Roman British, for the 'Quest for the Holy Grail' represents the personal journey towards *Gwynvyd*, or blessedness, which is attained through personal individual experience rather than as a dispensation of divine grace.

The Church Fathers soon retaliated against these radical ideas. It was Augustine who began the process of vilifying the Pelagians. Coelestius, who was an Irish travelling companion of Pelagius, was accused of seven counts of heresy and found guilty on all counts. With his friend excommunicated, the attack on 'Brito' himself commenced. By AD 415 Pelagius was living in the Holy Land, perhaps near to his then friend St Jerome in Bethlehem. Augustine wrote a castigating letter to Jerome, and then sent his ally, Osorius, the man who had prosecuted Coelestius, to Jerusalem, where he seems to have intimidated Jerome into a denunciation of the Briton.

The case against Pelagius was not proven, and so a further synod at Diospolis in December AD 415 was convoked. This synod also failed to condemn Pelagius, but Augustine was determined to anathematise his former friend. Eventually, and no doubt by the application of considerable political pressure, Pelagius was condemned at Carthage in AD 416 and 418 and in Milevius in 416. Pope Innocent I was suborned or flattered into endorsing these condemnations, but when the pope died his successor, Zosimus, made a point of studying the offending doctrines of Pelagius personally. He found no points of fundamental error, and so the Briton was exonerated. What had originally been a dry theological dispute with a hint of a personal vendetta

---

11 Romans, 6:1.

had now become a sensation. The obscure radical philosophy which had once relied on a Sicilian 'underground press' now had the support of high-ranking churchmen in Italy itself, and one of the most famous theologians in history had failed to make any headway against it.

It is perhaps no accident that this dispute with a British theologian was being debated at precisely the time when *Britannia* was under severe attack from the tribes beyond Roman control, by both land and sea. The empire was by this time visibly tottering. The Roman legions comprised in large part 'barbarian' tribes who had agreed to act as *foederati* or *laeti*, effectively mercenaries in the pay of the emperors. The same pressures which apply to the senescent Western world in our day were evident during the decline of the Roman imperium. As Bruce Chatwin observed:

> The same thing happened in the Roman Empire in the third century AD and later. The rich abdicated the responsibilities of their wealth; the cities became unendurable and at the mercy of property speculators. Wealth was divorced from its source. A strong state took over and collapsed under the strain. The rich wore their wealth, and the governments passed endless laws against extravagance in dress. Compare the diamonds and gold boxes of today, and the aura attached to portable possessions. The mobile rich were impossible to tax, the advantages of no fixed address were obvious. So the unpredictable demands of the tax collectors were laid at the feet of those who could least afford to pay.[12]

So there would have been a willing audience for the proto-socialism of Pelagius and his followers, and perhaps some sympathy for these ascetic Britons whose homeland was already being attacked. As the power of the legions waned, and barbarian chieftains were hired in their stead, what had been 'hard' Roman power gave way to 'soft' power – the Roman Catholic theocracy of the pope and his cardinals. The challenge to this reconfigured Roman authority represented by Pelagius and his followers was as serious in its way as Boudicca's ill-starred rebellion.

On 24 August AD 410, Alaric, King of the Visigoths, sacked Rome itself. Emperor Honorius had moved his capital to Ravenna, a place much easier to defend, and when he was brought news by his eunuch that 'Roma has perished' he thought this referred to a favourite chicken of his which he had named Roma. When told that it was the 'eternal city' which had fallen, he is said to have been relieved that his pet bird was still safe and well. This was the same man who responded to desperate British pleas for aid with a response that they should look to their own defence (it may be that he was advising the people of *Bruttium* in Italy, rather than Britain, according to more recent scholarship). The details hardly matter, though. Sometimes a myth proves

---

12 Chatwin, B., *Under the Sun*, Vintage, London, 2011.

truer than fact. Rome had indeed fallen, for the first time since Brennus the Gaul had sacked it 800 years before. *Britannia* had become increasingly isolated, an abandoned outpost of a decaying and doomed empire.

It was the Emperor Honorius who took drastic action against Pelagius. In AD 418 the emperor tired of the endless theological wrangling and acted against Pelagius on grounds of political subversion. Pope Zosimus had no choice but to follow suit and, once again, Pelagius was anathematised. This volte-face angered many eminent churchmen who rallied to his defence, including Julian, Bishop of Eclanum, and eighteen other Italian prelates. The debate about original sin intensified. The Celtic peoples originally had no concept of sin as such, and equally suspicious to them was the notion of divine grace. It was of the utmost importance to the Pelagians that no idea of sin be imputed to God. In the Lord's Prayer, He is enjoined to 'lead us not into temptation' – which implied that mankind has *choice* between committing evil or good actions. Augustine countered that such an interpretation encouraged the deadliest sin of pride, for 'good' actions would be attributed to the intrinsic excellence of the individual's character, rather than divine grace. St Paul had been explicit that man does not receive grace because of the 'good' in him, but has 'good' in him because he has received grace. Regardless, with the powerful figures of the emperor and the pope arrayed against him, and all his possessions seized by imperial edict, Pelagius disappears from the historical record in AD 420.

His fate is a mystery, but his legacy was crucial, for one of his British followers, Agricola, son of a British bishop, set about converting all the British prelates to Pelagian doctrines in about AD 429. By now there was no Roman military presence of any kind in *Britannia*, and the island was in danger of disintegrating into anarchy and chaos. With the 'native' appeal of the heresy's foundation in Druidism the Catholic authorities were extremely alarmed, because the half-Christianised or semi-pagan laity may easily revert to Druidism in its more unadulterated form.

By now there was a Christian presence in Ireland too, and the Church Fathers feared that this new outpost of the faith may become contaminated by the neighbouring British churches. Although its old 'hard' power was now long gone, Rome resorted to a compromise by sending Germanus, Bishop of Auxerre, to Britain with a mission to destroy the heresy there. A famous and eloquent debater, Germanus was a former Roman general and had a distinctly military bearing. He gave us the last clear account of life in post-Roman Britain before it descended into darkness. Following a vision of St Alban in a dream, Germanus visited *Verulamium*, where he dedicated a shrine to this early British saint, the shrine eventually growing into the town of St Albans.

Germanus confronted the Pelagian bishops in a public debate, and it is noteworthy that these British prelates and the 'fawning multitude' who followed them were 'richly attired' and wealthy. So we know that in AD 429 Britain still had a functioning Church hierarchy with the backing of a wealthy and ostentatious upper class and that town life was still going on in some form. Germanus apparently condemned Vortigern, the 'overlord' of the Britons, who may have been a Pelagian heretic, for the sin of incest. Vortigern is supposed to have sent a daughter of his who was pregnant to publicly accuse Germanus of being the father, but the ploy failed. It seems that Germanus defeated the heretics in open debate through his superior powers of rhetoric, and then went on to lead a campaign against a barbarian incursion in Wales. After this, conventional historical records fall silent, and we enter the realm of legend.

The grinding poverty of the rustic underclass had encouraged the growth of bands of peasant insurgents, brigands, military deserters and runaway slaves collectively known as the *Bacaudae*, or 'fighters'. Although this unrest was most widespread in Gaul, there can be little doubt that similar bandits were at large in Britain. Their concealed encampments in remote areas were ideal centres for heretical or pagan practices to flourish. These sporadic uprisings were, however, the least of Britannia's problems. In AD 383 another British-based usurper 'emperor', Magnus Maximus (the aforementioned 'Macsen'), declared himself as emperor of 'the Prefecture of the Gauls', which was made up of Britain, Gaul and Spain – he was himself a Celtic Spaniard from Galicia. He took a British wife, Elen (the so-called 'Helen of the Hosts' we encountered in chapter 2), and decided to remove the entire Roman military complement from *Britannia*, many of whom were by now Britons by birth. He marched to Rome, which he captured in AD 387, but the following year he was defeated by the Eastern Roman Emperor, Theodosius. His exploits passed into Welsh legend as a 'The Dream of Macsen Wledig'.

The situation whereby Britain had been over-militarised for centuries was now exchanged for the opposite case. Conventional Roman military forces ceased to exist, and only poorly trained and equipped militias remained, though perhaps retaining their impressive-sounding unit designations. This vacuum immediately encouraged Irish slave traders to attack Britain's western coasts on a regular basis, and it would not be long before they began to settle in south-west Wales. The northern wall, for so long an effective barrier against the fearsome Picts, now provided no protection, and on the eastern coasts Saxon and Jutish raiders plundered far inland. The one indisputable benefit of imperial membership had always been security from barbarian attack or peasants' revolts, but now that Rome could no longer provide even this basic protection many in Britannia looked to *tyrannoi*, local warlords, for protection.

We have seen how Allectus had recruited large numbers of Franks to fight for him at the close of the third century, and other Germanic mercenaries had been deployed in the fourth century. A Germanic king, Fraomar, and his entire tribe had been moved to the north of Britain in AD 372. Another Germanic group called the *Gewissae* protected the rich agricultural areas of the Thames Valley as *laeti* militia. These foreigners were settled alongside the host communities and shared a fairly common way of life with the locals, almost certainly interbreeding with them. In AD 407 another British-backed usurper, Constantine III, took what forces he could still muster from Britain to Gaul. His military commander was a Briton named Gerontius, or Geraint, and he began to intrigue against Constantine III. Gerontius had a large force of British-born soldiers with him and seems to have secured the backing of the remaining British political authorities. His rebellion failed, and 'the dream of Gerontius' died. From now on Britain was on its own.

Constantine III is remembered in British legend as 'Custennin Vychan' or 'the little'. According to these legendary sources – and remember, from now on we have little else to guide us – Constantine had two brothers, Ambrosius or 'Emrys' and Uther 'Pendragon'. Following Constantine's downfall, the most powerful of the British *tyrannoi*, Vortigern, son-in-law of the usurper emperor Magnus Maximus, took control and banished these brothers to Armorica, modern Brittany. This information is derived from a Welsh triad recorded by a ninth-century Welsh monk from Bangor named Nennius in his *Historia Brittonum*. This was one of the sources for Geoffrey of Monmouth's *Historia Regum Britanniae* of around AD 1136. The latter historian was to create one of the most important legendary personalities in history out of these garbled tales of internecine warfare: Arthur, the supreme Celtic hero.

This mythical or semi-mythical 'king' was attended by a wizard, also loosely based on a real character, 'Merlin', whose magical activities and vaticinations closely resemble those of the Druids. Vortigern is also said to have consulted Druids, and the entire atmosphere of the Arthurian epic is permeated by magic, a re-emergence of the vivid Celtic imagination after centuries of Roman 'order' and rationalism. Even the 'Christian' elements of the stories are magical, and especially the 'Quest for the Holy Grail', perhaps the most mystical interpretation of the faith of all time, a truly elemental myth. But above all else, Arthur was said to be a British national resistance leader who raised armies to staunch the inflow of barbarians, and especially the Saxons, which had begun at about the time Germanus made his visits. Vortigern is said to have hired these Germanic mercenaries just as his Roman predecessors had done long before him. Since these legends were to have such a profound impact on the national, and indeed global, imagination up to the present day, it will be useful to examine what evidence there is for a British national resistance, a heroic struggle which certainly has some basis in historical fact. Zosimus Historicus, a Greek historian from Constantinople who was writing shortly after these events, says:

> The barbarians from beyond the Rhine attacked without hindrance and prompted those living in Britain and some of the Celtic peoples to leave Roman control and live their own lives, free of Roman laws. The Britons took up weapons, and facing every danger themselves, liberated their cities from the barbarian threat.[13]

---

13 Zosimus, *Historia Nova*.

In fact, Bishop Germanus (or 'Saint Garmon' as the Welsh remember him) had commenced military hostilities against the intruders during his visits. A field outside Mold in Flintshire called *Maes Garmon* is traditionally the site of his famous 'Allelulia Victory'. Learning of a large-scale raid, probably by the Irish or Picts rather than the Saxons, Germanus reverted to his former military status and gathered a British militia of some kind together. As the barbarians were making their way through a steep-sided valley he ordered his men to await his signal, and when he sighted the pagan force he shouted out 'Allelulia!' three times. Immediately the British host responded with the same cry, echoing around the hills – and the surprised raiders panicked and fled, leaving all their booty behind them in their haste to reach their ships.

This bloodless victory was interpreted as a miracle, but the Irish could not be kept at bay so easily for long. The Cornish historian Charles Thomas made a strong case for Irish settlement in western Britain exceeding that of the Germanic immigrants arriving in the east during the fifth and sixth centuries.[14] If the designation of Cornwall and the south-west as Arthur's traditional heartland is correct then his military struggles may well have been against his Irish cousins rather than 'Saxons'. So, before we journey into the magical realm of King Arthur's Britain, a brief overview of the 'real' world of fifth and sixth century Britain will prove instructive.

Geoffrey Ashe, one of the foremost experts on the Arthurian period, was in absolutely no doubt that behind the myths and legendary accretions of the intervening centuries, there was an Arthurian fact:

> As the legend is unique, so the fact is unique. In essence, it is this. Britain, alone among the lands of the Roman Empire, achieved independence before the northern barbarians poured in, and put up a fight against them – a very long, and at one stage successful, fight. Between Roman Britain and Anglo-Saxon England there is an inter-regnum, which is not a chaos as historians once imagined, but a creative epoch with a character of its own. This rally of a Celtic people in some degree Romanised and Christianised is the reality of Arthur's Britain.[15]

But what evidence is there for such a Romano-British resurgence? Unfortunately, the promulgation of the Arthurian myth itself may have had the effect of skewing our perspective, because a myth of national resistance needs an antagonist, preferably a demonic, wicked, pagan antagonist. The fall of Britain was ascribed to the treachery and scheming of Vortigern, who allegedly invited Jutish and Saxon mercenaries into Britain and these latter peoples became the bête noire for the British scribes and historians such as

---

14 Thomas, C., *Britain and Ireland in Early Christian Times, AD 400–800*, Thames & Hudson, London, 1971.
15 Ashe, G., *The Quest for Arthur's Britain*, Pall Mall Press, London, 1968.

Gildas and Nennius, whose testimony forms our only, rather indistinct and partial view of the facts. In fact, Gildas is more than partial, he is deeply prejudiced, describing the Saxons as 'wolves' and rejoicing in victories against 'the gallows crew' as he calls them. As we will see, Gildas was the main source and moral inspiration for the later Bede, the 'father of English history', and his 'history' was actually a polemic against the immorality of the *tyrannoi* or Celtic warlords and their apostasy.

The myth Gildas propagated, in simple terms, is this. God has appointed the kings to rule over Britain, which to him is analogous to the Holy Land. His so-called 'complaining book' *De Excidio et Conquestu Britanniae* ('On the Conquest and Ruin of Britain') is a diatribe against the major British kings. Just as the prophets of ancient Israel had castigated wayward kings, so now Gildas takes it upon himself to do likewise. If these kings fail in their duty then God will send punishment upon his chosen folk, and the form of this punishment was, according to his interpretation, the pagan Saxons. Later, when Bede came to read Gildas, he was profoundly influenced by the idea that the Celtic peoples had lost their rightful dignity as heirs to the sovereignty of Britain precisely because of their apostasy and sin. He took up the theme as a justification for Anglo-Saxon hegemony, but later, during the Viking depredations, Archbishop Wulfstan of York reiterated the theme in his *Sermo Lupi ad Anglos* ('the Sermon of the Wolf to the English') in the early eleventh century. I make this point only to emphasise how easily 'historical facts' can be predicated upon partial and personal interpretations, and how these traditional perspectives are transmitted automatically for many centuries. There is no doubt in the author's mind that these national cultural myths exercised a strong influence on the 'Brexit' debate, for example.

But if the 'wolfish' Saxons were not responsible for the downfall of Britain, who or what was? The steady exodus of the wealthiest people from Roman towns to palatial villas on extensive country estates meant that British urban culture was never a great success even at the best of times. Even *Londinium*, the largest city by far, had a population of at most 50,000, and the smaller provincial centres like *Camulodunum*, *Eboracum* and *Corinium* (Cirencester) between 10,000 and 20,000. As the cities went into decline, Roman culture, which was pre-eminently urban, began to lose influence, and with it so did Christianity. Ashe presents an interesting perspective on this:

> The old religion, though doomed as such, also acquired a brief vigour that enabled it to live on in another form. At Lydney, the god Nodens inhabited a temple which was still fairly new ... Arthur, in one of his weirder guises, is a Wild Huntsman who rides through the clouds snatching the spirits of the dead; and his companion is Gwyn-ap-Nudd, Gwyn the son of Nodens. Gwyn is the King of the Fairies and the underworld. Another transmuted god was Maponus, who became the hero Mabon. Another was Belinus, who became Beli son of Manogan ... one of the results was the slow formation of the

legends of Glastonbury, where Christian hermits were possibly already living. Gwyn-ap-Nudd was eventually said to have an unseen palace on Glastonbury Tor, and Bran reappeared as Brons, the keeper of the Holy Grail.

Just as in more recent times, the decline of a distant supranational authority bred resentment, and a corresponding celebration of all things national and 'traditional', including their ancient tribal identities. As the towns decayed and their defensive walls collapsed or their circuits proved too large to be adequately manned, the local warlords resorted to the hill forts of their Iron Age ancestors, restoring them with massive new ramparts. A case in point is South Cadbury hill fort in Somerset. Archaeological digs in the late 1960s revealed that some mighty British warlord had constructed revetments of wood and stone, huge gateways and watchtowers, large residential buildings and a hall, as well as foundations for a unique cruciform church within the defences. Local people were never in any doubt about who the architect of these wonders was. John Leland, the English antiquary, recorded in 1542:

At South Cadbyri standith Camallate, sumtyme a famose toun or castelle. The people can tell nothing thar but that Arture much resorted to Camallate.

South Cadbury was not alone. A network of huge hill forts with beacons for signalling between them spread all across the south-west – a signal from South Cadbury seen from atop Glastonbury Tor would have reached Brent Knoll hill fort within a matter of minutes, weather permitting. Whoever ordered these fortresses to be refurbished was in possession of considerable authority and large resources of manpower. It is more than tempting to admit that the medieval folk of South Cadbury had a point when they thought 'Arture' had been that man.

Considerable controversy has arisen concerning the initial Anglo-Saxon immigration. Gildas left us in no doubt that the 'wolfish villains' were the culprits when it came to sheer wanton violence and destruction. He describes the whole of southern Britain as going up in flames following the Saxon revolt against Vortigern 'until it burnt nearly the whole surface of the island, and licked the western Ocean with its red and savage tongue'. Martin Welch, writing in his *Anglo-Saxon England*, seems irritated by the revisionism of modern historians on this point:

In recent years some archaeologists seem determined to believe that very few immigrants from northern Germany and southern Scandinavia were involved in the creation of Anglo-Saxon England from post-Roman Britain ... there are real problems in accepting such a viewpoint. Firstly it argues that we know much better than contemporary or slightly later commentators who wrote about the events in Britain ... Bede felt secure in the belief that he was not of British descent and that his people, the Northumbrians, were Angles.

But in the case of Gildas, we have seen how the deep prejudices and cultural preconceptions of a Christian cleric with his own agenda could have the effect of exaggerating a personal and particular bete noire, just as modern 'tabloid' newspapers excoriate despised groups in our day. Bede's certainty that no British blood ran in his veins does not tally with recent genetic research, which estimates that as few as 10 per cent of the population of sixth-century Britain were of Anglo-Saxon origins. Gildas accepted that Britons were still living within areas of Anglo-Saxon settlement, but thought they would have been 'better off dead'. But was he right? For many of them, perhaps, a reversion to a simpler, more economically sustainable way of life, a pagan pantheon which closely resembled that of their Celtic ancestors, and the security offered by a tribal warlord with a strong retinue of warriors, may have been preferable to the alternative.

Just as Angles, Saxons, Jutes, Frisians and Franks were arriving, so too Britons were emigrating, some to Armorica or Brittany, others to Britonia in Galicia, in Spain. It has been estimated that the maximum number of Germanic immigrants into Britain over a century cannot have amounted to more than 100,000 persons. True, these people were well-armed, fearsome and occasionally cruel 'barbarians', but sheer logistics tell us that they could not have been responsible for an absolute genocide on the scale Gildas hints at. The collapse of a money economy, an outbreak of severe plague, climate change and many other factors played a role in the decline of Britain.

There had long existed a cultural link between those Celtic-speaking nations connected by the Atlantic, a seagoing trading culture which had existed since the very earliest times, as we saw in earlier chapters. The extraordinary thing is that these ancient links now experienced something of a renaissance. All over the south-west, including at Tintagel, Cornwall, traditionally the birthplace of Arthur, and at South Cadbury, archaeological finds reveal that high-status goods were being regularly imported from the Eastern Roman Empire, which was still prospering despite the collapse of its western counterpart.

During the actual Roman occupation the north and west of Britain had been poor relations, marginal and 'difficult', always under the heel of military occupation. Now, suddenly, they were free to reassert their ancient cultural unity. In this light, it may be that the empire began to exert an emotional pull from a distance that it had failed to achieve when it was a tangible reality. Likewise the Christian faith, which had never caught on among the rural population, and which was strongly influenced by heretical ideas, became now a cypher for 'civilisation' as against the 'barbaric' paganism of their new national enemy, the *Sais* or Saxons. This may explain the enduring legendary connections to Arthur in the south-west and north of England in particular. In effect, Britain had divided into two cultural entities.

The Welsh have a word, *hiraeth*, for which there is no literal English translation, but an approximate meaning is 'a deep yearning or longing for a place or time which no longer exists, and so can never be restored or visited'. It is a sad word, but it sums up, I think, the odd emotional atmosphere of the Arthurian tales, for these legends express just such a yearning. The ultimate sorrow of Arthur's passing is ameliorated only slightly by his promise to 'come again to my kingdom, and dwell with the Britons with mickle joy'. We know that this promise will never be fulfilled in our own lifetimes, like the second coming of Christ. But before the barge emerges from the mists of Avalon, and 'two women, wondrously formed ... took Arthur anon, and bare him quickly, and laid him softly down and forth gan depart', we must set the scene for the magical drama which has obsessed the human imagination for 1,500 years.

Gildas is probably correct to say that there was some sort of rebellion by the mercenaries Vortigern had hired, but it was almost certainly more like an extensive Viking raid than a full-scale invasion bent on conquest. Even he concedes that after they had done their worst they returned to their limited reservations in Kent and eastern Britain. The analogy with the Vikings is interesting, because one feature of Anglo-Saxon 'barbarism' which differentiated them from, say, the Franks, Goths, Alans or Burgundians was their absolute devotion to pagan gods. The latter were all Christians – heretical Arian Christians, true, but nonetheless they shared in some degree the standards of 'civilisation'. The Anglo-Saxons, however, were more like the later Vikings and viewed Christianity as an unmanly, servile, alien religion.

Among these peoples there were strict rules of conduct, particularly about honourable agreements between allies. Vortigern had undertaken to make payments of foodstuffs in kind called *Annona* to ensure that the growing mercenary colony was well provisioned. For reasons which remain obscure – perhaps economic disruption, political division, plague, labour shortages, poor harvests, or just calculated treachery – these payments failed to arrive. To the Saxon chieftains this was not a mere delay or inconvenience but a personal dishonour to them. There is little reason to condemn the Anglo-Saxons as cruel sociopaths or genocidal maniacs, but their anger at a situation like this should not be underestimated.

Geoffrey of Monmouth in his *Historia Regum Britanniae* tells us that Vortigern was called to account for his actions at a grand council between the leading men of both the Britons and the Saxons:

> When Hengist saw that a suitable moment had come for his act of treachery, he bellowed out '*Nimet oure saxas!*' ('Saxons, draw your knives!'). He himself immediately seized hold of Vortigern and held him tight by his royal robe. The moment they heard this signal the Saxons drew their daggers, attacked the leaders standing near them and cut the throats of about four hundred and sixty counts and earls ... afterwards the holy Eldadus buried

the corpses and said the last rites over them according to the custom of the Christian Church: this was not far from Caercarraducc, which is now called Salisbury ... the Britons had come there all unarmed, thinking of nothing but the peace conference.

This so-called 'treachery of the long knives' became notorious in British and later Welsh history. The saying 'Never trust an Englishman in long sleeves' survives in Wales, but this entire event may be a literary device to account for the disappearance of Vortigern. Following the massacre he dishonoured himself further by marrying the beautiful daughter of Hengist, Rowena. Not only did Vortigern put away his legitimate wife (perhaps Severa, a daughter of Magnus Maximus), by whom he had three sons, but he had married a pagan foreigner. Ever afterwards, the inhabitants of *Lloegyr* or England have been known in Wales as 'the children of Rowena'.

According to Geoffrey, Vortigern retired in disgrace to his own fortress of Gwertherynion in Radnorshire, or possibly Little Doward, Herefordshire. He tried to construct a mightier fortress but in the night the mortar disintegrated and the stones kept collapsing. Vortigern consults a Druid to find the solution to this problem, and is advised to find a male child of a human mother and an Otherworld father who must be sacrificed, so that his blood can set the mortar. A search is made throughout the land of Wales, and eventually, at Carmarthen, the prophesied boy is discovered. This is no ordinary boy, but a powerful magician, *Myrddin Emrys* or 'Merlin'. He is the result of a union between a nun and an *incubus*, a demon in male form who seduces women in their sleep. Merlin is therefore 'a fatherless child', and not strictly human. He convinces Vortigern that beneath the castle there is an underground lake in which two dragons fight every night, causing the structure to collapse. This is the very first mention in history of 'Merlin', one of the most powerful magical personalities of all time; a convenient point to conclude a strictly 'historical' account and enter the magical world of King Arthur, the Round Table, and Camelot – a liminal world half real, half imagined, but totally captivating.

6

The Mists of Avalon

In the western confines of Britain there is a certain royal island of large extent, surrounded by water, abounding in all the beauties of nature and necessities of life. In the first neophytes of Catholic law, God beforehand acquainted them, found a church constructed by no human art, but by the hands of Christ Himself, for the salvation of His people.

> Letter of St Augustine of Canterbury
> to Pope Gregory the Great, AD 600

The letter above is authentic. St Augustine of Canterbury landed in Kent in AD 597 with a small band of followers. He did not arrive in a completely pagan land, for the British/Celtic Church had survived in the west – it was only the Anglo-Saxon kingdoms which were still pagan. His initial success was so limited that Augustine set out on a mission to the western borderlands with the Britons, to meet their bishops at Great Witley in Worcestershire. One of Augustine's followers, Paulinus, arrived at *Ynys Witrin* or Glastonbury, the 'island' referred to in the letter. Here he found a tiny wattle-and-daub structure, an oratory or chapel, which by tradition had been constructed by Christ Himself during one of the eighteen 'missing years' of His life when we hear nothing about His activities. It is claimed that this was the first church built above ground anywhere in the world.

Neither Augustine nor Paulinus were credulous fools, but highly intelligent and educated men. Paulinus was so impressed that he paid for a sheet-lead covering to be erected on an awning over the little church so that it might be better protected from the elements and thereby preserved for posterity. These stories were known in Britain well before Augustine's Roman Catholic mission. Gildas was aware of the tale of Christ's sojourn in the island: 'Jesus' light and precepts were afforded to this island during the last year of the reign of Tiberius.' This would have been in AD 37, a few years after the crucifixion and resurrection. Joseph of Arimathea, Christ's great-uncle and next of kin following the death of Mary's husband Joseph, had gone to Pilate to plead for His body so that it could be laid in his own tomb. Joseph had a vision in which the Archangel Raphael commanded him to take the 'Holy Grail' to the 'blessed isles' in the west. The apostle Philip commissioned Joseph to return to Britain to spread the faith after the resurrection.

Joseph had been a wealthy merchant in the tin trade, or *nobilis decurion*, according to Maelgwn of Llandaff, and we have already seen how a very long-standing trade in tin had existed ever since Pytheas and his expedition at least 300 years before. In addition to tin, there were also rich deposits of lead and copper in the Mendip Hills, just up the Bristol Channel. A village in the Mendips, Priddy near Glastonbury, has a long tradition of Christ having visited there. The villagers have a saying: 'As sure as Christ walked in Priddy.' Most of the lead in the Roman world originated in these hills; the lead pipework of Pompeii, for example, came from Somerset.

Joseph used exactly the same river routes as Pytheas, from Marseilles up to the Breton coast and thence the crossing to Falmouth or the *Mor Hafren* or 'Severn Sea'. The Cornish miners used to chant 'Joseph was a Tinner' or 'Joseph was in the tin trade' while purifying the molten ore until the nineteenth century. The town of East Looe in Cornwall still displays Joseph and the boy Jesus sailing in a small ship to St George's Island just off the coast as its town emblem. All over the former tin-mining areas, curious stone crosses called 'Tunic Crosses' depict a young boy wearing a short tunic on the reverse, supposedly a representation of the youthful Christ. He was expected.

The Druids already worshipped a god called *Yesu* or *Esus* and worshipped one God in three aspects; St Columba, when he arrived on the lonely island of Iona off the wild Scottish coast found two Druids already there, claiming to be Christians. Doubting their authenticity, he asked them to leave, which they did. The Irish Druids too were expecting the new religion, and there are hints in stories like *The Children of Lir* that Irish magicians had foreknowledge of the coming of Christ. St Patrick found the Irish Druids to be co-operative, so that there was an almost seamless transition from Druidism to Christianity, so much so that the first Irish-born bishops were former Druids. What Rome had failed to achieve with four full legions, the Christian missions accomplished with astonishing celerity.

A British king of the Silures tribe named Arviragus granted Joseph 12 hides of land outside Glastonbury where he and his twelve followers built a small religious community on the site where Jesus had once resided. This Arviragus was, according to Geoffrey of Monmouth, a son of Cunobelinus, or 'Cymbeline' as Shakespeare called him, and a cousin of the British national hero Caratacus. It was believed that during the latter's captivity with his family in Rome they had been converted to Christianity, and that his daughter Gladys, renamed 'Claudia' by the Roman emperor, had married a Christian convert called Rufus Pudens, a Roman senator. It was in the latter's apartments in Rome that St Paul spent his final years. The couple allegedly returned to Britain, and Claudia became a saint of the early church. Arviragus continued the Silurian resistance to the Romans after Caratacus had been betrayed, and they won a great victory against a full Roman legion, possibly *Legio* XX, *Valeria Victrix*. As the leaders of the British resistance, the Silurian royal house became 'high kings' of Britain, and it has been claimed that Arthur was a descendant of Arviragus. Joseph is said to have baptised the king, and presented him with a shield 'bearing a cross of Christ's blood, which from his neck did run'. Unfortunately, much of Geoffrey of Monmouth's 'history' is a subtle mix of garbled facts and his own imagination, but the stories are intriguing nevertheless.

Jesus was said to have travelled with Joseph to Britain on several occasions in His youth, for he was the legal guardian of Mary and the boy. Jesus traditionally stayed behind with His mother to commune with nature and meditated on matters spiritual in Glastonbury, where He built the oratory 'with His own hands' (He was, after all, a carpenter). When William the Conqueror sent men to Glastonbury to assess the abbey for tax purposes for his Domesday survey of England in the eleventh century, they found a monastery known as 'the Secret of the Lord', with 12 hides of land which had always been exempt from tax since the time of King Ine of Wessex, who in about AD 700 (according to the historian William of Malmesbury) had written to the abbot saying, 'To the ancient church situate in the place called Glastonbury, which church the Great High Priest and Chiefest Minister formerly through His own ministry, and that of the angels sanctified by many and unheard of miracles, to Himself and the eternal Virgin Mary.' William of Malmesbury was well known for his meticulous exclusion of dubious material from his histories, and the Domesday assessors were notoriously efficient and cynical. But the question we must ask is the same one William Blake immortalised:

> And did those feet in ancient time,
> Walk upon England's mountains green?
> And was the Holy Lamb of God,
> On England's pleasant pastures seen?[16]

But there were also, it was alleged, physical proof of Joseph's mission. He supposedly brought with him two phials – one containing Christ's sweat, the other one His blood – and also a small olive-wood bowl or cup, that which had either held the wine at the last supper or Christ's blood, which was collected in it at the crucifixion, the so-called 'Holy Grail'. Robert de Boron,

---

16 Blake, W., *Milton*, London, 1804.

a twelfth-century French poet, in his *Joseph d'Arimethe* says the vessel performed both functions. These extraordinarily holy relics were eventually bequeathed to the abbey, as proofs of its primacy as the oldest Christian foundation in the world.

Whatever we may now think about such stories, by the fifth century their purchase on the imagination of a culture liberated from the long Roman hegemony, yet at the same time oppressed by the *realpolitik* of a new and potent pagan enemy, was absolute. This is why, I believe, the Arthurian resistance was a real historical process – and the ideology which gave it its enduring strength derived from a particular cultural paradigm peculiar to the British Celts. The 'civilisation' Arthur defended was not 'Roman', 'Catholic', 'British' 'or 'Celtic' but a particular hybrid peculiar to the western Britons, a melange of conventional Christianity, Druidism/Pelagianism, and a phoney nostalgia for a vanished empire which, it was believed, had itself once relied on Britannia as a bulwark against barbarism. The myth of the 'Holy Grail' was an attempt to euhemerise and syncretise all these themes into one overarching story.

Joseph was supposed to have concealed the Holy Grail in secret caves beneath the Tor, traditionally at or near the 'Chalice Well', which has never yet run dry, and which runs red like Christ's blood. Another theory is that it was concealed at the nearby 'White Well'. There are almost certainly caves beneath the Tor, and in the twelfth century a party of monks were dispatched into them to search for the chalice. Only three returned alive, one struck dumb, his two companions insane. No person of impure heart can behold the vessel and live to tell the tale, for it is the ultimate 'holy communion', conferring everlasting life and healing all physical and spiritual sickness.

I emphasise 'western Britons' for a particular reason. Although Arthur's legend is ubiquitous now, originally it was concentrated in two main regions: northern and western Britain. However, it is only in the latter that we find traditions which point to places where he is definitely said to have lived – Tintagel in Cornwall, where he is said to have been born, or South Cadbury in Somerset, said to be the original 'Camelot', for example. The River Camel, which rises on Bodmin Moor and meets the sea at Padstow Bay, was identified by the Anglo-Saxon poet Layamon as 'Camlann', site of the 'last dim, weird battle of the west', and Arthur's Cornish base was at Kelliwic nearby. Dozmary Pool on Bodmin Moor is supposed to have been where Bedwyr, the prototype for the 'Sir Bedivere' of the medieval tales, threw Arthur's magical sword, Excalibur, into the grasp of an undine hand. So deep in the folk psyche were these traditions that in AD 1113 a party of French monks were almost lynched in Bodmin when they scoffed at the idea of Arthur being a 'real' personage who was immortal. An old Welsh poem in the *Black Book of Carmarthen*, the oldest literary manuscript in Welsh, seems to be derived from an earlier Brythonic original which may be one of the earliest references to Arthur in history:

At Llongborth I saw Arthur's heroes who cut with steel
The Emperor, ruler of our labour
In Llongborth Gereint was slain, heroes of the land of Dyfneint,
Before they were slain they slew.

Some believe that 'Llongborth' was Portsmouth, where a British prince named Natanleod was allegedly killed with 5,000 of his men by the West Saxons. Unfortunately, this reference in the *Anglo-Saxon Chronicle* is almost certainly a later interpolation. The *Elegy for Gereint* refers to a native prince of Devonshire, not Hampshire, and Llongborth is more likely to have been Langport in Somerset. And there is one other telling location.

A hagiography of St Gildas, the historian we have encountered before, was written by Caradoc of Llancarfan in Wales in the twelfth century. Poignantly, Gildas failed to mention Arthur at all in his *Liber Querulous*, or 'complaining book' as he called it, but Caradoc relates that Melwas, the king who ruled in Avalon or Glastonbury, 'the land of summer' or *Aestiva Regio* (Somerset), had kidnapped Arthur's wife, Guinevere or Gwenhwyfar. This extraordinary confluence of two of the greatest stories ever told, the Christian and the Arthurian, in one place in the British south-west is the magnetic pull which draws so many pilgrims to this day. The enigmatic Tor, rising above the Somerset Levels, is itself a natural omphalos, right at the heart of the most hallowed ground in Britain. Godney Island (it is now no longer an 'island', since the levels were drained) means 'God-marsh' island, from which etymology we may infer that this area was a holy sanctuary from the earliest times. The theme of sacred islands is very ancient indeed, and the ritual deposition of weapons, particularly swords, near insular causeways is a continuation of practices from the Iron Age.

In this place called 'Avalon' or *Ynys Afallon*, meaning 'the isle of apple trees', was concentrated the entire magical force of that culture which had endured along the western-facing coasts for thousands of years. It was here, where Joseph of Arimathea, or possibly even Christ Himself, had constructed the earliest Christian sanctuary in the world, where Arthur, the supreme hero of the British Celts, was buried with his wife *in insula Avalonia* – 'in the isle of Avalon'. Apples were the sacred fruit of the god Apollo, the same god the Britons called *Beli* or *Belinus*. We have seen how Apollo/Beli was the supreme god of the British Celtic pantheon, he who 'visited the island once in every nineteen years' according to Diodorus.

In this natural sanctuary, separated from the profane world by the holy waters, and shrouded in ethereal mists, the most extraordinary myth ever devised by the human race was conceived. Arthur calls together twelve of his most trusted companions, and charges them with a mission to find the Holy Grail and return it to Avalon. Note the familiar number of twelve followers and one leader, so redolent of both the twelve disciples and Christ – but also the twelve zodiacal constellations and the Sun we have observed earlier. Only three of the companions finally approach the sacred cup: Percival, Bors, and the young Galahad. The latter is the illegitimate son of Lancelot and Elaine, daughter of Pelles, the so-called 'Fisher King' who is the maimed and cursed keeper of the Grail at his fortress of Corbenic. He has foreknowledge that the child begotten in sin, his own grandson, will be the 'perfect knight' who will find the cup. This is confirmed when the lad takes his seat in the so-called 'siege perilous' at the Round Table. All who have dared to sit in the cursed chair previously have died, but Galahad is unharmed, the sign that he alone will attain the Grail, as the only 'perfect knight'. But as we have seen, no man can behold the Grail and live, and only Bors survives to tell the tale, Percival and Galahad having met with their apotheosis. These are the bare bones of the enduring myth, but what possible relevance can such tales have for us today, in our fallen age?

In 1539 the last abbot of Glastonbury, Richard Whiting, was dragged to the top of the Tor and hanged, drawn and quartered. His crime was to have refused to surrender the abbey's treasures, valued at 200,000 crowns, to the agents of Thomas Cromwell, acting on behalf of King Henry VIII and his iniquitous policy of the Dissolution of the Monasteries. Cromwell took the sick old man into custody at the Tower of London and tried to intimidate him, but Whiting stood his ground. Following his execution the abbey was razed, but the greatest treasure of all was never found. A party of former monks from the abbey made their way to Strata Florida Abbey in Wales, but this institution was also destroyed during the Dissolution. Some adjoining outbuildings, however, were restored, and the monks were employed by the Powell family, long-standing benefactors of the abbey. In exchange for their labour, they were allowed to remain there as 'guests'.

One by one the monks died, until just one remained. On his deathbed the last monk from Glastonbury gave a small olive-wood bowl, blackened with age and heavily damaged by pilgrims having torn chunks out of it with their teeth throughout the long centuries, into the care of the Powell family. They were asked to guard it well, for it was the monks' 'greatest treasure'. Ever since, miraculous cures have been ascribed – many hundreds if not thousands – to its restorative and healing powers. These are well attested, and are still reported to this day, including cases which medical science thought to be incurable.

The so-called 'Nanteos Cup' remained in the care of the Powell family for hundreds of years, but when the family line died out it was given into the care of the Mirylees family, also of Nanteos. The family eventually moved to Ross-on-Wye where, hearing of the plight of a local lady with a degenerative disease, they allowed her access to the cup. Unfortunately, the cup was stolen in transit, and the family contacted the BBC's *Crimewatch*, which made a desperate appeal for its safe return. A secret rendezvous was arranged with West Mercia police officers, and on Friday 19 June 2015 the cup was handed over anonymously. So devastated were the family by this frightful drama that they resolved to give the cup into the custody of the National Library of Wales in Aberystwyth, where in the summer of 2016 it went on display to the general public for the first time – suitably protected by the most up-to-date security technology.

So the ancient legend still has the power to grip our collective imagination. It has transmuted and been embellished many times during the intervening centuries until it has outgrown the prosaic 'history' which birthed it. But what was the history? The fact is that despite all the advances in archaeological and historiographical expertise in the last fifty years or so, we are still very much in the dark. What little we do know is generally inferred from unreliable or legendary sources, though this does not deter endless speculation. Every year of so a new candidate is proposed as the 'real King Arthur'. If such an important king existed, we would expect him to turn up in the most important near-contemporary history of the time, that of Gildas, but he is totally absent. We will examine the possible reasons for this shortly, but a contemporary leader Gildas does mention seems to be someone approximating to Vortigern, whom he calls a 'proud usurper' or *superbus tyrannus*, not a 'king' but the chairman of a committee of tribal and civic leaders comprising a national council.

The word 'usurper' may be related to a story related in Geoffrey of Monmouth's history that Vortigern had ruled through the surviving son of Constantine III, Constans II. He allegedly arranged to have Constans murdered by the Picts. Gildas is not as critical of Vortigern as later historians, but merely says that he was *infaustas* – 'unlucky'. His reign is recalled as being prosperous and secure for the most part, which may suggest a brief economic boom as imperial taxes no longer came due. This may explain the apparent prosperity Germanus witnessed. Gildas certainly had access to Saxon sources, for he uses the first English word in our national literature to describe how the Saxons came in three 'keels', or longships. This tells us that the first group could have comprised as few as 120 men in total. Gildas also relates a story that it was foretold by a wizard in the Jutish or Saxon homelands that they would plunder the land of Britain for 150 years, and occupy it for 300, a story consistent with devices used in Anglo-Saxon oral storytelling.

Vortigern's character gradually deteriorated over the centuries, until he became an archetypal 'villain'. William of Malmesbury has him importuning his own daughter into sexual intercourse with a promise that he will bestow half of the kingdom upon her. The girl bears him a son begotten in incest, and this is clearly related somehow to the events related in the life of Germanus of Auxerre. William portrays Vortigern as a libertine, a wastrel and a scoundrel, and while we must be aware that such one-dimensional characters are usually suspect in history, they do sometimes turn up. King John of England, for example, was as notorious in reality as in any later fiction.

Vortigern has three (or possibly four) sons, one of whom, Vortimer, takes command of the British armed forces in several battles against the Saxons. Following Vortigern's divorce of his mother, and his subsequent marriage to Rowena, Vortimer and his two brothers rebel against Vortigern. Vortimer succeeds him as the British national leader and leads the Britons in a hard-fought battle at *Episford* in Kent in which his brother Catigern is killed, as is Horsa, Hengist's brother. Vortimer died shortly afterwards, apparently by poisoning; traditionally the culprit was Rowena, his father's new Saxon wife, and Horsa's niece. Vortigern was then reinstated as the British national leader, but only as a puppet of the incoming Saxons, who now numbered in the thousands. This much, then, I think we can say – the traditions about Vortigern seem credible, even though they are slightly obscure and contradictory. The policy of introducing mercenary troops had been resorted to for a long time before the Roman departure from Britain, and it would have made sense for an indigenous ruler to continue it. But Gildas gives us the next part of the story too, of how a great British commander succeeded to Vortigern, and began a programme of national reconstruction and defence – Ambrosius Aurelianus.

It is probable that Vortigern was a Pelagian or some other kind of heretic, because his relations with Germanus are portrayed as being hostile. The expedition against the Irish or Pictish pirates which Germanus led into Wales may have been the first sign of the Romano-British Catholic party organising its own militia force. Ambrosius Aurelianus recalls very powerfully the name of Aurelius Ambrosius, or St Ambrose, a fourth-century Doctor of the Church whose theology had been a strong influence on St Augustine of Hippo – the adversary of Pelagius. It has been inferred from this that Ambrosius represented the orthodox wing of the Romano-British rural aristocracy. These were the fifth-century 'super-rich', whose huge estates in the Cotswolds and south-west England were threatened by the Saxon rebellion.

St Ambrose was the scourge of the Arian heretics, and perhaps Ambrosius contemplated a similar purge of the Pelagians and others in Britain. He must have had some sort of military training or background, or perhaps came from a family with strong military traditions, because we know that he mustered an army. This in itself was an astonishing feat, replicated nowhere else in the post-Roman Western Empire, but Ambrosius also constructed a fleet to secure the sea lanes between Armorica (Brittany) and south-west Britain. Gildas says that his family had 'worn the purple', meaning that he may well have been one of the brothers of Constantine III. A society which is on the verge of collapse naturally looks to a strong leader with a traditional pedigree, and it would seem Ambrosius was that man. Welsh legend remembers him as *Emrys* and he is called a *gwledig* or commander – a regional warlord with a base in the mountains of Wales. But when he arrives with his retinue in the south and raises his standard his appeal is to the 'citizens', those who still adhered to the traditions of Rome and the official religion. This undoubtedly historical figure was the Winston Churchill of his day, and the Britons rallied.

Eventually the Saxon threat was contained in the late 450s, and Germanic settlement was halted – and even went into reverse. Sir Frank Stenton in his *Anglo-Saxon England: Oxford History of England* noted that many Germanic settlers in the south-east of Britain decided to leave for northern France and Normandy around this time. The reason for this seems clear: Ambrosius and his forces had fought the Saxon invaders to a standstill and inflicted severe defeats on them, culminating in a crushing victory over them at a place Gildas calls *Mons Badonicus* or 'Mount Badon'. Gildas says he was born in the year of this glorious feat of arms, giving us a date of about AD 490. But there is an anomaly, because that date comes too late for Ambrosius to have been the commander of the British forces. If it was the culmination of a war of national liberation, and the apogee of a Romano-British 'imperial' renaissance, then the person who was its figurehead was not Ambrosius Aurelianus.

Robert de Boron, the twelfth-century French poet, gives us the interesting information that Ambrosius had adopted the title 'Pendragon', meaning 'head-dragon', after witnessing a comet in the form of a dragon. 'Pendragon' was a title conferring absolute authority, and when Ambrosius died without heirs it passed to his brother, Uther, who succeeded to him as overall commander. Uther is of course the father of Arthur 'Pendragon', making him a nephew to Ambrosius, and nephew or great-nephew of the last British-based emperor, Constantine III. In the poem *Elegy for Gereint*, the word *ameraudur*, meaning 'emperor', is explicitly used in connection with Arthur. One way of instilling an *esprit de corps* among previously untrained troops would certainly have been the revival of obscure but important-sounding military offices and titles.

The historian John Morris in his *The Age of Arthur: A History of the British Isles 350–650* made it his life's work to prove that Arthur was the last sub-Roman emperor of Britain, desperately trying to turn back the tide of history. Whatever else we may think of these stories, the fact remains that Saxon progress was stopped in its tracks for about forty or fifty years and British civilisation was preserved – by someone.

Was it Arthur? The problem with disentangling the legendary from the historical personage is this. The legendary character is 'real', but the historical personage is either absent or illusory. This in itself is a particularly pleasing aspect of the myth. Unfortunately, the banal investigations of literalist historians who insist on 'finding' a 'real' historical 'king' called Arthur using conventional means such as archaeology have given rise to endless speculation, unproven assertion and wishful thinking. Arthur's name is connected with countless ancient sites all over Britain, and every antiquarian is fiercely protective about their own 'local' candidate.

In my neck of the woods that candidate is an historical prince named Owain Ddantgwyn, who lived in the old Roman city of *Viroconium Cornoviorum*, or Wroxeter near modern Shrewsbury. Owain ruled at the beginning of the sixth century, precisely at the time Welsh annals record the Battle of Badon (dated 490–516) and 'the fight at Camlann' (dated 511–537). All over Britain urban life had gone into marked decline by this time. Even London was largely abandoned, and its great church of St Paul's on Tower Hill was a burned-out ruin. But Wroxeter was an exception to this rule. The ruins of the huge 'old work', as it is known, can still be seen here; it was once part of a Roman basilica the size of a cathedral nave.

By AD 350 the marked decline in urban life meant that the grand old buildings were in ruins, but then, during the prosperous reign of Vortigern, Wroxeter experienced a post-Roman renaissance. Although the lack of Roman masonic expertise meant that the buildings were constructed in timber rather than stone, a massive timber-aisled hall was constructed in place of the basilica, 125 feet long by 52 feet wide. Onto this an 80-foot-long extension had been added. Around this hall was clustered a new complex of shops and arcades and residential buildings of lesser importance. Whoever ordered and paid for this renovation was someone imitating the Roman imperial ideal, and tradition states that it was Vortigern, who is cited as a progenitor of the kings of Powys on a monument known as the 'Pillar of Eliseg' erected about AD 850, but the centre may have remained as the seat of the kings of Powys for some years after Vortigern. Powys was not, as now, a large Welsh county but a British kingdom extending well into the eastern Midlands.

It has been speculated that the refurbished city could be the template for 'Camelot'. Enniaun Yrth, the name of Owain's father, sounds similar enough to 'Uther' to have fuelled speculation that Owain may be 'the real King Arthur'. Gildas helpfully tells us that his battle-name or 'nickname' was 'the Bear'. Now, *Arth* or in Latin *Artorius* means 'bear', and it was a common practice among Celtic warriors of this time to adopt the name of a totem animal. Owain's ancestors, the kings of Gwynedd, were descendants of a tribe called the *Votadini* or *Gododdin*, which was relocated from the Scottish borderlands to North Wales with the objective of expelling Irish settlers there. They were known as 'head dragons' or 'Pendragons', and the bard Llywarch Hen describes the princes of a small local statelet called Pengwern as being descended from Arthur.

Quite near to Wroxeter there are places which may be 'Camlann'. There is a valley called Camlann outside Dolgellau, and a river called the Camlad runs very near to Mitchell's Fold stone circle near Priestweston on the Shropshire border with Powys, where, tradition states, Arthur drew the sword Excalibur from the stone. All these tantalising clues tempt local enthusiasts to surmise that 'Arthur' was a 'local hero' – but I am convinced that the connections with the south-west, Cornwall and Somerset in particular, are too strong to ignore. Archaeological proof may never emerge which will confirm my intuition, but the legendary connections and folk beliefs which have passed down to us for many centuries make it clear to me that 'Arthur' is not an historical person as such, but a magical figure, the personification of a unique culture created from a fusion of Celtic mysticism, past Roman glories and Christian imagery. That is why the material search is doomed; the Grail cannot be discovered in the exterior world, but only by an exploration of 'inner-space' – a magical process.

It is a common presumption among the English to dismiss the Arthurian traditions as the compensation myth of a defeated, emasculated Brythonic adversary, but while Arthur may be legendary the battle of Mount Badon was all too real. Later Welsh annals are explicit that Arthur was the victor:

490–516: Battle of Badon in which Arthur carried the cross of our Lord Jesus Christ on his shoulders for three days and nights and the Britons were victorious.

During the ninth century, Wales, like its English neighbour, was in the process of unification. A monk at Bangor named Nennius was determined to establish Arthur as the 'historical' ancestor of several important Welsh dynasties. Nearly all that was known about Arthur had been passed down through oral storytelling and poetry, the traditional devices of the bards. Nennius decided to 'make a heap of all I could find' in relation to Arthur, and the battle of Mount Badon becomes not just a great victory against the *Sais* but the culmination of a nationwide campaign to liberate the former Roman provinces from interlopers such as the Saxons, Irish and Picts.

Curiously, this list of twelve major battles, geographically widely dispersed, does not make Arthur a 'king' at all. Instead he is described as the *dux bellorum*, 'the leader of battles'. This seems such an awkward fact to disclose in any attempt to create a myth of a king, that it must be a genuine record of some old Roman military command. Nennius and his *Historia Brittonum* written about AD 828 formed the main source for Geoffrey of Monmouth's *Historia Regum Britanniae* 300 years later. Whereas the latter writer was consciously and deliberately conflating history with his own imaginative fiction, Nennius was at least only trying to pin Arthur down as an 'historical' person. His list of twelve battles seems real, because the places he mentions do exist – though they are a long way from each other.

In chapter 4 we saw how the Brythons had a military tradition which disputed river crossings as a central strategy. There are six such river battles: one on a river called 'Glein', no less than four on a river called 'Dubglas', and one on a river called 'Bassas'. The last named may well be Hammerwich Water near Lichfield, beside which the 'Staffordshire Hoard' was discovered in 2009. The seventh battle is in the 'wood of

Celidon' – that is the Caledonian Forest near to Hadrian's Wall. The next battle is a great slaughter of the enemy at a place called Castle Guinnion near what is now Bishop Auckland in County Durham. Clearly Arthur's force is a long way from south-west Britain, and its operations are mobile, using some kind of cavalry. Arthur is said to have 'carried on his shoulders an image of St Mary Ever-Virgin' a confusing passage which inclines one to think that the Welsh word *scuid* or 'shoulder' has been incorrectly transcribed for *scuit* meaning 'shield'. Another battle takes place at 'the City of the Legion' meaning either Chester or Caerleon. Other battles are fought, one at a river named 'Tribruit' and another on a 'Mount Agned'. But the culmination is Mount Badon where 'there fell in one onslaught of Arthur's, nine hundred and sixty men; and none slew them but he alone, and in all his battles he remained the victor'.

The eminent historian John Morris interpreted this battle list as evidence for a real King Arthur who was the last glorious representative of the imperial pretensions of sub-Roman Britain. In his view, Arthur was nothing less than an imperial figure, desperately attempting to reunite the former Roman provinces under Christian authority. These battles, he thought, were part of a campaign to liberate areas which had fallen to the barbarians – this not only meant Saxons, but also Picts on and beyond the northern wall, and the Irish who had occupied south-western Wales. The region of Dyfed had been occupied by an Irish tribe called the Deisi, and Morris was certain that some powerful authority had enabled the liberation of that area just at the right time. A local memorial stone to a man called *Votepor* calls him a *Protector*. This is a specific Roman military rank, and it meant someone who acted as a personal bodyguard to an emperor. Stilicho, the half-Vandal general who became known as 'the last of the Romans', had been a *Protector* of the Eastern Roman Emperor not long before – but if Votepor was really a *Protector*, this begs one question: on whose behalf was he acting? If Arthur really did adopt the title and style of an 'emperor', then perhaps the British recovery really did recapture the glory days of empire, if only briefly.

But as with Carausius and his mini-empire before it, Arthur's Britain was doomed. Mount Badon was a real British victory, but it didn't win the war. Some sort of territorial partition was enforced on the Germanic invaders, and if John Morris was correct the northern wall was stabilised, the Angles contained in their northern settlements, and the Irish were expelled from Dyfed and the south-western peninsula of Devon and Cornwall. The *Annales Cambriae* contains two brief and enigmatic entries about Arthur. The final entry dated 516 just states, 'The fight at Camlaun in which Arthur and Medraut were slain; and there was death in England and Ireland.' The contrast between the centuries-long romantic literary canon and this almost derisory entry is extraordinary, and can only be accounted for in two ways. Either this entry is a later addition, designed to confer some sort of 'historical' credibility on the legends, or it is genuine.

The reason for a later addition may be that, within a few years of his death, Arthur 'the Soldier' as he was known was a standard hero in many British ballads. His name appears in Brythonic poems very soon after his alleged passing. By AD 600 the bard Aneirin was composing a long poem about a band of 300 mounted British warriors who set out on a suicide mission against the Northumbrian Angles called *Y Gododdin*. One of the heroes killed in this battle at *Catraeth*, or Catterick, in Yorkshire is described as 'sating the ravens with the enemies he killed, although he did not compare to Arthur'. Not very long afterwards we see another poetic reference to Arthur, which may not be so straightforward, in the *Canu Heledd* composed after AD 656 somewhere in Wales. It is attributed to a surviving royal princess of Pengwern, Heledd, all of whose brothers have been slain by the Saxons: 'Brothers I had, better it was when they lived, the whelps of Arthur, our mighty fortress.' It is often alleged that little evidence exists for the 'original' Arthur, but it is there, even if it relates to a mythical character rather than an historical person.

Arthur also occurs frequently in mnemonic triads, groups of themes arranged into three, a traditional Celtic device inherited ultimately from the Druids. Arthur occurs in them more often than can be explained for an entirely fictional character, and curiously he is not always portrayed as a hero. In the Welsh compendium of stories called the *Mabinogion* there is one story which has Arthur as a central character, 'Culhwch and Olwen'. This is a 'pre-Galfridian' (pre-Geoffrey of Monmouth) story which provides the original Celtic names for some of Arthur's followers, such as *Gwalchmei* (Gawain), *Cei* (Kay) and *Bedwyr* (Bedivere).

Arthur is mentioned in many lives of Welsh saints, including, as we observed earlier, the *Life of St Gildas* by Caradoc of Llancarfan. Unlike his later medieval persona, Arthur is usually portrayed in a poor light by these Celtic holy men, and particularly as one who oppressed the Celtic Church with heavy taxation. From this we might be tempted to draw some conclusions about the silence of Gildas in respect of Arthur. A *Life of St Padarn* written in the twelfth century describes Arthur as a *tyrannus*, and it seems he was not alone in this perspective. It is very possible that the glaring omission of Arthur from Gildas' history can be accounted for by the fact that Arthur had killed Hueil, his eldest brother. Gildas had demanded and received compensation from Arthur for this, as was his right. We have already noted how Gildas displayed a tendency to prejudice in his depiction of the Saxons. Perhaps the temptation to calumniate Arthur would have been simply too great, and so on the sore subject of his brother's executioner, Gildas elected to remain mute.

However, Arthur was remembered with more effusive affection overseas, in the increasingly British colony of Armorica or Brittany. The *Life of St Goeznovius*, a Cornishman who became bishop of Leon in Brittany, is one of our best insights into the Breton emigrations from Britain. He declares that the victories against the Saxons were attributable above all to 'Arthur, the great king of the Britons'. Goeznovius describes him as being one 'not in the roll of common men', for he is immortal, a sort of god who has not 'died' but has been 'summoned from human activity' to the Otherworld in the west. Within a few years of his passing, Arthur had become legendary among his own countrymen.

For the time being, the Saxon advances were renewed by vigorous kings leading strong armies. But as the stories increasingly implied, Arthur was not dead, but merely sleeping. In time he was to return in a more potent form, a semi-divine being – one of the greatest legendary personalities of all time.

7

The Weave of Wyrd

It is an acknowledged fact about the British that they are obsessed with the weather. Foreigners note this idiosyncrasy with a wry amusement but it is, I believe, a legacy or folk memory of a caste of Druids who claimed the power to control the weather by magical invocations. It was said they could bring down dense mists and fogs and foment fierce storms. St Patrick himself was a victim of such magic; the Druids conjured a blizzard to prevent him reaching their holiest sanctuary. Owain Glyndwr, the self-proclaimed Prince of Wales in the fifteenth century, was thought to have inherited this ability to influence the weather. When Henry IV of England sent an army against him Alex Gibbon tells us:

> In the downpour which followed, as the English army struggled miserably across a swollen river, the king himself was almost swept away by the tremendous force of the torrent which poured from the mountains. Day after day vast storms of appalling power raged above their heads, lightning leapt from peak to peak, and the river valleys of the Dee, the Severn and others turned to seas.

Shakespeare has Glyndwr gloat at his supernatural abilities:

> Three times hath Henry Bolingbroke made head
> Against my power. Thrice from the banks of the Wye
> And sandy-bottomed Severn, have I
> Sent him bootless home, and weather-beaten back ...

In his *The Mystery of Jack of Kent & the Fate of Owain Glyndwr*, Alex Gibbon reminds us of the 'Neolithic mechanics' of the sympathetic magical ritual of dashing water from a fountain onto a magic stone to cause intense storms. When Shakespeare has Glyndwr claim 'I can call spirits from the vasty deep and teach thee to command the devil', this is no mere dramatic flourish:

The first line here implies the creative darkness of the Celtic 'deep', its ultimate union with the waters of the sea (*Mor*), and its deep relationship with the dark aspect of the Triple-Goddess often known as the Morrigan. Accordingly we find Morvran (i.e '*mor-bran*, or 'sea-raven) in the *Mabinogion* ...

Glyndwr possessed a stone, called 'the Raven Stone', which gave him the power to become invisible. Another of his inherited magical powers was the ability to communicate with birds, and as Gibbon states, these were ultimately Druidic magical powers. The Druidic *dicheltair* was literally a 'cloak of invisibility'. Berresford Ellis claims that when the Druids were in transition to Christianity they brought with them their ancient magical powers, and this 'cloak' or 'cloud' of invisibility in particular. The bards carried with them a wand with tinkling bells which was a badge of office but also conferred supernatural abilities such as shapeshifting. If these powers were still in evidence in the fifteenth century, then it stands to reason that they were commonplace in the fifth and sixth centuries.

We have hints that the Druids were resurgent in the characters of the Druid Vortigern consults and ultimately in Myrddin or Merlin the magician, and also in the conflation of Druidism with wizardry or magical power. Merlin has been seen as 'the last of the Druids' because his 'real' historical character, Myrddin, was a sixth-century bard whose patron was a pagan king named Gwendoleu. In AD 573, Gwendoleu was involved in a terrible battle at *Arfderydd* or Arthuret. The pagan king relied on Myrddin for prophesies and magical protection against his Christian enemies, but Gwendoleu was killed and his pagan army was heavily defeated. For a magician of Myrddin's calibre this was a catastrophe, but to compound his failure, the bard ran away from the battlefield in disgrace. In a self-imposed exile, Myrddin fled into the forest of *Celidon*. Here he lived among the animals as a *Homo Sylvester* or 'wild man of the woods'. In the depths of his despair and madness Myrddin resorts to plundering birds' nests and rummaging with the pigs in the forest mud. The pagan world of his forebears has been overwhelmed by the Christ-god and his psychical link to the Goddess, 'the swan-white woman', has been severed.

Gradually Myrddin recovers, and he is granted extraordinary gifts of prophesy and clairvoyance. In his guise as Lailoken he prophesies the death of King Rhydderch Hael of *Alt Clut* or *Hen Ogledd*, 'the Old North'. St Kentigern is said to have visited Lailoken in his refuge near Partick. The entire ambience of this magical retreat is suggestive of Druidic practices which are in transition to Christianity, and I think it is poignant that the 'myth' conveys this much more satisfactorily than any history could. In Ireland St Patrick basically wages a magical war on the Druids, whom he ultimately defeats and then converts. As a result of his magical victory Patrick is ascribed all the powers of the former wizards. As the Irish Druids became

Christianised they began to dedicate their powers to Christ, and acts of magic which had once been performed by the Druids were portrayed as miracles of healing. St Columba was explicit: 'Christ is my Druid.' This fusion of Druidic and Christian ideas seems to be the dramatic underpinning for the legendary character of 'Merlin', for example, but the magical revival in the island was not just confined to the Celts.

At the turn of the century I returned to my own tribal roots when I took up employment with Worcestershire County Council. My work took me up to the hill villages of North Worcestershire, and the contrast with my former urban life was pleasant. My journey home took me via many places I had not seen since my boyhood days, including St Kenelm's Well at Romsley. The ancient rhyme about this place still echoed in my head:

> In Clent, by Cowbatch
> Under a thorn,
> Lieth Kenelm, kingborn
> His head off-shorn

It was about a young prince of Mercia in the ninth century, Kenelm, who was murdered at this spot. He had received a warning in a dream that he was to die, but was lured out hunting on the Clent Hills with his sister's lover, Askobert. Cwenthryth or Quendrida, the boy's sister, meant the prince harm. She had arranged that Askobert would murder him, and the lad was dragged to a hawthorn tree, forced to kneel and decapitated. At the moment his head was smitten from his body a magical spring emerged at the spot. A white dove witnessed the killing and flew to Rome, where it dropped the verse above on the pontiff as he was at his devotions. Cardinals were sent to England and the boy's body was discovered when magical 'white' animals led the papal legates to the isolated spot.

As my visits became more regular I began to think about this legend, which contains many ancient Celtic magical elements – but it was about an Anglo-Saxon, Mercian ruler. I began to upload some of my thoughts about this on to *The Modern Antiquarian* website, the excellent resource pioneered by Julian Cope of *The Teardrop Explodes* fame. A theory began to emerge, which was not very sophisticated, but ran something like this. The people who ruled the Clent Hills were a tribe calling themselves the *Hwicce*, pronounced 'witch-a'. They were Germanic, though not necessarily Anglo-Saxons. Clent seems to derive from a word in Old Swedish meaning 'wooded slopes'. Gradually they pushed into Oxfordshire, where their name is recalled by the Forest of Wychwood.

When the local British chieftains who still controlled Gloucestershire were destroyed at the Battle of Dyrham in AD 577, the *Hwicce* seem to have displaced the former *Dobunni* tribe of Gloucestershire and Worcestershire. But the word 'displaced' is perhaps misleading, for, as I have observed, the total numbers of incoming Germanic-speaking folk could not have been very great. A document called the *Tribal Hidage* of the ninth century lists thirty-five tribes, suggesting approximate numbers for population. My intuition, which seemed very powerful just at this time, suggested to me that the *Hwicce* may have had to make compromises with the pre-existing population, and that they may have eventually 'gone native', as it were, like the Anglo-Norman chieftains in Ireland who became 'more Irish than the Irish'. The hills when approached from the south unmistakably resemble female breasts, 'paps' as they are called in Ireland, and when one ascended and looked down on the Severn Valley below and out to the Cotswolds and the Malvern Hills there was a strange feeling of organic continuity. Such were my musings, for what they were worth, but these local magical and pagan intimations were not just a thing of the distant past.

In April 1943 four young boys went out collecting birds' eggs on the Hagley Hall estate of Lord Cobham, near to Wychbury hill fort, a place with very ancient folklore and magical traditions. They came to a large, hollowed-out tree, a wych-elm, which appeared ideal for nests, and so one of the boys, Bob Farmer, climbed up and peered inside. He immediately saw a skull, and conveyed this news to his companions below, shouting, 'It's a mon's skull!' In fact the skull was that of a female, still with hair adhering to it. The boys, fearful to disclose that they had been trespassing on the estate, pledged to keep the discovery a secret, but one of them eventually told his parents. The skeleton was removed and remains of some clothing, a wedding ring, a shoe and a piece of taffeta which had been used to suffocate the woman were found. She had been put into the tree just after she had been suffocated, while the body was still warm – or, conceivably, still alive.

A year after the discovery, strange graffiti began to appear indicating that someone knew, or wanted others to believe they knew, who the woman was. They read, 'Who put Bella down the wych-elm at Hagley Wood?' or 'Who put Luebella in the wych-elm?' This question has never been satisfactorily answered, but there are many theories. One was that she was a prostitute from Birmingham's Hagley Road, not too far away. Somebody claimed that a girl called Bella had gone missing in autumn 1941 at exactly the time the body was hidden. Another story has it that she was a German agent who had been involved in espionage concerning the vital war industries in the Black Country and Birmingham area. Josef Jakobs, another Nazi spy, was captured by the Home Guard in January 1941. He carried a photograph of a young woman, his lover, whom he identified as fellow Nazi agent – and accomplished occultist – Clara Bauerle.

Bauerle was apparently a cabaret artiste on the Birmingham and Black Country club scene before the war and knew the area well, so well that she had acquired the distinctive regional accent. It is claimed that she was known locally as 'Clarabella'. He claimed she was due to parachute into the area in spring 1941, but was never heard from again. Jakobs was not believed, and became the very last person to be executed for treason at the Tower of London. The anthropologist Margaret Murray intervened in the case, pointing out that a detached hand had been discovered near the tree, which she thought suggested a ritual magical execution, a so-called 'hand o'glory killing'. Murray hypothesised that the pagan religion had survived underground since the early medieval period, a theory which, until quite recent times, was viewed with incredulity by mainstream academia.

In February 1945 another possible 'ritual magical killing' had taken place near to the Rollright Stones on the border of Warwickshire and Oxfordshire not very far away. Murray suggested there might be a link to witchcraft covens in both cases. A jobbing farm worker called Charles Walton was brutally murdered on 14 February 1945. His gruesome fate recalled the ancient ordeals of the 'triple death'. He had been brutally beaten with his own walking stick, his throat slashed with his own slash hook for hedging, which was buried deep in his neck, and finally a pitchfork had been thrust in on either side of his almost-severed neck – an ancient ritual, it was claimed, which kept the spirit of a witch beneath ground. Margaret Murray was convinced that the entire case was a classic example of pagan 'blood sacrifice', and that Walton was either himself a witch who was thought to have cursed local farm animals or blighted crops – or was a victim of a local witches' coven whose code of silence was so ingrained that it proved impossible to penetrate. Chief Inspector Robert Fabian 'of the Yard', as he liked to be known, was clearly deeply affected by the sinister ambience of the case:

> I advise anybody who is tempted at any time to venture into Black Magic, witchcraft, shamanism – call it what you will – to remember Charles Walton and his death, which was clearly the ghastly climax of a pagan rite.

It is strange, perhaps, that these two extraordinary murders still remain unsolved to this day. In the case of 'Bella', her remains mysteriously went missing. It is a phenomenon long observed by sociologists and anthropologists that in times of severe societal stress, such as wartime or economic catastrophe or famine, there is a psychical reversion to powerful folk archetypes, what the anthropologist Adolf Bastian called *volkergedanken*. We will probably never discover all the answers to these intriguing mysteries, but as one interested in the potential continuity of elemental folk ideas through the centuries, my question is: is there any evidence for a survival of very arcane pagan activities in the area? It turns out that there is.

At about the same time I was absorbing the folk history of the *Hwicce*, totally unbeknown to me, an Oxford academic, Stephen J. Yeates, was intensively researching 'the tribe of witches' as he called them. His research was finally published in 2008, entitled *The Tribe of Witches: The Religion of the Dobunni and Hwicce*. Subsequently Yeates has followed up his research in other studies, but this original book, he claims, was inspired by 'the Muse', an intuition this author understands implicitly. As soon as I read the book, which I discovered entirely by chance, my idea of some ancient pre-Christian folk religion, personified in the form of a goddess who is embodied within the natural contours of the local landscape itself, were powerfully confirmed.

The first thing to note is the name of the tribe itself. *Hwicce* means 'sacred vessel' and is directly related to the Old English *wicce*, 'witch'. In his *Religion and Literature in Western England, 600–800* Patrick Sims-Williams suggests that the name was adopted because of the curious topography of the region, which is in the form of a bowl or cauldron. He thought the origin of the word was something like 'a meal-ark'. The best place to observe this is from the Wyche-cutting above Malvern (itself named after the tribe). To the east Bredon hill fort marks the beginning of the upland massif of the Cotswolds. To the north the suggestive contours of the Clent Hills and Wychbury mark the far frontiers of the tribal region, but in the hollow depression of the Severn Valley below, a fertile and verdant plain extends.

Yeates proposes that the incoming *Hwicce* essentially constituted a 'change of management' in cultural terms rather than a wholesale influx of new people, and that they adopted a pagan nature-cult which had existed in the area since prehistoric times. This cult, he argues, had literally deified the landscape and all its natural features, which they worshipped in the form of a goddess named *Cuda* who gave her name to the Cotswolds. This theory is now widely accepted in academic circles as correct. Another pagan goddess with a similar name, *Godda*, was worshipped by the pagan Mercians to the north. Her name is recalled in the legend of 'Edric the Wild', an English renegade who resisted the Normans just after the Norman Conquest in Shropshire. Edric's fairy bride, 'Lady Godda', is clearly the tribal goddess of that name, whom he has abducted as his unwilling wife. The pair are still said to ride out across the Stiperstones and Shropshire Hills whenever England goes to war. It is also possible that the character of 'Lady Godiva' was based on some folk memory of *Godda*. Shropshire itself was known in ancient times as *Goddeu*, a dense forested area.

Localised iconography of three male figures known as *genii cucullati* have been discovered all across the area. They are depicted as cloaked and hooded devotees worshipping an enthroned goddess, the *Matribus et Genioloci*, 'the mother goddess and the genius of the place'. I have already postulated the survival or re-emergence of paganism in the Roman period in the rural hinterland and Yeates thinks these occult religious practices went on right through the Roman occupation. In fact, the arrival of the Germanic *Hwicce* may have encouraged a renaissance of pagan practices as the Christian infrastructure based on the towns declined. The ancient forests of the area – Arden, Wyre, Kemble, Kingswood, Dean, Morfe and Kinver – were the last strongholds of paganism in England; Morfe and Kinver had 'witches' oaks' until late medieval times. These were the haunts of animals sacred to the 'wild hunt' such as the wild boar. Arden is derived from the same root as the Ardennes region of France and south-eastern Belgium. The name recalls the huntress goddess Diana, whom we encountered in the introduction.

The Great Mother Goddess presided over all. This is why it was imperative for the devotions to continue, underground if necessary, because the folk and the land were magically united in her person, and also the sacred forests and rivers, especially the Severn or Hafren, the longest river in Britain. Fish was a very important part of the early medieval diet, and the Severn was then an abundant fishery yielding lampreys, eels and elves, porpoise, sturgeon, whale calves, trout, turbot, herrings and the sacred salmon, 'the leaper'. The Lower Severn was home to what the Welsh monk Nennius described as 'the fifth wonder of Britain', the Severn Bore, a large surge wave which is funnelled up the Severn Estuary. It has been known to reach 50 feet as the water flows upriver and people regularly surf on it, the second biggest tidal surge in the world. It is not difficult to imagine how this phenomenon was interpreted by the Druids, for whom rivers represented the flow of time itself. The springs and headwaters were symbolic of the urgency and vitality of youth, the middle section of maturity, and the lower reaches of senility and ultimate mergence with the greater scheme. Very probably the Druids and their pagan successors knew the secret of predicting these tides, and that a sexual motif was applied to the infusion of tidal spume into the narrowing estuary of the sacred river, 'Sabrina'.

The incoming aristocracy of the *Hwicce* adopted their name from the folk who preceded them – and who continued to live alongside them – the *Dobunni*, 'the people of the sacred vessel'. Yeates points out that Bede in his writing refers to the *Hwicce* as a British, not Anglo-Saxon tribe. We will return to the connotations of the 'vessel' or 'cup' or 'cauldron' later, but Yeates is most concerned with the concept that the 'vessel' was none other than the Severn Valley itself. The name was synonymous with *wicce*, 'female witch', and with *wicca*, 'warlock'. This is curious, but Yeates comes up with an ingenious solution. Few if any early medieval tribes defined themselves in terms of a pre-Christian religion, particularly one so devoted to goddess worship. If Cunliffe is correct that pre-Christian, Druidic Celtic culture was diffused from Britain to mainland Europe, the sacred landscape venerated by the *Dobunni* may well have given rise to religious practices at considerable distance from the tribal homeland.

The idea of a 'sacred vessel' is one we have encountered previously, in the myth of the 'Holy Grail'. It is well known that the motif of a cauldron resonated strongly in the Celtic imagination. In 1891 a large cauldron was unearthed near Gundestrup in Jutland from a peat bog. It was probably manufactured in Thrace around 150 BC and depicts many typical Celtic themes. A seated god, resembling *Cernunnos*, assists a line of warriors, apparently the spirits of deceased comrades who have previously sacrificed themselves, to immerse a still-living warrior who will shortly join his companions in the other world. This is 'the cauldron of rebirth', a theme which certainly influenced Celtic conceptions of the Holy Grail. In the *Mabinogion*, King Arthur sets out on a quest to find a sacred cauldron belonging to a local ruler called Diwrnach. This is no mere medieval romance, but comes from one of the oldest stories in Welsh literature, 'Culhwch and Olwen', and in Ireland, too, this theme of an ever-replenishing cauldron is recurrent – the *Dagda*, chief god of the Irish, possessed a cauldron which could hold 80 measures of milk, 80 of fat, 80 more of meal and still had room to accommodate entire pigs, sheep and goats – which the god blended into his breakfast porridge. The god Bran also has a magic cauldron so capacious that no one ever leaves his table unsatisfied, no matter how many guests arrive. Yeates comments on the stone reliefs excavated from around the Cotswold region:

> The reliefs show the goddess in a single or triple form and associate her with a cult or sacred vessel. Often, in English literature, for example in Shakespeare's *Macbeth*, three witches are shown around a cauldron. This image is believed to have been developed from the Germanic myths of the Wyrd sisters, or Norns; three women who lived at the root of the world tree ... a native British goddess in her many forms was linked with similar Germanic deities. This would have paralleled the actions of the earlier Roman culture. If all these things were true then it would imply that there had not only been a major survival of British people but that there was also an influx of Germanic people, but who may have held senior positions in society, who were trying to comprehend the native religion within their own traditions.[17]

Sims-Williams in his study of the region notes that there is evidence that as Germanic settlers moved west, out of the region Yeates has investigated, into Herefordshire and Shropshire, they may have been converted to Christianity by a still-functioning British Church. East of the Severn it was a different story. The most notoriously pagan Mercian king, Penda, was a native of Pebworth in Worcestershire, for instance. He is supposed to have offered refuge to a company of dissident warriors from Northumbria and allowed them to settle in Worcestershire, even though they were Christians, implying this was exceptional for the region. The cauldron was the symbol of life and death, the ultimate source of creation and rebirth, and the people who inhabited the great vessel of the Severn Valley considered themselves to be a 'chosen people' with magical powers – literally 'witches'. The negative connotations of the term would have been completely lost on the Germanic incomers, who were staunchly pagan anyway.

---

17 Yeates, Stephen, J., *The Tribe of Witches*, Oxbow, Oxford, 2008.

The more surprising aspect of the theory Yeates promulgates is the extraordinary continuity of the cult through the millennia, surviving even the imprint of Roman power, and which was only finally extinguished after AD 679 when Theodore of Tarsus, the Archbishop of Canterbury, founded the diocese of Worcester to minister to the *Hwicce*. By then the tribal area had been annexed by the Mercians, but although the pagan cults were superseded eventually, this must have been a slow process. By the eighth century the name of the goddess, *Cuda*, had become a personal name for girls, suggesting that the divinity had degenerated into a character in oral storytelling or folklore which it was now permissible to use in the profane world. But the people of this part of the world are notoriously conservative. In the Black Country a dialect is still spoken which has recognisable links to Middle English, and it shows no sign of dying out any time soon. It is by no means impossible that occult practices, having an origin in pre-Christian paganism, have survived in the area.

Like Yeates I believe that somewhere in the region, perhaps not far from Wychbury ('the burial place of the *Hwicce*'; each of the twenty-eight yew trees in the sacred grove there represents a fallen warrior-king of the tribe), the Great Mother Goddess still resides, bestowing her blessings upon her people – even in this cynical era. One potential implication of this is that Margaret Murray's theories regarding a putative survival of pre-Christian religious practices, so long the object of academic derision, may become (at least partially) rehabilitated. So, the Germanic settlements may not have always been a matter of Anglo-Saxon paganism displacing British Christianity as was traditionally taught in our schooldays, and it may be that the tardiness of Penda in converting to the Christian religion was partly rooted in his devotion to a pre-existing British paganism, rather than that which his ancestors brought with them. But what was the nature of these Germanic pagan beliefs?

The population estimates for late Roman Britain have recently been revised upwards. There may have been 3 million inhabitants at its peak, but following the collapse of the imperial structure and the influx of Germanic immigrants this fell quite rapidly, probably through the ravages of a great 'yellow plague' which arrived in the island from Mediterranean trading ships in the early sixth century. Because the Britons traded with the Eastern empire but the Anglo-Saxons did not, the latter were preserved against this plague, because there was little contact between the hostile British kingdoms and their Anglo-Saxon neighbours, or indeed the *Lloegrwys* – those of British descent who now lived under Anglo-Saxon overlords in 'Lloegr', 'the Lost Lands'. The population, particularly in the western half of the island, plummeted. The Anglo-Saxons thought of towns as cursed, unclean places, denizens of ghosts and evil spirits. Before very long urban life ceased, and the drainage ditches and canals which had reclaimed the fens and marshes silted up and reverted to impassable bogs. The great Roman highways became overgrown with weeds and the vast public basilicas and bathhouses stood as empty shells, crumbling to ruin. An Anglo-Saxon *scop* or bard stood in wonder as he gazed at the ruins of the once great city of *Aquae Sulis*, what is now Bath:

> Splendid this rampart is, though wyrd destroyed it,
> The city buildings fell apart, the works
> Of giants crumble. Tumbled are the tall towers
> Ruined the roofs, and broken the barred gates,
> Frost in the plaster, the ceilings gaping,
> Torn and collapsed and eaten by age
> And grit holds in its grip, the hard embrace
> Of earth, the dead departed master-masons
> Until a hundred generations now
> Of people have passed by. Often this wall
> Stained and grey with lichen has stood by
> Surviving storms while kingdoms rose and fell.
> And now the high-curved wall itself has fallen
> Resolute masons, skilled in rounded building
> Wondrously linked the framework with iron bonds.
> The public halls were bright, with lofty gables,
> Bath-houses many; great the laughing company
> And many mead-halls filled with human pleasures,
> Till wyrd the mighty changed all that ...

'Till wyrd the mighty changed all that'; the word *wyrd* is often rendered as the equivalent of 'fate' or 'destiny' – but there is much more to it than that.

One of the world's most esoteric and primordial religions, Tantra, derives from a Sanskrit word meaning 'to weave'. The cult practices are focused on an image of, or an apotheosis in human female form of, the Goddess. The adoration of the incarnated Goddess is the most sacred goal of the Tantrika, or male aspirant, as she dances in an ecstatic celebration of love. In unbinding her hair she creates the living universe, but as she gathers it up again all created things are destroyed. Our modern obsession with sex has debased and cheapened this extremely subtle philosophy, which may be the most elemental religious impulse known to the human race. The poet Robert Graves, in his *The White Goddess*, captured something of the ultimate devotion the Goddess elicits in his dedication:

> All saints revile her, and all sober men
> Ruled by the God Apollo's golden mean –
> In scorn of which I sailed to find her
> Whom I desired above all things to know,
> Sister of the mirage and echo.

As Philip Rawson explains, the charm of the inner divine image is far greater than that of any actual woman:

> Women, therefore, play a crucial role in Tantra. They are carriers of that female energy which occupies the central place in Tantrik imagery, and in ritual practice it is only by co-operation with women that the male Tantrika can progress ...[18]

But this dissolution of the self in ecstatic creation is not the whole story:

> The loving Goddess of Creation has another face. As she brings man into time and his world, she also removes him from it. So she is his destroyer as well. All those things which cripple and kill – disease, famine, violence and war – are an inevitable part of her activity, seen from the viewpoint of man as victim. No-one can be a successful Tantrika unless he has faced up to this reality, and assimilated it into his image of the Goddess. Many Tantrik icons therefore show her as the black-faced and terrible Kali, her tongue lolling and her fanged mouth dribbling blood. She may be hideous, but she must be no less loved.

The Anglo-Saxons, too, depicted female 'mother' archetypes whom they called 'the Wyrd Sisters'. The primordial connection to weaving is recalled in the Old English word *geweaf*, 'to weave'. Our modern English word 'wife' is related. Many Anglo-Saxon houses had a weaving shed with a sunken floor where the women kept their looms and the small girls watched and learned the art of weaving from their mothers. The complex process of creating patterns out of the warp and weft of yarns held in tension on a frame may have encouraged an early form of meditative practice, but by analogy, weaving came to be seen as a metaphor for the whole of creation – and it was a metaphor whose recondite meaning resonated especially with women. Professor Brian Bates, in his *The Real Middle-Earth: Magic and Mystery in the Dark Ages*, says:

> Through the centuries, stories about the three Sisters persisted. In England, they are mentioned by the medieval poet Chaucer, and famously a few centuries later by William Shakespeare in his play *Macbeth*. In the Norse culture they were known as the Daughters of the Night ... The mythology also pictured the Norns as having sway over creation, measuring and ending of individual life. The Greek version of the Three Sisters were depicted as having separate functions: one who spun, another who measured the strings, and a third who cut them to lengths. It is likely that the Sisters of Wyrd were believed to operate in the same way; one creating the golden

---

18 Rawson, P., *Tantra: The Indian Cult of Ecstasy*, Thames & Hudson, London, 1979.

strings, another laying them out in ways which reflected and determined the life unfolding, and a third who cut them off to length and so determined the life-span of each thread, and/or each life.

The strange threads which make up the fabric of each individual life were interlaced in patterns which were subject to the intervention of *wiccecreaft* and *drycraeft*. The 'negative' practices we associate with witchcraft, such as spellcasting, were only one aspect of the social functions performed by these women – they also provided vital services to the community such as healing, midwifery and divination by runes and other devices. It is often alleged that the pre-Christian Anglo-Saxons were fatalistic as a result of this submission to 'fate' or 'destiny', but this is, I believe, to misunderstand the matter. Fate was indeed hard to alter, but it was possible to moderate or subtly ameliorate its effects, though a humble and honest acceptance of one's condition is implied in the Anglo-Saxon poem *The Fortunes of Men*:

> Hunger will devour one, storm dismast another,
> One will be spear-slain, one hacked down in battle,
> One will drop wingless, from the high tree,
> One will swing from the tall gallows,
> The sword's edge will shear the life of one
> At the mead-bench, some angry sot
> Soaked with wine. His words were too hasty,
> One will delight a gathering, gladden
> Men sitting at the mead bench over their ale
> One will settle by his harp
> At the feet of his lord and be handed treasures,
> One will tame that arrogant wild bird
> The hawk on the fist, until the falcon
> Becomes gentle enough for jesses.

What distinguished the witches and wizards was their ability to *see* the pattern, the infinitely subtle interlocking golden threads which constitute the perceptible cosmos. This conception of the universe, far from being a quaint survival of 'primitive' beliefs, is now powerfully confirmed in the theoretical physics known as 'String Theory'. In the early medieval period, the Roman goddess Diana became synonymous with various northern European fertility deities which had been worshipped for many centuries. These ceremonial practices, conducted at night and illuminated by eldritch moonlight, may be the unconscious template for the much later phenomenon of the 'witches' sabbat'. The fear of witches was not confined to Christians, but arose out of powerful unconscious emotions evoked by inexplicable and mysterious forces. Russell and Alexander note the awe and revulsion evoked by the witch in the popular consciousness:

Usually, however, she represents an elemental natural force possessing enormous and unexpected powers against which a natural person is unable to prepare or defend himself, a force not necessarily evil, but so alien and remote from the world of mankind as to constitute a threat to the social, ethical, and even physical order of the cosmos. This manner of portraying the witch is very ancient and probably archetypal. The witch is neither a simple sorceress, nor a demonolater, nor a pagan. She is a hostile presence from another world. The gut terror inspired by this archetypal witch helps to explain the excess of hatred and fear that welled up during the witch craze.[19]

Chief among the Anglo-Saxon gods was *Woden*, whom the Romans equated to Mercury. In Norse mythology he is known as Odin. As Bates points out, he is 'the archetypal template for the initiation of shamans in Middle-earth'. A Norse poem called the *Havamal* decribes Woden's quest to the Otherworld to obtain shamanic wisdom:

> I know that I hung on the windswept tree for nine full nights,
> Wounded with a spear and pledged to Odin
> Offered, myself to myself;
> The wisest know not from whence spring
> The roots of that ancient tree.
>
> They did not comfort me with bread
> And not with the mead-horn;
> I peered downward,
> I grasped the runes, screaming I grasped them;
> I fell back from there.
>
> Nine powerful spells I learned
> From the famous son of Bolthor,
> Father of Bestla,
> And I got a draught of the precious mead,
> Poured from magic Odrerir.
>
> Learned I grew then, lore-wise,
> Grew and prospered well:
> Word from word gave words to me,
> Deed from deed gave deeds to me.

The tree from which Woden/Odin hung for nine days was a gigantic ash called *Yggdrasil*. In its upper branches were the abodes of the gods and

---

19 Russell, J. B. & B. Alexander, *A New History of Witchcraft, Sorcerers, Heretics and Pagans*, Thames & Hudson, London, 2007.

goddesses; in the middle branches and the trunk was our familiar world, 'Middle-earth', which was connected to *Asgard* the god-realm by a rainbow bridge called *Bifrost*; and the roots were a dark underworld called *Nifleheim*, the abode of chthonic entities and spirits of the dead. Each of its three vast roots was nourished by the 'Well of Wyrd', next to which the 'Wyrd Sisters' lived. The Anglo-Saxon world was then a profoundly magical one, and its cosmology and religious pantheon derived from almost unimaginably ancient roots, focusing primordial psychical archetypes. The Roman ways were utterly abhorrent to them. The rational, materialist, hegemonic world view dishonoured the unseen, spiritual upper world of the gods, and the abodes of the underworld, containing the wisdom of the deceased ancestors. Crucially, it sought to constrain, control and dominate this Middle-earth, with its 'straight' roads and gigantic buildings.

The Anglo-Saxons were reacting to an exploitative, decadent and environmentally destructive culture which they perceived as corrupt, greedy and wasteful. As we have seen, many Britons would have shared this view of Rome, and it is quite possible that rather than letting themselves be conquered, they chose to adopt the language, folkways and religious practices of the incomers, so-called 'cultural appropriation'. Our deeply ingrained cultural prejudices, and an educational outlook suffused by a subconscious veneration of all things rationalist and scientific, has meant that the 'dark ages' have become synonymous with all that is primitive, brutal and uncivilised. But the Anglo-Saxons were not 'barbarians'. The only 'dark' thing about the dark ages is our perception of them. Within a century of their arrival the Anglo-Saxons had founded seven kingdoms ('the heptarchy') which would eventually merge into the nation we call England. The next 'invasion' was to come from the west in the form of holy men and individual saints who arrived as missionaries – Christian magicians.

8

Out of Darkness

Originally, the Celts worshipped ancestor spirits which developed into god or goddess forms, with the Druids acting as intermediaries. Gradually the Christian saints and martyrs, those who were undoubtedly in heaven, took on the protective role in their stead, with the priest replacing the Druid or Druidess. In the early Celtic Church women had been co-equal with men, just as they had been within Druidism. Women could say the Mass, for instance, and powerful abbesses like St Hild and St Brigit controlled large, complex institutions where men women and children lived together in egalitarian communities called *conhospitae* or 'double houses' where they devoted their lives to God. This particularism and individualism was viewed askance from Rome, but the 'Celtic fringe' of Europe was allowed to develop its own peculiar style of Christianity without too much interference – at least at first.

As the influence of the Roman Catholic Church grew, what had been tolerated as harmless folkways which enhanced the human experience were denounced as foul heresies and the role of women in the Church was downplayed, but before its later suppression and persecution the Celtic Church became for a while a shining beacon of all that is noblest in the human spirit. There were undoubtedly minor matters where the Celtic traditions were irregular or eccentric, such as the style of the tonsure, for instance, or the computations used for calculating the date of Easter, but the Celtic Church considered itself to be part of the worldwide Christian communion. It was inevitable that many of the monks, nuns and priests in local areas would be drawn from the same social strata and powerful individual families which had formerly supplied the Druidic novitiates, especially in Ireland. The local traditions of gods and heroes were bound to encrust around the saints, and effectively the magical functions of the Druids were transferred to them. Just as the Druids had fasted against their enemies and cursed them, the Celtic monks had no compunction about using such methods in an emergency. At the Battle of Chester in AD 616, 1,200 monks gathered as spectators in order to pray for a British victory. King Aethelfrith of Northumbria was convinced they were muttering magical incantations against his army and slaughtered them even though they were unarmed.

All across Britain and Ireland we find place names like Dyserth, Dysart, or Dyzard in Cornwall. The word *diseartan* literally means 'desert' and referred to remote, inaccessible communities or hermitages where the Celtic monks retired to get closer to God. The example they followed came from Egypt. This self-exile recalled in some ways the austerities, disciplines and spiritual exercises practiced by the former Druids and magicians, but for the Irish, Cornish, Welsh and Breton monks the sands of Egypt were exchanged for the watery deserts of the ocean as they sought out isolated caves and headlands along the craggy coasts, or sailed out to uninhabited islands such as Skellig Michael.

Skellig Michael is the pinnacle of an undersea mountain shaped like a pyramid 8 miles off the west coast of Ireland, amid some of the stormiest seas in the world. A tiny community of monks settled here and built small huts of stone shaped like beehives, and a tiny but solidly constructed chapel. These men were extraordinary. The sturdy, compact huts could only be accessed by the narrowest of paths, on which they built stairways from gigantic slabs of stone. The buildings themselves are so cunningly designed that not a breath of wind stirs within them even amid the howling gusts of an Atlantic gale. The monks' diet consisted of fish and gull's eggs, and seaweed was gathered and mulched to provide a species of thin topsoil in which a few vegetables were grown.

Perched upon an 800-foot-high rock in the open Atlantic, these monks had found a deserted place indeed, but they had also chosen to desert the world, like St Anthony before them, and they were as far away from the worldliness and sophistication of Rome as it was possible to get. Their Christianity was—and is—different, emphasising a direct personal relationship with God, a profound celebration of the natural world, tolerance of human weakness and difference, mysticism (and to some extent magic), combined with a humility, kindness and asceticism in the face of gruelling hardship which won respect and admiration from the common folk. The models for this exemplary branch of the Christian vine were the so-called 'desert fathers'.

Earlier we saw how in all cultures throughout the world the notion of withdrawal for purposes of sanctification and purification was central to the development of spiritual or magical proficiency. The Jews had a long tradition of such magical retreats, and one such group, originating near to Alexandria, were called the *Therapeutae* or 'attendants upon God', who worshipped a Graeco-Roman god called *Serapis* whom they may have conflated with 'Christ'. Philo of Alexandria in his *De Vita Contemplativa* remarks on the utter simplicity of their way of life: 'They laid down temperance as a sort of foundation for the soul to rest upon, from which other virtues may be built up.' The name of the sect was also connected to healing and serving the outcast and unfortunate by offering spiritual aid, like the *yazatan* or guardian angels of Zoroastrianism. Another such desert community, the Essenes, were apocalyptic visionaries who believed in the immortality of the soul, forbade slavery, and practised rituals of purification by water.

Although these sects were Judaic, not Christian, they provided the templates for the first communities of Christian monks when they sought isolation in the desert. Some were undoubtedly fleeing the terrible Diocletianic Persecution by Rome in which 500,000 Copts and others who refused to comply with imperial edicts lost their lives. Many of the Egyptian Christian monks were then influenced by ideas which found a strong resonance among the Irish – because the Druids also practised healing and believed in the immortality of the soul, the survival of the human essence beyond death, purification by water and a mystical communion with God. The Coptic Christian father Hierax of Leontopolis in Egypt in the third century taught that only the celibate would enter the kingdom of heaven and that the spiritually inclined must eschew all sexual temptation. A corollary of this ascetic doctrine was that monasticism would become the refuge for the true spiritual seeker, a sanctuary against Satan where he or she, through constant self-abnegation, temptations and conflicts with demons, would develop their own magical inner power, and through the martyrdom of the body attain everlasting bliss and joy in God.

In third-century Egypt, following the death of his parents, St Anthony took the words of Jesus literally and gave away all his considerable worldly goods before isolating himself to purify his mind from the temptation of demons. These demons lurked everywhere, and could shapeshift into any form they pleased. They were real enough; Anthony was beaten almost to death by them on one occasion. The constant trickery and malevolence of the demons only intensified Anthony's efforts. For twenty years he confined himself in a ruined ancient Egyptian tomb where he incarcerated himself as if he were himself entombed, completely cut off from his friends, who finally broke down the door, expecting him to be insane. But Anthony emerged calm and well balanced. He obtained spiritual liberation and as an old man became a living saint, revered for his extraordinary holiness, tranquillity and wisdom. Indeed, he became a sort of celebrity of his time and so many were drawn to join him in his desert retreat that he was forced to find solitude once more.

Following a Bedouin camel-train across the desert, after three days Anthony discovered a retreat he called his 'Interior Mountain', where he isolated himself for another forty-three years, but as a concession to his followers he would occasionally emerge to meet with them and instruct the monks who were arriving in their thousands at Nitria on the edge of the desert. Here monks lived in 'Cells' where they lived austere, prayerful lives, meeting once a week for worship and a communal meal. Unlike their Celtic counterparts these early monastic communities were segregated by gender; women lived in separate convents apart from the men. St Anthony's monastery is still thriving today, where modern monks confront Satan in turn, but what was the link between the Coptic and Celtic Christian traditions?

In the last years of the Roman occupation of Britain in the early fifth century, a sixteen-year-old boy was captured in a raid by Irish slavers. His name was *Patricius*, in Irish *Padraig*, known to history as St Patrick. There are several theories about where he was from; some say the south-west, others south Wales, but there may be a connection to the area around Birdoswald Roman fort on Hadrian's Wall – the Irish raided heavily in all three areas. Patrick was taken far into Ireland, to a place called *Foclut* in Mayo, where he was kept in slavery for six years as a swineherd.

Patrick's parents were wealthy Christians and his grandfather had been a priest, but he was not strong in his faith. Nevertheless, his misery and loneliness encouraged him to pray in his darkest times and he began to feel that these were being heard. In the sixth year of his captivity he heard a voice in a dream announcing that a ship was waiting on the eastern coast and would take him home. Convinced that this was indeed a message from God, Patrick slipped away and walked 200 miles across dangerous country until he reached a port, probably Wicklow, where a ship was waiting to sail to Gaul. Patrick pleaded with the captain to take him aboard, and he eventually relented when he noticed Patrick's talent for calming the fierce hunting dogs which comprised his cargo.

When Patrick reached Britain another epic journey commenced, and for twenty-eight days Patrick, by now famished and in rags, marched until he was joyfully reunited with his parents. A 'happy ending', we might think – but Patrick's adventures had only just begun. A few years later Patrick had another dream. A man called *Victoricus* came to him and handed him a bundle of mysterious documents. One of them was entitled 'The Voice of the Irish'. All at once he felt he could hear the voices of the people of *Foclut* appealing to him: 'Come to us holy servant-boy, and walk among us again.' By now Patrick's faith was strong, and he resolved to follow a religious vocation.

By AD 432 he had been consecrated as a bishop by that St Germanus who had visited Britain to suppress the Pelagian heresy. It is very probable that Patrick was sent to Ireland to ensure that the heresy did not gain a foothold there. In fact, Patrick was not the first pioneering Christian in Ireland despite his designation as the 'apostle' of that country. The year before Patrick was consecrated bishop, Pope Celestine I had sent a bishop from Gaul, Palladius, to Leinster, probably with the same motive of suppressing heresy among the thousands of Christian slaves there. Some historians think that Palladius and Patrick became conflated by early Irish writers, but it seems that Palladius displeased the local Irish king and was exiled to Scotland.

Patrick had travelled to Gaul to do his monastic training, and the monastery he chose was St Honorat on the Isle de Lerins off the Mediterranean coast. This monastery was very strongly influenced by the example of the desert fathers, and one their chief guides was John Cassian, a man from the borders of Romania and Bulgaria who had lived as a hermit in the Holy Land and at Nitria, where St Anthony had once preached. Cassian was a profound mystic, influenced by many of the Gnostic, Hermetic and Alchemical ideas which still had considerable purchase on the Coptic imagination. He proposed a three-step approach to God – *purgatio*, *illuminatio* and *unitio*. The first step, purgation, incorporated self-isolation, abstinence and ascetic practices until the novice felt they were entirely sustained by the grace of the Holy Spirit. The second stage was spiritual practice in the world, using the example of Christ as the supreme teacher. Finally, having applied spiritual illumination in the world, the monk or nun retires to a remote place and, as *The Cloud of Unknowing* so eloquently puts it, becomes 'Onyd wid God' – *unitio*. The mind must be constrained to one single thought: 'O God make speed to save me. O Lord make haste to help me.'

It is perhaps too much to say that these exercises are magical, but they are very similar to some of the practices of the 'mystery schools'. When he returned to Ireland Patrick's Egyptian monastic influences, combined with folk traditions derived from the Druids, morphed into the hybrid we call 'Celtic Christianity'. Half of western Britain remained Celtic for centuries to come, and the British Church welcomed Irish monks and pilgrims. Patrick's brand of Egyptian influenced Christianity had come home.

A great deal of what we know about Patrick's mission in Ireland is legendary, but there can be little doubt that its astonishing success was facilitated in large part by co-operation from the Druids. A Fenian named Cailte became Patrick's constant companion, regaling him with stories of the ancient days and the gods and heroes as they progressed across the country. These tales were collected into a compendium called the *Colloquy of the Ancient Men*. A Druid named Dubtach became one of the bishop's stalwart counsellors and another, Fiacc, later became the first Irish-born bishop. Nevertheless, the Church hierarchy Patrick established was Roman through and through. Four vast sees exercised supreme Catholic authority over parish priests and monks and nuns. But when Patrick died his system could not outlast him. The Celtic Church developed along its own lines, a situation which Rome was determined to remedy by whatever means necessary, as Jean Markale points out in his *The Celts*:

> When discussing the disappearance of the Celts there is very seldom any reference made to the Roman Catholic Church, its attempts to destroy the Celts politically and its intention to reduce them to a life of wretchedness. In the early days Christian dogma was still too insecure to be able to countenance the existence of free spirits like the Celts. Only Wales escaped reform, though it fell prey to other kinds of subjection. And once the Irish and Bretons had been tamed, in Ireland's case one might say almost enslaved, they became the most conservative of religious believers.

The monastic foundations challenged Roman Catholic authority and power. Their autonomous abbots were more powerful than the bishops, and the monks took precedence over the priests. The monasteries and convents were themselves direct heirs to the Druidic *bangors* or colleges, centres of intellectual, artistic and scientific excellence as well as spiritual centres. Now that the spiritual and intellectual treasures of the Celts could be committed to writing in Latin and Greek, and the esoteric and scientific knowledge of Egypt and Greece collated in scriptoriums, Ireland, for so long considered as peripheral to the civilised world, suddenly became its centre.

The subtle blend of ancient recondite knowledge combined with a genuine evangelical mission was soon to spread throughout Europe. Britain, of course, was soon evangelised by Irish monks, but they were to be found in places much further afield – Gaul, Brittany, Germany, Switzerland, Italy, Ukraine, Iceland, Palestine, Egypt and Syria; legends say that St Brendan even sailed across the Atlantic and made landfall in America centuries before Columbus, or indeed the Vikings. The scene was now set for one of the most bitterly ironic twists in British history, for this remarkable and deeply spiritual Celtic Church was to be undermined and ruined by Rome, using the emergent Anglo-Saxon kingdoms as its instruments. The process by which the latter became Christianised will now be examined.

The story began, again, in Ireland. In AD 521 at Galtan, County Donegal, *Columcille*, 'the Dove of the Church', known to history as St Columba, was born into the powerful royal family of the *Ui Neill* clan. He was himself a direct descendant of the mighty king known as 'Niall of the Nine Hostages'. He was fostered and trained by priests who gave him his sobriquet, but his original birth name had been *Crimthann*, 'the fox'. By this time the monastic movement was established all over Ireland, and each institution guarded its own relics and precious books as sacrosanct. Columba committed the serious crime of copying out a psalter which belonged to a neighbouring monastery without obtaining the permission of the abbot, St Finnian. This dispute led to the pitched Battle of *Cuil Dreimne*, fought between armed monks, and many were killed.

Columba had a claim to the Irish high kingship in his own right, and he was in a strong position to challenge the last pagan High King, Diarmait of Tara. However, tortured with guilt over the battle fought due to his transgression, he accepted self-exile, vowing that he would not rest content until he had won as many souls for Christ as had been lost at *Cuil Dreimne* – well over 3,000 men. The *peregrinatio* or self-exile was a form of martyrdom among the Celts, for exile from one's kin and estrangement from the clan was for them the ultimate punishment. To ameliorate this bitter blow, King Connall of Dalriada, a kinsman, gave Columba the tiny island of Iona, originally called *Iova*, which is derived from the Gaelic *iogh* or yew tree. Iona had once been a sacred sanctuary of the Druids.

Overlooking the Ross of Mull, Columba and his twelve companions cleared a 20-acre site enclosed with a bank and ditch and built a settlement of wattle-and-daub sleeping cells thatched with reeds, a church, a cookhouse, barns, a building set aside for guests, and a kiln for drying corn. Later a cemetery was consecrated as the monks' years advanced. They kept cows, sheep and Columba's personal favourite, a horse. The monks produced a variety of craft goods with which to trade, and soon the little community was thriving, protected and blessed by the crowds of angels who were observed to gather around Columba as he prostrated himself in solitary prayer at a place known then as 'the mound of the fairies'. It was only fitting that angels should attend him; Columba had brought the stone called *An Lia Fail* or the 'Stone of Scone' with him to Iona, reputedly the same stone which Jacob had used for a pillow in the Book of Genesis (28: 10–15) when he dreamed that he saw angels ascending and descending a 'stairway to heaven' or 'ladder' at Bet-El. The thirty-three rungs of the ladder represent the thirty-three vertebrae in the human spinal column, as well as the thirty-three degrees in Freemasonry. This rarest of sacred treasures was to have a long and chequered history as we shall see.

On this magical island a tiny community lived a simple but holy life completely apart from the mainstream Christian world. Mass was said on Sundays and on important feast days only, and practical daily work and study were seen as holy tasks in themselves, acceptable as offerings to God. The controversial Celtic tonsure, worn bare from ear to ear after the manner of the old Druids (the Romans wore theirs in a coronal fringe), was the only fashion they knew, and they were content to calculate the date of Easter according to the tables which had been handed down to them from Patrick's time. These rather quaint details may seem like trifles to us, but soon they were to become vitally important to the fate of Britain.

Curious legends with a distinctly magical flavour attached themselves to Columba. That he was seen in the company of angels is well attested, but he was also said to have drowned out the chorus of a large company of hostile Pictish Druids by using just his own voice, and was said by Adamnan, a later Abbot of Iona, to have banished the 'Loch Ness Monster' by making the sign of the cross, commanding it to 'go back with all speed', which it dutifully did. He made the same sign of the cross over pails of milk on Iona which mysteriously never soured. In fact, Columba was an extremely accomplished politician, whose efforts transformed the Gaelic kingdom of Dalriada in his lifetime, and established it as a successful regional state in both Ulster and Argyll. His expeditions to the Picts, though they did not result in a mass conversion, were at least a hopeful beginning.

Behind Columba's saintliness there was, undoubtedly, a tortured soul. He regretted not having a wife and children. He never ceased yearning for his native land, his kinsmen, or grieving for the dead combatants on both sides at *Cuil Dreimne*. As his extraordinary life neared its end, Columba announced that he would soon die. He went out one last time to look out over the Ross of Mull, and to visit his precious white horse. The poor creature followed Columba to the side of the road where he was resting and laid its head in his lap, wetting the old man with its tears. His companion tried to lead the horse away, but Columba made him relent, and comforted the poor animal before he died.

This year, AD 597, was one of destiny for the Christian faith in this island. At the same time, another Christian mission – this time from Rome – had arrived hundreds of miles away in the pagan Anglo-Saxon kingdom of Kent. Iona was soon to be of considerable importance to the conversion of the Anglo-Saxons, but our focus must now shift to events in the south.

It was a chance meeting in Rome which sowed the seed for St Augustine's mission in AD 597. As a young man, Pope Gregory 'the Great' was walking through the slave market when he noticed a small group of charming children for sale. They all had piercing blue eyes and blonde hair. Gregory was so intrigued that he asked the dealer where they came from. He was told that they were Angles, from the nation of Deira, what is now Yorkshire. Gregory responded that to him they looked more like 'angels' from God, which caused considerable mirth. The dealer told Gregory that for all their charming looks, the parents of these infants, so far from being 'angels', were fearsome barbarians who knew nothing of God. Gregory became a Benedictine monk, and eventually became the first monk to achieve the highest office in the Church. It may be true that Gregory's yearning to convert the fair-faced barbarians on the 'pagan' island stayed with him, but there were other pressing reasons for expediting a Catholic mission. The Irish monastic movement was a direct challenge to the Benedictine order.

In AD 595 Gregory dispatched a monk, Augustine, and forty followers on a mission to convert the King of Kent, Aethelberht, who was married to a Christian princess of the Franks, Bertha, the daughter of King Charibert I of Paris. As the party progressed north, Augustine's nerve failed him. Tales of Saxon barbarism and their strange pagan religion unnerved the monks, and after a few months they pleaded to be allowed to return to Rome. Gregory was adamant, though, and Augustine and his comrades set off again. The mission was too important – not to convert the Anglo-Saxons, but to stop the contagion of Celtic monasticism, and especially Columba. The latter, this man who had walked with the angels and cradled injured seabirds to tend to their wounds, was described to Augustine in derogatory terms, traduced by 'fellow Christians' who can have had no personal experience of the man they calumniated.

Generations of schoolchildren grew up with the story of how Augustine and his forty companions processed ashore on Thanet in 597, under the watchful gaze of armed Kentish warriors. With great trepidation they progressed inland, singing the litany as they went to keep up their courage, bearing before them a silver cross and an image of Christ painted on a board. The king awaited them seated outdoors, beneath the protective shade of an oak, in case these Roman monks brought magic of their own which may bewitch him. But Augustine was never in any real danger. Aethelberht had already allowed his wife to restore an old Roman church, St Martin's, where she and her Frankish retinue worshipped. Aethelberht permitted Augustine's party to stay and to proselytise but decided to assess the project as it developed before committing to baptism himself. They were billeted near to St Martin's, which they set about rebuilding, and a grant of land between the church and Canterbury town was developed into a Benedictine monastery. In AD 601 King Aethelberht was baptised at St Martin's, and at a blow the whole kingdom of Kent had been won for Roman Catholicism. But this hard-won success was not the triumph it seemed, because the slender thread of one man's life was all that stood between the Kentish people and apostasy. There can have been few genuine Christian converts.

The news of Aethelberht's baptism was joyfully received in Rome. Pope Gregory immediately wrote to the king, enjoining him to unite himself to Augustine 'with all your mind', and to do his utmost to further his endeavours. Gregory only had knowledge of Britain from old maps of the Roman provinces on which great highways, thriving cities and gigantic fortresses were marked. Gregory was very familiar with Gaul, and he fancied that Britain must be something similar, and that the Anglo-Saxons were similar to the Franks. London, he knew, had been a great city, with the most impressive civic buildings and temples in the former empire outside Rome. All these impressions, as we have seen, were very wrong. The entire Roman apparatus had crumbled. The only Christians were to be found among the Britons in the far west, and the civilised Roman provinces had fallen under the sway of fearsome heathens. London was a burned-out, virtually empty ruin whose remaining inhabitants remained staunchly pagan.

Gregory suggested Augustine make London his archbishopric, but, this being impossible, Canterbury was chosen for his seat in its stead, where it still remains. Gregory helpfully advised Augustine that parish churches should be built atop the local pagan temples, so that the people would associate the new God with the old pantheon, and more readily and cheerfully worship there, in effect a 'rebranding' exercise. All of these thoughts must have seemed very far from Augustine's daily experience of the real Anglo-Saxon world. He and his few companions were getting older, and they could not convert the pagan Anglo-Saxons on their own. Augustine had no choice but to make an approach to the bishops of the British Church. As Christians, he thought, it was their sacred duty to help him evangelise 'the brethren' as he called the Anglo-Saxons, oblivious to the notorious hostility between the two peoples. Nevertheless, in AD 603 a meeting between Augustine and seven British bishops was arranged which took place at Great Witley in Worcestershire beneath a great oak, known as 'St Augustine's Oak'.

The meeting was clearly one which unnerved the Celtic bishops, so much so that they resorted to magic. On the way to the meeting they consulted a seer or holy man, one of the heirs to the Druids who still retained immense respect among the Britons. He advised them that if when they approached 'the bald man', as the Britons called Augustine, he rose from his episcopal chair to greet them fraternally, then he was a man with whom they should do business; but if he sat imperiously in his seat he was to be distrusted, and his proposals should be rejected. Augustine was determined that the British bishops, whom he regarded as virtual heretics, should defer to his status as the emissary of the Pope, and so he arrogantly refused to rise to greet them. The knowing glances of the British delegation made for a very difficult atmosphere.

Augustine was somewhat conciliatory, and said he would tolerate all the other things the Celts did differently if they would only conform about the dating of Easter and the tonsure problem. But his insistence on a joint project to evangelise the Anglo-Saxons was the explosive issue. Augustine refused to see the obstacles to this, and saw the British objections as bloody-minded, petty and uncharitable, despite the fact that the two peoples were traditional and implacable enemies in a state of unceasing warfare. It is true that we should love our enemies, and do good to those who hate us, but this is very difficult to do at the point of a spear. The Britons decided to depart, but as they left Augustine cursed them, shouting in 'an imperious and threatening manner', that the Britons would one day suffer 'the vengeance of death' at the hands of 'the brethren'. The later slaughter of the 1,200 monks at the Battle of Chester was interpreted rather gleefully by Bede, the Northumbrian scholar and saint, as being the fulfilment of this curse. The British prelates must have known Augustine's pomp was just for show, and their experience of the 'Saxon devils' was that their faith was shallow; they would soon revert to their old gods when 'the bald man' died.

In recognition of Augustine's difficulties, Pope Gregory made him archbishop, and in AD 601 reinforcements of monks were sent to him. One of them, Mellitus, was to become the first Bishop of London, and later Archbishop of Canterbury. Gregory wrote a letter to him, advising a gradualist approach to converting the Anglo-Saxons, and even that pagan practices be integrated or interweaved with Christian worship. Such a shallow faith could not endure long beyond Augustine's death, and when this day came, on 26 May AD 604, Kent immediately apostatised. Mellitus and Justus, Bishop of Rochester, fled to the Continent. Although they later returned, London remained obdurately pagan and would not co-operate with its bishop. Only Augustine's successor, Laurentius or St Laurence, remained at his post, having had a vision of St Peter admonishing him as he was preparing to flee. He had been consecrated as archbishop in Augustine's own lifetime, which was strictly uncanonical, and he never received a pallium.

In AD 616, Aethelberht, Augustine's patron, died. His son, Eadbald, was staunchly pagan, but Laurence eventually converted him. This was precious little to show for almost twenty years of hard work, but the foothold in the heel of England was maintained. Besides, there was another achievement to show for the mission, one which was to have powerful ramifications for the whole island. Aethelberht's daughter, Ethelburga, had married the King of Northumbria, Edwin. She was allowed to take her personal chaplain, Paulinus, with her as part of her personal entourage. Later Bishop of York, Paulinus was determined to do in Northumbria what Augustine had done in Kent and win the entire country for the Roman Church by converting its king. But Edwin was too preoccupied with establishing and extending his temporal power to be too concerned with spiritual matters. Hedging his bets, Edwin permitted Paulinus to proselytise and win converts, but he remained faithful to the pagan gods. A measure of Rome's investment in this mission is that Pope Boniface IV sent a personal letter to Ethelburga, in which he explicitly said that her marriage could not be considered as a true sacrament while her husband still worshipped 'abominable idols'. Boniface advised her to pray continually for her husband's soul, and sent her splendid gifts designed to appeal to a woman's vanity – a silver mirror and a gilt and ivory comb.

Edwin, who had spent much of his youth in miserable exile among the courts of Gwynedd and Mercia, was ostentatious, ambitious and ruthless. Every year, the two kingdoms he combined to form Northumbria, Deira and Bernicia, raided into the territories of their neighbours to obtain tributes of treasure, food and slaves. Gradually Edwin's authority extended until a vast swathe of Britain from the Cheviots to the Mersey was under his direct control. This expansionism was a threat to the kingdom of Wessex, whose king, Cwichelm, sent an assassin north to York. This assassin attacked Edwin with a poisoned dagger; the blow was deflected but still landed, and the wound festered. As the poison coursed around Edwin's body and he lay gravely ill, Edwin vowed that if he should survive he would convert to the Roman Catholic faith. Edwin did recover, and he was faithful to his pledge. All across the kingdom of Northumbria, especially in Yorkshire, Durham and Lincolnshire, vast crowds of converts came to be baptised in the cold fast-flowing rivers that wind through the dales.

Edwin's chief advisors – even Coifi, the chief priest under his former faith – were completely acquiescent, encouraging the king's conversion. One of the pagan priests compared this earthly life to a sparrow's flight through a warm, brightly lit mead hall on a cold night in winter – a brief spell of warmth and light between vast expanses of darkness. Coifi stood up and said that the pagan gods had done nothing to make him any happier or more prosperous, even though he was their greatest advocate. He decided that the time had come to smash the old gods, and, breaking centuries of taboo, he asked for the king's white horse. Pagan priests were forbidden from riding, and white horses were reserved exclusively for kings. Then, in full view of the company that had gathered to attend the king, Coifi broke yet another taboo. Arming himself with a spear, he rode into the pagan shrine and speared the idols through, symbolically breaking their power. The way was now clear for Paulinus to make mass conversions all over the north.

At Edwin's huge palace at Yeavering a massive timber-built auditorium was erected, where thousands of people at a time came to hear Paulinus preach before processing down to the nearby River Glen to be baptised. Because our national story has been so strongly influenced by the 'Venerable Bede', the so-called 'father of English history', it is usual to see this coup for Roman Catholicism as a victory in the struggle against barbarism. Perhaps controversially, this is a perspective the author does not share. My contention is quite the opposite, for Edwin's conversion, and his collusion in an imperialist plot to win the whole island for Rome, led to a series of long and brutal conflicts which engulfed the entire island in a religious war – a calamitous war between Christians and pagans, Roman Catholics and Celtic Christians, Celts and Anglo-Saxons. For Bede, the hero of this war was his illustrious countryman, Edwin. For me, Bede's villain is my countryman – Penda.

On 21 March 1974, my mother and I settled down to watch *Play for Today*, the showcase BBC drama series. The play was written by David Rudkin and directed by Alan Clarke, and was entitled *Penda's Fen*. Two hours later my life had changed. The play was a powerful evocation of what it means to have absorbed the complex conflicted messages of English history. Perhaps the play had such a profound effect upon me because the main character, Stephen Franklin, is a lonely, somewhat precocious, but also priggish and immature schoolboy, whose age temperament and education were rather similar to my own. Unsure of his sexuality, political standpoint, but above all of his essential identity – Stephen is adopted – the boy takes refuge in art and music, especially Elgar's *The Dream of Gerontius*, which narrates the story of the journey of a man's soul towards judgement. The boy also has a series of magical encounters, apparitions and dreams of various kinds, in which guardian spirits of the land – including Elgar – appear to him. The ultimate guardian of the spirit of the land is Penda, a character from history with whom I was also somewhat obsessed.

The play takes place on Penda's own home estates, near Pinvin in Worcestershire, the 'Penda's Fen' of the play's title. A sub-plot concerns a long discourse between Stephen and his adoptive father, an Anglican clergyman, about Manichaeism, a similar dualistic religion to that once practiced by the magi. In the eternal war between light and dark, Stephen realises that his soul is the battlefield, and he is not a creature 'belonging' to either, but to both. In contrast to the traditional view of Penda as a villain, when he is depicted in the final scene of the play – enthroned at the peak of the Worcestershire Beacon – he is a wisdom spirit, a protector of the land, a link in an unbroken spiritual chain which yokes the land and people together. *Penda's Fen* stimulated my long interest in the king as an historical person. Another 'encounter' with Penda came about as a result of events which took place a few miles from my home, on 5 July 2009.

Even in the deracinated culture of the twenty-first century there are some moments which come as epiphanies. I experienced such a moment in September 2009. I had just become a full-time carer for my parents in Staffordshire. My father was then old, ailing and losing his mental faculties. Those who are familiar with dementia will know that sufferers lose the ability to recall recent events and people, but can sometimes remember events from their own distant past – and also historical events they learned about before the onset of the illness. When I was a schoolboy, my father and I would venture out with a cousin and her father who was a metal detectorist. My father had a theory that somewhere in the area, perhaps near to Pinvin or Pebworth, a vast treasure lay hidden, spoils of war. Penda had looted these treasures or had them delivered as tribute from the many nations he subjected to vassalage. He was the most feared warrior of the time. Bede calls him 'a very able fighting man of the royal stock of the Mercians who ruled the people of that region through various fortunes for twenty-two years from that time', referring to 633 or thereabouts. A notorious pagan, Penda personally slew many enemies in battle and took Mercia from obscurity to a powerful polity which eventually came to control all England south of the Humber.

On 5 July 2009, another metal detectorist, Terry Herbert, was detecting in a field in Barracks Lane near Hammerwich in Staffordshire. The field was on Fred Johnson's farm, which is situated on top of a ridge overlooking the modern A5 road, in ancient times 'Watling Street', a Roman highway which remained in use centuries after their departure. Hammerwich is only 2 miles from a small but busy Roman town called by them *Letocetum* and now called Wall-by-Lichfield. There are still extensive visible Roman ruins there. Terry began to pick up signals, and before long, without even having to use his trowel, he began to pick up precious artefacts which were literally lying in the topsoil. When he washed away the mud which adhered to them he was astonished. Exquisite gold jewels, inlaid with thousands of individually worked blood-red cloisonné garnets, of a quality to rival the famous find at Sutton Hoo in 1939, turned up by the boxload.

Having found over 500 items, Terry informed Fred Johnson, the farmer whose land the treasures had been buried on. He also informed Stephen Dean, the Principal Archaeologist for Staffordshire. An excavation team was secretly deployed and focused on a tiny area where, it transpired, a bag or holdall of some kind had once been buried. Fred Johnson had ploughed over the top of it, and erosion of the topsoil over centuries had finally brought the treasure to the surface, where it had been scattered by Fred's ploughshare. The finds kept coming, until nearly 4,000 individual objects had been excavated. They were small, some tiny, but in all there was over 11 lbs of gold, and 3½ lbs of silver. Out of darkness, a great light now shone.

The workmanship demonstrated in the items was breathtaking, and it soon became clear that they must once have belonged to some 'high-status' individual. Fragments of stamped silver foils depicting marching warriors came from a gilded helmet as fine as the famous example from Sutton Hoo. The majority of the finds were pieces from pommels and hilts of swords, examples which must have belonged to the warrior elite of the seventh century. There were no sword blades.

As we listened to the announcement on our local news programme, my father was convinced that here, after so many years, was the vindication of his theory. Here was a treasure fit for a pagan Anglo-Saxon king. Christian crosses had been found among the finds, mangled and distorted, treated with seeming contempt. A gold strip with a Christian inscription was also found; the words from the Book of Numbers (10:35) read, 'Rise up, O Lord, and may thy enemies be dispersed and those that hate thee flee from thy face.' But the strip had been detached, as if the 'enemies' had been victorious. There was something about my father's absolute conviction that this was Penda's personal treasure which affected me. Some years after my parents died, I volunteered to work at the Staffordshire Hoard Gallery at Birmingham Museum and spent many hours among works of art so staggeringly beautiful that the legendary seems to have introjected into our mundane reality. But this is the reality, the confirmation of the glorious sagas like *Beowulf*. It was this magical quality which inspired me to write about the Anglo-Saxons and their civilisation, and particularly the contribution of Mercia, my own country. But the treasures are not just 'bling', in the modern argot. They tell a story of a time when this island was convulsed by a savage war of religion – and of the rise and fall of the last pagan Anglo-Saxon king.

9

The Last Pagan King

And they buried torques in a barrow, and jewels, and a trove of such things as trespassing men had once dared to drag from the hoard. They let the ground keep that ancestral treasure, gold under gravel gone to earth, as useless to men now as ever it was.

Beowulf

A recent study by the University of Oxford called *People of the British Isles* has confirmed that in the seventh century a small independent Brythonic kingdom called Elmet ('the elm forest') extended as a salient, jutting east into Anglian-held territory and bordering Deira, modern-day Yorkshire, from whence Pope Gregory's blonde blue-eyed children hailed. The centre of the little realm was *Loidis*, modern Leeds. In AD 590 they had contributed forces to the northern alliance of Celtic-speaking Britons which had rallied around the heroic King Urien of Rheged. This was a Celtic kingdom extending from Galloway all the way to Rochdale. Urien's alliance almost succeeded in pushing the Bernician Angles into the sea, but at the moment of triumph he was assassinated by one of his rivals.

Elmet was exposed – too exposed. The predatory Edwin of Northumbria was looking for a pretext to invade, and to the south a Mercian chieftain, Eowa, was only too conscious of the dangers of having a powerful Northumbrian 'super-state' as a neighbour instead of a compliant British statelet. Eowa was the brother of the dreaded Penda, who ruled in southern Mercia, so an attack on one was an attack on both.

Until recently, these little micro-kingdoms hardly mattered in historical terms. They seemed somehow ethereal, other-worldly – realms like *Gore* in the Arthurian legends. Small clues remind us that they were real; place names like Sherburn-in-Elmet outside Leeds, or organisations like the West Mercia constabulary. The ethnogenesis of the people of Britain in the seventh century is very complex, and what the Oxford study has revealed is that Elmet, now West Yorkshire, contains a surprisingly high number of inhabitants with

Brythonic or Celtic ancestors. As a young man I traversed the Pennine region on a fairly regular basis and I knew that the poet Ted Hughes (itself a Welsh surname) was a native of the area. Some of his poems were combined into a book, with photographs by Fay Godwin, called *Remains of Elmet*, which had a strong influence on me at that time. But the real remains of Elmet, it seems, are its people, islanded amid the hills and dales. There is something reassuring about the research too, because it broadly confirms a traditional account based on Bede that a series of catastrophic wars engulfed Britain as soon as Edwin converted. Despite its obscurity, this tiny hill-kingdom was to be the scene for the first hostilities.

In 619, Ceretic ap Gwallog, the King of Elmet, had allowed a Deiran exile, a nobleman called Hereric, to reside within his protection. Hereric was poisoned, and Edwin immediately accused Ceretic, using Hereric's death as his excuse to invade. There was a brave but futile resistance on the River Idle, but the Northumbrian army easily brushed the Britons aside. Ceretic escaped by riding west over the Pennines, the last of a line of kings stretching back to the legendary 'Old King Cole' or *Coel Hen*. The defeated man did not live long. His sad tale was greeted with gloomy silence at the court of Gwynedd, and the news reverberated in Mercia too. Suddenly the stakes were raised. Although Sussex remained semi-pagan for a little longer, Mercia was one of the last places in Europe where the old gods were still honoured, and its people were thoroughly pagan. With Edwin's conversion, Northumbrian dominion must mean the demise of the ancient gods. So, by an extraordinary twist of fate, the Mercian kings increasingly looked to an alliance with Gwynedd against their fellow Anglians. The Celtic Christians of Gwynedd, meanwhile, looked for alliances throughout the Celtic lands, and looked to the bards, and especially the 'Prophesies of Merlin', for guidance.

An early thirteenth-century manuscript in the keeping of the National Library of Wales at Aberystwyth, the *Black Book of Carmarthen*, contains an ancient Welsh poem called *Cyfoesi Myrddin a Gwyndydd ei Chwaer*, or in English 'A Conversation between Myrddin [Merlin] and his Sister Gwyndydd'. This is the earliest existing written document in the Welsh language. Readers of my earlier works will perhaps forgive me if I recapitulate this story, because it illustrates powerfully, I think, the strange threads which interweave when one comes to examine the magical history of Britain. This is why, for conventional historians, archaeologists and social anthropologists, a great many important themes can be overlooked or misinterpreted or simply consigned to oblivion – the most important 'history' actually missed. For the ancient Celts, time was not perceived in the way we now understand it. The past, present and future were combined, interoperative. Robert Graves proposed that all creative processes were predicated upon 'proleptic' and 'analeptic' thought, a suspension of the conventional boundaries of time, something akin to the ancient Greek concept of *Anamnesis* or 'loss of forgetfulness'. As he remarked, 'It is possible to have memory of the future, as well as the past', a state of 'trans-personal constancy'. His *The White Goddess* is a 'historical grammar of poetic myth' which explores the evolution of the creative consciousness since the old Stone Age Palaeolithic.

We have already encountered Myrddin, the north-country bard sometimes called *Lailoken*. Geoffrey of Monmouth conflated this character with the historical personage of Ambrosius Aurelianus, whom the Welsh called *Emrys*. The composite personality, *Myrddin Emrys* or 'Merlin Ambrosius', was the fictional character with whom we are all familiar, a half-human half-demonic wizard who magically engineers the rise of Arthur but is then infatuated with and bewitched by Nimue or Vivien, an undine fairy woman, and entombed in a tree at Barenton in the forest of Broceliande in Brittany – 'the Nemeton of Beli'. Geoffrey's 'history' was, of course, no such thing. It was derived from history, but soon took on a magical life of its own. His works were enormously popular in Wales, and it is very probable that many of the so-called prophesies uttered by Merlin were retrospectively intruded into Welsh annals as if they were historical events. The innovative way in which the Celts perceived time was, perhaps, one way in which they could transcend a world which seemed to be conspiring against them.

Despite a most gallant and prolonged resistance, the Saxon enemy and the Roman Church were steadily gaining power as Celtic energy waned. Geoffrey of Monmouth claimed that while he was a *magister* or master at Oxford in the 1130s an archdeacon had lent him a very rare book 'in the British language' – meaning either Welsh or Breton – which he used as the foundation for his extraordinary literary career. We don't know if this book ever really existed, but a consensus is that it must have been a copy or recension of *Historia Brittonum*, a ninth-century work attributed to a Welsh monk named Nennius. There are other influences too, but as Geoffrey needed more and more such material he resorted to literary inventiveness and whimsy. This melange of fact, fiction, romance and prophesy was the literary 'blockbuster' of its time. But these ideas and characters were not entirely fanciful, or indeed unhistorical. Many events Geoffrey mentions which were once dismissed as his inventions have subsequently proven to be factual. Disentangling this complex web of history, prophesy and magical lore is frustrating – but it can also be immensely rewarding.

One of the most ancient names for Britain is *Clas Myrddin* – 'Merlin's Enclosure'. According to the Welsh Triads, the name is even older than 'Albion'. This implies that Myrddin was originally the name of some elemental god-form who was identified with the destiny of the 'Island of the Mighty'. It is also possible that rather than being a personal name, a 'Myrddin' was a title used among a specific class of persons whose task was to utter vaticinations while in trance states. The ancient poem called *Cyfoesi Gwyndydd a Myrddin ei Chwaer* recounts how Myrddin's sister asks her brother to demonstrate his powers of prophesy. She asks him to tell of future British kings and their fates, and of the destiny of the Britons as a nation.

Myrddin then gives a long regnal list of kings to come, and says that there will be a resurgence of the Britons under a 'Great Eagle', a mighty warrior who will recapture the sources of the rivers Trent and Mersey – and extend the frontier with the Saxons to the eastern bank of the Severn throughout its entire length. This new frontier was to be fixed at an ancient grove called *Onnenau Meigion* or 'the ash trees of Meigion', on the high road between Bridgnorth and Kinver. This mighty British leader would then reconquer the 'Lost Lands' and restore the rightful dignity of the Britons as heirs to the sovereignty of the island.

There are many elements in this account which seem too old to have been invented by Geoffrey of Monmouth. The Celtic name, the references to control of sacred rivers and the gathering of a 'great army' of Britons under a 'Great Eagle' or commander sound like they belong in the seventh century, and another legend has it that the king supposedly prophesied, Cadwallon ap Cadfan of Gwynedd, defeated Penda in a fierce battle at *Onnenau Meigion* (modern-day Six Ashes). This was one of the fourteen battles and sixty skirmishes Cadwallon allegedly fought as he re-established his power when he returned from exile. All these events may be completely legendary, and they may as well be, for Six Ashes is today a sleepy hamlet on the border of Staffordshire and Shropshire. No one there seemed to know the legend, and there were many raised eyebrows when I mentioned the fact that it had once been prophesied that it would be the Welsh border one day.

On 28 February 1405, three men signed a document called the 'Tripartite Indenture'. Two of the men were English, Edmund Mortimer and Henry Percy the Earl of Northumberland. The third was the self-proclaimed Prince of Wales, Owain Glyndwr. The three men plotted to overthrow King Henry IV of England and divide the country in three between them. Henry Percy would take all England north of *Onnenau Meigion*, Mortimer all of England south of the place, and Glyndwr would be ruler of a Welsh state encompassing everything west of Six Ashes, including Shropshire, Worcestershire, Herefordshire and Cheshire, along with an enclave in the Peak District. Glyndwr's bards referred to the ancient prophesy as the basis for legitimating these territorial demands. In their eyes the Prophesy of Myrddin was sacred and inviolate. This tiny obscure hamlet, which motorists speed by without a second glance, was once of quintessential importance to the magical-political history of Britain. Nothing came of the project of dividing the realm in three parts. In 1415, Glyndwr disappeared into the Welsh mountains. He was never found. The ash trees remained as silent witnesses of a border that never was, and the whole affair was forgotten – until now.

During my researches to find out more about *Onnenau Meigion* over the last five years I was often struck by the mismatch between its present obscurity and its past magical-political significance. It seemed to me unconscionable that such an inheritance should be entirely obliterated, and I resolved to do something about it – in fact took a magical vow to that effect. By a serendipitous meeting with a local celebrity I was enabled to put forward a proposal to the Owain Glyndwr Society to erect a small but tasteful monument at Six Ashes which gives the historical context of the place in both the Welsh and English languages. The donor for the project is as modest as he is generous, and must remain nameless, but by immense good fortune he was familiar with the legends and as passionate as I in wishing to restore them from oblivion. At last, as the monument says, 'the past, present and future are intertwined'.

But this is not just a story about protecting our heritage. During the 1960s and 1970s, the conceptual artist Joseph Beuys proposed 'an expanded conception of art' expressed in social process works or 'social sculptures' he called 'actions'. Beuys was profoundly influenced by German and Austrian mystics such as Novalis, Fichte, Goethe, Schiller and Steiner. His artistic 'materials' included speech, thought, will and the written word. It is an attempt to mobilise inherent dynamic action and recapture meaning. Many of these works, such as the famous *7000 Oaks*, incorporated trees, and so I conceived the project as a kind of 'guerrilla social sculpture' celebrating the ash trees, a modern *nemeton*. What I propose is an active, imaginative antiquarianism, something along the lines of Watkins' 'foot archaeology', a kind of 'spiritual archaeology'. The monument has been designed as a focus for walkers, ramblers and cyclists. Julian Cope's *The Modern Antiquarian* is a pioneering project of this type.

Later on we will return to the significance of these ideas as prototypes for a new approach to the teaching of history, but it seems to me important that we not only analyse and 'study' history, but act in it creatively – not as a 'science' but an art, a challenge to what the philosopher George Steiner called 'the organized amnesia of present primary and secondary education'. As a constellation of ideas and events which have coalesced in time, history itself forms a 'material' from which we can restore meaning to a paralysed world, in which people are cut off from their vital cultural roots. Such a movement would be more than mere history; it might be called magical.

But we must return to more conventional historical analysis. Edwin's conquest of Elmet opened the door to the Irish Sea. This was what Cadwallon most dreaded, and another kingdom, *Ulaid* or Ulster, also had serious concerns. Its king, Fiachne, mounted an invasion of Northumbria and his forces made their way across country to Bamburgh, which they put under siege, but Edwin's forces rallied and drove them out. In AD 629 the Northumbrians attacked Gwynedd. Cadwallon was taken by surprise and forced to retreat to the tiny island of *Glannauc*, now called Priestholm off Anglesey. According to the *Moliant Cadwallon*, a Welsh praise-poem composed in his honour, Cadwallon escaped to Ireland but his kingdom fell to Edwin, who garrisoned it with a Northumbrian army and a fleet.

Edwin's marriage alliance with Kent was a powerful counter to King Cwichelm of Wessex, and now that Gwynedd had been defeated any Mercian hopes of a common cause with Cadwallon were irrelevant. Edwin seems to have invoked his technical dominion over the Mercians by sending Penda on an expedition against Wessex in AD 628. Penda forced the kingdom of Wessex to come to terms, and according to Geoffrey of Monmouth he was besieging the city of Exeter when a surprise landing by an army of Breton and Irish mercenaries took place, led by the exiled Cadwallon.

The return of the 'High King of Britain' after a long exile in Ireland, Brittany and Guernsey seemed to the Britons like the promised return of the god-king Arthur, the hero of what was by now a very real cultural mythology. The man himself is historically vague, misty and semi-legendary, but he undoubtedly existed. The wars which commenced immediately following his return are reminiscent of the wars for 'Middle Earth' in Tolkien's *The Lord of the Rings*, and Tolkien was certainly an expert in this strangely obscure period of British history.

What happened next is frustratingly obscure, but it seems that Penda, who was acting as a proxy for Edwin on a mission of plunder and exacting tribute, suffered a defeat. For all his ferocity and military skill, Penda's force would have been a large raiding party. Cadwallon's mercenary force must have been larger, composed, we must presume, of Irish and Bretons, but the men of Dumnonia or Devon rallied to him and many British kings pledged him fealty. The list of fourteen battles and sixty skirmishes Cadwallon is supposed to have fought in one year to establish his authority seems inflated, probably derived from some ancient ballad.

There now occurred one of the most dramatic turnarounds in British history; Penda, the despised pagan, threw in his lot with Cadwallon against Edwin. How this came about we simply do not know. It is possible that Cadwallon's army invaded Mercia and defeated its army in a series of battles. The legend of *Onnenau Meigion* says that Penda was defeated there, but it is equally possible that the Mercian and British forces combined there before embarking on the campaign to liberate Gwynedd, Cadwallon's homeland, which was still occupied by Edwin's forces. Two small British statelets, Pengwern in Shropshire and Luitcoit in South Staffordshire, were among the many Brythonic peoples who welcomed the return of the king.

With thousands of British levies, and the fearsome Mercian forces, Cadwallon crossed the Severn near modern Welshpool and confronted Edwin's forces at *Cefn Digoll* or Long Mountain. It is not known if the Northumbrian force was commanded by Edwin himself or one of his ealdormen. The result was a defeat for Northumbria either way, and Gwynedd was finally freed. The tables had been dramatically turned. For Northumbria, and for Rome, the great project for establishing Edwin's hegemony over the entire island had collapsed. On 12 October AD 633 Cadwallon and Penda's forces combined again at a place called *Heathfelth* or Heathfield, usually identified as Hatfield Chase outside Doncaster (another strong candidate is the village of Cuckney near Warsop – not far from the place still named Edwinstowe). The result was a catastrophe for Northumbria. Edwin was killed alongside his son Osfrith, and his other son, Eadfrith, who fled, was later hunted down by Penda and put to death.

The Prophesies of Myrddin and the bards had finally been fulfilled. Cadwallon was now 'High King of Britain' in reality, and he marched his British army into a cowed York like a latter-day Roman emperor. Penda's pagan marauders looted and ransacked every church and monastery, and extracted everything of value there, the places functioned in the same way as modern safety-deposit boxes for noblemen. Bede, whose bias will become evident, was writing some years after the events, and according to him Cadwallon was actually a more brutal oppressor of the Northumbrians than Penda. He states that Cadwallon intended to 'exterminate the whole English race within the island of Britain', and that he ravaged and destroyed regardless of age or sex, 'a barbarian crueller than any pagan'. Northumbria could not survive, and the queen took ship with her children and chaplain to find refuge in her homeland of Kent.

As the kingdom disintegrated into its former constituent parts, Bernicia and Deira, the claimant kings of the regions reverted to the pagan gods. The Christian God had failed them, or so they thought, and they probably attributed Edwin's downfall to his renouncing the pagan gods. Eanfrith, the Bernician king, was invited to negotiate with Cadwallon and treacherously murdered. Osric of Deira lost no time in raising an army and besieged Cadwallon's forces in 'a large town', unfortunately it is not known which town. Cadwallon's army broke out and destroyed Osric's army, putting an end to any hopes of a Northumbrian revival. The Britons were now an army of occupation, and it may well be true that they visited brutal depredations on the nation which had formerly occupied their homeland. There seemed no prospect of hope, and as famine took hold the cowed folk of Northumbria had few consolations. Only James 'the deacon', as he is known, remained as a solitary witness of Christ, doing what he could to comfort the desolated wandering refugees.

But there was hope. On the tiny island of Iona, where Columba had lived and died, two young boys had fled for refuge from Edwin. They were the sons of Aethelfrith, Oswald and Oswy, and had been educated as Christians by the Celtic Christian monks. Oswald gathered an army in Lothian and the borders, composed for the most part of Irishmen from Dalriada. His army was miserably small, but tough, and also inspired by Oswald's absolute conviction and faith. He proclaimed that Columba had appeared to him in a dream and promised him victory. He had a huge wooden cross erected at a place known by the Northumbrians as Heavenfield and by the Britons as *Catscaul*, the 'strife beside the Wall', meaning Hadrian's Wall, just outside Hexham. Cadwallon marched his vast army from York, and must have been confident of victory, but Oswald's forces surprised him in a dawn assault. The Britons fled in disarray for over 5 miles, and few of them ever returned to their homelands. Cadwallon was found hiding in a burn at a place called Denis Brook and killed. The great dream of a British resurrection died with him.

A unique situation now presented itself. The two great Christian kings in the island, Cadwallon and Edwin, had both been slaughtered in battle, and the new Northumbrian king, Oswald, although he was a devout Celtic Christian, inherited a charred wasteland full of desperate refugees. It was the obdurately pagan Penda who now held the destiny of the island in his hands.

The relatively late devotion to the heathen idols in Mercia demonstrated by Penda has been noted in previous chapters. Mercia was an Anglo-British kingdom, as was Northumbria, and indeed Wessex. The survival of a pre-existing British pagan or semi-pagan magic called by the Anglo-Saxons *drycraeft* is implicit in the theories promulgated by Stephen J. Yeates, as we have seen. Bede complained bitterly about what he perceived as hostility and incivility from the *Celi-de* or Culdees – the ascetic 'servants of God' who have been seen as an intermediate stage between the Druids and Celtic Christianity. Bede said that these monks would proffer the same honour to pagans as they would to Christian 'brethren' of the Anglo-Saxon race, which is *ipso facto* an admission that paganism still flourished among the Britons as well as the Saxons. The Germanic *Hwicce* and *Mierce*, the 'border folk', were often interbred with the local British stock. Penda's own name could be British. Pontesbury and Pontesford in the Shropshire Hills may be named after the Welsh version of his name, *Panta*. It is postulated that he was bi-lingual. A class of persons called *walhstods* acted as interpreters with the British, but in West Mercia these may not have been strictly necessary. To this day the area containing the highest number of people with the surname Wall is the West Midlands.

In earlier books I have postulated that Penda's peculiar paganism may have been linked to the cult practices of the 'tribe of witches'. It was precisely the area around the Severn Valley, the heartland of the *Hwicce*, which was Penda's base. One of Penda's sons, Merewalh, has a name containing the word *walh*, meaning 'a foreigner' or 'a stranger'. The *Volcae* were the first Celtic tribe the Germans encountered on the Continent in ancient times, and so the Germans used this name for any Celtic folk – *Waelisc* or 'Welsh', individual Celts being called *walh*. To Bede these Culdees or Celtic Christians seemed like Christians in name only. They associated with the pagan Mercians, and indeed had allied themselves with the pagans during the merciless sack of Northumbria almost a century before he was writing his account. St Bernard doubted that these Culdees were really Christians at all:

They are beasts, absolute barbarians, a stubborn, stiff-necked, and ungovernable generation, and abominable; Christian in name, but in reality pagans.

Bede depicted Penda as a ruthless, greedy, bloodthirsty, ferocious demon, much as later Christian monks were to portray the heathen Vikings. It is usual, of course, for victorious nations to calumniate the leaders of enemy nations, and I do not berate Bede on that account. But his portrayal of Penda as demonic is, I think, an oversimplification. Penda permitted individual Mercians to practice Christianity. He never interfered to prevent his Brythonic allies and satellite states, Pengwern and Luitcoit, practising their Christian devotions, and some say that he took a princess of Pengwern, Heledd, to wife. He assented to the Christian baptism and marriage of his heir, Peada, to the daughter of the Northumbrian king, Oswy, and did not demur when four Christian missionaries from Northumbria were settled at Peada's court. He is said to have declaimed that having foresworn himself to the gods of his ancestors, he would not break faith with them – and that the only people he truly despised were those who, having been baptised, became backsliders.

As we will see, Penda's downfall became part of a 'national story' devised principally by Bede, which associated the outworkings of divine providence with the establishment of an 'English' national destiny. Penda, as a pagan, was the archetypal villain of this 'story', but his British allies were equally suspect – heretics whose hatred for the English race and the Catholic Church ran so deep that they would combine with unclean heathen forces rather than conform. Henry of Huntingdon, a twelfth-century historian, wrote that a gleeful rhyme was sung after Penda's grisly death, celebrating the demise of the hoary old warlord who had personally killed five other kings in battle.

Penda's reputation for ferocity in battle may be linked to his devotion to Germanic Wodenism. This was what gave Penda his baleful reputation. Like the later Vikings these warriors believed they could shapeshift into animal forms associated with ferocity, particularly the wild boar, but also the wolf and the bear – the *ulfhednir* or *berserkar* respectively. The blood-red garnets which inlaid the dazzling gold fittings for swords, helmets, horse trappings and similar war gear were designed to purify and protect the wearer in the eventuality that they were wounded – a form of sympathetic magic. Christian warriors (and perhaps these included at least some Mercians) wore crosses or inscribed prayers such as the one discovered in the Staffordshire Hoard. The pectoral cross discovered in the hoard is of such rare quality that it may have belonged to a churchman or noble of high rank – perhaps even King Edwin or King Oswald.

Before the battle of Hatfield Chase, Penda seems to have been a relatively obscure, if much feared, warlord. After this, though, his power grew until he was the acknowledged over-king of all England south of the Humber. Oswald could not stand aside, especially following Penda's ruthless invasions of East Anglia, three of whose kings he personally slew. In AD 642 Oswald appears to have invaded into the area at the junction between Penda's power base of West Mercia and Powys, his main Welsh ally. There is strong reason to suspect that Penda's brother, Eowa, had gone over to the Northumbrians, and that a northern Mercian contingent served in Oswald's invasion force. In his scholarly work *Wales and the Britons 350–1064*, Thomas Charles-Edwards asserts that there was a long-standing Northumbrian policy going back to Edwin's and Aethelfrith's reigns which was predicated on annexation of the former territory of the Brythonic *Cornovii* tribe, Cheshire, Staffordshire and Shropshire. If the theory that the Battle of *Maserfelth* or Maserfield was fought in modern-day Oswestry ('Oswald's Tree') is right, this is exactly where Oswald struck his blow.

Oswald's army of combined Mercians and Northumbrians confronted Penda and his Welsh and Brythonic allies at a place the Welsh called *Croesoswallt* or *Maes Cogwy*, traditionally Oswestry. The client-kingdom of Pengwern and its illustrious king, Cynddylan, also mustered to assist Penda; as a Welsh poem states, 'when the son of Pyb [Penda] requested – he was so ready!' The pagan king was in his element, and his forces stormed Oswald's position and broke his line. When he could see that all was lost, Oswald sank to his knees in prayer for his doomed soldiers before being hacked to pieces by enraged Mercian warriors. Penda ordered that his head and limbs be cut off and set up on poles on the branches of a great oak – 'Oswald's Tree' as an offering to Woden. The Christian Welsh were as disconcerted about this as the later Bede, and they attributed Penda's military prowess to a diabolical pact. But now the man they called *Panta ap Pyd* or 'Penda, Son of Danger', was undisputed overlord of all Britain south of Hadrian's Wall.

Oswy, who succeeded Oswald as King of Bernicia, sent a raiding party to the battlefield to recover his brother's remains and remove them for Christian burial. In retaliation, Penda invaded Bernicia the following year, 644, and besieged Bamburgh. This strong fortress defied Penda, who in frustration ordered faggots to be stacked and lit around the palisades. St Aedan, the great Celtic missionary Oswald had introduced to rebuild Christianity in Northumbria, observed the Mercian incendiaries and exclaimed, 'Lord! See what evil Penda does!' Immediately the wind changed and blew the smoke and flames onto the pagan attackers, saving the town from immolation. Could this be an example of the ancient powers of control of the weather which the Culdees inherited from Druidism?

After another campaign of looting and pillaging and exacting rich tributes of gold and jewels Penda withdrew, but these raids were not just wanton violence, nor were they motivated by greed. To understand the context of the Staffordshire Hoard or the Sutton Hoo treasures we need to appreciate their magical context in Anglo-Saxon society. In his *The Real Middle-Earth: Magic and Mystery in the Dark Ages*, Professor Brian Bates sums up the philosophy neatly:

> Gold, in particular, was used as the mark of the success of a kingdom, whether it was gained as war booty, as tribute from subservient kingdoms, or through trade. But this level of success dealt with a deeper dimension than mere material wealth. For a person's degree of success was a result of

that individual's luck, or personal charisma or mana ... but this luck was more than we would mean by it. The Anglo-Saxon terms '*eadig*' and '*saelig*' are used to mean both 'lucky' and 'rich', and wealth is taken as a token of that quality on which the gods shower their blessings. The king was the charismatic holder of the tribal 'luck'.

Professor Bates goes on to say that the tribal king kept the treasure in trust on behalf of the tribe; gifts from kings, such as expensive and rare swords, for example, were regarded as being in a sense 'on loan', bestowed by the king on behalf of the wider community. These customs had a particular resonance, perhaps, among the Mercians, who were an obscure frontier folk, of mixed Anglo-Brythonic blood, and whose parvenu kings had all too recently been freebooting warlords whose swords were for hire. Now, Penda sought to establish his newly united Midland kingdom as a genuine Anglo-Saxon nation – the equal of Wessex, Northumbria, East Anglia and Kent. All these kingdoms were invaded and looted by him, and truly vast quantities of gold removed. I am not alone in thinking that the possibility of the Staffordshire Hoard as being in some way connected with these constant Mercian depredations cannot be easily dismissed.

Penda's fearful martial reputation and his grim veneration of Woden are well known, but he may well have utilised seers and other pagan magical aids. Such magic, what we would call today 'psychological warfare', undermined the confidence of the terrorised vassal kings of neighbouring countries. The awesome reputation of the Mercian king was itself enough to intimidate the bravest monarch, but wizards casting spells could exert even more subtle pressure. Bates says:

Such spellbinding in the historical Middle-Earth was a practical matter. Wizards cast spells on people by placing or releasing magical bonds which held them fast – literally spellbound. And like the wizards for whom he was the deity, Odin had spells which spun people's threads into knots, so that the interwoven forces of life became stuck. The knots shackled the mind, and paralysed movement and will. These spells rendered his enemies helpless in battle.

This deep-rooted paganism was not eradicated, even after Penda's demise. Witchcraft, *drycraeft*, and divination by specialist seers, usually women, who could induce trance states survived in the folk culture of the British Isles all through the Anglo-Saxon era. But the Church exacted heavy penances on any who practised 'the craft', and on those who sought out the services of 'cunning folk'. One penitential suggests five years' penance for a clergyman and three for a layman, including a whole year on bread and water, as punishment for dabbling in the dark arts. All this was to come, but in AD 655 there was a real prospect that a substantial part of Britain might revert to paganism. This term, 'paganism', has always been used in a pejorative sense until recent times, but it is worthwhile to consider what it was that was about to be extirpated – the essence of that native culture which had endured here since the Neolithic era. My view about this, as will become clear, is strongly influenced by the English philosopher and philologist Owen Barfield. He suggested that

> the most striking difference between primitive figuration and ours is that the primitive involves 'participation', that is, an awareness which we no longer have, of an extra-sensory link between the percipient and the representations (observed natural phenomena).[20]

This 'original participation' began as 'the unconscious identification of man with his creator'. Since 'God' was perceived as being in all, so idols were erected to the manifold representations of the divine spirit which permeated, and was immanent in, all nature. Hitherto, even under the iron grip of Rome, Britain had retained a powerful legacy of magical-religious ideas predicated on such primordial beliefs. But even for the mighty Penda, the weave of *wyrd* was about to unravel. In 655, the ageing heathen king summoned forces from thirty Anglo-Saxon and Brythonic nations to muster for an invasion of Northumbria – yet another foray into the far north for plunder and tribute. This mighty host was unstoppable, and King Oswy of Bernicia withdrew himself into *Iudeu* or *Iddaw*, a place identified as the Rock of Stirling. Penda had taken Oswy's son as a hostage and so Oswy offered up 'all the treasures which he had with him in that place, which (Penda) distributed among his British allies'. As the autumn came on, Penda was content to turn south. He was never to see his Mercian homeland again.

Penda's heterogeneous polyglot forces made slow progress on their homeward journey, burdened no doubt by the vast quantities of booty they carried with them. They were making for the old Roman road which wound across the Pennines from York to Manchester when news came that Oswy was close behind them. The Bernician king had a small army, but he knew the country well enough to know that Penda's cumbersome force would struggle to cross the numerous small streams and becks which became fast-flowing rivers when they were swollen by autumnal storms. Oswy promised that if he won a victory he would endow a dozen new monasteries and give up his favourite daughter to a nunnery. On 15 November 655 Penda's army was confronted by a raging stream called the *Winwaed*, possibly the River Went, but just outside Leeds another stream, the Cock Beck, runs through a large modern housing estate traditionally named Pendas Fields.

---

20 Barfield, O., 'Imagination and Inspiration', in Hopper, S. R. & D. L. Miller (eds), *Interpretation: the Poetry of Meaning*, New York, 1967.

As a fierce rainstorm flooded the proposed ford, Penda prepared to stand and fight. But during the night Penda's Welsh allies, led by the King of Gwynedd, Cadfael, deserted him and made their way west by another route. Cadfael's own countrymen traduced him with the sobriquet *Cynfedw* or 'battle-shirker' for this act of treachery. As Oswy's army came into view through the driving rain, Penda's other ally, Aethelwald, King of Deira and the son of Oswald – the man whose body Penda had ordered to be hacked in pieces and suspended from a tree – decided to stand aside from the battle and observe which side was winning. The only non-Mercian contingent to remain loyal was that of the East Anglians under their king, Aethelhere. He was trenchantly aware of the fate of his three predecessors, all of whom Penda had personally killed.

Even though his army was now half the size it had been in the summer, Penda would be no pushover. The old man was still the most feared warrior in all Britain. But Oswy's soldiers hacked their way through to the mighty pagan and surrounded him, finally bringing him down, as the veteran king hewed around him to the last. Oswy's prayers had been answered. Bede relates, rather gleefully, that 'having cut off the wicked king's head (Oswy) converted the Mercians and the adjacent provinces to the grace of the Christian faith'. Penda, having lived by the sword, perished by violence at the Battle of *Winwaed*, his body violated and dishonoured as Oswald's had been. It is a fate such a man would have accepted implicitly. He had risen from humble origins to become the mightiest king in Britain, and his sons would raise Mercia to even greater glories.

But as Oswy's men hacked off the old man's gory head, they also decapitated the pagan religion in Britain. It would continue, of course, but now underground, proscribed, a faith to be practised in utmost secrecy in remote locations. Contrary to the notions of many neo-pagans, later Anglo-Saxon England was not strongly influenced by paganism or witchcraft; following Charlemagne's lead, Alfred condemned anyone found guilty of the 'craft' to death. His more lenient grandson, Athelstan, only required those found guilty of causing death by witchcraft to be sentenced to execution. Strong nation states under powerful kings, combined with a growing and militant Church, gradually eroded the influence of the so-called 'Old Religion', until it became a feeble simulacrum of original pagan practices. This process began in earnest following the Battle of *Winwaed*. This obscure battle in the Yorkshire countryside, probably unknown to the majority of school students nowadays, marked the end of an era.

The magical and pagan practices we have examined hitherto carried with them no serious stigma or popular opprobrium, unless of course the magical workings caused others harm. But the establishment of strong nation states under the influence of the Roman Catholic Church meant that the earlier belief systems were, quite literally, demonised. Any concourse with spirits was, by definition, an invocation of Satan, 'the obstructor'. The success of magical operations undermined the uniqueness of Christ's miracles, inviting the thought that He may have been no more than a powerful magician Himself. The elimination of the last pagan king was, then, a major coup for the Christians.

The late survival of paganism in the Midlands was not exceptional. Germany was not converted until the ninth century (achieved in large part by English Christian missionaries) and Scandinavia was not completely Christianised even in the twelfth century. Even when the ruling dynasts had converted, the new faith was initially an overlay on a semi-pagan culture. Ironically, it was the later incursions of the heathen Vikings which consolidated the Christian religion among the English, who saw the Scandinavians as God's just punishment for their sins.

Christian theologians taught that the gods and goddesses of the former pagan pantheon were in fact devils, bent on preventing mankind's ultimate salvation. This unsophisticated approach effectively meant that all forms of 'cunning' practices such as the administration of herbal remedies, divination, spellcasting and the like, were lumped together with more pernicious forms of diabolism and sorcery. Christ had proclaimed that those who were not for him were against him, and so the common folk contrived an ingenious solution. They began to attribute the former powers of the pagan deities to a host of localised Christian 'saints', many of whose exploits, or indeed sometimes their very existence, were extremely spurious. A reputed grandson of Penda, Rumbold, became such a saint. The youngest saint in history, he was miraculously born with the ability to speak. He asked for communion and declaimed long passages from scripture, gave a sermon, and prophesied that he would die after three days – which he duly did.

Having disposed of one dangerous enemy, Oswy now turned his attention to his remaining opponent, the Britons, who would shortly become 'the Welsh'. Ever since the Roman departure the Britons had persisted in calling the island *Britannia*, but the momentous wars which had raged for over twenty years began processes of cultural identification which culminated in state formation. The nations of 'England' and 'Wales' did not exist as yet, but the seeds of national consciousness were there. This new consciousness did not come out of nowhere, for it was predicated on magical and mythical interpretations of history, partialities, misrepresentations and prejudices, themes taken up by bards and monks which culminated in the British 'national story' with which we are familiar. It was an amalgam of all that had gone before, and as the national consciousness coalesced and evolved, particularly in Wales, this consciousness became more than a veneration of the past – it also provided the prophetic template for the 'manifest destiny' of British expansionism.

The heroic age had passed. Now Britain had entered into an aeon dominated by religion and political machinations, the prototype for the modern world. There was no place for a man of Penda's stamp, but across the northern sea the ancestors of the Vikings still retained their pagan way of life. One day the old gods would return. There was little to show for Penda's turbulent years as the lord of all Britain, but perhaps the Staffordshire Hoard gives us a brief tantalising glimpse into the last years of pagan Britain. The finds are all of the correct period, of the most exquisite quality, seemingly taken by violence. While it cannot be definitively proven that these were once treasures personally concealed by the king, who for obvious reasons never came to recover them, it is rather satisfying that the conventional archaeological and historical academic community cannot disprove it. If such a man concealed one cache of buried treasure, it is conceivable that he may have deposited more, and that further hoards could come to light, splendid, dazzling relics of the so-called 'dark ages'.

10

Mythogenesis

In previous books I have analysed both the gradual emergence of England out of the Anglo-Saxon heptarchy and the long wars waged by the Anglo-Saxons, Normans and the English kings to subordinate and finally conquer the Celtic-speaking tribes and nations. The most extraordinary aspect of these long and bitter struggles was that the eventual victors, the Anglo-Normans, adopted the heroic mythology of the Celts as their own. This interpenetration of Celtic and Germanic mythic elements, supposedly predicated upon 'historical' genealogies of royal dynasties and traditions derived from bards and *scops*, was the basis for the first and most important history of 'England' – Bede's *Ecclesiastical History of the English People*.

The notion of 'Englishness' was something new in the seventh century. *Engle-lond*, the 'homeland of the Angles' (or English), was at least in part a response to a need felt by the English to differentiate themselves from both the Continental Saxons (who were still notorious pagans), and their Celtic neighbours, who were considered as heretical by Rome. In 673 an elderly Greek, Theodore of Tarsus, convoked the Synod of Hertford in his capacity as the Archbishop of Canterbury, a groundbreaking measure William Stubbs called 'the first constitutional measure of the collective English race'. In 680 Theodore convoked another synod, at Heathfield, and representatives from King Ecgfrith of Northumbria and the kings of East Anglia, Mercia and Kent attended. Although these nations were fiercely independent and engaged in constant warfare with one another, in matters of religion they were now of one mind, for Penda's sons, Peada, Wulfhere and Aethelred, who succeeded to him in turn, were all Christians.

Local folklore in Staffordshire suggests that, at least in Wulfhere's case, Mercia was conflicted about the new faith. Wulfhere was supposed to have slain his two sons in a fit of temper when they revealed they had converted to the Christian faith. But to cleave to heathenism was political suicide. In the struggle for political supremacy between the Anglo-Saxon realms, the support of the papacy and the Roman Catholic Church was absolutely vital. Wulfhere can have been under no illusions. His brother Peada had been poisoned on Oswy's orders by his own wife, Aelflaeda, who was Oswy's daughter. But following the conversion of the Mercian kings, and especially after Aethelred's victory over the Northumbrians at a huge battle fought on the banks of the River Trent in 679, this conception of an *Engle-lond* dominated by the Mercian royal dynasty gradually took hold of the imagination of the Mercian monarchs – especially the two long-ruling kings, Aethelbald and Offa, who between them ruled for eighty years continuously.

As Sir Winston Churchill pointed out, despite his redoubtable services rendered, Theodore was never canonised. However, Churchill was surely mistaken to call the 'remarkable Asiatic ... the earliest of the statesmen of England ... who guided her steps with fruitful wisdom'. There was, as yet, no 'England'. But that obscure monk from Jarrow, Bede, did become a saint, an accolade richly deserved for all his remarkable contributions to historical, theological and scientific knowledge – the 'Venerable' Bede indeed. Yet it behoves me to challenge Bede's history, exemplary though his achievements were. Bede's account is biased towards the Northumbrians, Rome, and the English as against British peoples. He was prejudiced against Mercia and its pagan king, Penda, in particular, and fiercely critical of Celtic Christianity, which he regarded as heresy. But most crucially, he inherited a historical perspective which saw historical events and processes as outworkings of divine favour.

Bede inherited this historiographical prejudice from the British monk Gildas, who in the sixth century had written his *On the Conquest and Ruin of Britain*. This strongly influenced Bede's own perspective, which legitimised the subordination of the Britons and 'Welsh' on the grounds that they had incurred divine disfavour due to their apostasy and sin. God had sent the Anglo-Saxon peoples as a punishment on the Britons for their manifold sins, and had finally dispossessed them in favour of the pagans – but He had also sent the saintly Augustine to deliver the English from diabolical forces. For Bede, God had acted in history to punish and impoverish the once mighty Britons and elevate the despised English race by His divine favour. It was nothing less than the will of God that 'the Welsh', as we must now call them, should be marginalised, oppressed and excluded, and the English peoples raised to ever greater heights of glory. But there was a caveat to this divine favour: if the English race became in its turn sinful, apostate, or morally decadent, then God would punish his chosen people and the English race would fall, just as the Britons had fallen before them.

King Oswy of Northumbria was now in a position to exert both his political and military pressure in addition to his 'spiritual' pressure. Peada, Penda's eldest son, had agreed to be baptised in 653 to facilitate his marriage to Aelflaeda, Oswy's daughter. Peada was the ruler of Middle-Anglia, the north-eastern territory of Mercia, but the *entente* between Middle-Anglia and Bernicia, the rump state in the north-east Oswy ruled, could not have supervened without Penda's tacit approval. It is hard to reconcile Bede's portrayal of Penda as an inveterate heathen with the fact that he allowed a Christian mission into Peada's territory consisting of four monks – the Anglians Adda, Betti and Cedd, plus the leader Diuma, who was either an Irishman, or a Gaelic-speaking Irishman from what is now Argyll.

Diuma had been consecrated as bishop by Finan of Iona, and it was envisaged that a see would be established for the Mercians based at Repton. This had profound implications, because the Mercian confederation had alliances with Brythonic tributary statelets such as Luitcoit and Pengwern, with a royal centre near Shrewsbury. These 'adjacent provinces', as Bede describes them, were not benighted pagans who stood in need of the Christian message; they were Celtic Christians who were now confronted not by an unsophisticated pagan 'frenemy' (in the modern argot) – but by a predatory Christian power whose 'foreign policy' had been hostile to them for generations.

One of the Brythonic princes who had contributed warbands to Penda's armies was Cynddylan, Prince of Pengwern. His technical overlord was Cadfael, King of Gwynedd, and it likely that his forces were among those that escaped the slaughter at *Winwaed*. I have postulated elsewhere that an attempt was made by Oswy to use his son-in-law Peada's local influence to annexe these former Mercian client kingdoms, and this resulted in the last Brythonic military expedition east of the Severn, in 656. This incursion was a large-scale cavalry raid in the finest Celtic tradition, much like Aneirin's *Y Gododdin*. In fact the raid resulted in a praise-poem, the *Canu Heledd*, supposedly composed by the grief-stricken sister of the band of brothers who set out on the final swansong of the Britons:

> Glorious was the battle,
> Great plunder captured
> Outside Caer Luitcoit,
> Taken by Morfael,
> Fifteen hundred head of cattle
> And five stewards, four-score fine horses
> Splendid shining armour,
> The bishops ran to the four corners
> Hugging their books, but it saved them not

It is a fact that *Caer Luitcoit*, modern-day Wall-by-Lichfield in South Staffordshire, is only 2 miles from Hammerwich where the Staffordshire Hoard was discovered. It seems to me only reasonable to consider the possibility that there may be a connection, especially given that this is precisely the time when the treasures were supposed to have been concealed. But the debacle seems to have signed Peada's death warrant. Even Bede concedes that Peada was an exemplary and sincere Christian, and regrets that he was assassinated over Easter by his wife, who arranged for him to be poisoned. Oswy now took personal control of the business with Pengwern. A raiding party was sent out which surprised Cynddylan and his family at their royal hall, *Llys Pengwern* outside Shrewsbury. The only family member not present was Heledd, Cynddylan's sister, who composed the heart-breaking *Canu Heledd*:

> The Hall of Cynddylan is dark tonight
> Without Fire, without light
> And O, what a silence surrounds it!
> There is no laughing throng here now
> And the panels are darkened
> Woe to the one who knows a sad end!
> The Grey-beaked eagle of Pengwern
> Cries most piercingly,
> Greedy for the flesh of my own heart's love!

This vicious attack culminated in the expulsion of the last free Britons in the lowlands, a vacuum which was filled almost immediately by a resurgent Mercia. A trio of Mercian nobles, Eadberht, Immin and Eafa, proclaimed Penda's son Wulfhere as the new King of Mercia. The Northumbrian governor and his retinue were killed or driven out while Oswy was preoccupied with a war in the far north. The Mercian border with the Welsh was fixed at a place called 'Wulfhere's Ford' on the upper Severn. Although the process was slow and extremely complex, the process of state formation which culminated in the nations of England and Wales had begun. Necessarily, the 'national story' promulgated by the Welsh had much more ancient roots than that in England, for they had yet to discard their ancient name for their country, *Britannia*, and in order to account for their national decline, and to ameliorate the gnawing grief at the loss of their ancient sovereignty, a myth of their having been undermined by treachery and of a future redemption under a godlike leader was gradually constructed. Professor R. R. Davies sums up the implications of this mythology for the Welsh national consciousness;

> Central to this mythology was an intense pride in the past or rather in a particular interpretation of it. Two aspects of the past were especially emphasised. One was the unbroken link between the Old North – the kingdoms of North Britain of the fifth and seventh centuries – and the contemporary political order of Wales ... it was a mythical, validating past and, thereby, a potent if gradually diluted part of the Welsh consciousness. The second point of reference in this native Welsh historical consciousness was a wistful memory of, and pride in, the Roman past of the country. This memory concentrated in particular on the legends which had encrusted around the figure of Magnus Maximus (d. 388), the Macsen

Wledig of Welsh lore. Several Welsh dynasties traced their descent whether directly in the male line or through marriage, to Macsen. He, thereby, served as a convenient bridge from native tradition to Roman glory and thence to Trojan origins; he also served both to embody and to explain the transition from the Roman political order to the political dispensation of native Wales.[21]

This mythology was resilient, and its ultimate implications went far beyond the borders of Wales. The national mythology of the Welsh eventually morphed into the romantic corpus which underpinned the Arthurian revival – a tapestry of chivalry, treachery, doomed love and magical outworkings which conquered the courts of all Europe – and nowhere more successfully than in England. As Professor Davies observes, this Welsh pride in a half-imagined past was balanced by 'a sense of loss and shame – the loss of the sovereignty of Britain, and shame at the oppressions which the Island of the Mighty had suffered at the hands of alien races. Such a sense of deprivation often led to despair, to a deep conviction of the Britons' sinfulness and a sense of shameful contrition in the face of ineluctable divine retribution.'

This 'divine retribution' seemed to be emphasised at the momentous Synod of Whitby in 664. King Oswy of Northumbria presided at the synod, which he called in order to iron out the inconsistencies regarding the style of tonsure to be worn by monks and more importantly the *computas* or method for calculating the date of Easter. Oswy, having been tutored by Celtic monks on Iona, had hitherto contented himself with Columba's traditions and the method for calculating Easter used by the Celtic *Quartodecimans*, but his marriage to the Kentish princess Eanflaed presented him with a new dilemma. Eanflaed and his son Alchfrith were both staunch Roman Catholics. Alchfrith had expelled Irish monks from monasteries he had endowed and Eanflaed made her point by continuing her fasting and celibacy even as her husband was celebrating the Easter feast.

The debate at the synod was the chance for a brilliant young theologian, Wilfred, to put forward the Roman case. He had spent many years studying on the Continent, and even in Rome, and contrasted the splendour and majesty of the apostolic see with what he perceived to be a peripheral sectarianism. Originally a Frankish-speaking bishop, Agilbert, was scheduled to argue the Roman case, but he objected that since he would have to speak through an interpreter he would be at a disadvantage (Oswy was a fluent Irish speaker). Wilfred was permitted to speak in his stead, a mere tyro, but his noble bearing, eloquence and good looks had charmed Queen Eanflaed – and he knew the Irish customs well from his days at Lindisfarne.

Colman, and the great 'mother' Abbess Hilda, faced a skilled opponent in Wilfred. As John Nankivell says in his *Saint Wilfred*, both Hilda and

---

21 Davies, R. R., *The Age of Conquest: Wales 1063–1415*, Oxford, 1987.

Colman had every reason to be confident: 'The Irish dating of Easter had the authority of the apostle and evangelist John, and it was ever the practice of St Columba and the holy fathers of Iona. Many of those present would have been moved by the power of his argument. Did they in Northumbria not owe their faith to Irish Aidan, whose gentle holiness was evident in all?' Wilfred acknowledged Columba's 'rustic simplicity and pious intentions' but this, he thought, was no excuse for continuing in erroneous and outdated practices. Addressing his main opponent in the debate, Bishop Colman, he declared, 'As for you and your companions, you certainly sin if, having heard the decrees of the Apostolic see and of the universal church you refuse to follow them.' It had not been Columba, but 'the most blessed prince of the apostles', St Peter, who had been chosen as the rock on which Christ's church was founded. This was an argument which swayed Oswy. Smiling, he turned to Colman, saying that since St Peter held the keys to heaven, he dare not offend him. The Celtic practices were condemned, and after a brief interlude Roman Catholic religion came to dominate in Northumbria. The defeat was a catastrophe for the Celtic party, but a triumph for Rome. Pope Vitalian wrote to Oswy exhorting him to subdue the whole island:

> We therefore desire your highness will hasten to dedicate all your island to Christ, establishing there the Catholic and Apostolic faith. Truly your highness seeks, and shall no doubt obtain, that all your islands shall be made subject to you, as is our wish and our desire.

This extraordinary betrayal legitimised Anglo-Saxon, and especially Northumbrian, lordship over the Celtic-speaking peoples, denouncing their ancient religion as heretical, even virtually pagan. The ancient folk beliefs in the fairy Otherworld were consciously equated with witchcraft and diabolism – a preposterous claim. Like the much later Cathars of southern France, the Celts were calumniated as agents of demonic powers whose stubborn, stiff-necked refusal to bow to the authority of Rome betrayed the presence of that deadliest of sins – pride. British and Irish monks were expelled from their *parochiae*, and British pilgrims were forbidden from visiting *martyria*.

These political machinations had profound consequences for the Celtic peoples. Their status was much diminished, and English raiding and depredations legitimised. But for all that, the author is happy to concede one point to the Catholic party, if only because it forms a central plank of my own argument – that Druidic practices had survived the coming of Christianity, and that they had morphed into the work of the Culdees. In his 1829 volume *The Celtic Druids*, Godfrey Higgins made a claim that the Druids incorporated pre-Christian philosophies predicated upon esoteric doctrines of Pythagorean and Essene origins, which, he thought, accounted for their seamless conversion to Christianity, for 'the Essenes were as nearly Christian as possible'.

There were certainly influences on the Celtic Church which were of extremely exotic origins. The splendid illuminations of the Book of Kells and the Lindisfarne Gospels display striking similarities with works of art from Syria and Egypt, and even Coptic Ethiopia. The mercantile intercourse between western Britain and Ireland and Egypt may be much more ancient than is generally supposed. Ancient Egyptian hieroglyphs speak of a race called the *Tam-Hou* or 'white men' who were devotees of the god Horus. An Egyptian princess named Aimee, known as 'Scota', was apparently betrothed to a Celtic warlord named Goidel Glas about 1500 BC. The Celts' military skills were deployed to suppress a rebellion against the dynasty of the Hyskos by the Ethiopians. Scota is cited in legend as the founder of the Scottish race. Her sons conquered Ireland, and the *Scotti* emigrated to northern Britain. This crypto-history is confused because there seem to have been two separate daughters of the pharaoh Nectanabus involved, but despite their garbled nature there does seem to be something in these accounts of ancient connections with Egypt. The Egyptian or Coptic 'wheel cross' has been found inscribed on ancient Scottish monuments and the so-called *Crux Ansata*, the Egyptian symbol of life, has been found depicted on stones in Ireland and Scotland.

The scope of this volume will not permit of a full account of the establishment of the English nation – a process which was, ironically, accelerated by the onset of the Viking invasions during the ninth century – but a brief overview will suffice. Of the original seven Anglo-Saxon kingdoms, only four remained viable by the time the *micel heathen here* or 'great heathen army' of the Vikings arrived in 865. For well over a century the dominant Anglo-Saxon nation had been Mercia. Offa, remembered to this day for the famous dyke between England and Wales named after him, had endeavoured to portray himself as an overlord of all England south of the Humber. He aspired to a marriage alliance between his son and Bertha, the mighty Charlemagne's notoriously spoiled daughter, and letters exchanged between the two discuss the regulation of English cloth exports to Francia and imports of 'black stones' from the Continent for revolutionary new mills Offa was building, including one excavated at Tamworth, the Mercian capital. This Mercian supremacy was not welcomed by the kings of what were now, in effect, client states – East Anglia, Kent, Sussex and Wessex, all of whom bitterly resented the Mercian hegemony.

The Mercian kings were feared rather than loved. Aethelbald, who preceded Offa, was murdered by his own bodyguards at Seckington near Tamworth as he slept. It is alleged that his fondness for seducing nuns had made powerful enemies among the male relatives of these ladies. Boniface, the English missionary to the Germans, had written to Aethelbald denouncing his sexual appetites and recommending Christian marriage. A brief civil war followed Aethelbald's death, the victor of which was Offa. He proved an equally controversial ruler, who notoriously ordered the execution of King

Aethelberht of East Anglia for the offence of minting his own silver pennies bearing his image. Aethelberht's murder outraged the common people everywhere, because regicide was regarded as a heinous sin. The East Anglian king was subsequently canonised. Alcuin of York, the foremost English scholar of the time, described Offa as 'a man of blood' and thought that the death of his precious son, Ecgfrith, within a few months of Offa's death (Ecgfrith left no heirs) was a judgement on Offa's cruelty, avarice and pride. Just before Offa died the great monastery at Lindisfarne had been raided by the Vikings. Alcuin foresaw the tribulations to come:

> An immense threat hangs over this island and its people. It is a novelty without precedent that pirate raids of a heathen people can regularly waste our shores. Yet the English people are divided, and king fights against king. Saddest of all, scarcely any heir of the ancient royal houses survives, and the origin of kings is as dubious as their courage. Study Gildas, the wisest of the British, and examine the reason why the ancestors of the British lost their kingdom and fatherland; then look at yourselves, and you will find among you almost identical causes.

Here the mythical history derived from Gildas, via Bede, is explicit. But Alcuin was not alone in sensing the gathering storm. In 793 the *Anglo-Saxon Chronicle* relates that

> dreadful forewarnings came over the land of the Northumbrians, terrifying the people most woefully … immense sheets of lightning rushing through the air, and whirlwinds, and fiery dragons flying across the firmament. These tremendous tokens were soon followed by a great famine; and not long after, on the sixth day before the ides of January in the same year, the harrowing inroads of heathen men made lamentable havoc in the church of God in Holy Island, by rapine and slaughter.

The terrified nuns had deliberately disfigured themselves by slashing open their lips and noses, hoping this would prevent their being dishonoured by rapine. Unfortunately, this did not prevent the Vikings from consigning them to death by immolation. The elder gods had returned – and in a terrifying form – for these 'heathen men' had no scruples about destroying Christian civilisation, indeed churches and monasteries were their main targets initially. Ireland and Wales also suffered heavy raids until 865, when Ivar and Halfdan, the sons of Ragnar Lothbrok, a notorious Viking chieftain, landed in East Anglia with an invading army numbered in the thousands. Their object was the military conquest of the Anglo-Saxon nations.

In recent years revisionist historians have sought to emphasise the positive aspects of the Viking settlements, and to downplay their fearsome reputation as raiders, incendiaries, and despoilers of churches and monasteries. Instead, we are asked to recognise their contribution as traders, explorers and farmers. These latter claims for their positive contribution to European and wider culture are quite true – but this perspective was certainly not shared by contemporary observers of the earliest raids. The onset of the Vikings was a terrible shock to Christian culture everywhere, from France to Ireland, and in Wales and the four remaining Anglo-Saxon nations, though it is true that the accounts that have come down to us were written almost exclusively by Christian monks, whose terror and resentment at these slavers, murderers and vandals was bound to prejudice their accounts. Gradually, and especially in northern and eastern England, the Danes (the Scandinavians in England were mostly Danish) did settle as farmers and merchants, and eventually adopted the Christian religion, but this was not how they were remembered by their stricken victims. The raid on the island of Lindisfarne in 793 was repeated on Iona in 825, and all the monks there were killed. Irish monasteries suffered a similar fate, with over thirty large-scale raids during the first half of the ninth century.

Criminals in every age always seek out 'soft' targets that promise a high yield of plunder or prospects for ransom, but there was perhaps another element to the raids – a deliberate attempt to destroy the Christian faith and its adherents, driven by a resurgence of Germanic Wodenism. Charlemagne had waged a war of extermination against the Continental Saxons, ordering mass executions of those who refused to convert to Christianity. The encroachment of an imperial Christian power on their borders may well have been the impetus for a resurgence of paganism in Denmark and Norway at just the time when the raiding commenced. Overpopulation, lack of viable farmland and vicious wars between rival clans also contributed to the overseas expeditions. So far as these tough northerners were concerned, the Christian faith was unmanly, slavish and alien.

The Vikings' ability to appear without warning in any coastal area, before opposing forces had time to concentrate and deploy, meant their superbly designed longships could beach quickly, plunder and take captives, and then escape without heavy loss with their loot. Their savagery and barbarism was legendary but they were not afraid to fight should this prove necessary. They were superb physical specimens, trained from infancy in the use of weapons and horsemanship. They could live off the land and erect invulnerable fortifications from which they could not be easily ejected. The British Isles had not faced such a deadly threat since the coming of the Anglo-Saxon peoples nearly 400 years before. Their valour in battle and disregard of personal danger, and their intrepid thirst for adventure took them from Russia to North Africa, and from Byzantium to North America.

In 845 they besieged Paris and demonstrated their legendary cruelty by hanging many hundreds of prisoners. This success emboldened them to attempt the invasion of England in 865, a Viking 'Blitzkrieg' which rapidly destroyed three ancient Anglo-Saxon realms – East Anglia, Northumbria and

Mercia. In November 869 the young King of East Anglia, Edmund, offered them battle at a place near Hoxne called *Haeglesdune*. Edmund's forces were heavily defeated, but he managed to flee. As Viking outriders scoured the countryside a young courting couple peered over a wooden bridge and saw the king's golden spurs reflected in the water. Edmund had concealed himself beneath the bridge, but the young couple betrayed him. He was taken to a tree and bound, as the Vikings used him for archery practice until his body bristled with arrows 'like the spines of a hedgehog'. Then he was cut down and his backbone hacked open, so that his lungs could be splayed out – the terrible rite of the 'Blood Eagle'. Finally the king's head was smitten from his body and thrown into a thorn bush as a final insult, and a warning of what would befall any who dared to oppose the heathen army. Aella, King of Northumbria, suffered the same fate, and Burgred, King of Mercia, fled to Rome for sanctuary, terrorised by these grim examples.

In the space of a few short years, two-thirds of England had fallen to the invaders. Only one last kingdom remained – Wessex. In autumn of 870 the 'Great Army' fortified themselves outside Reading, confident that yet another easy victory would soon follow. Alcuin's warning had been vindicated, and an effete, senescent people seemed doomed, but in this most desperate hour the West Saxons discovered their own 'King Arthur', a national saviour – 'England's darling' as he became known – called Alfred. He was an unlikely hero. Since childhood he had been afflicted with chronic disabilities which plagued him daily. He never expected to become king, and probably never desired power, but in this supreme crisis the man who had been anointed by the Pope in Rome as a four-year-old boy rose to the challenge against the most incredible odds, a true story of courage and determination stranger than any fiction.

In early January of 871 the Viking army set out along the ancient trackway known as the Ridgeway to confront and destroy the West Saxon forces under King Aethelred of Wessex and his younger brother Alfred at a place called Ashdown. The king refused to lead the army against the enemy until he had finished Mass, and so it fell to Alfred to take the initiative. He rallied the West Saxon warriors and led them in a furious assault up a steep hill against the Vikings. On the slopes dominated by the ancient chalk figure of a white horse, a grim struggle took place which went on all morning. Around a stunted thorn tree, a Danish king and five of his chieftains were killed before Aethelred arrived with his personal household troops to seal a great victory over the pagans, who left many thousands of their dead comrades behind them as they fled the field of slaughter.

But the Danes were nothing if not resilient. When Aethelred died in April, leaving only young boys as potential heirs, the crown passed by a unanimous vote of the West Saxon *Witan* to Alfred. After nine battles in one year, Alfred was exhausted and sued for peace, paying the 'Great Heathen Army' to depart his realm. No one, especially Alfred, expected this agreement to be honoured, but the Danes had learned a hard lesson. Guthrum, their king, was shrewd enough to realise that another summer campaign would prove so costly that it would be a better policy to decapitate Wessex by eliminating its new king. Guthrum undoubtedly employed spies, who reported that Alfred intended to spend the Christmas feast with his family and close retainers at Chippenham in Wiltshire. Guthrum was at Gloucester, and 'after Twelfth Night' he sallied out over the Cotswolds with a large force which surprised the West Saxon guards. In the nick of time, Alfred and his immediate family escaped to the Somerset marshes, into the wintry mists of Avalon.

At Easter 878, Alfred, with a tiny force of no more than 200 men, built 'something of a fort' on a tiny 'island' in the marshes called Athelney. The Danes, meanwhile, were ravaging the whole countryside of Wessex, desperately hunting for the troublesome king and his family. The miseries of the West Saxons were compounded by the fact that it was not at all clear if Alfred was still alive. But at Easter, after Mass, rumours spread that the king was not only very much alive, but that he had begun a guerrilla war against the Danes, and was visiting terrible revenge on any who collaborated with them. Viking war bands were ambushed and killed and their supplies taken. One legend tells that Alfred even joined one of their raiding parties disguised as a travelling musician. But the most enduring folk legend, and the one which has stuck in the popular imagination to this day, was that on one particularly miserable day he arrived with a few companions at the hovel of a cowherd. The herdsman's wife was commanded to prepare food for the disguised king as he warmed himself by the fire and attended to his bow and arrows. The lady of the house had told the king to watch that the bannocks cooking on a griddle over the fire did not burn, but Alfred foolishly forgot to turn them, only to be admonished in no uncertain terms by the 'wretched woman'; 'Hey fellow, can't you see the cakes are burning? Why didn't you turn them over? You'll be quick enough to swallow them when they're ready!' As William of Malmesbury recorded, 'The miserable woman little thought she was speaking to the famous King Alfred, who had fought so many battles against the pagans, and gained so many victories over them.' But the greatest victory of all was yet to come.

In May 878 Alfred sent out messengers to the leaders of the West Saxon resistance movement to gather the fighting men of Wiltshire, Hampshire and Dorset to assemble at an ancient monument known as 'Egbert's Stone'. When he arrived the mustered warriors were ecstatic, and immediately the men marched to confront the Danes at *Ethandun* or Edington on Salisbury Plain. The infuriated Englishmen smashed the Viking force. Asser, Alfred's Welsh biographer, recounts the events:

> Fighting ferociously in dense battle-order, and by the divine will (Alfred) made a great slaughter among them, and pursued them to their fortress. Everything left outside the fortress, men, horses and cattle, he seized, killing

the men, and encamped outside their gates. After fourteen days the pagans were brought to the extreme depths of despair, by hunger, cold and fear, and they sought peace.

The terms of the peace were explicit. The Danish king and thirty of his *jarls* were required to convert to Christianity. Alfred himself stood as godfather to Guthrum, who, adopting the baptismal name of Athelstan, was received from the font as if he were indeed a 'new man'. The chastened Danes, at least those who had survived, withdrew to Cirencester, and after a year moved on to East Anglia where they settled down as farmers.

It had been a miraculous comeback, and confirmed the West Saxon royal house as the repository of divine power. The pagan Anglo-Saxons had seen their kings as literally the descendants of the ancient gods such as Woden. But now the mythology of their Christian descendants identified their kings as executors of the universal divine will. Wessex was the last such Anglo-Saxon royal house to have survived, and although he was never to rule outside his own native kingdom, all free Englishmen looked to Alfred as a 'national' deliverer from the Danes. This was the foundation of a unified English nation which emerged under Alfred's capable son, Edward 'the Elder', and his daughter, Aethelflaed, who became the 'Lady of the Mercians'. Under this warrior queen's able leadership the Midlands was recovered from Danish domination. She also fostered the illegitimate son of her brother Edward, Athelstan, Alfred's mighty grandson, who became not only a 'King of England' in name, but the 'Emperor of Britain'.

Athelstan was not content with subduing the Danes, but invaded Scotland and Wales, forcing their kings to accept humiliating terms. This was a huge gamble, for it invited the prospect of a grand alliance of the Celtic nations and the Viking King of Dublin, Olaf Guthfrithson. In the autumn of 937, the forces of King Constantine of Scotland, the Prince of Strathclyde, and Olaf Guthfrithson combined at *Brunanburh*, probably modern-day Bromborough on the Wirral. Athelstan assembled a gigantic army of combined West Saxons and Mercians, and in a desperate two-day battle the invading armies were almost totally destroyed. In the space of two generations the *Cerdicings*, or West Saxon royal line, had extended their power from a tiny patch of bog land in Somerset to encompass the entire island – and indeed beyond. Athelstan's sisters married some of the most powerful kings on the Continent, and his fleets assisted the Bretons and even threatened Ireland and Scandinavia.

These remarkable exploits confirmed the English in their belief that they were agents of the divine plan. The *Anglo-Saxon Chronicle* saw these developments in historical terms: 'Never before in this island, as the books of ancient historians tell us, was an army put to greater slaughter by the sword, since the time when the Angles and Saxons landed, invading Britain from across the wide seas from the east, when warriors eager for fame, proud forgers of war, the Welsh overcame, and won for themselves a kingdom.'

This perspective seemed to confirm the myth promulgated by Bede – that the English race was divinely ordained to conquer the island of Britain, under kings ruling as Christ's ministers on Earth.

Athelstan died two years after 'the Great Battle' of *Brunanburh*, and within a few years of this Olaf of Dublin returned and the wars resumed. But the immense power, both economic and military, of the English state would enjoy a brief period of supremacy which birthed an abiding myth of a country ruled by kings who were God's anointed agents, and whose people were His chosen race. These divine blessings, however, were conditional, as Bede had implied, upon the righteousness of the people and the *fortuna* and virtue of its kings. Should the king prove to be apostate or weak, cowardly, lascivious or unjust, then the divine compact would be broken, and God's just punishment would be visited on the English.

In 959 England achieved the zenith of its powers. Its new king, Edgar, known as 'the peaceful', ruled unchallenged for sixteen precious years, but as had been prophesied, the seeds of national decline had already been sown. Edgar was, for all the acclamations which followed his death, something of a libertine. His womanising was deftly concealed by the high churchmen who were his ministers, such as St Dunstan, but rumours abounded that he had become so infatuated with Elfrida, allegedly the most beautiful woman in England, that he had arranged to have her husband, Aethelwold, murdered so that he could take her for his queen.

So besotted with Elfrida was Edgar that in May 973 he arranged a second coronation ceremony at Bath, where this paragon of beauty was crowned as the first Queen of England. The couple were desperate for a legitimate son and heir, but unfortunately their firstborn son, Edmund, died. Soon afterwards Elfrida became pregnant again, and produced a healthy boy, Ethelred. From this moment the tide of England's fortunes turned, and the 'golden years' of English supremacy faded. The unravelling of Anglo-Saxon England commenced soon afterwards. All this was presaged by the appearance in the heavens of a 'hairy star', or comet, shortly after Edgar's death. For the superstitious English the stars had been fixed in their stations by the divine will, so comets seemed to them to be an unnatural phenomenon, if not actually diabolical. The *Anglo-Saxon Chronicle* was explicit:

> Then too was seen, high in the heavens, the star on his station, that far and wide wise men call Cometa by name. Widely was spread God's vengeance then throughout the land, and famine scoured the hills.

Christianity was itself imbued with a world view which was deeply superstitious and predicated upon apocalyptic beliefs – and never more so than in these crucial years as the first millennium approached. It was widely expected that the Antichrist would be unleashed in AD 1000, as had been prophesied in the Book of Revelation, and that this would be followed immediately by the

Last Judgement. When this failed to materialise, some theologians postulated that these events would supervene a thousand years after the crucifixion of Christ, in 1033.

Edgar's eldest son by his first marriage, Edward, succeeded to the throne; Ethelred was only a minor of seven years. Edward himself was a mere youth of sixteen. He was tempestuous and arrogant, as teenagers are wont to be, but he was surrounded by wise statesmen and loyal ealdormen such as St Dunstan and Byrhtnoth, a warrior of the 'old school'. Elfrida, the queen-dowager, plotted against him from the beginning of his reign, with the intention of replacing him with her own precious son, but Edward's inner circle were loyal. Unfortunately, Edward chanced to go out hunting one day near Corfe in Dorset, quite close to one of Elfrida's residences. He decided to arrive with his small retinue and sent messengers ahead to alert the household. When he arrived, Elfrida awaited him at the gateway with a goblet of mulled wine, a traditional greeting for a royal guest. As Edward stooped down in the saddle to accept the goblet, Elfrida's household ostlers grabbed hold of his bridle and repeatedly stabbed him in the stomach. The young Ethelred was on the premises and allegedly became so hysterical that Elfrida had to thrash him to keep him quiet. Edward died of his wounds shortly afterwards, and his body was buried in a shallow grave 'without royal honours'. This brutal regicide, the most grievous sin imaginable to the common folk, simply stunned the nation, but Elfrida kept her composure. The *Anglo-Saxon Chronicle* recorded the national shock:

> No worse deed than this was ever done by the English nation since they first sought the land of Britain. Men murdered him, but God hath magnified him. He was in life an earthly king – he is now after death a heavenly saint.

The evil deed done, Elfrida faced down her accusers, protesting her innocence, but whether justified or not her reputation was damaged beyond repair – as was that of her son Ethelred, who was probably innocent. She retired to a convent at Wherwell in Hampshire, and endowed many monasteries and nunneries, almost invariably a device for salving a guilty conscience following a royal murder. In the popular mind she became demonised, and many muttered that she was a witch. This sinister reputation attached itself, deservedly or not, to her young son. It was known that the boy had sullied the font at baptism, a notorious ill omen. Of course, the lad was much too young to rule in his own right, and relied on trusted ministers to govern on his behalf until he came of age.

Ethelred 'the Unready', as he became known, ruled with a brief interlude for thirty-eight dramatic years. 'Unready' was a popular pun on his name; *Aethel-raed* means 'noble counsel', but the people called him *Un-raed*, meaning 'no counsel' or 'bad counsel'. In truth, he was more 'unlucky' than 'unready'. He lacked confidence and authority, was lazy and self-indulgent, and an inveterate coward. This latter failing was a mortal sin for an Anglo-Saxon king, especially in the context of a renewed threat from the Vikings, who soon arrived in vast fleets to extract the Danegeld, a tax Ethelred increasingly levied on his subjects to buy off the raiders. This is, of course, a somewhat cursory analysis of the king's personality – but the course of his reign was marked by such terrible misfortune that the only thing to remark about it was that despite almost four decades of national humiliation the English people remained loyal to him throughout, except for a brief four-month exile in 1014. The meltdown of the Anglo-Saxon state had commenced.

In 991, Ethelred's loyal veteran commander Byrhtnoth confronted a larger Viking army at the Battle of Maldon. The old warrior was killed, and despite the heroic poem composed to commemorate his sacrifice the martial spirit of the English had degenerated, mainly due to Ethelred's vacillation, cowardice and intransigence. The Danegeld increased exponentially, and as the common people were squeezed for the tax, hatred towards the Danes who had been settled in England grew. On 13 November 1002, St Brice's Day, Ethelred sent out sealed orders for a pogrom against these innocent Danes, many of whom were law-abiding and loyal citizens. Thousands died, among them the sister of King Sweyn 'Forkbeard' of Denmark, Gunhilde. Sweyn swore on the 'bragging cup' to avenge her death and conquer England.

Once again, it fell to one of Ethelred's local commanders, Ulfkytel of East Anglia, to oppose the Viking marauders, but despite a valiant resistance he was compelled to withdraw. Ulfkytel's bravery only served to emphasise Ethelred's weakness. Eventually Ethelred responded, ordering a huge fleet to be built, and 24,000 coats of mail for a well-equipped new army. A dispute between English admirals led to a tragic farce in which eighty state-of-the-art warships were wrecked in a storm. The Vikings took the Archbishop of Canterbury, Alphege, prisoner and demanded a £3,000 ransom. When Alphege refused to co-operate in the plan he was cruelly murdered and English hearts sank.

Shortly afterwards the new Archbishop of Canterbury, Wulfstan, wrote a sermon which was distributed to be read out in churches throughout the nation. Called *Sermo Lupi ad Anglos*, 'the Sermon of the Wolf to the English', a pun on his own name, it was an excoriating critique of the state of the English nation, and a barely concealed indictment of Ethelred and his ministers. Taking his lead from Bede and Alcuin of York, Wulfstan ascribed the plight of the nation to the collapse in the moral order in the country. He was particularly concerned at the decline in effective jurisdiction since Edgar's day. People were sold into slavery and prostitution to the Danes, and many ancient churches and monasteries lay in ruins. Most pernicious of all was the revival of paganism and witchcraft, but sexual immorality and vices such as drunkenness were condemned as well, being rife at the time. All these sins fed the growing power of the Antichrist. Just as the Anglo-Saxons had displaced the Britons because of their sins, now the Vikings came to visit God's just revenge on the English for their manifold iniquities.

Seeing his opportunity, Sweyn invaded southern England from his base in the Danelaw–northern England. He had given orders that everything in the path of his army should be destroyed, and Ethelred's authority seeped away rapidly. On Christmas Day 1013, the English nobles offered the crown to Sweyn, and Ethelred was forced to flee into exile in Normandy, the homeland of his second wife, Emma. By a miracle, Sweyn died at the beginning of February 1014, just before he was to be crowned. His young son, Cnut, was still in the north of England with the Viking fleet, but the English nobles had a change of heart. They wrote to Ethelred, expressing their desire to restore him to the throne with the proviso that he should 'govern them more justly than he had before'. In spring 1014 Ethelred returned to a rapturous reception in London, one of the most remarkable political turnarounds in history. For once he acted with resolve and raised a huge army. Marching north, he devastated those areas which had collaborated with the Danes, and Cnut's fleet put to sea.

But this short-lived triumph was illusory. One of Ethelred's ministers, Edric Streona, lured nobles from the Danelaw to a conference in Oxford under false pretences and had them murdered. Not long afterwards an undersea earthquake in the Atlantic caused a huge tidal wave to inundate the Severn estuary and many thousands died. Ethelred's son, Edmund 'Ironside', began a rebellion against his ailing father, and on St George's Day 1016 the king did the best thing he had ever done for his countrymen – he died. A terrible war between the new king, Edmund, and Cnut immediately commenced. The dashing young man won several important victories, but at the Battle of Ashingdon on 18 October 1016 Cnut defeated Edmund, whose forces suffered heavy losses. A partition was arranged at Deerhurst in Gloucestershire, and Edmund was allowed to retain Wessex, with the rest of the country going to Cnut. On 30 November 1016, Edmund was assassinated while he was on the lavatory, and by the terms of the Treaty of Deerhurst Cnut became king of all England. The facts were inescapable; England had fallen to a foreign conqueror.

The price was very high. Cnut demanded £72,000 in silver and £10,500 in silver for the departure of his fleet. Edmund's baby sons were exiled, and an elite force of Viking warriors were retained as Cnut's personal bodyguard. The omens were dark, but in one of those strange ironies of history, the half-Danish, half-Polish king proved himself an exemplary Christian ruler. The famous story of his being carried to the seashore, where he commanded the tide to turn, was recorded by Henry of Huntingdon in the twelfth century. Very often misunderstood, this tale was intended to exemplify the king's 'great and magnificent actions'. He restored the laws of Edgar, and was guided by the learned and upright Wulfstan – the archbishop who had been so critical of Ethelred's regime.

Cnut's influence was international, and he ruled an empire which extended from Norway and Denmark to England. He even took a largely English army to Sweden and attempted to conquer that country. By his death in 1035, England had been restored to a prosperity and security it had not enjoyed since Edgar's day. But his two sons, Harald 'Harefoot' and Harthacnut, who succeeded him in turn, were violent, greedy and cruel oppressors. Harthacnut drank himself to death at a wedding feast in 1042, leaving no heir. To the delight of the English people, Ethelred's son, Edward, was recalled from a long exile in Normandy, his mother's homeland, to be crowned king at Winchester on 3 April 1043. The last of the *Cerdicings* had been restored, and there were high hopes for this pious and learned monarch.

The story of the last years of Anglo-Saxon civilisation can be briefly told. Edward had spent so long in exile in Normandy that he had become, to all intents and purposes, Norman. His knowledge of England and its politics was limited and he relied on the main political player, Earl Godwin, for crucial political and military support. Godwin was a parvenu who harboured high ambitions for his family. He arranged to marry Edith, his daughter, to Edward, intending that he should be the grandsire of kings, but Edward did not prove compliant in the plan. Although he agreed to the marriage, he refused to sleep with his wife on grounds of chastity. In truth Edward despised Godwin, and feared his five sons, especially the tempestuous Sweyn, the eldest. As a counterweight to Godwin's power, Edward increasingly imported Norman friends and allies, who formed a coterie around the king. Sweyn died on a pilgrimage to the Holy Land, but the next eldest son, Harold Godwinson, was equally ambitious and much more astute politically than his brother had been.

In September 1051 an incident brought matters to a head. A party of French knights entered Dover and demanded billets. When they were refused, an innkeeper was killed and this provoked a furious riot in which nineteen Frenchmen were slain. Count Eustace of Boulogne, Edward's brother-in-law, immediately demanded that Edward punish Dover for this aggression, and Edward ordered Godwin to expedite this retribution. Godwin, who portrayed himself as a patriot, refused to do so, and this gave the king the excuse he needed to repudiate his marriage to Edith and banish the entire Godwin clan. Godwin fled to Flanders, Harold to Ireland. But just one year later, Godwin and Harold would combine their fleets and sail up the Thames.

The national mood had changed, and the chief nobles of the realm forced Edward into a humiliating climbdown. It must have seemed that Edward was doomed to become a powerless puppet of the man he hated, and he was forced to reinstate Edith in the royal apartments. Perhaps out of sheer spite, Edward refused to produce an heir, and it became clear that Godwin intended to have his son, Harold, installed as his successor. The latter was extremely popular, handsome and brave, with a keen intelligence to boot. Godwin died in April 1053, and to thwart Harold's ambitions Edward recalled Edward 'the Exile', the son of Edmund Ironside, to England with the intention that he, a *Cerdicing* should inherit the throne. Unfortunately, 'the Exile' died shortly after his return to his homeland. Edward seems to have accepted that Harold's position was a strong one at this point, and gave him more and more responsibility. But in Normandy, Duke William also had an eye on the succession. Harald Hardrada, the gigantic King of Norway, also pressed his own dubious claim.

In 1064, Harold was shipwrecked off the coast of France, and was delivered up to the 'protection' of Duke William of Normandy who, allegedly, exacted a sacred oath from Harold that he would support his claim to the English throne. When Harold's brother Tostig was driven from his earldom of Northumbria, the country was brought to the brink of civil war. The ageing King Edward 'the Confessor', worn out by cares, took to his deathbed in December 1065. He claimed that he had seen a vision of two monks who told him that England would fall 'to the agents of the devil' within the year. England would only be restored to liberty when 'a green tree stricken in twain by lightning, shall be restored as one, and put forth fresh leaves'. When he finally died, on 5 January 1066, Harold immediately seized the throne, with the unanimous support of the English nobles. The rival claimants in Norway and Normandy began their military preparations with celerity, and as the anxious English nation awaited the onslaught, in April 1066 a bright comet, a 'hairy star', appeared in the heavens for more than a week. The rest, as they say, is history.

11

Arthur Reborn

The Celtic traditions considered that kings were sired by the light-god *Lugh*, who inhabited the physical form of their fathers at the moment of conception. Thus, they were 'placed' into space and time by the operations of divine destiny. Arthur, as the ultimate such incarnation, was not dead, but merely sleeping. While England had become established as one nation, survived the Viking threat, risen to hegemony, and then declined and fell, Arthur's quiet slumber in the west had continued. Wales too had united, and Arthur had become more than a figure of legend to the Welsh; he was a crucial historical personage, whose real existence no true Welshman doubted.

The monk from Bangor, Nennius, visited the border realm of *Ercing*, or Archenfield, where he was shown the grave of Arthur's son, Anir. Arthur had killed his own son and built a burial mound, 'and when men come to measure the length of the mound, they find that it is sometimes six feet, sometimes nine, sometimes fifteen. Whatever length you find it at one time, you will find it different at another, and I myself have proved this to be true.' Now, it is easy to dismiss this as Welsh whimsy, but the author heard a similar tale about the Rollright Stones in Oxfordshire. In this variant there are never the same number of stones when counted again, and 'I myself have proved this to be true'. Charles Williams, the poet and member of the important philosophical group in twentieth-century Oxford known as 'the Inklings', was not alone in thinking the tale of this miracle to be 'mind-shattering'.

This is a magical history, and so nothing happens by accident. Charles Williams, who will return in a later chapter, was immersed in Celtic and Arthurian myth, which he used as the backdrop for his 'sub-creation' *Logres*, a magical realm resembling Britain and borrowing from earlier conceptions of John Milton and William Blake. This idealised country is part of a larger 'empire' which forms a gigantic humanoid body, the 'head' of which is *Logres*. A Celtic bard, Taliessin, loosely based on the historical Welsh bard Taliesin, is on a mission to unlock the mystery which will reveal the Holy Grail and restore the Island of the Mighty to its true glory, a mystical kingdom of heaven on earth.

Williams himself is often described, wrongly, as a magician. He practised a form of healing based on the theoretical philosophical process he called 'co-inherence, substitution and exchange'. He felt that the pain and disease of another person could be transferred onto oneself, relieving them but inviting the suffering onto the host. He joined the Christian mystical fraternity known as the 'Fellowship of the Rosy Cross', founded by A. E. Waite. Waite had been one of the founding members of the Hermetical Order of the Golden Dawn, but had gradually become unhappy about the ethical implications. His discomfiture arose from the same basic objections we encountered in chapter 1; that magic, being concerned principally with controlling nature for 'practical' results, was a grave temptation to all that is base in the human spirit. Mysticism, by contrast, had much to commend it, and could be reconciled with membership of the Christian Church – indeed, may even, in this wickedest of epochs, prove the spiritual weapon which would establish the kingdom of heaven on earth. So, these ancient myths, constantly reinvented over the centuries and millennia, have been a touchstone for a certain class of obscure intellectuals, 'Guardians of Albion', whose task is not exclusively confined to 'historical' interpretation. History, to be sure, is one aspect, but they are not just concerned with the past – these reinterpretations and refinements are also deeply spiritual, mystical, and magical, and refer to future events also.

Much has been written elsewhere about the events of 1066 in England. In the traditions of the island race, Harold 'looked to his moat' as the mainstay of England's defence. The *fyrd*, or part-time militia, were mobilised during the crucial summer months, and a force of up to 20,000 men patrolled the south coast. The English fleet was at sea in rough weather. The summer of 1066 was unusually stormy. Winds from the north kept Duke William, 'the Bastard' as he was known, pinned down in his harbours in Normandy, but the same wind assisted Harald Hardrada of Norway, who sailed for the Orkneys. As harvest time approached, King Harold Godwinson, the last Anglo-Saxon king, had no choice but to order the militia to stand down so that they could go to their homes to get the harvest in.

The autumn equinox came, and the English people breathed a collective sigh of relief. The equinoctial storms which had wrecked Caesar's fleet in his day still blew strong, and William's army had the additional problem of transporting 4,000 warhorses, huge beasts trained to kick and bite their opponents, on a perilous Channel crossing. During winter, Harold would have precious time to organise, hire Danish mercenaries, and establish his new regime. Any delay to the Norman project would sap morale and energy, and dissipate crucial political support for the crusade – for such it was – against England. However, in mid-September a spell of good weather shook this sudden complacency. Hardrada, the Norwegian king, in alliance with Tostig, Harold's embittered and vengeful brother, landed at Riccall in Yorkshire, 9 miles south of York. The giant Viking king was a legend throughout Europe, and his piracy and ruthlessness made him a vast fortune in gold. As a mercenary in Byzantium he had been paid with a block of gold weighing as much as a man, and he took this with him everywhere.

King Harold was in the south, too far away to immediately assist. Edwin and Morcar, the earls of Mercia and Northumbria, led an English force to Gate Fulford just outside York to try to defend a narrow causeway between two marshy areas. The 10,000-strong Norwegian force smashed through the English and trampled their bodies into the fen, using their corpses as stepping stones. York immediately offered to capitulate and to send hostages and food, so the Norwegians retired to their encampment at Riccall to celebrate the victory. Hardrada and Tostig had arranged to meet the delegation from York at a place called Stamford Bridge to collect the supplies and take charge of the hostages. They took with them about half of their army, and since 25 September was a hot day, none of the men had bothered to wear their mail shirts. As the men basked in the glorious sunshine, a distant dust cloud, and the sunlight reflecting off thousands of helmets and spearheads, revealed the presence of the English army. Harold had marched an army 10,000 strong from Sussex to Tadcaster in five days – an astonishing achievement.

The Vikings defended themselves manfully, and when their comrades from Riccall ran almost 20 miles to save them a terrible carnage ensued. But the English had not come so far to be denied, and the Viking force was annihilated. A cairn of human bones, Viking bones, was still visible at Stamford Bridge a century after the battle. Hardrada and Tostig were both killed, and Harold captured their vast treasures, including Hardrada's huge block of gold. All this was taken into custody in York, where the king and his warriors held a great victory feast. No gold was actually distributed at the victory feast, and many of the Danish mercenaries, professional axemen who wielded the 'Danish Great-Axe', a razor-sharp, foot-long blade on a 5-foot helve which could easily decapitate a horse, were resentful. As the men feasted and cavorted, a grim-faced messenger arrived from London. William's Norman force had landed at Pevensey Bay in Sussex, right in the middle of Harold's own personal estates. The king lost no time in riding hard for London. Whatever else history may say of him, he was no coward.

The Battle of Hastings on 14 October 1066 is so well known that the briefest account will suffice for the purposes of this volume. Harold attempted the rapid march and surprise attack he had used with such success at Stamford Bridge. But William's pickets were alerted to English infiltrators during the night, and the duke quickly donned his armour, so quickly in fact that he put his mail coat on back to front, an ill omen he laughed off. While it was still dark, the Normans and their French, Breton and Flemish allies took up their position before a 1,000-yard-long ridge which extended between boggy ground on the flanks. Harold stood with his banners in the centre of the ridge with an army of about 12,000. William's army was of comparable size.

The first attack went in around 9.00 a.m. The English and their Danish allies stood firm and inflicted grievous casualties, particularly on the Breton contingent, who fled. Unfortunately, Harold's ill-trained soldiers disobeyed his strict orders not to break ranks, and ran after the Bretons. William, seeing his opportunity, wheeled his cavalry round and annihilated the English right flank on a small hillock where they had gathered to defend themselves. Although the battle went on all day and into the dusk, this indiscipline sealed Harold's fate. Further relentless attacks wore down the English centre, until four knights broke through to Harold, who had been hit in the eye with an arrow. He was hacked into pieces, and the news spread all through the English ranks. Harold's personal bodyguard stood firm, allowing the rest of the army to dash into the woods behind their position. A force of Norman cavalry pursued them, but fell into a concealed ditch, where the delighted English returned to slit their throats.

As night fell, Harold's lover, Edith 'Swan-neck', came to plead for what was left of his body. She could only recognise him by 'certain secret marks, only known to her'. A myth grew up that Harold had not really died at the battle, but had escaped, the age-old story told by every defeated people. He was said to have been treated in Winchester for two years by a 'Saracen woman skilled in surgical arts'. Like Woden, the one-eyed Harold wandered through Europe canvassing support for an invasion of his lost realm, but finally accepted his fate as a punishment for his broken oath to William. He made his way to St John's Church at Chester, where he lived into the twelfth century. He was supposedly visited there by William's son Henry I. These tales were a compensation myth of an occupied people, unable to come to terms with the much harsher reality. Although English resistance went on for some years, it was desultory and was never likely to dislodge the Normans, who stamped their authority with an efficiency and ruthlessness which reduced the English to a slave race, second-class citizens in their own nation.

It took the Normans, or 'French' as the English preferred to call them, 300 years to bother to learn the native language, and they lived as a privileged elite, apart from the despised English, even building separate 'French towns' and worshipping in separate churches. Rebellions were brutally suppressed, and in Yorkshire and Durham William's harrying during one of the harshest winters for centuries left over 100,000 dead. Gradually even the most tenacious guerrilla fighters like Hereward 'the Exile' and Edric 'the Wild' capitulated. William employed the services of a witch to defeat Hereward, but Edric's fate was more mythical. He fell in love with a fairy woman who bore him a half-human half-fairy son. When Edric broke his oath to her, Lady Godda, his bride, dematerialised. He searched desperately for her, even in the fairy underworld beneath the Stiperstones in the Shropshire Hills. In legend, the pair ride out at the head of the 'Wild Hunt', with Edric taking Woden's place at its head, blowing his horn and leading a pack of red-eared hellhounds. This sight has been regularly reported whenever England goes

Above: Stonehenge: 'A magnificent precinct or temple of Apollo, in round form ... where the people bring many consecrated gifts ...' (Photograph by Al King)

Below: Avebury: 'And there is also a city, sacred to the same god (Apollo), where the people process and offerings are made, and harpists sing the praises of the deity ...' (Photograph by Nigel Parker)

Knowth Passage Tomb, County Meath, Ireland. At 6,000 years old it is the oldest megalithic monument in Europe. (Photograph by Nigel Parker)

'Entopic' designs on gigantic slabs at Knowth, where an elite communed with the ancestors in a 'spirit-house'. (Photograph by Nigel Parker)

Newgrange Passage Tomb as seen from nearby Knowth. The extraordinary astronomical and geodesic knowledge displayed in its construction is truly astonishing. (Photograph by Nigel Parker)

The Rollright Stones on the Warwickshire/Oxfordshire border. Many legends attached themselves to these monuments. In 1945 there was an alleged 'ritual murder' quite nearby. (Photograph by Iain Simpson)

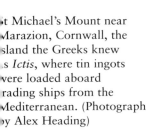

St Michael's Mount near Marazion, Cornwall, the island the Greeks knew as *Ictis*, where tin ingots were loaded aboard trading ships from the Mediterranean. (Photograph by Alex Heading)

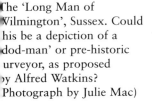

The 'Long Man of Wilmington', Sussex. Could this be a depiction of a 'dod-man' or pre-historic surveyor, as proposed by Alfred Watkins? (Photograph by Julie Mac)

Above: Glastonbury Tor. Without doubt, the most magical site in Britain. Its elemental power has inspired the magical consciousness of Britons for thousands of years. (Photograph by Nige Parker)

Below: St Patrick. Croagh Patrick, Ireland's Holy Mountain, is in the background. As a young man Patrick was a slave nearby. (Photograph by Nigel Parker)

Above: Boudicca statue on the embankment, London. As the personification of 'Andrasta', the goddess of victory, she visited a savage revenge on the Roman invaders. (Photograph by Carole Raddato)

Below: Saxon Shore Fort at Portchester, Hants. Originally explained as a defence against the 'Saxons', actually the forts are a legacy from the first 'Brexit'. (Photograph by Nigel Brown)

Above: Abbots Bromley Horn Dance, Staffs. Each September this ancient ceremony is faithfull re-enacted. Could it be a legacy of devotions to the 'horned god'? (Photograph by David)

Below: Mitchell's Fold stone-circle, Shropshire. This remote spot on the Welsh border is suppose to be the place where Arthur drew the 'sword from the stone'. (Photograph by Nigel Parker)

Glastonbury Abbey ruins. Ruthlessly destroyed during the Dissolution of the Monasteries, it is nevertheless the most sacred sanctuary in Britain, allegedly founded by Christ. (Photograph by David Merrett)

Above left: Arthur's grave in the grounds of the abbey ruins at Glastonbury. 'Here lies the famous King Arthur in the Isle of Avalon …' (Photograph by Michael Gaylard)

Above right: The Chalice Well, Glastonbury. The waters run red, like Christ's blood, and have never been known to run dry. The source is a mysterious underground reservoir beneath the Tor. (Photograph by Avariel Falcon)

Hagley Hall, Worcs. The body of 'Bella in the Wych-Elm' was found nearby in 1943. (Photograph by Tony Hisgett)

Wychbury Hill near Stourbridge. Each tree in the yew grove there represents a fallen warrior of the 'tribe of witches'. (Photograph by author)

ONENNAU MEIGION – SIX ASHES

Mae'n debyg i'r cytundeb gael ei lunio yn Chwefror 1405 rhwng Owain Glyndŵr, Tywysog Cymru, ei fab yng nghyfraith Edmund Mortimer a Henry Percy, Iarll Northumberland. Bwriad y cytundeb oedd disodli Harri IV fel brenin a gosod aelod o deulu Mortimer ar yr orsedd. Credai llawer fod gan y Mortimeriaid well hawl i orsedd Lloegr na Harri IV.

Yr oedd y cynghrair â Ffrainc yn golygu bod Owain Glyndŵr mewn sefyllfa gref ac felly dynodai'r cytundeb ffiniau i Gymru a ymestynnai y tu hwnt i Glawdd Offa hyd at afon Hafren

Seiliwyd y ffiniau ar broffwydoliaeth a soniai am rannu Prydain yn dair rhan, syniad a geir yng ngwaith Sieffre o Fynwy. Soniai proffwydoliaeth a briodolwyd i Fyrddin am Onennau Meigion fel y man lle byddai'r Eryr Mawr yn cynnull byddin y Cymry. Hwn, mae'n debyg, oedd lleoliad buddugoliaeth gan y Cymry dros y Saeson, dan arweiniad Cadwallon. Y proffwydoliaethau sy'n egluro'r defnydd o 'Cambria' a 'Loegria' yn y cytundeb ac nid 'Cymru' a 'Lloegr'.

Yr oedd gan Owain Glyndŵr weledigaeth glir ar gyfer dyfodol Cymru, gweledigaeth a seiliwyd ar chwedlau a mytholeg ei genedl

CYTUNDEB TRIDARN
TRIPARTITE INDENTURE

 Glyndŵr   Percy   Mortimer

Owain and his heirs shall have the whole of Cambria or Wales, within the borders, limits, and boundaries underwritten, divided from Loegria, which is commonly called England; namely, from the Severn coast where the River Severn leads from the sea, going down to the North Gate of the city of Worcester; and from that gate directly to the ash trees commonly called Onennau Meigion in the Cambrian or Welsh language, which grow on the high road from Bridgenorth to Kinver, thence directly by the high road, which commonly is called the old or ancient way, as far as the head or source of the River Trent; thence directly to the head or source of the river commonly called the Mersey; and thence, as that river leads to the sea, going down within the borders, limits, and bounds written above.

And the aforesaid Earl of Northumberland shall have to himself and to his heirs the counties written below; namely Northumberland, Westmorland, Lancashire, Yorkshire, Lincolnshire, Nottinghamshire, Derbyshire, Staffordshire, Leicestershire, Northamptonshire, Warwickshire, and Norfolk.

And the lord Edmund shall have the whole of the remainder of England entirely to himself and his successor.

(Lladin oedd iaith y ddogfen)
(The document was written in Latin)

Cymdeithas Owain Glyndŵr
www.owain-glyndwr.cymru

The Owain Glyndwr Society
www.owain-glyndwr.wales

It appears that the Tripartite Indenture was agreed in February 1405 between Owain Glyndŵr, Prince of Wales, his son-in-law Edmund Mortimer, and Henry Percy, Earl of Northumberland. Their aim was to replace Henry IV as king of England with a member of the Mortimer family. Many people felt that the Mortimers had a stronger claim to the throne than Henry.

The alliance with France meant that Glyndŵr's bargaining position was strong and the indenture accordingly extended the Welsh border well beyond Offa's Dyke to the river Severn.

The Welsh boundary was defined in the indenture in accordance with prophetic tradition and the tripartite division of Britain echoed the works of Geoffrey of Monmouth. A prophecy attributed to Merlin had stated that the ash trees of Meigion would be the place where the Great Eagle would muster the warriors of Wales. It was also the supposed location of a Welsh victory under Cadwallon against the Saxons.

Glyndŵr had a specific vision for the future of his nation but he was also rooted in its mythology and prophecies. The past, present and future was intertwined.

Above: Monument at Onennau Meigion or Six Ashes on the Staffordshire/Shropshire border. From such small projects, perhaps we can restore a collective spiritual meaning? (Image courtesy of the Owain Glyndwr Society)

Right: Skellig Michael, off the coast of Co. Kerry, Ireland. From remote outposts such as this, the light of Christianity blazed again. (Photograph by Arian Zwegers)

...ona, Inner Hebrides. Another ...nsular beacon of Celtic ...hristianity, it was originally ... Druidic sanctuary – 'the isle ...f Yew trees'. (Photograph by ...im Regan)

Above: Lindisfarne. Yet another bastion of Celtic Christianity. It became a spiritual and artistic powerhouse, until it was pillaged by the heathen Vikings. (Photograph by Chris Combe)

Below: Whitby Abbey. Here Celtic Christianity was decisively defeated at a famous synod presided over by King Oswy. (Photograph by John Campbell)

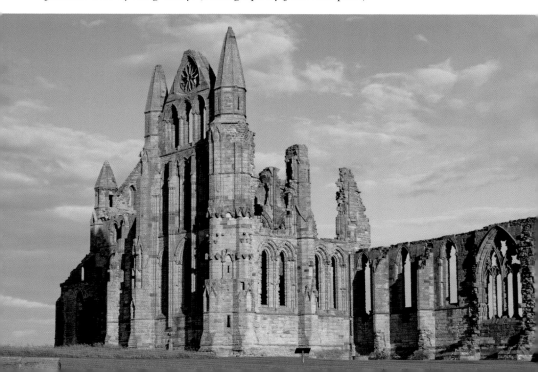

The Stiperstones, Shropshire. When the last Anglo-Saxon resistance ceased, Edric 'the Wild' disappeared into the lead mines beneath. When war threatens England, he rides out with his fairy bride in the 'Wild Hunt'. (Photograph by Jonathan Stonehouse)

The University of Oxford. This esteemed institution began in late Anglo-Saxon times. Within a century of Hastings, Geoffrey of Monmouth was teaching here. (Photograph by Alison Day)

Arley Redstone Worcestershire. Here the lay preacher and poet Layamon first translated the ancient history of Britain into English, (Photograph by author)

Ludlow Castle, Shropshire. Henry Tudor's first-born son, deliberately named Prince Arthur, died here shortly after his marriage to Catherine of Aragon. (Photograph by author)

Left: Worcester Cathedral. Prince Arthur's body was rowed down the Severn here, where he was laid to rest in a lavish tomb. (Photograph by author)

Below: Fountains Abbey, North Yorkshire. The gigantic ruins stand as a testament to a more spiritual age, as haunting and desolate as Stonehenge. (Photograph by Rob Ellis)

Right: Despite his extraordinary achievements, little now remains to mark the life of John Dee, greatest magician of his age. (Photograph by Matt Brown)

Below: Carisbrooke Castle, where Charles I was 'close confined' before his eventual execution. (Photograph by Dave Mills)

Bottom: Dudley Castle. The area around the castle was gradually denuded of woodland; innovations by 'Dud Dudley' anticipated the 'Industrial Revolution' by almost a century. (Photograph by Matt Johnson)

William Blake's tombstone. During his lifetime Blake was obscure and little understood, but his 'mental fight' against 'the Beast' was a battle for the soul of 'Albion'. (Photograph by Matt Brown)

Osborne House, Isle of Wight. Queen Victoria withdrew to this isolated residence following the death of her beloved husband Albert. The poet Tennyson consoled her. (Photograph by Barry Skeates)

Aleister Crowley's infamous 'Abbey of Thelema', Cefalu, Sicily. The death of Raoul Loveday here in 1923 led to scandal in the British press. (Photograph by Nigel Parker)

Another view of the 'Abbey'. Crowley's pornographic murals were whitewashed, but are now partially visible again. The fascist authorities expelled Crowley and his group. (Photograph by Nigel Parker)

The 'Eagle & Child' public house, Oxford. In a scullery called the 'Rabbit Room', the 'Inklings' met to discuss their writings and reimagine the world. (Photograph by Jim Linwood)

Perrott's Folly, Edgbaston, Birmingham. Tolkien was inspired by such landmarks, on which the 'Two Towers of Gondor' were based. (Photograph by Tony Hisgett)

Kali, destructive aspect of the Goddess, depicted in her usual fashion. (Courtesy of the Metropolitan Museum of Art)

to war, and the hunt rides in the direction of the enemy nation. It was seen before the Napoleonic Wars, when they rode south, and the Crimean War, when they rode east. Edric cannot die, for he must expiate his guilt for having surrendered to William, the 'Cong Kerry' as he was known in Shropshire.

The myth of God's judgement on a sinful English race had been fulfilled, and now a new and brutal regime took control of England, which before long threatened the Celtic nations also. And it was this interface between the newcomers and the Welsh which gave birth to a remarkable renaissance of the Arthurian legends – one of the most influential mythical hybrids in history.

An Anglo-Saxon settlement had grown up on the borders of West Mercia and Wessex called *Oxen-ford*. Legend has it that when they first came to the place the Anglo-Saxon settlers discovered a huge statue of a bull, sacred animal of the god of the Roman legions, Mithras. This idol stood at the confluence of several sacred rivers and streams, and the place grew into a campus where young men from noble families were tutored and socialised. West Mercia and Wessex were the foundations of the state which became England. This informal arrangement grew into the University of Oxford, one of the foremost centres of learning in all Europe.

About seventy years after the Battle of Hastings, a man named Geoffrey ap Arthur from Monmouth in Wales became a secular canon at St George's College in Oxford, where he was employed as a *magister* or teacher. Geoffrey's own father had been called Arthur, and his colleagues called him 'Geoffrey Arthur', possibly because of his inordinate interest in the 'pseudo-historical' king of antiquity. According to Sir Frank Stenton, Geoffrey was not in fact a Welshman, but from a Breton family. Geoffrey and Arthur are names which were popular among the Bretons, but little used in Wales. After the Norman Conquest, many Breton knights were rewarded with lands in the south-west of England, Devon and Cornwall – and the Welsh Marches. *Marche*, the Norman French word for these intermediate borderlands, comes from the same root as the Anglo-Saxon *mierce*, which gave Mercia its name.

One rationale for this plantation of the Bretons was that they spoke a language so similar to Cornish or Welsh that they could easily communicate with their Celtic neighbours. The Bretons were descended from those emigrants who had been forced to flee the island following the Anglo-Saxon invasions, and to them this 'homecoming' seemed like a dispensation of divine justice. The Arthurian tales were deeply ingrained in the Breton national myth, and Monmouth was one of the main centres of Breton settlement. Geoffrey 'of Monmouth', as he called himself in his books, was profoundly interested in the ancient history of the British Isles, the mysterious times before the Christian era. By Geoffrey's time a degree of intermarriage and cultural assimilation had commenced between the Norman aristocracy and the substrate Anglo-Saxon population, and a Benedictine monk, William of Malmesbury, had become the first serious post-Conquest historian.

William was a librarian at Malmesbury, and so he had access to many crucial sources. He was also a regular visitor to Glastonbury Abbey, where the history and legends of the foundation of the 'Secret of the Lord' were recounted to him. In 1125, William published a book called the *Gesta Regum Anglorum* or 'History of the Kings of the English'. Half-English himself, William's motive may have been an attempt to mollify the resentment and wounded pride of the English element of the population who had been so cruelly oppressed and dispossessed since Hastings, but he was also half-Welsh and had a Welsh-speaking wife. Surely the glories of the Celtic kings and heroes deserved their proper place in the august history of the island and its fate, the so-called 'Matter of Britain'?

During his researches for the book, William, taking hints from Gildas via Bede, became aware of the shadowy history surrounding a Celtic commander who had defeated the Saxons at Mount Badon. Combined with traditional tales and the testimony of the Abbot of Glastonbury, Henry de Blois, these clues convinced William that Arthur was no mere legend but a truly historical personage, and should be treated as such – 'a man worthy to be proclaimed in true histories'. William became a patron of Geoffrey of Monmouth who took William at his word. In his *Historia Regum Britanniae* or 'History of the Kings of Britain', Geoffrey makes a conscious effort to present Arthur as an indigenous Celtic hero whose glorious reign is the climax of the book. Geoffrey's books were written in Latin, the language of the intelligentsia, almost all of whom were clergymen, but the intention behind the foundation of the University of Oxford was to ensure that members of the elite noble class should also acquire at least a modicum of learning.

The Norman elite were a tight-knit group, and the thing which bound them closely together as an exclusive class was their military method, the cult of the mounted knight. To bond the knights together, and to inculcate the virtues and obligations of the code of chivalry, a body of 'romance', tales sung by minstrels in the great halls of the new castles, grew up. These tales were sung in French, and initially referred to the 'Matter of France', heroic poems celebrating such heroes as Roland and Charlemagne. The French court was the main centre for the development of the cult of knighthood, and this conferred on it a certain international cachet.

The parvenu Norman kings of England, who were still technically vassals of the French king, desperately sought for an equivalent myth, but to resurrect the heroic tales of the Anglo-Saxon heroes such as Alfred or Athelstan would doubtless encourage English dissent against their regime, even subversion or rebellion. Arthur, however, was an entirely different case, so far removed in time, and his compatriots so marginalised and powerless, that he could be lionised with minimal risk. Moreover, as the enemy of the fallen Saxons, it was legitimate for the Norman knights to identify themselves with him. Robert Graves in his *The White Goddess* realised the profound cultural implications of this process: 'The troveres or "finders" translated them into contemporary French and adopted them into the Provencal code of chivalry, and in their new dress, they conquered Europe.' One of the bitterest ironies of this co-option of the Arthurian myths by their enemies was that the Welsh, the descendants of the people Arthur had once ruled, were *excluded* from the neo-Arthurian corpus. Lady Charlotte Guest, in her introduction to her masterly translation of the *Mabinogion* makes this quite clear:

> In the twelfth and thirteenth centuries there arose into general notoriety in Europe, a body of 'Romance', which in various forms retained its popularity till the Reformation. In it, the plot, the incidents, the characters, were almost wholly those of Chivalry, that bond which united the warriors of France, Spain, and Italy, with those of pure Teutonic descent, and embraced more or less firmly all the nations of Europe, excepting only the Slavonic races, not yet risen to power, and the Celts, who had fallen from it. It is not difficult to account for this latter omission. The Celts, driven from the plains into the mountains and islands, preserved their liberty, and hated their oppressors with a fierce, and not causeless, hatred. A proud and free people, isolated both in country and language, were not likely to adopt customs which implied brotherhood with their foes.[22]

For the Welsh, Arthur was an entirely historical king, and the linchpin of their claims to national liberty and independence. The 'romantic' tales seemed to them frivolous, and the corruption of their sacred history and its co-option by foreigners just one more insult to add to many other injustices, part of the *gormesoedd*, the oppressive psychical plagues inflicted on them by hostile alien forces with whom they were in a state of unceasing warfare.

But the almost immediate success of the reinvention of Arthur did amount to a kind of rebirth. The ancient Egyptians revered a mythical creature, a bird known as the phoenix. Every 540 years the bird was destroyed by fire, only to renew itself. The resurrection of the phoenix was linked to an astronomical concept known as the 'Great Year'. The ancients were familiar with the phenomenon known as the Precession of the Equinoxes, the retrograde motion of equinoctial points along the ecliptic in each successive year. So, every year the Sun appears to rise approximately one minute earlier than in the preceding one. Over what seem to mortals vast periods of time, these minute differences amount to a quite significant movement backwards around the Zodiac. A 'Great Year' consisted of 25,920 earthly years, and was divided into twelve 'months' or 'aeons' of 2,160 years, each corresponding to the astrological signs. Each degree of precession, then, consisted of seventy-two years – the average length of a human life. The Christian 'aeon' corresponded with the astrological sign of Pisces, 'the fishes'; the motif of the earliest Christians had been a fish. This concept was to have momentous

---

22 Guest, Lady C. (trans.), *Mabinogion*, London, 1906.

consequences for our present age, as we will discover, but it is curious that Arthur's death, as recorded in Welsh annals, occurred in 537, and his 'rebirth' and restoration to glory occurred at precisely the time his 'national enemy', the Anglo-Saxons, were finally vanquished 540 years later. The periodicity is not precise, and the date of Arthur's death cannot have been known with any degree of accuracy, but, like the phoenix, the ancient Celtic mythology and its hero king had risen, in a strange way, from the ashes.

The astonishing international success of the refurbished Arthurian mythos was due in no small part to the incorporation of an exciting new element – romantic love. This was not the banal sexual 'love' of the modern imagination, but a complex, ritualised 'game of love', whose participants were under the spell of *fin amor* or 'refined love'. In the south of France there was a region called *Occitania*, which had its own language called Occitan. With its extensive Mediterranean trading contacts, the region attracted many and various religious sects, including the Bogomils, Gnostic dualists who believed that matter was evil in itself, and that Christ could not have incarnated in a material form but was a spiritual apparition giving the appearance of materiality. This base material world was the province of *Rex Mundi*, the 'King of the World', the Devil. The tempter had offered Christ dominion over all the kingdoms of the world, after all.

Another, possibly foreign, influence came with the troubadours or 'composers', poet-musicians who performed songs before the nobility in which the elaborate rituals of 'courtly love' were exalted. The essential motif of this love was that it encouraged spiritual transfiguration or ennoblement. At its core was an elevation and idealisation of women, which offered a frisson of suppressed sexuality to the participants in the 'game of love'. Duke William IX of Aquitaine became one of the earliest troubadours, and his granddaughter, Eleanor, who became queen consort of both France and England, presided over 'courts of love' which formalised the elaborate 'games'. The revolutionary aspect of the cult was that women were in control, elevated to the status of distant, unattainable objects of a fanatical love which may be unrequited, usually because the lady was already married or loved another. Nevertheless, the suitor was obliged to press his tortured affections on his beloved, and be ready to endure the utmost humiliation, disappointment, and heartache.

In the age of the Crusades, and indeed before that time, noble marriages were purely political and economic. A knight might not see his wife for years if he was on a distant military expedition, and it was by no means assured that he would return. There could be no *fin amor* in a conventional marriage. Therefore adultery, or the potential for adultery, far from being regarded as socially disruptive and sinful, provided the dramatic tension which fuelled the relationship between the suitor and his lady. Actual sexual intercourse was not the object, but in many cases this undoubtedly occurred, though only when the cult had degenerated.

The Arthurian stories were overlaid with these themes, and the character of Lancelot, and his doomed and tragic love for Arthur's queen, Guinevere, was invented and intruded into them as the epitome of the pseudo-erotic drama. The four marks of the true lover were his humility, his courtesy, a sensual desire and, crucially, an overwhelming beatification of the beloved woman to a point of quasi-religious devotion. By intensification of the erotic emotional impulse, the hard crust of individual selfhood was disintegrated, and a psychical unity with the beloved achieved. As with Tantrik Buddhism, this ecstatic union of the male and female pointed beyond the material to the divine. Courtly love was, then, a 'religion of love' which was, perhaps, a compensatory psychological mechanism for releasing a deeply suppressed longing for goddess worship, with its aim a return to a state of prelapsarian ecstasy and bliss. The Grail quest became symbolic of the trials and travails of the knight-errant who has embarked on his journey and whom love alone could sustain. We may judge how deeply primordial this psychical theme is when we consider that the human ovum will receive just one spermatozoon from among many millions to generate the ultimate 'Magick' of human life.

The Welsh were not alone in feeling excluded from the Arthurian revival. The English, although they doubtless heard oral folk tales of Arthur or saw mummery of his deeds by roaming players, had no access in their own language to written versions of Geoffrey of Monmouth or the Norman Robert Wace, who translated him. But at some time in the early years of the thirteenth century, an obscure lay preacher or clerk known as Layamon decided to redress matters personally. It is certain that he had access to a copy of Wace's *Roman de Brut*, and he used this verse poem as the template for his own *Brut* in the English language, what he called a *Chronicle of Britain*.

But the story does not end there. Layamon's *Brut* is not just a straight copy. It contains new elements and versions of the Arthurian tales, which must have derived either from Welsh drovers who came to him for blessing as they made the dangerous river crossing at Arley Redstone on the Severn, or – and this is a fascinating possibility – they could have been transmitted by indigenous 'Welshry' who survived deep in the forest of Wyre into the thirteenth century. His 16,000-line poetic history of Britain, commencing with the arrival of Brutus of Troy at Totnes in Devonshire in the twelfth century BC, is regarded as one of the seminal works of early English literature. But who was Layamon, and why did he take on this herculean task in such an obscure place?

A long time ago I toyed with the notion of writing an historical novel based on exactly this question. I was living quite near Arley Redstone, where Layamon wrote the poem by candlelight in a cave next to the rock-hewn chapel where he ministered to the forest folk, river trow men, charcoal burners and Welsh drovers on their way to London. The collapsing sandstone cave is situated behind a caravan park beside the Severn and is not easy to find. The site attendant's Alsatian growls menacingly. There is nothing to show to mark Layamon's epic labour, though one of the roads in the adjacent housing estate is named after him. All that can be discerned from the historical record is that he was licensed to 'read book' by the rural dean of Martley in Worcestershire, rather like a lay reader in the modern Anglican Church. He was not ordained, but could lead prayers and offer blessings. He must have had a sound education because he could read French, the language of the Norman elite, but his name is Anglo-Saxon.

Layamon was probably a clerk. One in twenty men in medieval England were clerks, and with his preaching license Layamon was in a position to minister beside the Severn ferry near modern Stourport-on-Severn. The 'simple-hearted Saxon priest' said that it seemed to him a good thing to compose his history of the island beside the great river. He was in good company. St Beuno had contemplated the dance of time in his day beside the Hafren, and Aethelweard, a member of the West Saxon royal house, had composed his *Chronicon* a few miles upstream at Bridgnorth. My novel was predicated on the idea of some connection between these riverside historians, and their guardianship of a recondite 'key', having to do with the more esoteric aspects of the 'Matter of Britain'. Although this ultimately came to nothing, I remain convinced that there is a mystery to be solved about Layamon. Since this is no ordinary history, but an attempt to 'euhemerise in reverse', I feel permitted to speculate from intuition in this case.

The truly innovative thing about Layamon's work was that it was in English, and this must have been an expression of some deeper need in the English national psyche to feel themselves an integral part of the dramatic epic which had captured the imagination of the entire Christian world – and not just the Christian world. On his way to the Third Crusade, King Richard I, 'the Lionheart', presented King Tancred of Sicily with a sword he made out to be 'Caliburn' or Excalibur, King Arthur's magic weapon. Arthur's tales were told among the Saracens, and the military monks called the Knights Templar were well acquainted with them. How ironic, then, that in the very land of Arthur's birth the ordinary folk were locked out of the story?

Richard's famous military exploits, his march on Jerusalem, and the huge sacrifices of the common people to raise his ransom when he was a prisoner all contributed to an emotional identification with the myth of a hero king among the English. But Richard's brother, John, who succeeded him, was quite another example of an historical archetype – that of the cruel, greedy, despotic, wicked tyrant. John had a nephew, called Arthur, Duke of Brittany. The Bretons still hoped for Arthur's reincarnation, and the boy had been named quite deliberately with this in mind: *Arturus Redivivus*, 'Arthur Reborn'. On 3 April 1203, the odious John flew into one of the furious drunken rages for which he is remembered, and personally strangled the sixteen-year-old Arthur before throwing his body over the castle parapets into the river at Rouen, weighed down with a heavy stone. This incident is a very little-explored aspect of Arthurian studies, but it is of interest, because

Layamon was writing at just about this time. In his analysis of the period, Frank McLynn remarks on the devastating emotional consequences of the murder for the Bretons:

> Brittany was in a ferment, for the cult of King Arthur was strong there, and the Bretons regarded the young son of Geoffrey and Constance to be *Arturus Redivivus*. The killing of Arthur was therefore akin to deicide, and his murderer was regarded as a second Mordred, the very avatar of evil and the destruction of hopes of heaven here on earth.[23]

But the loathing for John was not confined to the Bretons. Because Arthur had now captured the hearts and minds of the entire Christian world, there was a spasm of disgust and outrage, a feeling of violation of all that stands for good. I have suggested that Layamon's portrayal of Mordred, the evil villain of the Arthurian tales, is a barely concealed indictment of John. Layamon writes:

> Mordred, wickedest of men; truth had he none, to ever any man. He was Arthur's relation, his sister's son. To his uncle he did treachery. This land he destroyed with numerous sorrows, and became odious in every land, so that no man would offer prayers for his soul. All that Arthur had he gave to him, his land, his people and his queen.[24]

Layamon's work was also very influential in another way. It democratised the stories in a wider sense, because the issue of language also reflected class. Layamon had reconciled what A. E. Housman called 'the ancient ill' by making Arthur a 'national' hero for the English, someone they could now think of as 'one of their own' like Alfred. He was now part of the emotional imagination of the English people, and they were free to take forward the combined myth and magic, all that had arisen from the momentous history of the island, in their own language. This was a relatively unheralded but truly great achievement. The English language had won out, against all odds.

The Arthurian myth became inextricably intertwined with the fate of the English monarchy. During his campaigns in Wales, King Henry II visited a Welsh bard whom he claimed had disclosed Arthur's secret burial place at Glastonbury to him. The king was told that the grave lay between two 'pyramids' in a cemetery just to the south of the Lady chapel. This information was highly convenient for Henry. Wales had proven a perennial problem for him. A coalition of Welsh princes under Lord Rhys of Deheubarth had lured the king's army into the bleak Berwyn mountains, and Henry, the most feared warrior in Europe, was forced to retreat because of the infamous Welsh

---

23 McLynn, F., *Lionheart and Lackland: King Richard, King John and the Wars of Conquest*, Vintage, London, 2007.
24 Madden, Sir F., *Layamon's Brut*, Society of Antiquaries, London, 1847.

weather. For the notoriously bad-tempered Henry this was bad enough, but the prospect of a resurrection of the Arthurian propaganda in Wales was even more dangerous. The myth said that he was not dead, but if it could be proven that Arthur had been a mortal human being who had lived and died like everyone else then his return was impossible.

Henry informed the Abbot of Glastonbury about the location of the grave. A disastrous fire in 1184 consumed the abbey, at the time the most prestigious pilgrimage site in England. The abbot urgently needed funds to rebuild the abbey. One way of raising it was to find a way of attracting pilgrims again in larger numbers. The monks initially claimed that they had found the remains of St Patrick but this was not widely believed, and the later discovery of St Dunstan's bones failed to capture the public imagination. The prospect of discovering Arthur's remains and displaying them as holy relics was the answer to the monks' prayers, and in 1191 the grave was excavated.

Henry died in July 1189, and his successor, Richard I, named as his heir the young Duke of Brittany, Arthur. This intensified the search, and as the bard had predicted, two bodies were discovered. The historian Gerald of Wales recorded that the bodies were enclosed within a hollowed-out oak trunk at a depth of 16 feet. A lead cross was discovered which was inscribed in Latin with the words 'Here lies the famous King Arthur, in the Isle of Avalon'. The skeleton was said to be that of a giant of a man, and the remains of Guinevere touchingly included wisps of her golden hair.

So fortuitous for the abbey was this discovery that it has been assumed that the entire incident was manufactured by the monks on the orders of King Henry. Unfortunately, the lead cross was lost, but an engraving was made of it. If it was a forgery of the Glastonbury monks then it was a very poor one. More recent excavations suggest that it may have been intruded by St Dunstan during his refurbishment of the abbey in the tenth century, and that originally a large stone monument or pillar marked the spot, typical of those erected to commemorate early British kings or princes. It is quite true that the king and the abbot both had ulterior motives for facilitating such a discovery, but this may be a mere coincidence.

The English royalty were now thoroughly enmeshed in the Arthurian drama. In 1278 Edward I transferred the relics to a magnificent new shrine at the foot of the high altar in the newly restored abbey. Edward was absolutely obsessed with the legends and he regarded himself as the heir to Arthur's realm in some mystical sense. His ruthless war against Llywelyn ap Gruffydd, 'the Last', Prince of Wales, culminated in a great victory pageant staged at Nefyn, the Welsh village where the 'Prophesies of Merlin' were written down. Arthurian themes were mimed to a desolated Welsh audience whose baby princess, Gwenllian, was immured in a nunnery in England for the rest of her natural life. Both her parents were dead, and she never even knew them. The poor girl knew no Welsh, or even how to pronounce her own name properly. The Welsh crown jewels, the *Croes Naid* (which contained a fragment of the

True Cross) and Arthur's crown were all removed to England, and the Welsh nation reduced to serfdom. Edward also removed what he thought to be the 'Stone of Scone' from Scotland to Westminster. This was not the original, but a locally procured substitute. The appropriation of the Arthurian tradition by the 'old enemy' of the Welsh was complete. An English canon, Pierre de Langtoft, made this explicit:

> Ah God! How often Merlin said truth
> In His prophesies if you read them!
> Now are the two waters united in one,
> Which have been separated by great mountains;
> And one realm made of two different kingdoms
> Which used to be governed by two kings.
> Now are all the islanders joined together,
> And Albany reunited to the royalties
> Of which King Edward is proclaimed lord.
> Cornwall and Wales are in his power,
> And Ireland the Great at his will.
> There is neither king nor prince of all the countries
> Except King Edward, who has thus united them;
> Arthur never held the fiefs so fully.

This earlier English imperialism, and the gradual subjugation of the Celtic peoples, was the precursor to a much larger imperial project which was to eventually encompass the entire globe, and this project was predicated upon and legitimated by the legends which had encrusted around Arthur. Yet these legends were, as yet, disjointed, sometimes contradictory, and always contested. The magical aura which had attached itself to the English monarchy was disputed by foreign scholars, and held in contempt by the Welsh, who still stuck stubbornly to their own version of events. Owain Glyndwr's uprising of 1400–1415 used the Prophesies of Merlin as a political weapon, as we have seen. The rebellion was a glorious failure, and for seventy years the character of Arthur returned to his former slumber. Then, in 1485, a momentous year in other respects, Arthur returned once again.

A prisoner named Thomas Malory, whose identity is still disputed, occupied his time by drawing together all the Arthurian material he could find into an entire myth cycle. The consensus of opinion is that Thomas was a notorious criminal, whose feud with and attempted murder of the Duke of Buckingham led to his incarceration. Almost certainly he was confined in Newgate prison, where a library existed which had been endowed by 'Dick' Whittington, the mayor of London. The main objection to the idea of Malory's authorship was that his highly moralistic and spiritually refined rendering seems so inconsistent with what is known about his dubious character, but these were heady and dangerous times – the so-called 'Wars of the Roses'. Many a bad character has discovered his hidden depths while imprisoned, and no one is a one-dimensional 'good' or 'bad' personality.

Whatever his other faults, Malory was a conscientious and industrious researcher and writer and his *Morte d'Arthur* became the first great prose work in English literature. For him the romantic entanglements of courtly love were relatively insignificant, ephemeral aspects of the legends. Malory was most concerned to promote a return to the chivalric ideal of the knight, and the theme of a golden age brought about by a dynasty which inculcated integrity, nobility and virtue. It may well be that this vision of an ideal realm was designed to stand in contradistinction to the ruined and divided England of his day. Malory's book became the defining text of Arthurian literature, and with the assistance of William Caxton's editing and his pioneering printing press, the book was published in 1485.

In that very year an event of huge significance took place, yet another of the weird coincidences which seem to coalesce around the myths. On 7 August of that year, a small army of Bretons and Normans about 2,000 strong landed at St Ann's Head in Pembrokeshire, led by Henry Tudor, a nobleman who claimed descent from Cadwallader, the seventh-century King of Gwynedd. Henry came to claim the English throne, and deliberately emphasised his somewhat dubious ancient Welsh pedigree. Under the banner of the Red Dragon, Henry drummed up support in Wales before crossing the border at Newport in Shropshire. At the Battle of Bosworth Field on 22 August, Henry Tudor was the victor – and now, yet again, Arthur was to be reborn.

12

The Giant Albion

Just as all seemed lost for the forlorn descendants of the Britons, a self-styled Welshman with a putative ancestral connection to Arthur had ascended the English throne. The Arthurian connection was made flesh when Henry VII was presented with a healthy firstborn son he named Arthur. In 1501 Arthur married Catherine of Aragon and the couple took up residence at Ludlow Castle, from where Wales and the Marches were governed. Within a few months Prince Arthur became ill and died, and Catherine claimed that the marriage had never actually been consummated, despite rumours which circulated that Arthur had been heard boasting to his friends, 'I was in Spain last night!' His body was taken to the Severn and loaded onto a barge near to Layamon's old jetty before being solemnly laid to rest at Worcester Cathedral.

Once again a prince called Arthur had died young, but his death was also extremely inconvenient politically. Spain and England were both desperate to repair the damage Arthur's untimely death had caused. A scheme to achieve this was devised by which Catherine, her virginity allegedly still intact, would marry Henry, Arthur's younger brother. The obstacle to this was that it was proscribed under Christian law for a man to marry his brother's widow. The pope was petitioned by both Spain and England to dispense with the law and allow the marriage to proceed, which he duly did. For a while the couple were happily married, but Henry's dalliances became more frequent as Catherine became older, less attractive and increasingly pious. When he became infatuated with Anne Boleyn and the alliance with Spain deteriorated, Henry sought a divorce, on the grounds that the Christian Bible had been right, and that the prophesy that any such marriage would fail to produce male heirs had been fulfilled. Henry's envoys conveyed this sentiment to the pope, but on this occasion he declined Henry's request. Henry VIII was renowned for his notoriously violent temper and was incensed that the ultimate spiritual power in Christendom seemed prepared to disregard holy writ, condemning him to live in sin, and his country to another century of bloody civil war – for, should he leave no male heir behind him, the bitter factionalism of the Wars of the Roses would surely re-emerge.

The Protestant movement which had commenced in 1517 was by this time advancing all over northern Europe, and a body of opinion, promulgated by the scholar Erasmus and others, existed which argued that the pope, rather than being the heir of St Peter and the chief vicar in this world, was legally no more than the Bishop of Rome. This being so, the so-called 'pope' had no right to intervene in the political or spiritual affairs of England, or to appoint bishops. Catherine was duly divorced, and Henry arrogated to himself the right to appoint bishops and to sunder the Church of England from the Roman Catholic Church. One of Henry's arguments was that the first church in the world had been established in England, at Glastonbury, and so it had primacy over Rome in spiritual terms.

Henry married Anne Boleyn in secret – she was already pregnant – and passed the Act of Supremacy in 1534 by which he became head of the Church of England. He liked to think that he had inherited the mantle of the spiritual remanifestation of Arthur, and Malory's ideals of a kingdom which would recapture the glories of Camelot were very popular. Unfortunately, within a few years, the spiritual foundations of the nation began to disintegrate, and the old medieval order was violently swept away.

Between 1536 and 1541, a violent attack was made on the ancient monasteries, convents, priories and friaries; it has since become known as the Dissolution of the Monasteries. The Acts of Suppression of 1536 and 1539 seized all their lands and assets, dismissing and dispersing their 12,000 members. Having destroyed the roofs of the buildings, the authorities left the ruins to be plundered by the local populace. It became apparent to those scavenging for beams, stones and tiles that no spiritual harm seemed to befall them, and this bred a new attitude of incredulity in the face of superstition, an impoverishment of respect for the sacred. One in fifty men had been in religious orders, so the economic and social dislocation was brutal. More than this, the cultural damage was immense. At Worcester Cathedral library only six of its 600 books survived. Many of the books, taken to be used to line wine casks and the like, were priceless Anglo-Saxon manuscripts. Between 1530 and 1600, virtually all English religious art was destroyed in an orgy of iconoclasm.

On 13 October 1536, an uprising among the conservative Roman Catholics of Yorkshire known as the 'Pilgrimage of Grace' began. A body of men 40,000 strong, all under arms, were led by Robert Aske, a London lawyer, and these 'pilgrims' were militant and angry at the policies of the 'base-born' Thomas Cromwell, Henry's chief minister. There were several similar rebellions around the country at this time, but this one was too strong to be contained by Henry's forces and so a truce was arranged.

Aske was given safe passage to London to negotiate with Henry. His main demands were the suspension of ecclesiastical reform, and Cromwell's dismissal. Henry gave an impression that he was prepared to comply with these demands, and Aske returned north. But shortly afterwards reports reached the king that hostilities had broken out again. Aske was arrested and incarcerated, and eventually executed for treason, at York on 12 July 1537. The rebellion had failed, and the old spiritual order passed away – but nature abhors a vacuum. A new order was necessary, and as so often before, the reimagined England of the Tudors was constructed from a subtle and potent blend of magic and myth.

In 1497, Henry VII had granted a charter to John Cabot, an Italian navigator based in Bristol, to discover 'new found land' to the west of Iceland and Greenland, its existence rumoured for centuries among sailors. In his tiny ship called *Matthew*, Cabot made landfall at Cape Bonavista in Newfoundland, the first European to do so since the Vikings. The discovery of North America opened up exciting possibilities for the English monarchy. Henry's ancestor, Cadwallader, seventh-century King of Gwynedd, was said to have prophesied the coming of a magical queen born of his line. Elizabeth I, Henry's granddaughter, was said to be this prophesied 'faerie queene' incarnate. A Welsh antiquary, Humphrey Llwyd, claimed that a son of Owain Gwynedd, Madog ap Owain Gwynedd, had discovered North America in the twelfth century. Other legendary 'history' alleged that Arthur, who had gone to some indeterminate place in the west, had also 'discovered' America. Since Prince Madog was, like Elizabeth, a descendant of Cadwallader – and therefore Arthur – it followed that Elizabeth was the rightful ruler of the newly discovered territories. These legendary devices may now seem quaint, but at the time they were in earnest, and the magical and mythical pretensions of the English court would soon grow into a full-blown magical cult, with a wizard to rival Merlin of old.

In spite of the long hegemony of the Christian faith in England since late Anglo-Saxon times, magic had never really gone away. In the thirteenth century Roger Bacon, known as 'Doctor Mirabilis', acquired the reputation of being a wizard. His pioneering empirical study of nature, and a 'universal grammar' derived from Aristotle and Arab mystical philosophy, anticipated the ideas of Goethe and Steiner, among others. Bacon spent many years at Oxford. The university, and another at Cambridge that was founded when Oxford became overcrowded, provided a respectable environment where philosophical enquiry was allowed to shade into more esoteric studies. Bacon referred to a mechanical brazen head with oracular powers, said to have been constructed by Albertus Magnus, a German friar who had been influenced by Archytas of Tarentum. Archytas was a fourth-century BC philosopher who designed mechanical avatars which, he thought, would liberate man from the domination of nature, and reveal the secrets of universal consciousness.

As the spirit of Protestantism with its focus on the liberty of the individual spread, this spirit of free philosophical enquiry was tolerated and even encouraged. Elizabeth became venerated as a kind of goddess, and she was given exotic magical names such as *Gloriana*, *Phoebe* and *Virginia*. In Edmund Spenser's *Fairie Queene*, dedicated to Elizabeth, her magical ancestor, 'Gloriana' is the fairy instructress of the young Arthur, with whom he is hopelessly in love. The 'Society of Archers', of which Spenser was a member, put on huge pageants and gala celebrations which presented the Elizabethan regime as a restoration of ancient Camelot. The queen herself was the incarnation of a magical destiny whose mission was to spread the true Protestant reformed religion of the Church of England across the globe, and so save the souls of the colonised peoples of the 'new world' from the false religion of papacy, now condemned as the Antichrist. The showdown between England and Spain when the Spanish Armada was defeated in 1588 was perceived as a microcosm of the larger cosmic struggle between the Protestant and Catholic faiths. In this holy war, all means, including magic, were employed, and Elizabeth was no stranger to the occult.

Doctor John Dee's family were of Welsh extraction. The family seat was near to Pilleth in Radnorshire but he was born in London in 1527. He inherited a tradition, very common among his compatriots, that he was of royal British descent, and that his line could be traced to Arthur. More than this, he claimed that since Arthur was a descendant of the mythical Trojan Prince Brutus, whom Geoffrey of Monmouth identified as the progenitor of the 'Kings of Britain', he was heir to certain occult prophetic powers. He claimed kinship through the Welsh royalty with the queen herself. He was a tutor to Robert Dudley, Elizabeth's favourite (and alleged lover). The ambitious Dudley family were zealous religious reformists who established Dee as a permanent member of the royal court, where he became one of the foremost intellects of sixteenth-century Europe.

While he was still a student at Cambridge, Dee designed a mechanical insect which appeared to fly into the rafters of the hall where it appeared in a student show. He studied at the University of Louvain in Belgium, a hotbed of radical philosophical ideas. He studied navigation and cartography with Mercator, the Fleming who revolutionised map-making. This skill was to be of utmost importance as England strove to expand its imperial project. A mathematical genius at a time when mathematics was regarded with the same suspicion as the occult arts, Dee became the royal astrologer to Queen Mary I, a fanatical Catholic. Dee's mathematical studies convinced him that the key to unlocking the secrets of the universe lay in numbers. But as Frances Yates says in her *The Occult Philosophy in the Elizabethan Age*,

Dee was intensely aware of the supercelestial world of the angels and divine powers. His studies in number, so successful and factual in what he would think of as the lower spheres, were, for him, primarily important because he believed they could be extended with even more powerful results into the supercelestial world. In short, as is well known, Dee believed he had achieved, with his associate Edward Kelley, the power of conjuring angels.

Dee's proficiency in casting horoscopes was brought to the attention of the Protestant Elizabeth while she was held under house arrest in Oxfordshire by her sister, Queen Mary. Dee cast two horoscopes, one for Elizabeth and the other for the queen. Elizabeth's chart was encouraging, promising that she would eventually succeed Mary and enjoy a long and glorious reign. Mary's, however, was just the opposite, and her early death was indicated. Such a conclusion was treason, and when the charts were discovered Dee was thrown into prison. Mary considered that her mother, Catherine of Aragon, had been murdered by Anne Boleyn, Elizabeth's mother, using witchcraft. Anne had been executed on trumped-up allegations that she had bewitched her husband, and for alleged fornication with her own brother.

Fortunately Dee survived, and his prediction of Elizabeth's accession came true. Elizabeth even asked Dee to choose a propitious date for her coronation ceremony, and once she was established Dee was employed as her 'noble intelligencer'. She referred to him as 'my ubiquitous eyes'. Elizabeth was, with some justification, paranoid, and lived in constant fear of Catholic plots and assassination attempts. Dee's role, then, was not dissimilar to that of the modern security services, and it is no accident that we still refer to these as the 'intelligence' services. Originally 'intelligence' in that sense was a form of scrying or magical divination, and in Dee Elizabeth had found a 'secret weapon' second to none.

But like many a clever man before him, Dee soon became obsessed with finding the ultimate key to the secret of universal consciousness, what he called his *Liber Mysteriorum*. In doing so he was prepared to sacrifice everything, to break all religious, moral and sexual taboos. His 'angel magic', as it became known, was ethically and morally questionable by any standards. It was to lead him into a series of disturbing adventures so strange that they still beggar belief. Yet Dee thought of himself as a 'Christian Cabalist', as Frances Yates puts it, whose magical experimentation was under absolute protection from God and his angelic representatives. In Dee's exegesis Arthur represented the 'mystical exemplar of sacred British imperial Christianity'. He was a mythical champion to inspire co-religionists on the Continent resisting the forces of the Roman Catholic Counter-Reformation.

Dee moved to his mother's house at Mortlake just outside London in 1565 or 1566. Here he assembled a library with reading rooms to rival any in Europe, with a large section devoted to magical, alchemical and other occult themes. In addition, there was a private 'oratory' and an alchemical laboratory. Many famous navigators came to consult Dee and to peruse his collection of maps and charts before commencing their expeditions. England's fate was now inextricably bound up with the development of global maritime trade. In 1577 Sir Francis Drake, with Elizabeth's financial backing, set out to circumnavigate the globe. Late in that year a comet, the so-called 'Great Comet', appeared. It was observed by the Danish nobleman and astronomer Tycho Brahe, who recorded that it was visible for seventy-four days between November 1577 and January 1578.

Drake set out on 13 December, as the comet made its closest approach, and sailors still dreaded comets as tokens of ill omen. Dee was considered an expert in the significance of celestial phenomena, and the queen broached the matter with him. During this consultation Dee suggested to Elizabeth that the comet was a sign that she should challenge Spanish imperialism. The year before, Dee published a book he called *Brytanici Imperii Limites* which developed Humphrey Llwyd's idea of a 'British Empire' – not an 'English Empire', it should be noted. Llwyd's claims about Welsh colonisation of the Americas in medieval times were, Dee claimed, corroborated by Mercator who confirmed that King Arthur had conquered much of Scandinavia, the polar regions, parts of America, and Ireland. Elizabeth's claim to a 'British Empire' rested on her direct descent from Arthur, and Dee's project was a magical restoration of this (entirely mythical) imperium. So John Dee's contribution was not confined to vulgar occultism. The magical history of Britain was about to change the geopolitical paradigm on a global scale.

For many centuries, legends of a lost continent called 'Atlantis' had been recounted. Less than a century ago the Nazi regime in Germany became obsessed by it, but in the sixteenth century English minds were drawn to the idea that the newly discovered Americas were, in fact, the 'Island of Atlantis' described in the *Socratic Dialogues*, the idealised state described by Plato. If it were an island, then a 'north-west passage' must be navigable, putting Muscovy, and more importantly China, within easy reach by sea. It was these possibilities which drove the British exploration of North America forward in the first instance, and Dee's imperial project was taken seriously by the queen.

All Dee's plans for English naval supremacy and a British Empire ultimately came to pass, but Dee's darker obsessions were henceforth to focus on worlds far more mysterious than the Americas. In 1582, Dee was introduced to a man calling himself Edward Talbot. Dee had been communicating with spirits through mediums for years, and it is likely that Mr Talbot had come highly recommended as a scryer. This 'Edward Talbot' was actually a notorious conman, forger, and necromancer (one who haunts graveyards to question spirits as to the whereabouts of buried treasures) called Edward Kelley.

The Elizabethan age was one of extraordinary celestial phenomena of many kinds. A new star, so bright it could be seen in the daytime, was observed – a sign that all was not well in Heaven and denoting, according to the Hermetic philosophy, corresponding turmoil on Earth. Every twenty years the planets Saturn and Jupiter form an astrological aspect called a great conjunction, and in 1583 this aspect took on a deep magical significance. It may well have been this expected event which intensified Dee's magical activities at this time, and which led to his fateful meeting with Kelley. Benjamin Woolley, in his excellent book about Dee, remarks on the cosmic significance of the expected event:

> In 1583, just such an epoch was to come to an end and be succeeded by another, with a conjunction predicted on 28 April of that year in the last face of Pisces, the final sign of the watery trigon. This, in astrological terms, was momentous enough. But this event was of even greater significance, because the conjunction also marked when the cycle had worked through all the combinations of signs in the zodiac and was about to return to the primary one – the 'fiery' trigon.[25]

This 960-year-long cycle had been completed on six previous occasions, each of them announcing the birth of a great prophet. The number seven had particular magical significance, and now the seventh great cycle was to commence. The great nova, or 'new star', signified the beginning of a great new project, and the rise of new empires. All these matters concentrated Dee's considerable talents – but he needed a breakthrough, a way to communicate with the intelligences he believed could reveal the secrets of the forthcoming epoch.

Despite his sinister appearance and demeanour, Kelley was a 'sensitive', a medium of rare talent. Shortly after their first meeting Kelley scryed into Dee's crystal ball and said he could see an 'angel' named Uriel. This was the angel who had instructed the prophet Enoch in the science of astrology. According to Coptic Christian tradition, a lost book of the Bible had been written in the original 'Adamic' language of humanity, literally the language of God. Kelley began to receive coded messages in this antediluvian language, in which the angel revealed forty-eight calls or 'keys' thought to correspond to the forty-nine magic squares in Dee's book *Liber Loagaeth*, the use of which would unlock the gates to wisdom and understanding. The final key was concealed.

These operations were carried out in an atmosphere of utter solemnity and secrecy, and the two men became completely obsessed with the secrets revealed to them in the 'Angelic' or 'Enochian' language. Dee felt himself in the grip of forces over which he had no control, and drove Kelley on for days at a time without rest, transformed from the intellectual giant of his age

---

25 Woolley, B., *The Queen's Conjuror: The Science and Magic of Dr Dee*, HarperCollins, London, 2001.

into a psychopathic personality. But the two men were almost magnetically attracted. Dee was convinced, as I think history must be convinced, that Kelley really did have unique and genuine ability in spiritual mediumship. It cannot have been possible for a poor young man from Worcester, perhaps a Catholic recusant forced for want of legal opportunities into a life of deception and crime, to have obtained the degree of education necessary to invent the angelic language, or indeed to have reported complex codes given in Latin written backwards.

Another spirit appeared, called Camara, who sent an angel in the form of a child with a gift of a magical crystal for Dee. This gift of the angels was to be Kelley's new scrying stone, and with its aid the two men were to venture into regions of almost ineffable magical significance. It is no accident that Dee was the inspiration for Prospero in Shakespeare's *The Tempest* and Marlowe's *Doctor Faustus*. Frances Yates described him as an 'inspired melancholic', a model for *King Lear*. His dark activities raised many uncomfortable moral questions. As Dee fell out of political favour and rumours of his thaumaturgical experiments spread, he and Kelley resorted more and more to the astral realm, and as the communications intensified both men became increasingly disoriented and paranoid. But the point had now been reached where there was no going back.

Now the angels gave proof of their extraordinary powers. A lost scroll written by the Anglo-Saxon St Dunstan, once Abbot of Glastonbury, was discovered by Kelley, possibly in the ruins of the abbey itself. A strange substance was also found there, a red powder which turned out to be the secret tincture used in alchemical experiments to obtain 'the philosopher's stone', which could turn inexpensive base metals into gold. Dunstan was known to have been a powerful wizard, despite his sanctification. A window at the Bodleian Library at Oxford depicts him grasping the Devil by the nose with a pair of tongs. The tempter came to him in the disguise of a lovely maiden, wanton and exquisitely beautiful, sent to try his vow of celibacy, but Dunstan was not deceived, and the monstrosity beneath the mask was revealed. Dee examined Dunstan's scroll and intuited that it was written in code in what he discovered to be Latin. Various locations of ancient buried treasures were revealed.

Dee's psychopathy drove Kelley to despair, and impending insanity. He begged to be allowed to rest, but Dee insisted on more 'actions', even when Kelley was physically attacked and seriously injured by the spirits. The work went on regardless. A new spirit appeared, a 'pretty girl child' named Madimi, and it was this spirit more than any other who would come to obsess Dee's imagination. She revealed intimate knowledge of Edward IV of York and his ancestors from 'Bewdley, Cleobury Mortimer, Wild Wenlock [and] Ludlow'. Pronounced 'Mah-*dee*-mee', this spirit was none other than that of 'Helena', the 'Deified Genius' and 'Daughter of Fortitude', the eternally incarnating woman sought by Simon Magus.

As his relationship with the goddess of wisdom developed over time, Madimi became a seductress, a young maiden who came to dominate Dee, where Dunstan had resisted. Once a devout man of God, Dee put his hands into the hands of the Goddess, and he was sorely troubled. He was right to be. The difficulty about all such spirit communications has always been that of differentiating between benign and malicious spirits, who may mislead and entrap the unwary. But these operations, if pursued, become addictive, to the extent that the intelligences have a habit of intruding or illuding even when unbidden. Kelley had already complained of this exhausting phenomenon, and when visions of 'all Serpents, Dragons, Toads and all hideous shapes of beasts' appeared, Kelley suspected that the communicating entity, Galvah, was an evil spirit.

Serpentine visions were explicitly infernal. After the Fall, the sentence on the serpent was that 'upon thy belly shalt thou go, and dust shalt thou eat'. In Islamic countries the legend is still told that the Devil begged all the animals to carry him into Paradise, that he might tempt Adam. Only the serpent, who in those days had legs, agreed, and carried him in between his teeth. As punishment for this, the archangel Michael was commanded by God to cut off his legs, and replace his teeth with poisonous fangs. The cursed serpent, then, is an archetypal symbol of evil, but Dee, an educated and religious man, was oblivious to this, where Kelley saw only too clearly the potential for demonic possession. In truth, neither man was in control by this point; the work was unfolding itself through them.

Madimi reappeared, this time with a dire warning that Elizabeth's principal secretary and 'spymaster', Sir Francis Walsingham, was preparing to search Mortlake, where he was bound to discover Dee's occult paraphernalia, not to mention the vital but extremely incriminating Enochian documents. On 21 September 1583, Dee, Kelley and their families decided to leave England secretly, bound for Poland. They arrived at the home of a friend, an occultist and alchemist named Olbracht Laski, on 3 February 1584 after an arduous journey. The spiritual apparitions and 'actions' continued during the journey, and as soon as they were established at Laski's home they intensified. An audience with King Stefan of Poland proved fruitless. Laski, Dee's sponsor, was bankrupt and politically out of favour. Stefan was staunchly Catholic and distrusted the Enochian revelations, though he was interested in Kelley and his precious 'red powder'. Dee, whose intimate relationship with Elizabeth I was well known, was understandably distrusted, but Kelley began to see how his alchemical services might bring him fame and fortune.

In August 1584 the small group arrived in Prague, where Dee hoped to meet Rudolf II, the Holy Roman Emperor. Madimi appeared at another 'spiritual conference', now 'bigger than she was' and full of woes. Then, much to Dee's consternation, she made the extraordinary demand that he should confront the emperor himself – he whom they had travelled so far to solicit for aid – and 'rebuketh him for his sins'. This seemingly suicidal command would have tested any sane man's resolve, but Dee complied with Madimi's instructions. He stood before the emperor and declared before God that he had 'a message from him, to say unto you; and that is this:

> The Angel of the Lord hath appeared to me, and rebuketh you for your sins. If you will hear me, and believe me, you shall triumph. If you will not hear me, the Lord, the God that made heaven and earth (under whom you breathe and have your spirit) putteth his foot against your breast, and will throw you headlong down from your seat. Moreover, the Lord hath made this covenant with me (by oath) that he will do and perform. If you will forsake your wickedness, and turn unto him, your Seat shall be the greatest that ever was, and the Devil shall become your prisoner: which Devil I did conjecture to be the Great Turk. This is my commission from God. I feign nothing, neither am I an hypocrite, or ambitious man, or doting or dreaming in this cause. If I speak otherwise than I have just cause, I forsake my salvation.

This impertinent message was in fact received with equanimity and humility by Rudolf, who, like Stefan, had one eye on Kelley's alchemical abilities. The papal nuncio in Bohemia, Franciscus Bonomo, denounced Dee as a black magician in a letter to the emperor which Dee managed to intercept. Madimi appeared again and commanded that Dee and Kelley return with their families to Krakow, which instruction was faithfully obeyed.

The Catholic authorities were by now very interested in Dee and Kelley. It was noted that their material circumstances seemed suddenly prosperous, and their accommodation more opulent. Where was the money coming from? During one of their 'actions', a spirit commanded Dee to destroy all his precious and irreplaceable scrolls, books and papers, but a few weeks afterwards a mysterious man appeared to Kelley in the garden of their house, who 'mounted up in a pillar of fire'. Dee was called to investigate and three of the books which had been destroyed were found lying there. The mysterious man returned and took Kelley with him. Subsequently Kelley came back with all the other documents which had been destroyed restored and intact. These extraordinary goings-on, the strong suspicion that Dee was a spy, and the political pressure from Rome finally resulted in Dee and Kelley and their families being banished. The 'Great Work' would have to be accomplished elsewhere.

The itinerant magicians next decamped to Trebon Castle, halfway between Vienna and Prague in the region of Hesse-Kassel. Their host there was Count Moritz, whose many influential friends included Vilem Rozmberk, a close advisor to Emperor Rudolf. The emperor was still very interested in Kelley's abilities in alchemy for obvious reasons, but

Rozmberk's interest in the subject was of a more esoteric kind. The 'philosopher's stone' was far more than a mere money-making machine. It was said to confer the secret of eternal youth, and the restoration of fertility to those barren of progeny. Rozmberk, who was without an heir, hoped that the vitalism inherent in the 'philosopher's stone' may assist him in this regard. As Kelley's reputation as an alchemist spread, many rulers pricked up their ears, and the relationship between the master and his scryer changed. Kelley began to feel uncomfortable with the 'angelic conversations', and that he was devoting far too much time to Dee's work when he could be applying his more lucrative alchemical skills in work on behalf of fabulously wealthy patrons. Dee was aware of all this, and desperately needed a replacement for Kelley.

Dee's eldest child, a seven-year-old boy called Arthur, perhaps as a result of the family's Welsh origins, was designated as Kelley's successor. The spirits commanded Kelley to relinquish his role in the angelic conversations and make way for Arthur. Under Dee's supervision the boy did his best, but failed to make progress. Kelley returned and instantly made contact with Madimi, in the presence of the young Arthur. But now, this spirit, once a sweet and innocent child, had grown into a wanton and shameless 'Jezebel'. She pronounced that henceforth the entire Christian moral order was to be set at naught. She revealed herself beneath her gown, sensual and naked, and the young Arthur suddenly swooned and fainted. Madimi, through Kelley, now asked Dee to countenance a procedure so profane, so sinful, that both adult men were horrified. Madimi commanded that Dee and Kelley should become 'wife-swappers'.

Not only was this ultimately sinful, in the prevailing morality of sixteenth-century Europe, but Jane Dee despised Kelley and was repulsed by him, though Kelley was attracted to her. Dee was mortified, but he had never yet disobeyed Madimi, even though Kelley had expressed many times his view that the 'angelic' entities may well be demons in disguise. Madimi explicitly inverted the concept of sin, saying that in God 'all things are possible and permitted' and that Jesus was of no more account than countless other prophets, and unworthy of any special reverence. This mystical antinomianism appalled the men, but to disobey seemed likely to put in jeopardy all the long and arduous work of the last few years, just as the final secret of secrets was about to be revealed. Just as he had obeyed Madimi's instruction to confront the Holy Roman Emperor, Dee felt he had no choice but to obey the spirit. He informed Jane that the couples should be 'cross-matched', as he called it. His wife's distress was evident, but she eventually relented with the proviso that all four should perform the act in one room. She did not trust Kelley alone. To our modern minds this quirky sexual behaviour seems a trifle bizarre, at most, but what was about to be enacted was, in a sixteenth century context, almost satanic. Once this Rubicon had been crossed there could be no going back, for any of the participants, and hellfire and damnation – or the ultimate bliss of divine enlightenment – must be the result. The 'cross-matching' was duly performed.

This sexual and moral iconoclasm resulted in the disintegration of the relationship between Dee and Kelley. Dee was left with a lasting souvenir of the act, however, when Jane gave birth to a child nine months later. Dee named the child Theodorus Trebonianus Dee in honour of the 'ceremony', raising him as his own, but Kelley was almost certainly the father. For Kelley there were immediate practical benefits from the 'working', as acts of ritual sexual magic are called. He was in demand in all the courts of Europe, including England, for his alchemical expertise. Dee's star, meanwhile, was fading, and his noble patrons were abandoning him. He was now over sixty, an old man for that time, and his magical apotheosis had yet to materialise. By contrast, Kelley had managed to produce, or appeared to have produced, large quantities of gold with his red tincture in front of reliable witnesses.

Rozmberk was suborned into recruiting Kelley to work for Emperor Rudolf, who was now convinced of his ability to produce alchemical gold. Kelley became wealthy and titled, but failed to produce gold in sufficient quantities and was imprisoned until this was achieved. Finally, in 1597, Kelley died while trying to escape from his prison, though rumours persisted that he was still alive, having acquired the elixir of life conferred by the 'philosopher's stone' like his alchemical predecessor Nicolas Flamel. Dee and his family returned to England, but the much-promised divine revelation failed to materialise. Now old, poor and out of favour, Dee was heartbroken to find his library and laboratory at Mortlake destroyed by vandals. His reputation at home was unsavoury, if not notorious. In 1608, or possibly early in 1609 (his gravestone was subsequently lost), this master magician died, almost unremarked. Yates sums up his bitter end succinctly: 'The descendant of British kings, creator (or one of the creators) of the British imperial legend, the leader of the Elizabethan renaissance, the mentor of Philip Sydney, the prophet of some far-reaching religious movement, dies, an old man, in bitter neglect and extreme poverty.' His life seems almost a caricature of the ignoble end of all those who 'sell their souls to the Devil', for as the Bible says, 'What shall it profit a man, if he gain the whole world, and lose his own soul? (Mark, 8:36)' The Renaissance magus had 'turned into Faust'.

But Dee left an enduring and very important legacy, as we shall see, and not just in geopolitical terms. The esoteric traditions were passed down from Dee to Francis Bacon, a founding father of the modern scientific method and an early exponent of Rosicrucian doctrines and the ideal of a 'Masonic Christ'. His concept of a 'New Atlantis' and his advocacy of a 'divine child' – that is, the 'Christ-child within' – were to ultimately transform the world in ways which Dee could scarcely have imagined possible. Dee was the original 'Agent 007' as immortalised by Ian Fleming's fictional character 'James Bond', for example. The two zeros represented eyes, and the seven the sacred magical numeral. Fleming was later to become the British intelligence handler for Aleister Crowley, who was to claim that he was Edward Kelley's reincarnation. For Dee, as Benjamin Woolley notes, magic was 'the strange participation, to use Dee's phrase, in which the body and spirit, the natural and the artificial, the real and the imagined were engaged'. This ideal of 'participation' has remained an enduring legacy of Dee's thought for the British magical tradition. The twentieth-century philosopher Owen Barfield used similar terminology in his analysis of human evolutionary consciousness, meaning that this powerful philosophical current retains a vital, and possibly world-changing relevance, even in the twenty-first century.

Meanwhile, religious reformation and dynastic change were about to convulse England. In 1603, King James VI of Scotland succeeded to the throne of England and Ireland as James I. James was said to be 'the wisest fool in Christendom', renowned for his learning and keen intuitive faculty but also given to intense prejudices such as his detestation of tobacco smoking. Another of his pet hates was witches. He was convinced they were a real threat, not only to the prevailing Protestant order but to him personally. He interrogated an alleged witch named Agnes Sampson. After cruel tortures, the poor woman confessed to 'sailing in sieves' with a large company of witches to North Berwick, where they performed a black mass in order to work magic against King James using toad's blood.

A keen Protestant, James exhorted his new English subjects to be especially circumspect in the matter of seeking out witches. From now on, persecution of witches, real or imagined, and the suppression of the more harmless 'cunning folk' was officially sanctioned and had royal approval. The ferment of the Protestant Reformation and the multiplication of heresies and weird sects led to a species of institutional paranoia. Women, whose social status was inferior to that of men, were extremely vulnerable to unfounded and malicious allegations of witchcraft. This witchcraft was not the same as the earlier 'craft' practised in Anglo-Saxon England, but was in effect a heresy of Christianity, whose rituals it aped. As early as 1486 a German professor, Heinrich Kramer (or Institoris), had published the infamous *Malleus Maleficarum* or the 'Hammer of the Witches'. There was and is a deep strain of misogyny within Christianity, and particularly Protestant Christianity. Kramer's intense paranoia and hatred of women was as rabid and vile as Hitler's rants against the Jews:

> The word woman is used to mean the lust of the flesh, as it is said: I have found a woman more bitter than death, and a good woman more subject to carnal lust ... women are more credulous, and since the chief aim of the devil is to corrupt faith, therefore he rather attacks them ... Women are naturally more impressionable ... they have slippery tongues, and are

unable to conceal from their fellow women those things which by evil arts they know ... Women are intellectually like children ... [they] are more carnal than the man, as is clear from their many abominations ... She is an imperfect animal, she always deceives ... [she] is by her nature quicker to waver in her faith, and consequently quicker to abjure her faith, which is the root of witchcraft ... Just as through her first defect in her intelligence they are more likely to abjure the faith, so through the second defect of inordinate affections and passions they search for, brood over, and inflict various vengeances, either by witchcraft or some other means ... Women also have weak memories; and it is a natural vice in them not to be disciplined, but to follow their own impulses without any sense of what is due ... She is a liar by nature ... Let us also consider her gait, posture, and habit, in which is vanity of vanities.[26]

To our modern minds this embittered and vicious propaganda elicits disgust, as it should, but we must not be blind to the motives, whether personal, political or theological, which underpinned the persecution of the witches in the seventeenth century. Much modern discourse on these matters inverts these prejudices, and so mirrors them, in its vitriolic and irrational disdain of Christianity and other Abrahamic faiths. But these unconscious prejudices, and the victimisation, marginalisation and dehumanisation of vulnerable people, they would retort, are, like the poor, always with us. In his *Warrant for Genocide*, Norman Cohn describes vividly how, interrogating captured SS officers implicated in the persecution and extermination of the Jews in the immediate aftermath of the Second World War, he was struck by the similarities between these men and the persecutors of the witches in the seventeenth century. Even today, in the twenty-first-century United Kingdom, hate crimes against foreigners of all kinds, and disabled people – any vulnerable minority, in fact – are becoming more common in the aftermath of the latest economic catastrophe. This, it seems to me, is a strong proof of human wickedness, ignorance and cowardliness, precisely as presented in the scriptures. No amount of progressive liberal education or legislation will eliminate human evil, but if we are to begin to understand these phenomena – and we surely must – then we have to engage honestly with those core beliefs and instincts which have generated and legitimised hate throughout human history.

The Tudor era had been one of astonishing transformation in England. The Protestant Reformation, the Dissolution of the Monasteries, the discovery and colonisation of the 'New Atlantis' and the remarkable reinterpretation of the Arthurian myths to legitimate a British Empire all contributed to a massive transformation of consciousness. To protect Elizabeth from Catholic intrigues and assassination attempts, a secret service, a fraternity known as the Rosicrucians (the Rosy Cross was an ancient symbol used in the 'invisible

---

26 Kramer, H., & Sprenger, J., *Malleus Maleficarum*, Speyer, 1486.

colleges' or mystery schools) was formed. There is reason to believe that the fraternity was founded by John Dee. Yates, in her *The Occult Philosophy in the Elizabethan Age*, states:

> It has been shown that the so-called Rosicrucian Manifestos, published in Germany in the early seventeenth century, are heavily influenced by Dee's philosophy, and that one of them contains a version of the *Monas Heiroglyphica*. The Rosicrucian Manifestos call for a universal reformation of the whole world through Magia and Cabala. The mythical 'Christian Red Cross' (*Christian Rosencreutz*), the opening of whose magical tomb is a signal for the general reformation, may perhaps, in one of his aspects, be a teutonised memory of John Dee and his Christian Cabala, confirming earlier suspicions that 'Christian Cabala' and 'Rosicrucianism' may be synonymous.

Dee was a secret agent of the queen, as was the younger Francis Bacon. In turn Bacon became a secret master of the occult society. He was unquestionably in contact with the spirits, possibly using Dee's 'Angel Magic', but he did not repeat Dee's mistakes. The political and religious currents were too volatile to openly practise magic, and so the society and its individual members became extremely secretive. Bacon gathered around him a network of poets, artists, actors, authors and playwrights such as Jonson, Shakespeare, Raleigh and Spenser. In the space of a generation these men transformed and refined the English language. Bacon has been suggested as the guiding mind behind Shakespeare's plays, or even their author. ('Shake-speare' was an allusion to Pallas Athena, the ancient goddess of wisdom who brandished her spear in the face of ignorance; she is the model for the goddess 'Britannia' on British coins. Shakespeare's plays are packed with Rosicrucian motifs and themes, and Bacon regarded Athena as his personal muse.)

Bacon's researches laid the foundation for the later Royal Society. His intensive study of the ancient mystery traditions, including the Cabbala or esoteric theosophy, led him to believe that it was possible to reverse the Fall of Man, and create the kingdom of heaven on earth. He proclaimed himself the 'Herald of the New Age' as the prophet Elijah had done, and dreamed of establishing a 'New Atlantis' on the American Continent founded on Rosicrucian principles. The secret societies incorporated the burgeoning cult of Freemasonry, which Bacon also pioneered, and many of the founding fathers of the United States of America were Freemasons, including Benjamin Franklin and George Washington. Thomas Jefferson exalted Bacon, along with Isaac Newton and John Locke, as one of his most important intellectual influences. It has also been plausibly suggested that Bacon was the 'love child' of a secret affair between Elizabeth I and Robert Dudley, Earl of Leicester. If so, this clandestine prince, forced to become a 'prince of scholars', was the unacknowledged descendant not merely of Elizabeth, but of Arthur himself.

The country had been torn apart by the Wars of the Roses for most of the century; when Henry Tudor was crowned in 1485, he ruled over a bankrupt, exhausted and divided nation. But now it had been transfigured into a powerhouse of revolutionary innovation and daring exploration. And it had all been achieved by magic, much of it *black* magic. In a sense, England had not just become a Protestant nation, but a Gnostic/Protestant empire. The descendants of the painted savages discovered by Pytheas of Massalia almost 2,000 years before were now to create a new *Britannia*, a 'Giant Albion' whose culture would spread across the entire world. But before the 'New Age' could properly dawn, a blood sacrifice was required. The intellectual, psychological and spiritual changes, the transition to a new consciousness, created deep unease and resentment. Religious, economic and political divisions deepened as the old certainties collapsed, until finally the centre could not hold. England was convulsed by a calamitous and tragic civil war.

13

War in Heaven

All war is tragic, but none more so than civil war – brother against brother, father against son – and especially when blood is shed in the name of the 'Prince of Peace'. But Jesus said, 'I come not to bring peace but a sword' (Matthew, 10:34). True, the old medieval order which had passed away had narrowed the individual, and offered little prospect of material advancement to the vast majority of the population. But it had also provided a sense of security, and a feeling of belonging, of being a member of a tribe or nation – a person's sense of themselves was derived corporately. The Renaissance and then the Protestant Reformation overturned these shibboleths, and a new breed of men emerged, filled with a spirit of initiative and purpose, greedy and ambitious for power. They were wealthy too, but this only went so far.

This new caste of 'upwardly mobile' middle-ranking burghers lived together, and usually worshipped together, in exclusive walled towns and cities, where they established close social and business networks. Although they aspired to greater social status, they resented the old established nobles and members of the royal family who still constituted the members of the royal court. These were still, even in the seventeenth century, almost all descended from the Norman families which had colonised the country after the Battle of Hastings. A myth of the 'Norman Yoke' grew up, to the effect that the 'free people' of England had been enslaved by a callous, brutal Roman Catholic foreigner, William, and 'his armed banditti'. Literacy had spread, and publishers produced thousands of tracts and handbills which were distributed around taverns and theatres, passed from hand to hand. Many of these were of a millenarian or apocalyptic nature, and others were politically radical, even downright seditious. People were obsessed with almanacs, horoscopes, witchcraft and magic of all kinds, and constantly in fear of comets, earthquakes, fire and flood. Beneath the surface of society, in rookeries and courts between vile open sewers and rat-infested alleys, desperate men, women and children lived squalid hopeless lives, as wretched as any on the planet. As this volatile mix came to the boil, a new king,

Charles I, ascended the thrones of Scotland, England and Ireland in 1625. His reign was to end on the scaffold on 30 January 1649.

Charles was diminutive and suffered with a pronounced stammer. He was headstrong and sometimes arrogant. From his father he inherited a belief in the concept known as the 'divine right of kings', which promulgated the idea that kings were appointed to rule by God, and that Parliament should provide merely an advisory function. A canard was rife that Charles was the first king to be crowned wearing white garments – Merlin had foretold of a *rex albus* or 'white king' who would eventually be dethroned. When Charles married a Catholic wife, Henrietta Maria of France, suspicions grew that he was a Catholic himself, and secretly took Mass in her private chapel.

However, our primary concern here lies in the psychological and magical effects of the conflict, not its military details. It was a small passage in *The White Goddess* by Robert Graves which made me begin to think of the war in these terms many years ago:

> The temporary reinstatement of the Thunder-god in effective religious sovereignty during the Commonwealth is the most remarkable event in modern British history: the cause was a mental ferment induced by the King James Bible among the mercantile classes of the great towns and in parts of Scotland and England where Celtic blood ran thinnest. The first Civil War was fought largely between the chivalrous nobility with their retainers and the anti-chivalrous mercantile classes with their artisan supporters. The Anglo-Saxon-Danish south-east was solidly Parliamentarian and the Celtic north-west was solidly Royalist. It was therefore appropriate that at the Battle of Naseby, which decided the war, the rival battle-cries were, for the Parliamentary army, 'God our Strength' and for the Royalist army 'Queen Marie'. Queen Marie was a Catholic and her name evoked the Queen of Heaven and of Love.[27]

Graves was not an historian but a philosopher-poet writing on historical themes, yet I do not think that the statement above is completely devoid of fact. Ultimately, people do not reach for pike and musket and gird their swords because they are inflamed with passions of a merely political or theological nature. To slay one's own neighbours and justify this to oneself, requires a resort to deep-seated archetypes, to submit to an ineluctable tide of emotional self-identification with a cause. As a young man, I was rather ashamed that at least one part of my family had been staunchly Royalist to the extent of aiding the escape of Charles II after the Battle of Worcester. But reading Graves changed all that. More and more I began to see that my heart, as it were, was more powerful than my head. I came to believe, whether rightly or wrongly, that the cheerless fanaticism of the rebels and their

---

27 Graves, R., *The White Goddess*, Faber & Faber, London, 1961 edn.

objective of 'turning the world upside down' was not actually to my taste. In a war between the old and the new, I too would have enlisted to protect the ancient ways – and the Goddess.

A strange tale is told in Worcestershire about Oliver Cromwell, the principal rebel general. The story goes that before the Battle of Worcester on 3 September 1651 Cromwell was supervising the positioning of his siege guns at Perry Wood overlooking the city. He received a mysterious visitor who beckoned him to meet a messenger. A Colonel Lindsay escorted Cromwell into an isolated glade, and to his horror, Lindsay knew all at once the identity of the hooded figure who stood there. The Devil, for it was he, stretched out his hand with a parchment for Cromwell to sign – a Faustian pact. Victory would be his this day, his 'fortunate day' on which he had never yet been beaten, but the price was his soul, which Satan would receive seven years from that day, 3 September 1658. Cromwell haggled, arguing that a term of twenty-one years was the normal arrangement, but the Devil had his way. The terrified Lindsay, in fear for his own soul, deserted the Parliament forces and refused to fight, even though he had hitherto served Cromwell loyally.

A sinister folk tale, no doubt invented by the citizens of Worcester who had little reason to love their 'Lord Protector'. Cromwell used the cathedral there as a stables, almost exactly nine years after rebel troops desecrated the same church on their so-called 'Lord's Day'. But the very fact that such a tale was invented, and is told to this day – the author heard it from a young woman only last year – tells us something of the deranged prejudices and fantasies which had now been unleashed in England, and which still lie deep in the national psyche. Each side, to be sure, thought that the other side were damned servants of the Devil. Each side described the other as 'heretics'. Prince Rupert, the principal Royalist general, was said to be 'shot free', meaning bulletproof, and rode into battle with his white poodle called 'Boy', which the rebel army thought was bewitched. It was rumoured that Rupert was a witch, and that the dog was his 'familiar spirit'. 'Boy' died at the Battle of Marston Moor outside York on 2 July 1644. Things went ill with the Royalist cause after this point.

Parliament's greatest strength was its swift possession of London, which could muster trained bands or militiamen numbering 20,000 men under arms with at least a modicum of military training. The rebels were well equipped with artillery, and many of their officers had served abroad in various campaigns. But London was also home to the most fanatical sectarians, the Anabaptists, many of whom had already infiltrated the Parliamentary army in anticipation of a spiritual revolution which would be evinced by the overthrow of the 'papist' Charles, followed by the coming in glory of Christ himself who would reign in splendour over a world transfigured into an earthly paradise. The king and all his ministers were all irredeemably corrupted by 'the world'. All forms of religious and moral compunction were to be rejected, and all worldly authority, especially kings and bishops, utterly eschewed.

In principle the Anabaptists were profoundly pacifist, but a myriad of other sects and heresies took their lead from the Anabaptist insistence on personal liberty of conscience. Many of these were more overtly militant, supporting physical violence in pursuit of the revolution, and even more profound in their rejection of the old order. Their Christian beliefs were often so radical that they departed entirely from traditional scriptural authority. Indeed, one group, the 'Ranters', often desecrated Bibles and suggested their use as lavatory paper, or offered Bibles for sale in taverns for a jug of ale. There was a resurgence in the national consciousness of that most pernicious British heresy, Pelagianism, the notion that there is no such thing as 'original sin'. This implied the corollary, that it was legitimate for those who had rejected corrupt worldly authority in the name of the spirit to sin as they pleased – a licence for wantonness and libertinism.

In 1534, the Anabaptists had taken control of the German city of Munster using force. For sixteen bizarre months the German town was redesignated as the 'New Jerusalem'. John of Leiden named himself the heir to King David and declared a state of pure communism. Polygamy was introduced, and John took sixteen wives, beheading one woman who refused to marry him. The anarchy was eventually extinguished, but this example of the most extreme form of radical Protestantism appalled all traditional ecclesiastical authorities. When Munster fell, all those who resisted were put to the sword. This affair represents the extreme end of the spectrum, but for those most marginalised and powerless in society the Anabaptist ideal of an earthly commune with no king but Christ following the *Parousia*, or Second Coming, retained its mystique. For those with a vested interest in maintaining a form of authority and order in the world, however, the extreme radicalism could only constitute a dangerous, even terminal threat.

The Battle of Powick Bridge on 23 September 1642, fought near the same fields where the Battle of Worcester was fought nine years later, was the first skirmish of the war, and a minor Royalist victory. But blood will come from blood, and madness from madness. Many Englishmen were now prepared to reject the institutions and hallowed doctrines of their forefathers, the monarchy and ecclesiastical authority. Indeed, there were those who rejected the claims of religion altogether, the pioneers of our modern apostasy.

Graves was correct in his intuition that the Parliamentary cause was a 'temporary restoration of the Thunder-god'. Misogyny was inherent in Christianity as a whole, as it was in other religions of the Middle East. The decline of the Christian Church in the West may be attributed in large part to its expulsion of the feminine principle from the deity; the reaction to this – the emergence of charismatic female religious leaders such as Joanna Southcott, a Devonshire prophetess, or later Madame Helena Petrovna Blavatsky, for example – drained away much popular support from the conventional churches.

Often, too, the esoteric beliefs and magical thinking behind the rival sects distorted Christian doctrine. Christianity has always found it difficult to reconcile the ambivalence in the nature of woman, that same difficulty encountered by the male Tantrik aspirant who must learn to love the creative and destructive aspects of the Goddess equally. But in Christianity, especially so after Protestantism, women were either saints or sinners. Their concept of God could not entirely encompass the female principle, or the principle of evil. This was the mainspring of the tradition of courtly love, which was a belated attempt to reincorporate female spirituality within the Christian tradition. The fantasy of the pure, chaste, idealised woman and the increasing veneration offered up to the Virgin Mary in the medieval period propitiated two of the three aspects of the female principle: the maiden or virgin and the mother. But the third, negative female aspect was not integrated – that of the destroyer, the malefactor, the hag. Consequently, all the hatred malice and loathing which people unconsciously felt towards the negative female principle was conflated with hatred of the Devil, whose absolute evil disbarred him also. Psychologically speaking, these feelings of loathing, contempt and hatred were projected onto scapegoats, in the shape of old, lonely, poor, unattractive or deformed women, whose other problems were now compounded by the fact that any communal or personal misfortune could be laid at their door. The 'witch craze' was about to reach its grim climax.

Resentment, contempt and hatred were not just projected onto witches. One of the main tenets of Calvinism (John Calvin had been one of the main proponents of the Protestant Reformation) was the *inequality* of man. Only an elect, predestined few will be saved – those practising Calvinist principles. The vast majority, however, are and always were destined to be consigned to eternal damnation. The implications of this philosophy have been violent and tragic over the five centuries which have passed since it was first propounded. Calvin identified particular virtues which marked out the chosen folk of God. They must be modest, just, moderate and pious. God has already selected his chosen, and nothing a man can do can alter that, but it is by their continual unrelenting effort and labour that the world shall know them as God's chosen people. Erich Fromm describes how this psychological compensation, really a kind of mental illness, gave rise to the underpinning drive of modern Western civilisation, the 'Protestant work ethic':

Effort and work in this sense assumed an entirely irrational character. They were not to change fate since this was predetermined by God, regardless of any effort on the part of the individual. They served only as a means of forecasting the predetermined fate; while at the same time the frantic effort was a reassurance against an otherwise unbearable feeling of powerlessness ... This new attitude towards effort and work as an aim in itself may be assumed to be the most important psychological change which has happened to man since the end of the Middle Ages ... What was new in modern society was that men came to be driven to work not so much by external pressure but by an internal compulsion, which made them work as only a very strict master could have made people do in other societies.[28]

Man had become his own slave driver, and perhaps we see in this perverse logic an origin for the modern media misrepresentations of the unemployed and the disabled mentioned before. Fromm goes on to remark upon the intense feelings of hostility and resentment felt by the Calvinistic Protestants towards those in the upper class, feelings they were obliged to repress – not only because they violated Calvin's four cardinal virtues but because Calvinists, too, had a vested interest in maintaining the emergent capitalist order. This pent-up resentment, Fromm argues, expressed itself as an 'all-pervading hostility' which 'pervaded the whole personality'. Their idea of a despotic, vengeful God, 'who wants unrestricted power over men and their submission and humiliation, was the projection of the middle-class's own hostility and envy'.

The Calvinists' moral indignation, however, was not just projected downwards, onto the allegedly feckless, idle or unfit, but also upwards, onto the equally idle upper class and its wasteful decadence and immorality. Attitudes such as this formed the underpinning moral atmosphere of the 'New Model Army' and the Parliamentarian cause. But the rebels were an alliance of two wings, one Presbyterian or Calvinist and the other more influenced by Baptists, Quakers and other 'Independents'. It was among these latter sects that radical ideas emerged which prefigured modern socialism, for example.

Into this heady mix of millenarianism and expectancy of a divine dispensation which would enrapture God's elect and transform the world, older spiritual elements supervened. Bernard Capp, in his chapter on the 'Fifth Monarchy Men' in *Radical Religion in the English Revolution*, alludes to the popular superstitions which contributed to extreme radical sectarianism:

Many of the prophesies circulating in the 1640s sprang from non-biblical sources, of which astrology was by far the most important. It was generally accepted in Europe that the stars were God's instruments and contained a key to the future, and the traditional link between astrology and the Apocalypse survived the Reformation little changed. Heated speculation on the conjunction between Saturn and Jupiter in 1583 produced assertions that the Last Judgement was at hand. A total eclipse of the sun predicted for 29 March 1652, 'Black Monday', aroused still more excitement. Many pamphleteers announced the end of the world, while others, including William Lilly, the most famous astrologer of the day, prophesied upheavals leading to a final, millennial age ... A series of Bloody Almanacks publicized

---

28 Fromm, E., *The Fear of Freedom*, Routledge, London, 1995 edn.

Napier's claim that Judgement Day was at hand and added an endorsement from a leading astrologer, John Booker. Distinctions between biblical and non-biblical prophesy became blurred, and even the Fifth Monarchist John Rogers was willing to use the prophesies of Nostradamus.[29]

In an agricultural society with limited literacy, almanacs and astrological tracts were the 'best-sellers' for the emerging publishing industry. In most rural households the entire library would consist of a family Bible and a host of such pamphlets, whose word was as unimpeachable as holy writ. Just as in our own times, sensationalism sold, and the last days were confidently expected. The ancient prophesies of Merlin were rediscovered, alongside alleged predictions of 'Old Mother Shipton', a soothsayer from North Yorkshire. Her vaticinations were almost a century old but were only finally published in 1641. Although she did not predict the end times in her lifetime, her sayings were conflated with other more apocalyptic tracts and chapbooks, giving the impression that the present troubles of England had long been foreseen by the wise.

One of the consequences of this religious and psychological ferment was a strong sense of English exceptionalism. The war became seen as a prelude to a worldwide revolution in consciousness, which the blood sacrifice of the struggle against Anti-Christ, in the shape of the king, would usher in. The New Model Army was seen as God's instrument to throw down papist domination, whether at home or overseas. John Rogers, a Fifth Monarchist preacher from Essex, declared that 'the blade of that sword which is presently held in England will reach to the very gates of Rome ere long'. It was envisaged that once a truly godly regime had been established in England, the 'Beast and Whore' would be overthrown in Continental Europe, with English troops as the vanguard. A Protestant Charlemagne was expected, who, like Arthur, would lead the soldiers of Britain against Rome, and liberate the world from the foul doctrines of popery. Cromwell was seen as he who had been sent to redeem the subjugated English people from the power of the 'Norman Yoke', 'Oliver the Conqueror'. Milton, the poet of the Puritan Revolution, envisaged the English as God's chosen, a 'Puritan occultism', and planned an epic poem on the theme of the Arthurian myths, which eventually transformed into *Paradise Lost*. He was the heir to Dee's Christian Cabala via its revival under the Rosicrucian Robert Fludd. From them Milton inherited the concept of England having a special messianic role – an idea which was a profound influence on William Blake's imaginative system. Such notions played into the incipient fanaticism of the radicalised Commonwealth army, and became a major contributory factor in the appalling cruelties inflicted upon the Irish during Cromwell's campaigns.

---

29 Capp, B., 'Popular Millenarianism' in McGregor, J. F. & Reay, B., (eds), *Radical Religion in the English Revolution*, Oxford University Press, Oxford, 1986.

The privations and depredations of war set the common people dreaming of an Arcadian utopia, much like the 'Land of Cockaigne' imagined by the medieval rural peasantry, where the harvest would be gathered endlessly without toil, sensual pleasures would be enjoyed openly and without restriction, and all compulsory authority overturned. This wish fulfilment was a natural reaction to the asceticism which was the daily lot of the rural peasantry, but the 'Age of Spirit' envisaged for the post-revolution Commonwealth went beyond even these fantasies. It was to be an earthly paradise where 'the Lion lay down with the Lamb'. A Ranter preacher, George Foster, claimed to his hearers that 'you shall be as so many kings and princes that shall reign here on the earth, every one of you no less than a king', and that the 'sons and daughters of Sion shall have of the best, they shall eat and drink of the best, and wear of the best'. When Christ came to rule in majesty, wrote John Fenwick in his *Zion's Joy in her King* of 1643, men of a 'wolvish, ravening, lionish, raging spirit' would become docile and peaceful. Others thought that the nature of carnivorous beasts would be changed, and that the lion would eat straw like the ox. Mankind would at last be freed from the curses of age, disease and death. Some even went so far as to claim that when the godly kingdom was established, all would become immortal.

Nor would there be any economic oppression. Taxes and rents would cease, and the insecurities and burdens of the old order would be abolished, along with private property, from which all exploitation and oppression sprang. In the context of these disturbed times these hopes and dreams of the uneducated poor may be excused, but there was also another strand of thought – that of outright atheism and irreligion. Many radicals thought that religion was 'a mere fiction' or 'fable' designed to 'keep the baser sort in fear'.

This sentiment was by no means new. As early as 1593, a Dorset cobbler declared that 'hell is no more than poverty and penury in this world; and heaven is no other but to be rich and enjoy pleasures; and that we die like beasts and when we are gone there is no more remembrance of us'. The antinomian Ranters believed it more lawful to 'sit drinking in an ale-house' than to go to church. Another cobbler (for some reason this trade was a magnet for radicalism) believed 'money, good clothes, good meat and drink, tobacco and merry company to be gods; but he was little beholden to any of these; for his God allowed him but 8 pence or 10 pence a day, and *that* he made him work for'. Christopher Hill, in his chapter entitled 'Irreligion in the "Puritan" Revolution' in *Radical Religion in the English Revolution*, reminds us that the Ranters Abiezer Coppe and Laurence Clarkson 'defended from the pulpit the view that adultery, drunkenness, swearing, theft, could be as holy and virtuous as prayer. Sin existed only in the imagination.'

As the revolutionary fervour intensified, there was a multiplication of unorthodox heresies and sects – Ranters, Diggers, Levellers, Familists, Seekers, Quakers, General and Particular Baptists, Socinians and Muggletonians, the latter named after Lodowicke Muggleton, a London tailor who believed that he and his cousin John Reeve were the two witnesses written of in the Book of Revelation (11:3) who would 'prophesy for 1,260 days dressed in sack cloth'. This tiny sect endured until the death of its last member in 1979. All these questioning sects, whether thoughtful and serious enquirers after truth or libertine 'fanaticks', promoted a general decline in belief in supernatural and super-sensible experience. The Puritan divine Richard Baxter thought that the 'horrid villanies' of these sects were promoted by secret agents of the Jesuits, with the specific aim of discrediting the true ministry of Christ.

However they emerged, these strands of Nonconformist and atheist thought remained strong, especially among the artisans of London and other large industrial and commercial towns. The proto-socialism of the Levellers and Gerrard Winstanley's 'Diggers', agrarian communists, planted the seeds of the modern British Labour movement. For the Levellers, 'false religion' was, to quote Brian Manning, 'a cloak for class interests' and disguised from the people their true interests or 'true religion'. All this had a secularising effect on the common people which corroded traditional religious certainties, and legitimised anti-clericalism or atheism on grounds of 'liberty of conscience'. But as these revolutionary creeds took root, other unconscious hatreds and prejudices were about to be unleashed.

Matthew Hopkins, the infamous self-styled 'Witchfinder General', was born in Suffolk in 1620. In March 1644 he and his associate John Stearne set out on a 'crusade' against witchcraft. In fourteen terrible months they sent 300 women to the gallows. Women were stripped naked and searched by the enthusiastic Stearne for 'witch's marks' or 'secret teats' which they used to suckle their familiar spirits or imps. The accused were 'pricked', starved, deprived of sleep and subjected to 'swimming', where they were immersed in water. If they floated they were deemed guilty and hanged, but if they sank, they were innocent – though they frequently drowned in the process. He swore on oath that he had frequently witnessed witches conversing with cats, dogs, mice, moles and squirrels, with exotic-sounding names such as 'Sacke & Sugar', 'Griezzell Greedigutt', 'Pyewackett' or 'Ilemauzar'. No one was safe once they had been denounced. Even a respectable clergyman, John Lowes, was accused of sinking a ship using a magical spell.

Hopkins wrote an account of his activities entitled *The Discovery of Witches*, saying his 'commission' began after he eavesdropped on an alleged conversation between members of a witch coven in his home town of Manningtree in Essex, where the women revealed they had made infernal pacts. He was very strongly influenced by King James I's *Daemonologie*, written in 1597, which presented the witches as a worldwide conspiracy of malefactors, mainly women, who made pacts with the Devil. Another influence was the money on offer. Hopkins and his confederates were well remunerated for their work. The moral insecurity and turmoil of the war provided a cover for his efforts, and his activities were concentrated in areas of East Anglia and the south-east with strong Parliamentarian sympathies, which were likely to be more credulous.

His excesses were so brutal, and the accused executed so numerous, that suspicion was aroused, and he was rumoured to be a witch himself. His campaign stalled towards the end of 1646, and the following year he died of tuberculosis. A rumour spread that he had been subjected to a 'swimming' himself and contracted pneumonia as a result. Although almost all his victims were innocent, some came forward to confess of their own free will, under the delusion that they were in league with infernal powers.

That other famous man who allegedly made a satanic pact, Cromwell, was meanwhile in the ascendancy. By the spring of 1644 he had risen to the rank of lieutenant-general leading a regiment of 1,500 cavalry. Nicknamed 'Ironside' by the Royalists, he had a reputation as a strict disciplinarian. After the death of John Pym in December 1643 he was the natural choice as the main Parliamentary commander, but many moderate Puritans opposed his elevation. He constantly schemed against his fellow officers, and despite being technically forbidden to hold a commission by the terms of the 'Self-Denying Ordinance' he was given command of the cavalry regiments of the New Model Army.

It was Cromwell's success at the Battle of Naseby on 14 June 1645 which quickly consolidated his position. The king's forces were thoroughly routed, being heavily outnumbered and Charles was effectively doomed. After the fall of Bristol, the main Royalist port, Charles decided to leave Oxford, his temporary capital, on 27 March 1646. He still entertained hopes that he may be able to take advantage of the split between Presbyterians and Independents, and come to terms with those of more moderate views. Oxford fell soon afterwards. Charles surrendered himself to the Scottish army, all of whom were strong Presbyterians. The Scots immediately gave him up to the English Parliament. Charles seemed insouciant about his recent defeat, and remained stubborn in his refusal to countenance an English Church organized along Presbyterian lines, as was Parliament's desire.

Cromwell had fondly hoped for a baronetcy as the price for his acquiescence in the restoration of Charles, but the king's obduracy, and the increasing militancy of the hard-line radicals in the army, prevented any significant progress in the negotiations. The Independent army regiments, packed with Levellers and other extremists, were still under arms, but had rarely been paid since hostilities had ceased. It became clear to Parliament that no accommodation with Charles could be accomplished while Cromwell remained in command, and a plot was hatched to have him arrested. Cromwell struck first.

On 5 June 1647 a young officer, Cornet Joyce, arrived to arrest Charles, who for the first time began to suspect the deadly danger he was in. He asked by what commission Joyce acted, and the cornet gestured through the window, pointing to a line of fully armed cavalry arrayed in the grounds of the house. Charles remarked, 'It is as fair a commission, and as well written, as I have seen in my life.' From that moment Charles was in dire peril, but would the English people really leave him to his fate? Did they really possess the resolve necessary to break with centuries of hallowed tradition, the ruthless will to kill an anointed king, the terrible crime of regicide?

In August 1647 the army escorted Charles to London in a show of strength designed to overawe Parliament. Charles was confined at Hampton Court, but in November he escaped to Carisbrooke Castle on the Isle of Wight. He hoped that the Parliamentarian commander there, Colonel Robert Hammond, might be sympathetic to his cause, but Hammond was too cautious. Charles was 'close confined' at the castle, but could still communicate with the outside world by smuggling out letters with his chambermaid. He attempted to escape, but the bars on the windows of his room prevented his squeezing through. Another attempt was made after the bars had been treated with a solution of nitric acid, but his guards became suspicious and this attempt failed as well. Letters had been sent to the Scots, encouraging them to invade. The Duke of Hamilton led a Scottish army as far as Preston, but in August 1648 the Scots and a few diehard Lancashire Royalists who had joined them were defeated by Cromwell.

The army were now firmly in control and resolved that 'it was their duty, if ever the Lord brought them back in peace, to call Charles Stuart, that man of blood, to account for all the blood he had shed and the mischief he had done'. Royalist risings in Wales, the northern borders, Essex and Kent were soon put down, and a mutiny in the fleet crushed. These insurrections undoubtedly had some support within Parliament itself; on 6 December 1648, Colonel Thomas Pride entered Parliament and arrested 101 members thought to have colluded with the king, in what became known as 'Pride's Purge'. The remaining members, the so-called 'Rump', could do nothing to prevent Cromwell from arraigning the king before a High Court with or without parliamentary approval. He famously declared, 'I tell you we will cut off his head with the crown upon it.'

A show trial took place in Westminster Hall. Charles refused to recognise the authority of the court, and offered no defence. Troops were on duty in the court with orders to open fire on anyone who protested at this travesty of justice. The outcome was a foregone conclusion, and under the circumstances it is remarkable that nine of the sixty-eight members of the commons selected to sit at the trial refused to sign the king's death warrant. The trial lasted a week, and Charles was obstinate and unyielding to the last.

The unthinkable now became a grim reality. The execution was scheduled for Tuesday 30 January 1649. The weather was dreadfully cold, and so Charles requested to put on two shirts, lest his shivering be misinterpreted as fear. He was accompanied to the scaffold in Whitehall by William Juxon, Bishop of London. Despite the freezing weather, a large crowd had gathered. Charles remained stubborn to the end, declaring:

As for the people, truly I desire their liberty and freedom as much as anybody whatsoever; but I must tell you that their liberty and freedom consists in having government, those laws by which their lives and goods may be their own. It is not their having a share in the government, that is nothing appertaining to them. A subject and a sovereign are clean different things; and therefore until you do that – I mean put the people in that liberty – they will never enjoy themselves.

As he stood before the block he addressed the gathered crowd: 'I go from a corruptible to an incorruptible Crown, where no disturbance can be, no disturbance in the World.' After the axe fell, and the body was removed, many people came forward to dip their handkerchiefs and scarves in the royal blood; it was still believed to possess magical properties. The ancient fertility oblation of the 'Killing of the King' had been performed, but would the land be fructified by the shedding of his blood?

Cromwell became an effective dictator, and, like so many other usurpers, soon became a bloody tyrant. In May 1649 a rebellion by Levellers within the army was crushed, and three randomly selected soldiers were taken out into the churchyard at Burford in Oxfordshire and publicly executed. Cromwell remarked, 'You have no other way to treat these people but to break them in pieces; if you do not break them they will break you.' The rebels had mutinied because of rumours that they were to be redeployed to Ireland. Cromwell's invasion of Ireland and his infamous massacre of the citizens of Drogheda and Wexford meant that he was detained in that country from August 1649 until 1653. Parliament used his absence to reassert its authority, but on his return Cromwell entered Parliament and addressed them. At first his manner seemed conciliatory, but gradually his demeanour darkened, until in rising fury he denounced them: 'You are no Parliament; I say you are no Parliament. I will put an end to your prating!' The doors of the chamber opened, and a party of musketeers entered, removing the speaker from his chair. Cromwell gestured towards the mace, the symbol of Parliamentary authority, instructing the soldiers to 'remove that bauble'. In 1653 Cromwell declined the offer of the crown, preferring the title of 'Lord Protector'. England was now under the heel of a military dictatorship.

Unquestionably Cromwell's iron rule gave England a degree of stability at home and a military prestige abroad, which ultimately benefited the nation, but his protectorate was very far from being a 'Merry England'. It was a joyless time for the common people. Christmas was abolished and dancing proscribed, for example, and Cromwell survived many attempts on his life. It is a common misconception that Cromwell was responsible for the return of the Jews to England. An edict of Edward I in 1290 had ordered all Jews to leave his realms, and it is quite true that Cromwell desired the return of the Jews, because as a Puritan he identified strongly with Old Testament prophesy. He was aware of the Jewish prophesy that the Messiah would come only when the Jewish people had been dispersed to the remotest parts of the Earth, which he took to mean England. Puritans like Cromwell shared a common expectancy of the coming (or second coming) of the Messiah with the Jews. Some extremist English Puritans left England to live among the Jewish enclave in Amsterdam where they actually converted to Judaism. But Cromwell was in fact forced to shelve his project for allowing Jewish settlements, and it was Charles II who quietly allowed their immigration in the early years of his reign.

On 3 September 1658 Cromwell died, perhaps in accordance with his alleged unholy pact. John Evelyn's diary recorded, 'It was the joyfullest funeral I ever saw; for there were none cried but the dogs, which the soldiers hooted away with a barbarous noise drinking and taking tobacco in the streets as they went.' He was succeeded by his son, Richard, as 'Lord Protector' but he resigned after only eight months. By now the common people hated the rule of the army and only awaited a signal to rise in support of Charles, son of the executed king. On 2 January 1660 General Monck led a Scottish army into England which reached London on 3 February. Parliament was recalled and on 8 May Charles was proclaimed as King Charles II. A desultory uprising led by Thomas Venner, a London cooper and a fanatical Fifth Monarchist, took place in 1661 with the aim of frustrating the Restoration, but this failed miserably. The English experiment with revolutionary politics was over. The Messianic hopes of both the Puritans and the Jews were unfulfilled, and a new age of science, rationalism and utilitarianism had begun, exemplified by the foundation of the Royal Society in 1660. The crystal stream of occult knowledge must perforce flow underground.

Charles II, 'Old Rowley' as he became known, ruled with financial assistance from Louis XIV of France, having secretly promised he would convert to Roman Catholicism at a propitious moment. He was obliged, however, to submit to the 'Clarendon Code', by which the Church of England was re-established as the 'national' religion. Although Charles had no legitimate heirs, his illegitimate children were so numerous that he was ironically dubbed 'the father of his people'. The days of Puritanism were now well and truly over, as the king openly cavorted with a succession of courtesans and demi-mondaines. His twenty-five-year reign was an uneasy truce between the former warring factions, but when his brother James, Duke of York, converted to Roman Catholicism, and Charles favoured him as his heir in preference to his illegitimate son James, Duke of Monmouth, a constitutional crisis would reprise the previous hostilities.

In 1681 Charles decided to dissolve Parliament. Two new factions emerged: the 'Tories', who supported the Duke of York, and the 'Whigs', who supported the Duke of Monmouth's succession. 'Tory' was originally an Irish term referring to mythical sea pirates who came ashore to ravage and pillage the land. A 'Whig' was a similar Scottish term for a border cattle rustler. When Charles died in February 1685, the old hostilities recommenced.

Monmouth made a surprise landing in Dorset and marched into Somerset, where at Taunton he proclaimed himself king. Though he had an army of at least 4,000, the Monmouth rebellion was crushed at the Battle of Sedgemoor on 6 July 1685, the last major battle to be fought on English soil. A terrible retribution was exacted on the people of the south-west by the infamous 'hanging judge' Lord Chief Justice George Jeffreys. Monmouth himself died in some style. He was executed at the Tower of London, famously offering the axeman 6 golden guineas before the decapitation, with another 6 to follow if he did his job efficiently. He promised that if the axeman botched the job, he would 'look him in the face'. When the first blow fell and failed, Monmouth was as good as his word, staring at the poor fellow and extending his hand to feel the blunt blade of the axe. It took five blows in all to decapitate him.

James II proved a king every bit as obstinate and arrogant as his father had been. He intended to restore the Roman Catholic faith, and petitioned Parliament to allow him a professional standing army of 15,000 men. The Whigs were outraged and secretly conspired to invite the Protestant William of Orange, the Dutch husband of Mary, James II's daughter, to invade England and depose the king. In 1690, at the Battle of the Boyne in Ireland, James II was decisively beaten. After forty-eight years, the wars of religion were finally over. William and Mary ruled as joint sovereigns over a Protestant nation, the so-called 'Glorious Revolution'. But the long and bitter struggles had left their mark on the English national psyche, scars which still endure to this day. In Ireland the ramifications of the conflict reverberated until the late twentieth century, and even now the deep religious divisions persist.

14

Romanticism and Resistance

One of the men who supported the Royalist cause during the civil wars was 'Dud' Dudley, the illegitimate son of Lord Dudley. The area around Dudley had been gradually denuded of woodland as the local charcoal burners spread out into the little villages beyond, cutting down the oaks and beech trees. The wars had greatly increased the demand for iron, and Dud's family owned large ironworks at Pensnett Chase. When Dud returned from studying at Balliol College in Oxford in 1618, his father put the bright young man in charge of these works. He immediately saw the potential solution to the problem of producing enough charcoal, which was to use 'pit-coal' instead. All over the region, a thick 30-foot seam of coal, the largest in England, was exposed, which local people accessed by digging drift mines into the slopes of the hills. This was then converted into coke, and this ingenious process received a royal patent in 1621 after the iron was tested and found to be of sufficiently good quality. Unfortunately Dud's works at Cradley were destroyed in one of the frequent floods which supervene on the River Stour. Another works, at Sedgley, was wrecked by a mob induced to attack it by his local rivals.

The Dudley family were out of favour during the Commonwealth, but on the very day Charles II returned to England Dud sent a petition to the king, reasoning that the restored monarch would be willing to support such a potentially lucrative enterprise. However, Charles was too busy with his courtesans to pay much attention to this new industry. Dud then wrote a book, *Metallum Martis* (1665), which purported to reveal the secret of smelting iron with coal, but teasingly failed to reveal the main process, only saying that he had done it at four different sites. He died in 1684 aged eighty-five. His tomb in Worcester is engraved with alchemical motifs and astrological symbols. Many people dismissed Dud's claims, and he faded from memory, but a Black Country historian, Carl Higgs,[30] has proven that

---

30 Dudley, D. & Darby, A., *Forging New Links*, The Black Country Society, 2012.

Abraham Darby, the man first credited by history with smelting iron with coal, at Coalbrookdale in Shropshire in 1709, was a descendant of Dud Dudley. Darby was a Dudley man, and it is possible Dud's secret was passed down through the family to him. The details are tantalisingly mysterious, but the outcome was to change world history. On these bleak uplands of South Staffordshire, and in the wooded vales of North Worcestershire, the 'Industrial Revolution' had begun.

One of Dud Dudley's contemporaries was Richard 'Fiddler' Foley. Foley was a pioneer of 'industrial espionage', if local folklore is to be believed. He travelled to Sweden disguised as a wandering musician. With a fiddle he had purchased in Dudley he entertained the workers at a revolutionary slitting mill which slit iron bars into thin rods for making nails. The Swedish plant was water-powered, and Foley memorised the details of the whole operation. On his return he obtained a lease on Dud Dudley's former works at Hyde near Kinver in Staffordshire. The slitting mill he built there was a great success, and soon the Stour Valley became a nexus for a thriving and lucrative (for the owners) nail-making industry. The conditions of the nail makers and their families were an affront to human decency. The criminal exploitation of the nail factors reduced the local people to iniquitous poverty and squalor unequalled anywhere, and the workers became so brutalised that they reverted to savagery. A Doctor Ballenden of Sedgley in 1868 described the industrial communities as 'the most immoral people in England'. He said that during thirty years of practice there he had frequently seen the women of the region besting their feckless menfolk in brutal drunken affrays.

These early experiments in industrial exploitation are a source of immense pride for the people of the 'Black Country', as the area around Dudley and Wolverhampton became known, but the sentimentality of hindsight should not obscure the grim reality of this disgraceful slavery. There were riots and on one occasion artillery was deployed in Dudley and the local yeomanry cavalry mustered. By the nineteenth century the entire region was a terrible swart-blackened wasteland, with perpetually burning pit fires and fiery blast furnaces continually belching smoke and steam. The 'cuts', or canals, threaded through the flame and stench like 'bleeding veins' according to Elihu Burritt, the American consul in Birmingham. He described the view from Dudley's ancient castle as 'the sublimest battle scene on earth'. Perhaps he heard the local rhyme:

> When Satan stood at Brierley Hill
> And all around him gazed,
> He said 'I never more shall be
> At Hell's bright flames amazed.'

Burritt was among the first to describe the region as 'the Black Country'. The actual title of his book was *Walks in the Black Country and Its Green*

Borderland, but it was the dark region which passed into myth. As Edward Chitham says in his *The Black Country*, it was Charles Dickens, in his *The Old Curiosity Shop*, who called it a 'black region ... where not a blade of grass was seen to grow, where not a bud put forth its promise of spring, where nothing green could live but on the surface of a stagnant pool'. All over England, and in Wales and Scotland too, once peaceful 'green borderlands' were being despoiled, exploited, polluted and raped of their natural resources. Vast fortunes were made for the few who owned the industrial infrastructure and profited from the sale of manufactured goods, but for the vast majority, the 'white slaves' of the industrial cities, the once idyllic landscape had been transformed into a hellish wilderness, a terrible exploitative machine which ground down both body and soul.

Nobler spirits refused to avert their eyes from the pitiless suffering of the poor. The poet William Shenstone refused to report a poacher he caught in the act when he heard the poor man's awful circumstances. He had a wife and five children, all of whom would starve while he was imprisoned. Such fine sentiments were rare enough, but they were growing. Shenstone was not the only poet whose heart was moved by the plight of the industrial working class, as an emotional and intellectual reaction against the grinding materialism of the age set in.

By the terms of the Acts of Union of 1706 and 1707, Scotland and England were united into 'Great Britain'. The newly combined state stood in need of a reconstituted history, a unifying myth which could reinvent the nobility and grandeur of the Ancient Britons, a fresh take on the magical history of the island as a whole. Two colonial models suggested the means by which this could be achieved – North America with its 'Noble Savages', and the Irish Celts. Stuart Piggott, in his *The Druids*, points to the implications of the romantic turn for the rediscovery of the Druids:

The discovery of the American Indians played its part in the development of a hard primitivism with regards to Ancient Britons and their religion, but although in fact the Elizabethans had met early Celtic society face-to-face in Ireland, the implications of this for a view of the world of the Druids in pre-Roman Britain or Gaul were not appreciated. Hard primitivism can perhaps be seen as an outcome of the mood of national confidence in the contemporary ethos; the psychological need for a past containing Noble Savages, Golden Ages, and primitive untutored intimations of immortality as part of Great Nature's simple plans, seemingly not felt by the Elizabethan and succeeding generations, came perhaps with a changed attitude of personal or social doubt and unease. From the middle of the eighteenth century it seems to have been increasingly felt by many that the rules of taste and the Age of Reason did not provide wholly adequate and inevitably satisfying standards for thought and emotion, and with the distrust of the ultimate validity of the doctrines of the Enlightenment, an alternative mood, emotive and romantic, seemed once more appropriate for the contemplation of the remote past. With this swing of mood, the accommodating Druids could change their character and take on a suitably romantic cast of countenance.

From such a perspective the Druids had been 'virtuous sages' in the mould of the Old Testament patriarchs, and even 'proleptically Christians'. Such an august body of men must surely have erected gigantic monuments and temples, and it was widely conjectured, especially by such antiquaries as John Aubrey and William Stukeley, that Stonehenge and similar megalithic monuments were, in fact, Druidic temples. The need for a spiritual grounding in a primordial and incorruptible religion was acute. The spiritual fracturing and sectarianism of the civil wars, and the rise of self-proclaimed prophets such as Joanna Southcott and John Wroe, had the effect of making people yearn for a 'true' religion, or 'Natural Religion' whose claims were universal and intrinsic. Stukeley proposed that the Druids had arrived in Britain shortly after Noah's flood where they introduced a 'Patriarchal Religion' which prefigured later Christianity. But it was not just in England that the Druids were being rediscovered.

A classically educated Welsh clergyman named Henry Rowlands made a specific link between Druids and cromlechs or stone circles on his home island of Anglesey in his *Mona Antiqua Restaurata* of 1723, at about the same time that William Stukeley began surveying Stonehenge, researches which culminated in his own book, *The History of the Temples of the Ancient Celts*. Stukeley also entered Holy Orders in 1729, and one of the motives behind his antiquarian research was to 'combat the deists from an unexpected quarter, and to preserve so noble a monument of our ancestors' piety, I may add, orthodoxy'. Deism, the belief in a 'Supreme Being' or 'Grand Architect', was a reprise of the 'natural' religion apprehended by gnosis we have encountered in earlier chapters. The Protestant Reformation led to a revolution in science. Orthodox Christianity permitted the study of only three pre-Christian philosophies, those of Plato, Aristotle, and 'Hermes Trismegistus'. But Aristotle's conceptions of science were predicated on both mathematics and magic. Mathematics, though tolerated, had always been treated with suspicion by the Catholic authorities, but magic was beyond the pale. To be a magician was to put oneself in opposition to holy writ and in danger of eternal damnation.

There was a reaction against Christianity exemplified by the writings of Voltaire. Voltaire was an acquaintance of the political philosopher Jean-Jacques Rousseau. The son of a Calvinist preacher from Geneva, Rousseau proposed a 'social contract'. According to this theory:

> If one removes from the social contract all that is not essential, one finds that it is reduced to the following terms: Each one of us jointly places his person and all his ability under the supreme direction of the general will;

and we receive in our body each member as an indivisible part of the whole. This act of association results in a moral and collective body ... this public person formed thus by the union of all the others was previously known as the City and now takes the name of Republic or body politic ... As for its members they are known collectively as The People, calling themselves in particular citizens as participants in the sovereign authority of the republic, and subjects in submission to the laws of the State.[31]

Sentimental and insecure by temperament, Rousseau's utopian political ideals culminated in the American and French revolutions. Both these latter developments were existential threats to the British imperial establishment. In particular, the claims of revealed religion needed to be substantiated if the revolutionary ideas were to be kept at bay in Britain itself. Stukeley was quite explicit about this: 'My intent is, besides preserving the memory of these extraordinary monuments, now in great danger of ruin, to promote, as much as I am able, the knowledge and practice of ancient and true Religion, to revive in the minds of the learned the spirit of Christianity.' What Stukeley did was to conflate the Natural and Christian religions and project them back in time – *analepsis*, or 'flashing back'– to a preceding patriarchal religious order which had flourished in ancient 'Albion' and was thus the 'natural' religion of the British race. He thought that the Druidic religion was 'so extremely like Christianity that the only difference is this; they believed in a Messiah who was to come, as we believe in him that is come'.

Although, as we have seen before, there were authentic connections between Druidism and Christianity, and it is possible that the architects of Stonehenge and the like may have anticipated the philosophies of the Druids, Stukeley's ideas were a very erudite romantic whimsy. Despite this, however, they seeped into the national consciousness, where they became embedded, so that at least in more tolerant times many thousands of people still converge at Stonehenge, where they participate in gatherings to venerate the sunrise on the summer solstice. Facts such as that the monument is oriented to the midwinter solstice and that white-robed Druids presiding over ceremonies there is an invention of eighteenth-century clergymen are details irrelevant to the worshippers. One of the motivations behind this book is to emphasise just this point; myth and magic possess a logic of their own. Once a certain point has been reached in the mass consciousness, 'facts' no longer matter. The magical history becomes more powerful than the 'scientific' history adduced by academics. The consequences of this strange power of myth and magic to overwhelm rational thought have been, and remain, extremely dangerous. Only eighty years ago the world was convulsed by a war caused in large part by a civilised industrial nation falling victim to a species of mass psychosis induced by warped interpretations of history, and it may happen again.

---

31 Rousseau, J. J., *The Social Contract*, 1762.

The emotional reaction against industrialism and materialism among a certain faction of the intelligentsia was a movement of the intellectual and propertied class, whose leisure and refined sensibilities were freely indulged while the workers toiled in soul-destroying mills or laboured six days a week in the fields on a diet of 'potatoes and water porridge'. Poetry was the main medium for expressing the romantic ideal, but the industrial and agricultural labourers were for the most part barely literate. What was extraordinary was the emergence of a great poet from the humblest and most constrained circumstances, the 'poorest of the poor', John Clare, the so-called 'peasant poet'. As Frederick W. Martin observed in his biography of the man, 'John Clare was a poet almost as soon as he awoke to consciousness. His young mind marvelled at all the wonderful things visible in the wide world: the misty sky, the green trees, the fish in the water, and the birds in the air. In all the things around him the boy saw nothing but endless, glorious beauty; his whole mind was filled with a deep sense of the infinite marvels of the living world.' As a boy Clare would run out into the woods and fens where he communed with the 'fairy-folk' whom he saw plainly, dancing around him. As a young man, nursing a broken heart after a frustrated love affair, Clare ran away with a gypsy band whose wild way of life attracted him.

A life of extreme destitution, romantic rejection and condescending patronage by social superiors took a heavy toll on the 'Northamptonshire Peasant'. Eventually he was admitted to a private lunatic asylum on 16 July 1837. Clare was separated from his wife and children and taken to Fair Mead House in Epping Forest. There he received care and kindly supervision by the standards of the time, but he was desperate to see his family and the beauty of his native Northamptonshire Fenlands once more. For years he received not a single visitor, and was discouraged from writing verse for fear that it would arouse his tendency to morbidity. When strangers visiting another inmate produced a pencil and a sheet of paper, Clare took them and immediately wrote down lines as fine as any that have been produced in English literature.

Clare was constantly tormented by visions of 'Mary', his first and most idealised love, whom he felt had been won away from him by evil spirits. He began to imagine that 'Mary' was his actual, rather than spiritual spouse, and under the spell of this delusion he designed to make his way home. He had no money, but wandered the roads until he met a gypsy who befriended him and set him on his right road north. After a few days a man took pity on the hapless wayfarer and threw him a penny, which enabled him to buy a tankard of ale. As he progressed he became so starved that he sank to his knees and ate grass like the beasts. As Frederick Martin rightly observed, 'a great many people passed – people rich and poor, on foot and in carriages, in clerical habit and in broadcloth; but not one gave him alms, or even noticed, or had a kind word for the dying man at the roadside. There was not one good Samaritan among all the wayfarers from the rich episcopal city.' By chance some folk from his home village of Helpston passed by and left him some pennies and a small amount of food. His real wife was alerted to his condition and came to collect him from the roadside, but he could no longer recognise her, longing only for his 'Mary'. He was committed to another asylum, to be kept under restraint 'after years addicted to poetical prosings', as the certificate of committal put it.

For twenty-two years Clare was imprisoned as a pauper lunatic, for the 'crime' of writing some of the most beautiful verse ever to have been composed in English. His wife never visited him, and only one of his children visited, and then just the once. He and the world were no longer connected:

I am! Yet what I am who cares, or knows?
My friends forsake me like a memory lost.
I am the self-consumer of my woes,
They rise and vanish, an oblivious host,
Shadows of life, whose very soul is lost.
And yet I am – I live – though I am toss'd

Into the nothingness of scorn and noise,
Into the living and the waking dream,
Where there is neither sense of life, nor joys,
But the huge shipwreck of my own esteem
And all that's dear. Even those I loved the best
Are strange – nay, they are stranger than the rest.

I long for scenes where man has never trod,
For scenes where woman never smiled or wept;
There to abide with my Creator, God,
And sleep as I in childhood sweetly slept
Full of high thoughts, unborn. So let me lie,
The grass below; above the vaulted sky.

John Clare died on 20 May 1864. His final words were 'I want to go home.' As Frederick W. Martin so aptly put it, 'There now lies, under the shade of a sycamore-tree, with nothing above but the eternal vault of heaven, all that earth has to keep of John Clare, one of the sweetest singers of nature ever born within the fair realm of dear old England – of dear old England, so proud of its galaxy of noble poets, and so wasteful of their lives.'

The angst exemplified by the Romantic movement was a mystical reaction against the stultifying and dehumanising domination of 'the Beast' or 'the Machine'. Strictly speaking, then, these matters impinge not only on historical study, but on theology, cultural and anthropological studies, and magic. The ancient Druidic veneration of water, pools, springs, wells and rivers runs deep in our island psyche. The man who did most to produce a 'philosophy' of Romanticism, Samuel Taylor Coleridge, is best known for his sublime poetical works, but the philosophy which underlay his poetical vision, intentional or not, amounted to a restatement of Druidic metaphysics updated for the industrial age. Richard Holmes was explicit that Coleridge needs to be considered not merely 'just a figure winding through the historical landscape, but a close and continuing presence – our contemporary. 'Truth ... may be conceived as ... a water source.' This 'Truth' is a much larger thing than a vague apprehension of past events through consideration of documentary, traditional and archaeological evidence. It is an *imaginative* and also *figurative* experience, in which the actor is emotionally invested:

> Coleridge shows one principle or fact of nature (the spring water) in contention with an opposite one (the freezing snow). The water and the snow are in dynamic opposition, working against each other's nature and tendency: the water trying to flow, the snow trying to freeze. The process of dynamic opposition is a dialectical one; and truth, says Coleridge, works like nature – dialectically. Moreover the result of this opposition is not a victory for one side or the other, but a kind of active reconciliation. The water changes into ice, and then the snow and ice change back into water: 'it turns the obstacle into its own form'. They flow on together, combined and mutually increased – the flow of truth 'increases its stream'. So the dialectical process in things leads to a synthesis: a reconciliation in a more powerful state, or higher reality.[32]

For Coleridge, these deep metaphysical contemplations on the wellsprings of the human spirit came to operate at the precise interface between mysticism and magic, and like the ancient bards the new breed of Romantics mediated their recondite philosophy in verse form. The musings of antiquarian clergymen on the origins of the Druids were fanciful and whimsical – but the visions of men such as Coleridge and Blake were, at least, an approach to the heart of the Perennial Philosophy. Vision was the faculty which made the world *vital*, which, 'brings life to a dead world'. Shelley, in his *Defence of Poetry*, thought that 'our greatest weakness' as modern Western 'civilised' people was that we lacked the 'creative faculty to imagine that which we know'.

The implications of the retardation of our imaginative faculty will dominate the remainder of this book, and a potential solution, derived in large part from the Romantic philosophy, adduced. But for Coleridge, the practical solution, at least in part, lay in the institution of a *clerisy* or 'National Church' comprised of 'scholars, scientists, learned priests and laymen, schoolmasters, writers, artists, teachers and thinkers of every kind, irrespective of their formal religious persuasions – the learned of all denominations'. What was being proposed – and what may yet come to pass – was a reinstitution of the ancient intellectual caste exemplified by the Druids.

---

32 Holmes, R., *Coleridge*, Oxford University Press, Oxford, 1982.

As the French Revolution came to influence a new breed of radicals, *Jacobins* or 'Old Jacks' as they became known in England, Coleridge was forced to reassess his youthful sympathies with the radical tradition. For him, the real revolution was a revolution of the soul, the heart and the mind, a transfiguration of the consciousness which would 'teach [the poor] their *Duties* in order that [the Philosopher] may render them susceptible of their rights'. This opposition to the emphasis on the 'rights of man' as articulated by Rousseau and Tom Paine identified, as Richard Holmes said, 'a fundamental misconception about State power: that external machinery could transform the inward nature of man … Jacobinism, in action, becomes the Juggernaut of pure, abstract reason, crushing everything in its path'. In his notebooks Coleridge commented, 'In looking at objects of Nature, I seem rather to be seeking, as it were *asking* for, a symbolical language for something within me that always and forever exists, than observing anything new.' For Coleridge, Blake, Wordsworth, Clare, Keats and Shelley it was the mind, or imaginative faculty itself, which conferred meaning, and which derived from a higher form of mind – that power which infused all living things, the very antithesis of the inorganic, measured, mechanical, and soulless universe implied by Newtonian science. Coleridge, hopelessly addicted to opium since childhood, was well placed to observe the transcendental, mystical world he perceived in nature, and like Schiller and Goethe he thought he could trace the lineaments of the spiritual world which underlay physical form. In dreams there were no constraints, no limits, no boundaries.

As the behemoth of industrialism and a vulgar materialism displaced the ancient spiritual order, a resistance movement began. There was physical resistance, machine-breaking in the industrial towns of the north of England and the East Midlands by 'the Luddites', and in the countryside the disturbances known as the 'Captain Swing' riots among the rural labourers. But perhaps the most profound resistance of all came from a poet, painter, engraver and prophet whose imaginative genius, though utterly unrecognised in his own time, became a testimony against materialism, and what he saw as the 'Antichrist' – William Blake.

The radical tradition of the English Revolution was not quite spent, and it was from this tradition that Blake sprang. I must confine myself to an explanation of the radical and Nonconformist background of the man, and his deep disdain of organised religiosity, which he thought suppressed natural desires by encouraging a hypocritical chastity, robbing Mankind of the development of spiritual understanding through the experience of joy. Blake's vision was an attempt to resolve the conflict between the prevailing religious literalism, and the spiritual imagination. But above all Blake's imaginative system was based on his belief in a primordial patriarchal and prophetic tradition, which he saw as unfolding through the operation of divine destiny in the affairs of an idealised and visionary 'Albion', whose fate was inextricably linked to that of the wider world and the entire human family.

To a culture of otiose mediocrity such as ours, Blake has become a mystifying, almost incomprehensible figure. One of our greatest Christian artists, he never went to church; he was a giant intellect who rarely went to school. He was born in Soho, London, on 28 November 1757 to a family in the hosiery trade. The lack of a formal education was in fact beneficial to the boy. He detested schools: 'There is no use in education – I hold it wrong – it is the great Sin.' His father indulged the boy's precocious artistic talent, and he began drawing while he was still a toddler. Another 'talent' the boy demonstrated was his ability to see disembodied spirits. This was no mere childhood fantasy, but a lifelong experience, a super-sensible imaginative facility. As he sat beside the deathbed of his beloved brother, Robert, he saw his spirit rise out of his body 'clapping his hands for joy'.

Robert's spirit continued to communicate with Blake, and inspired his illuminated sketching technique. Many other spirits appeared to William, to the extent that he would often include them in conversations when corporeal persons were present. Such unusual goings-on (to a modern perspective) were tolerated by William's parents, who may themselves have been influenced by the ideas of Emanuel Swedenborg (1688–1772), a Swedish geologist turned mystical occultist whose radical religious ideas were widely admired in London at the time.

Swedenborg, like Blake, often saw the spirits all around him and conversed with them. He was definitely clairvoyant, describing a terrible fire which was consuming Stockholm to guests at a dinner party while many miles away in Gothenburg, well before any messenger could have been dispatched. These hypnagogic states led him to a meeting with a disguised Christ in the back room of a London tavern in 1744, an encounter which was to completely change his life. When the pioneer of Methodism, John Wesley, expressed a desire to meet with Swedenborg, the latter declined because the date of the proposed meeting fell after 29 March 1772, which he casually predicted was to be the appointed day of his own death. Swedenborg died on the day and at the time predicted, and presumably his spirit departed to the heaven to which he had already been introduced by various angels

It is important that we realise the extent to which such experiences were tolerated as normal in Blake's day, where now they seem extraordinary, eccentric or 'mad'. During his lifetime Blake was, indeed, obscure and unrecognised except by a few faithful and perceptive friends, and after his death his work was almost forgotten until its rediscovery by a fellow poet, and practising occultist, W. B. Yeats. Yeats was a strong influence, in turn, on the poet Kathleen Raine, whose extensive study of Blake led her to believe that, far from being a brilliant autodidact, Blake's 'vision' was the product of a long tradition derived from the 'Perennial Philosophy', Platonic, Gnostic and Hermetic thought. Others, such as the historian E. P. Thompson, demurred, and proposed that he was a product of the political radicalism of the English revolutionary tradition, at precisely the time when the French

Revolution of 1789 and its violent aftermath circumscribed the scope for effective political action, diverting this into artistic and literary movements such as Romanticism. However we choose to view him, Blake's relevance to my own argument is that he was a prophet in the true sense of the essential spiritual nature of England – or, as he preferred, 'Albion'.

In 1772 Blake became apprenticed to James Basire, an esteemed London engraver. For seven years he learned the complex techniques which he was to utilise in his visual art, but did not neglect his intensive Bible study or his precocious literary talent. His *Poetical Sketches*, a collection begun when he was just twelve years old, was published in 1783. As Kathleen Raine observed, 'His craftsman's training was also, almost accidentally, to put into his hands the technique which enabled him to create his unique illuminated books.' The intense debate as to the ultimate sources for Blake's ideas which unfolded in the twentieth century seems to me to have proceeded on the basis of 'either/or' thinking, whereas it might be more profitable to consider Blake from a 'both/ and' perspective. Thompson is right to suggest that, even given his early and prodigious reading, it would have been difficult, though not impossible, for Blake to have obtained access to actual Gnostic texts, and that any Gnostic influence was more likely to have come from antinomian or Moravian thought and from the Behmenists, or followers of the German mystic Jacob Boehme (1575–1624). There is little doubt that Boehme was a primary influence on Blake's religious thinking, but there was another strand of contemporary thought which, I believe, must have imprinted itself on his imagination.

In 1801 an odd pamphlet circulated, called *The Strange Effects of Faith*. It was the work of Joanna Southcott (1750–1814), a self-appointed 'Prophetess' who proclaimed that she was the 'Woman of the Apocalypse' prophesied in the Book of Revelation. The times were indeed dark. The misery and privation of England during the Napoleonic Wars portrayed so diligently by E. P. Thompson in his *The Making of the English Working Class* produced an atmosphere of millenarian expectancy. Napoleon was (and still is) widely believed to be one of three personifications of Antichrist as predicted by Nostradamus, and to be 'the Beast' incarnate. Joanna promised her followers, on payment of a fee, 'a seal' which would guarantee their membership of the elect 144,000 souls who would be taken up to heaven after the Apocalypse.

Over 100,000 'Sealed People' were convinced, some would say gulled, into handing over as much as 12*s*, and among them were friends of Blake such as William Sharp and William Owen Pughe. Pughe was one of the twenty-four elders appointed by Joanna Southcott to oversee the 'church' of the 'Sealed People', which at one point became a serious challenger to Methodism. Pughe had an eclectic interest in all manner of arcane mysteries, including the works of the self-described Welsh 'Druid' Iolo Morganwg, whom we have encountered before. According to Robert Southey, it was through his acquaintance with Pughe that Blake and his wife became persuaded of the notion that 'Ancient British Christianity was strongly tinctured with Druidism'.

Blake's mind was already open to the veracity of these ideas as imaginative and spiritual, as well as historical 'facts': 'The antiquities of every Nation under Heaven is no less sacred than that of the Jews. They are the same thing. As Jacob Bryant and all antiquaries have proved.' Stuart Piggott quotes from Blake when he asks, 'Was Britain the Primitive Seat of the Patriarchal Religion?' 'Your Ancestors derived their origin from Abraham, Heber, Shem and Noah, who were Druids, as the Druid Temples (which are Patriarchal Pillars and Oak Groves) over the whole Earth witness to this day.' The final page of Blake's *Jerusalem* is illustrated with an engraving of Stukeley's depiction of the Avebury complex The Serpent Temple. Even E. P. Thompson concedes that Blake 'had a quirky interest in Druidism'. Blake combines this with the trilithons of Stonehenge, which in another of his engravings from the same book loom over the figures of Newton, Bacon and Locke, dwarfing these indistinct pygmies Blake so reviled. E. P. Thompson in his *Witness Against the Beast* refers to Blake's 'comminations' against the above trio, those whom he thought

> Deny a conscience in Man & the Communion of Saints & Angels
> Contemning the Divine Vision & Fruition, Worshiping the Deus
> Of the Heathen, The God of This World, & the Goddess Nature
> Mystery Babylon the Great, the Druid Dragon & hidden Harlot ...

In connection with Blake's prejudice against Newtonian science, it seems only fair to point out that research into Newton by Michael White published as *Isaac Newton: The Last Sorcerer* has radically altered our view of this 'father' of modern science. White has demonstrated beyond any doubt that Newton was a magician and alchemist who devoted the majority of his intellectual researches to esoteric and religious matters, and that the 'scientific' philosophical and mathematical advances he pioneered were a corollary of his occult interests:

> Ironically, although Newton was largely responsible for the development of the scientific enlightenment which swept away the common belief in magic and mysticism, he created the origins of empirical science and the modern 'rational' world in part by immersing himself in these very practices.

Newton was obsessed with the idea that the Bible contained encrypted codes and mathematical formulae which he was determined to decipher. Before he commenced his alchemical experimentation, Newton spent literally years reading himself into the subject. He was convinced that the Old Testament prophets and the Egyptian Hermetic practitioners of ancient Alexandria had possessed the secrets of transmutation of substances. Therefore, it was possible, theoretically, to change any one material into another by subtly altering the constituent elements of which it was composed. This knowledge, derived ultimately from Aristotle, was lost to Western Europeans for centuries but the Arabs reintroduced it via Spain.

Newton's 'heretical' religious position – he was an Arian – led him into religious speculations which can only be described as profoundly mystical. He proposed that the 'incorporeal ether' which was the medium for the operation of gravity was 'the body of Christ'. Since, as he said, 'God does nothing by himself which he can do by another', Christ had facilitated the creation as the divine agent. In short, Blake's view of Newton was as skewed in his day as ours. He thought him a cold-blooded 'measurer', a rationalist, a calculating machine – as we do. But ironically he was no such thing – he was a magus.

Blake's interest in ancient Britons had little to do with history or archaeology of the Druids as such. 'The Nature of my Work ... is Visionary or Imaginative; it is an endeavour to Restore what the Ancients called the Golden Age.' The spiritual epicentre of this 'Golden Age' was 'Albion', 'All things Begin & End in Albion's Ancient Druid Rocky Shore.' The 'Giant Albion' or 'the Eternal Man' is the sleeping embodiment of the spirit of a magical Britain, whose awakening will transfigure the world and all creation. A recent book by Jeffrey John Dixon, *Goddess and Grail: the Battle for King Arthur's Promised Land*, reminds us that Albion's fate as the 'Eternal Man' is to become the redeeming figure of Arthur, recalled from the faerie Otherworld:

> Blake's vision is of a web of imaginative sympathy that links the material, human and spiritual worlds in a way that neither the Net of Religion nor the 'fixed' rationalism of science can. At its heart is the human, embodied in the Eternal Man whose Spectre, fallen in time and space, is Arthur.

All that is contained in the previous chapters leads us here, to an apotheosis of the British national spirit expressed in specifically religious and mythical terms. And as so often before, it was the native god-man, Arthur, who will return to 'dwell with the Britons with mickle joy'. Blake was explicit enough: 'The stories of Arthur are the acts of the Giant Albion.'

In ancient British mythology Albion was a giant son of the sea god, Poseidon. Blake used the ancient myth as a template for his own more imaginative mythology in which Albion's fall has him fracture into four 'Zoas' or aspects. One of these, Urizen, represents the idea of reason, boundary and measurement, the aspect which personified the spirit of the Newtonian age. Another Zoa, Los, an anagram of 'Sol' or Sun, represents the divine aspect of the imagination, which has fallen into the material realm. As Europe was convulsed by revolution and war, Blake's ideas developed along less political lines, although not because his radicalism and dissent had diminished – this was not a retreat. His mythogenesis was itself a form of resistance, in fact the weapon of resistance par excellence:

In *The four Zoas* (1795–1804), *Milton* (1804–8) and *Jerusalem* (1804–20) Los and Enitharmon are more fully realised, and – with Blake's progressive loss of faith in revolution, recedes into the background. Urizen, still retaining the venerable features of 'aged ignorance', becomes the Satan of Milton. He makes his last, terrible appearance as the cloven-footed false image of God ... the four Zoas and their Emanations – the pantheon of Blake's interior cosmos – take their final forms.[33]

We saw in earlier chapters how the Druids had developed a complex system of shamanic magic, whereby the nature of things could be changed or transmuted by use of mantras, called in Welsh *Glam Dicin*. Intuitively Blake knew that it was possible to change the states of things; 'Every Natural Effect has a Spiritual Cause. Not a Natural; for a Natural cause only seems.' Like Coleridge, Blake had grasped the need to go beyond philosophy, politics and theological, literal religion. He decided instead to concentrate on spiritual combat, 'mental right' against the oppressive powers, what he called 'the one thing needful'. This was no evasion of reality, but an imaginative process of creation involving all his prodigious talents, something often described as 'mystical' but also magical. In her book *William Blake*, Kathleen Raine says of his *Marriage of Heaven and Hell*:

> The poem itself is a sombre satire of Milton's account of the Creation; according to Blake, the Seven Days of Creation represent seven phases of the imprisonment and 'binding' of 'the caverned man' within the limitations of a world experienced only through the five senses. Urizen, thus limited, becomes the self-deluded and anxious demiurge, engaged in the 'enormous labours' of imposing his 'ratio of the five senses' on rebellious life, whose nature he has not understood. Such, according to Blake, is the 'human reason', the false God of the Enlightenment, and, in France, of Rousseau and Voltaire.

What Blake was trying to accomplish was nothing less than to construct an inner cosmology of the imagination, what J. R. R. Tolkien called 'sub-creation', a spiritual world rendered so vivid, so complex, that it assumes a 'reality' of its own: 'I must Create a System or be enslav'd by another Man's.'

From the beginning of his career, Blake had been obsessed by the Glastonbury legends, and for him the true ruler of the world was 'Jesus the Imagination' or 'the Jesus within', whose marriage with the individual soul is the key to mystical revelation and illumination. Blake certainly had access to and studied a translation of the ancient Vedic text called the *Bhagavad Gita*, and his spiritual contemplations resemble very much the practices of Raja or 'royal' yoga. I do not suggest that Blake modelled his 'system' on

---

33 Raine, K., *William Blake*, Thames & Hudson, London, 1970.

Vedantism, any more than that he 'copied' Druidic practices. Rather, it seems to me that since the Hindu and Celtic spiritual systems were very similar, as the classical writers observed, it follows that underground channels in the race consciousness existed, which Blake's imaginative power flowed into, like water through a conduit.

It would not be going too far, in my opinion, to describe Blake's work as a 'sub-creator' as magic. He was more than just a poet, an engraver, a philosopher and prophet, as Raine pointed out: 'Blake's uniqueness lies in no single achievement, but in the whole of what he was, which is more than the sum of all that he did.' These maverick polymaths of Romanticism seem almost like a last flare of the Druidic candle before the excrescences of the rational-scientific, industrial and commercial age engulfed the world. But people like Coleridge and Blake were out of their time in another way – they were imagining the future: 'The past, present and future are intertwined.' It was Newton's science which prevailed, not Blake's 'Work of the Imagination', in the war of cultural ideas. But the wheel turns. It is not too late for Romanticism to come of age, and as I hope to show, that process may already be underway.

The similarities between the economic and cultural transitions and conflicts of the eighteenth century and our own plight today are striking. In our day, we feel like we have become batteries for machines, that the time is coming where no organic contribution will be strictly necessary, a prelude to the 'Great Tribulation'. Electronically generated hallucinations, the 'powers of the air', seem more valid, more 'real' than our authentic human experience, leading to an epidemic of mental illness, psychosis and drug addiction – all the blooms in the garden of consumerism. Our eighteenth- and nineteenth-century forebears, especially the working class, experienced just these same insecurities, felt the same fears for their future. E. P Thompson, in his *The Making of the English Working Class*, says:

> Again and again in these years working men expressed it thus: 'they wish to make us tools', or 'implements', or 'machines'. A witness before the parliamentary committee enquiring into the hand-loom weavers (1835) was asked to state the views of his fellows on the Reform Bill:
>
> Q. Are the working classes better satisfied with the institutions of the country since the change has taken place?
> A. I do not think they are. They viewed the Reform Bill as a measure calculated to join the middle and upper classes to Government, and leave them in the hands of Government as a sort of machine to work according to the pleasure of Government.

They were right, of course. They were being converted into machines as we are being converted into 'avatars'. The discontent and unease with the 'utilitarian' system was not just felt by workers and radicals, dreamers like

Coleridge and visionaries like Blake. A traditionalist and ex-soldier, William Cobbett, author of *The Political Register*, lamented the demise of the rural England he loved so well, and despite his own deep prejudices, even bigotry, he became a convert to the radical cause.

Cobbett was the 'salt of the earth', a farm labourer's son from Farnham in Surrey, but he was never going to follow in his father's footsteps. He enlisted and was posted overseas to Canada, where his diligence, enthusiasm, reliability, and an abiding honesty and detestation of corruption, ensured he rose through the ranks. While his comrades-in-arms dissipated their pay on drunken debauches and whoring, he sat and educated himself by lantern light. But his complaints of embezzlement and dissatisfaction with the army made him discharge himself. Ironically, he went to France with his new bride, but was forced to leave because of the French Revolution, an event inimical to all the traditional values he held so dear.

As an ex-soldier, Cobbett began to feel that the British government was not prosecuting the war against France with sufficient vigour, much like the later George Orwell in the Second World War. But soon, he felt there was more to this desultory attitude than mere inefficiency. He became convinced that the British political establishment was deeply corrupt. He read the works of Tom Paine, and was especially impressed by his critique of the financial system. Cobbett's obsession with the corruption of a system of paper money is strangely apposite for our times, and although his intellectual grasp of economics was rudimentary, he knew the smell of venality, corruption and hypocrisy well enough. For the rest of his life he devoted himself to a campaign to oppose those forces he believed to be putting his beloved England in jeopardy – a radical patriot. Cobbett was deeply prejudiced against urban life, which he thought encouraged moral degeneracy, crime, and disease both spiritual and physical. The supreme centre of pestilence was London, 'the Great Wen'. The same city which Blake saw as 'the New Jerusalem', the prophesied City of Revelation, seemed to Cobbett a cesspit of vice, corruption, fraud and speculation. But Cobbett's England was vanishing, and by 1830 half of the population were town dwellers (worldwide this has only recently been replicated).

Britain had been the first nation to industrialise, and as a global imperial power its great capital became the hub of the international financial and mercantile network. Wellington's victory against Napoleon at Waterloo outside Brussels in 1815 meant that the British Empire was to enjoy almost a century of dominance. But 1819 saw 'Peterloo', where the Yeomanry Cavalry charged a political demonstration in St Peter's Fields, Manchester. Sixty thousand unarmed people, including many with their families, had attended the gathering to hear 'orator' Hunt, a famous radical. Fifteen people were sabred to death, and almost a thousand seriously injured. Imperial pomp and swagger could no longer hide the obvious divisions in the nation. As the Victorian era dawned, the old spiritual certainties were under challenge as never before. The Church seemed to the working people a bastion of privilege, and the failure of its bishops to support the Reform Bill of 1832 was seen by many as a betrayal. The revolutionary scientific theories of Charles Darwin on evolution radically undermined the foundations of Christian faith. The process which began at the Reformation, the emphasis on the individual, liberty of conscience, internal and external exploration – was reaching its climax. As exotic religions and cults were encountered all over Britain's far-flung empire on which the Sun never set, there was great interest in spiritual systems other than Christianity. And now a 'rough beast, its hour come round at last', slouched towards Bethlehem to be born – or rather to 30 Clarendon Square, Royal Leamington Spa.

15

The 'New Aeon'

Just as the Arthurian myths had been reinvented in the Anglo-Norman period, and enjoyed an astonishing revival under the Tudors, so in the Victorian era, the 'Golden Age' of the British Empire, they were reinterpreted once more. Through the influence of William Morris, the Pre-Raphaelite movement of artists took up the romantic theme of the Grail quest. But it fell to yet another poet, the Poet Laureate in fact, to present the myth anew, in terms which reflected the mood of the times – a mood of proleptic lament for a civilisation on the brink of destruction, basking in the fading twilight of a fast vanishing magical kingdom. The poet was Alfred Lord Tennyson, one of the most widely read poets of all time. Tennyson was haunted by another Arthur, Arthur Hallam, to whom he wrote his requiem *In Memoriam A.H.H.*, completed in 1849.

At Cambridge Tennyson had fallen into the company of a group known as 'the Cambridge Apostles', a debating society which met every Saturday in term times. Arthur Hallam was the epitome of the imperial ideal – startlingly handsome, perfectly poised, academically brilliant, and an accomplished poet, all by the age of twenty. At Eton he had been admired by all his contemporaries, indeed beloved. To Tennyson he seemed the perfect specimen of the noble Arthurian ideal, and, what was more, his admiration of Hallam was reciprocated. Hallam encouraged the rather gauche Tennyson, two years his junior, to write poetry and join in the weekly meetings of the 'Apostles'. A friendship developed which was predicated on adoration on Tennyson's part. There was nothing sordid about this 'David and Jonathan' relationship – this was a masculine *fin amor*. To complete Tennyson's happiness, Arthur fell in love with his sister, Emilia, and the two became engaged to be married. Alfred, Emilia and Arthur planned a book of poetry to which all three would contribute.

But then, on 15 September 1833, Arthur suddenly died while touring Austria. He was just twenty-two, and despite suffering a slight chill he seemed in good enough health. His father returned from a walk to find him reclining on a couch. At first he thought him asleep, but he then noticed Arthur's head was in a curious position. He had died in his sleep of a stroke, the *jeune homme fatal* of his generation. Tennyson and Emilia were devastated, emotionally eviscerated. Arthur's body was placed in a sealed coffin and sent to England by ship as the young brother and sister waited anxiously for his return. To them, it seemed that the king was dead, that life could never be the same – and that a darkness had fallen on which no dawn could hope to break. Tennyson could not will himself to let go of his grief: 'Let darkness keep her raven gloss.'

His grief was lifelong, and destiny had decreed that Alfred was to be one of the most widely read poets of all time. The obvious course was to channel his grief into his poetry, but he could not bring himself to openly express his emotions, which for years were too raw. He had already planned a long poem on an Arthurian theme before his friend's untimely death, but it was only afterwards that he used the *Morte d'Arthur* as the template for expressing his desperate feelings of loss. Queen Victoria's new husband, Prince Albert, was an avid admirer of *In Memoriam*, and her beloved husband's predilections were ever close to her heart. Royal patronage ensured that in 1850 Tennyson became the Poet Laureate. By now, seventeen years after Hallam's passing, Tennyson had become engrossed with the Arthurian legends, and especially the tragic denouement of the collapse of the fellowship of the Round Table, the fatal battle at Camlann and the weird circumstances of Arthur's passing. This was not just the maudlin sentimentality we have come to associate with the Victorian era, but something more – an anticipation of the unravelling of all that was beautiful and good, the inevitability of dark night.

Then, in 1861, the whole terrible process was repeated. Albert, the queen's darling and Tennyson's sponsor and dear friend, died of typhoid fever at Windsor Castle just before Christmas. Victoria could not be consoled, and withdrew herself from public life to such an extent that there were real fears for the future of the monarchy. The whole empire grieved with her. Tennyson visited Victoria in her retreat at Osborne House on the Isle of Wight where he recited lines from *In Memoriam* and his *Idylls of the King*. Nothing, seemingly, could truly console the morose monarch, and to add to the gloom the Prince of Wales became ill with typhoid fever, his death seemingly imminent. Popular sympathy for Victoria ensured that republican agitation ran out of steam. The Prince of Wales recovered.

Tennyson, the loyal bard, guarded his monarch with a fierce loyalty, and in the popular imagination the Arthurian and Victorian dramas merged into one. This was no longer the passionate, sexually suggestive drama of the 'courts of love', but conveyed a respectable, somewhat dour atmosphere, which made the term 'Victorian' a pejorative for those of my generation. The slightly nauseating sentimentalism, the hypocrisy around sexual mores, the sense of subordinating oneself to 'duty' and propriety and the denial of self-indulgence were not to everyone's taste. On 12 October 1875, a child was born at 30 Clarendon Square, Royal Leamington Spa in Warwickshire. His name was Edward Alexander Crowley, and he was to make it his life's work to set about the destruction of the Christian religion and replace it with a new world faith, but above all to tear down the sanctimonious, canting, restrictive and hypocritical Victorian edifice.

On 13 October 1884, the day after Crowley's ninth birthday, Pope Leo XIII suddenly entered a trance state. For ten minutes he sat ashen-faced and transfixed. When he came to, he related that he had heard two voices, one he knew to be Christ, the other Satan. Satan boasted that he could bring the Church to its knees and destroy it within 75 to 100 years, to which Christ responded that the said time would be allotted to him. The beginning of Satan's campaign is disputed. Catholics believe that the apparitions and miracles at Fatima in Portugal in 1917 mark the beginning of the tribulations. The First World War of 1914–18, with the gruelling slaughter on the Somme and at Verdun and Ypres, would seem a good candidate. My paternal grandfather related that many thousands of men of all combatant nations witnessed a celestial sign of a cross on the last evening of the Somme battle.

Crowley came to believe that he was a prophet of a 'New Aeon', and that communications he received in Cairo on 8, 9 and 10 April 1904 from an intelligence he called 'Aiwass' marked the commencement of a 'new age', a post-Christian era corresponding to Satan's boast. There are good reasons, I believe, for taking his claims seriously. There is not space in this small chapter to give a full and adequate account of Crowley's extraordinary life, nor to dwell too much on his notoriously decadent lifestyle; indeed, it would perhaps be indelicate to do so in a book of this type. Rather, I wish to concentrate on the religion Crowley founded, Thelema, in response to the communications received in Cairo in 1904, *Liber Al vel Legis*, 'The Book of the Law'. For Crowley this was the supreme moment of his magical career, the revelation of his life. This was not just some trick of the so-called 'Wickedest Man in the World', and even if Crowley was 'A Man We'd Like to Hang', as the newspaper *John Bull* put it, we would be wise to pay heed to the words of the entity called Aiwass, prophesies of a forthcoming age of 'Force and Fire' so cruel and brutal that Crowley himself was appalled by them.

In August 1903, Crowley married Rose Edith Kelly after eloping with her to save her from an arranged marriage. The two then embarked on a drunken, drug-fuelled romp which brought them to Cairo as part of an extended honeymoon early in 1904. Crowley set up a temple in their apartment, and tried to impress Rose with his magical powers by performing the 'bornless ritual' or 'Invocation of Goetia', to summon his 'Holy Guardian Angel'. Rose was completely ignorant of magic but she swooned into a light trance state, probably induced by hashish and cocaine. During this reverie she began to repeat the phrase 'They are waiting for you'. Crowley questioned Rose further. Who were 'they'?

Rose identified the Egyptian god Horus, and Crowley was intrigued enough to take Rose to the Boulak Museum in the city. He then asked Rose to pick out an image of Horus and she made straight for an image of him on a funerary stele of a priest of the XXVI dynasty, Ankh-af-na-khonsu. The deceased priest is shown offering sacrifice to Horus, and the chances of Rose correctly choosing the 'Stele of Revealing', as Crowley called it, and identifying the attributes of the god during interrogative sessions with her husband were astronomically low, so the mystery deepened. But the 'clincher' for Crowley was the catalogue number on the stele, 666. Crowley's own mother had dubbed him 'the Beast' when he was a child, disgusted by his appalling behaviour, and he had self-mockingly called himself 'the Beast 666' (of the Book of Revelation) ever since. (There is a legend that he was born with three hairs on his breast forming the numerals 666, the 'Number of the Beast' prophesied by St John 'the Divine'.)

The coincidence seemed genuinely extraordinary, and Crowley began to trust his wife's utterances. Now under the guidance of Thoth, the god of magic, further instructions were received via Rose. Crowley had been chosen to receive the prophesy of the 'New Aeon' of Horus. He was to go into a room at noon on three successive days, 8, 9 and 10 April. There he was to sit at his desk and write down words spoken by an entity who stood behind him for one hour. He was commanded not to glance over his shoulder. A deep male voice then spoke, Aiwass, the minister of 'Hoor-paar-kraat' or Harpocrates, 'Horus the child'. The revelation, when complete, announced the end of the 'Age of Osiris', and the commencement of the reign of the 'Crowned and Conquering Child', Horus. In his *The Book of Thoth*, written forty years later when many of the prophesies of Aiwass seemed to be coming to pass, Crowley says of *The Book of the Law*:

It is also important to study very thoroughly, and meditate upon, this Book, in order to appreciate the spiritual, moral, and material events which have marked the catastrophic transition from the Aeon of Osiris. The time for the birth of an Aeon seems to be indicated by great concentration of political power with the accompanying improvements in the means of travel and communication, with a general advance in philosophy and science, with a general need of consolidation in religious thought. It is very instructive to compare the events of the five hundred years preceding and following the crisis of approximately 2,000 years ago, with those of similar periods centred in 1904 of the old era. It is a thought far from comforting to the present generation, that 500 years of Dark Ages are likely to be upon us. But if the analogy holds, that is the case. Fortunately, to-day we have brighter torches and more torch-bearers.[34]

---

34 Crowley, A., *The Book of Thoth*, Samuel Weiser, York Beach, 1988 edn.

So a sense of foreboding, of dread even, portended the coming of the twentieth century. Tennyson's proleptic gloom was not the only poetry to penetrate through time. A. E. Housman's *A Shropshire Lad*, published in 1896, eighteen years before the First World War, seemed so remarkably prescient of it that British soldiers were given a pocket edition to take into battle;

> On the idle hill of summer,
> Sleepy with the sound of streams
> Far I hear the steady drummer
> Drumming like a noise in dreams.
>
> Far and near and low and louder
> On the roads of earth go by
> Dear to friends and food for powder,
> Soldiers marching, all to die.

An assault by Satan, a 'New Aeon', '500 years of Dark Ages' seems a daunting prospect indeed, and after a century of slaughter, 'Force and Fire', perhaps it is time we examined *The Book of the Law* more carefully.

In Part Four of his preparatory introduction to *Liber Al vel Legis* entitled 'The New Aeon', Crowley begins by apologising for 'the characteristics of the Period on which we are now entered', saying that 'superficially they appear appalling'. The 'Equinox of the Gods', the change from one era or aeon to the next, which occurs in occult belief every 2,160 years, had been announced through the proclamation of *The Book of the Law*. But for all his anti-Christian prejudice, Crowley's 'revelation' is not couched just in those terms. The entire magical ambience is suitably Ancient Egyptian in character, and the 'aeons' are those of Isis, 'the mother', Osiris, 'the father', and Horus, 'the child, in which we come to perceive events as a continual growth partaking in all its elements of both these methods, and not to be overcome by circumstance. This present period involves the recognition of the individual as the unit of society.'

Crowley had been brought up in an exclusive Christian sect, the 'Plymouth Brethren'. This extremely conservative evangelical 'church' (the Brethren prefer the term 'Assembly') was founded in Dublin in the 1820s. The Brethren, and especially the 'Darbyite' faction of which Crowley's parents were members, were particularly fastidious about scriptural study, and the outworking of Biblical prophecy in history. Young Edward (he changed his name to 'Aleister' later, spelt 'Ale-ister' as a pun on the family brewing business) was expected to read a chapter from the Bible at every family mealtime. Crowley accompanied his father on his preaching tours and was inculcated early on with an immense respect for the Book of Revelation. Although he came to loathe and despise Christianity, and to actively compass its downfall, all these early influences are clearly evident in the apocalyptic tone of *The Book of the Law*, as is the influence of the philosopher Friedrich Nietzsche (1844–1900). The most telling characteristic of the new era, Crowley states, is the infantilization of the culture:

> Observe for yourselves the decay of the sense of sin, the growth of innocence and irresponsibility, the strange modifications of the reproductive instinct with a tendency to become bi-sexual or epicene, the childlike confidence in progress combined with nightmare fear of catastrophe, against which we are yet half unwilling to take precautions ... Consider the outcrop of dictatorships, only possible when moral growth is in its earliest stages, and the prevalence of infantile cults like Communism, Fascism, Pacifism, Health Crazes, Occultism in nearly all its forms, religions sentimentalised to the point of practical extinction ... Consider the popularity of the cinema, the wireless, the football pools and guessing competitions, all devices for soothing fractious infants, no seed of purpose in them ... Consider sport, the babyish enthusiasms it excites, whole nations disturbed by disputes between boys ... Consider war, the atrocities which occur daily and leave us unmoved and hardly worried. We are children.

There is little in the above statement with which the author would not concur, except that during his lifetime the process has increased a hundredfold, and appears to be exponential.

The neo-pagan revival exemplified by Crowley had commenced long before. The Prussian publisher Karl Ernst Jarcke in the nineteenth century convinced himself that the Germanic peoples were intrinsically anti-Christian, and that their 'true religion' was a subliminal paganism which had subsisted underground in the form of witchcraft. This was precisely the position the anthropologist Margaret Murray promulgated later, and the implications of Jarcke's romantic view were to culminate in the upsurge of occultism which engulfed Germany following the First World War. The English occult revival of the eighteenth century gained a following of dissolute and libertine spirits in the form of the 'Hellfire Club', whose patron was Sir Francis Dashwood, and whose members included such luminaries as Benjamin Franklin. Underground caverns were adapted to the uses of Dashwood for his debauched orgies, where excess of all kinds was the rule. Whoring, drinking, exotic feasting, gambling and cock- and dog-fighting were among the perverse diversions of the members and toasts were drunk in honour of the Devil. As a jest the members adopted the motto 'Do What Thou Wilt'. The motto recalled the rule of Francois Rabelais whose sixteenth-century *Abbaye de Theleme* was a decadent reversal of all Christian virtues. The original *Abbaye de Theleme* had been a satire and Dashwood's 'club' a bawdy joke of degenerate English aristocrats, but for Crowley the concept of *Thelema* or 'will' became the touchstone of his new religion.

Paganism and witchcraft had been reinterpreted in the aftermath of the French Revolution as a survival of a somehow 'democratic' religion of the medieval peasantry, which had heroically resisted the persecutions of the *ancien régime*. In France the occult revival flourished, and occult orders such as the Martinists soon established lodges in England, alongside various other Masonic, Cabbalist and Rosicrucian orders and temples inspired by the French revival. The most influential of these was the revolutionary Hermetic Order of the Golden Dawn, which took the unprecedented step for a Freemasonic order of admitting women into its ranks. Evelyn Underhill and Maud Gonne were among the many celebrities of literature, art and magic who became initiated. W. B. Yeats was a member, as were William Wynn-Westcott, Algernon Blackwood, H. Rider Haggard, Arthur Machen, Bram Stoker, and A. E. Waite. The organisation was inspired by the Rosicrucian Sir Edward Bulwer-Lytton, author of the novel *The Coming Race* (1871), which was to later have such catastrophic consequences for world history.

Of the four founder members of the Golden Dawn, three had formerly belonged to the 'Societas Rosicruciana in Anglia'. The Revd Adolphus Woodford, an Anglican priest and high-ranking Freemason, obtained cypher manuscripts which, once decoded, were found to comprise five previously unknown Rosicrucian rituals. An address was encrypted which purported to be that of a lady called Anna Sprengel of Nuremburg, Germany. Woodford, Westcott and Mathers decided to contact Frau Sprengel, who authorised them to establish the Isis-Urania Temple in London in 1888. Freemasonic orders were particularly attractive to members of the middle class, many of whom became interested in esoteric ideas through reading the works of Madame Blavatsky's Theosophical Society. She claimed to have contacted the 'Secret Chiefs'.

Frau Sprengel made similar claims, and in 1892 Mathers claimed that he made astral contact with these Secret Chiefs, whom he claimed conferred upon him supreme authority of the order, which he retained until his death during the influenza epidemic of 1918. He was succeeded by his widow, Moina Mathers, but Samuel Liddell MacGregor Mathers became a magical adversary of Crowley, who was initiated in 1898. Crowley's membership of the order was controversial in every way, as we will see, and may have been contrived by British intelligence. At any rate, Crowley's interpretation of 'Do What Thou Wilt' was no mere jest, but the supreme commandment for the 'New Aeon', the 'whole of the Law'.

Thelema, the Greek word for 'will', was to become the defining logos for the coming age of 'Crowleyanity'. This was not an injunction to wantonness and libertinism, as the 'hippies' of the 1960s were wont to interpret Crowley's ideas, but rather a restatement of the ancient magical method of harmonising or bringing into rapport the individual and divine will. Since another injunction of *Liber Al vel Legis* was that 'every man and every woman is a star' whose cosmic destiny is potentially perfect, then it follows that the person who has achieved such a rapport must be completely liberated by exercising their true will. The 'Stele of Revealing' when translated was found to include a passage from the so-called *Egyptian Book of the Dead* which contained the secret of remanifestation from one material form to another. Crowley, the 'Prince Priest the Beast', was now indwelt by Aiwass, the messenger of Horus, whom he identified as his personal Holy Guardian Angel. But the 'Equinox of the Gods' presaged a terrible calamity: 'Now let it be understood that I am a god of War and of Vengeance. I shall deal hardly with them.' The new law was the ultimate extension of Protestant individualism:

> There is no law beyond 'Do what thou wilt.' This means that each of us stars is to move on our true orbit, as marked out by the nature of our position, the law of our growth, the impulse of our past experiences. All events are equally lawful – and every one necessary, in the long run – for all of us in theory; but in practice only one act is lawful for each one of us at any given moment. Therefore Duty consists in determining to experience the right event from one moment of consciousness to another ... Each action or motion is an act of love, the uniting with one or another part of 'Nuit'; each such act must be 'under will', chosen so as to fulfil and not to thwart the true nature of the being concerned.

In the immediate aftermath of the communications their cosmic significance was not realised, even when the newly-wed couple sailed aboard a ship aptly named *The Osiris* on their homeward journey with the Theosophist Annie Besant as a co-passenger. Crowley had always been keenly aware of his own genius, but also of his failure to succeed despite his exemplary accomplishments. He made himself into a noted mountaineer despite quite fragile health. He was a chess prodigy and seriously considered concentrating on the game with a quite achievable aim of becoming a master. As a poet he displayed an early talent, with some of his works such as *Hymn to Pan* enthused with a genuine passion which will endure. Despite extraordinary intellectual capacities he failed to take a degree at Cambridge, and although he was a prodigious author many of his earlier works were self-financed from the fortune he inherited (and rapidly squandered) from his parents.

His decadent and extreme lifestyle, his notorious drug habits and his constant global perambulations all dissipated his inheritance. But for all the persecution and ostracism he was forced to endure, especially later in life, Crowley was convinced that all experiences, whether 'good' or 'bad', were necessary correctives designed to align him with his true will. After years of magical training and initiation he had finally attained the supreme magical apotheosis, the grade of 'Ipsissimus', a spiritual being completely freed from all constraints of material necessity, perfectly in balance with the universal will. When he had been initiated into the Hermetic Order of the Golden Dawn he had taken the magical motto *Frater Perdurabo*, 'I will endure until the end.' Now, as head of his own world-changing magical organisation, the 'Esoteric Magickal Order Astrum Argentum', he had become *To Mega Therion*, the 'Great Beast', the 'Master Therion'. Not since John Dee had any magician aspired to such dizzying heights, but an abyss loomed ahead.

Crowley's new-found status immediately brought him into magical conflict with Samuel Mathers, the (disputed) head of the Hermetic Order of the Golden Dawn. Under instructions from the shadowy 'Secret Chiefs', a group of hidden masters said to reside in a monastery located in a remote area of the high Himalayas, Crowley usurped Mathers. Crowley had been recruited into the British intelligence services while a student at Cambridge, and it is possible that he infiltrated the Golden Dawn with the specific aim of undermining Mathers, who was a strong supporter of the Spanish Carlist movement, which sought to restore a separate line of the Bourbons on the Spanish throne and enforce traditionalist Roman Catholic values there.

Mathers immediately responded with a magical attack on Crowley. At his sinister residence at Boleskine House on the shores of Loch Ness in Scotland, inexplicable events began to occur. There was a plague of strange black beetles, of a species previously unknown to science. Crowley's hunting dogs all died suddenly. Crowley retaliated by invoking the demons of Beelzebub and sending them to attack Mathers and his wife in Paris. Whether there was a political agenda or not, the original Golden Dawn was effectively defunct. In 1905 Crowley arrived on the borders of Sikkim and Nepal to attempt the ascent of Kanchenjunga. The expedition was a disaster, in which four people were killed after Crowley was deposed as leader for allegedly beating the porters. Crowley cynically denied any responsibility for the deaths, but his reputation in the British press began to assume a certain notoriety. These were not the acts of an English gentleman. Crowley contented himself that he had reached 22,000 feet – higher than any human being had ever climbed up to that time. The next great adventure was a walk across China with his wife and baby Lilith. The laws of lesser men did not apply to the Master Therion. Little Lilith died on the trip.

Our prurient twenty-first-century Western culture, obsessed with the salacious, has encouraged a puerile interest in Crowley's 'sex magic', but in reality these practices and ritual 'workings' which Crowley persisted in throughout his adult life derive from extremely arcane and secret doctrines passed down to initiates for thousands of years. We have already seen how in Tantrik Buddhism, Indian Shaktism and in the *fin amor* of the 'courts of love' of medieval Europe, the sexual act had been exalted into a method for achieving the ultimate ecstasy of divine union. This recondite philosophy passed down a kind of occult language, as Lama Anagarika Govinda says:

> In which very often the highest was clothed in the form of the lowest, the most sacred in the form of the ordinary, the transcendent in the form of the most earthly, and the deepest knowledge in the form of the

most grotesque paradoxes. It was not only a language for initiates, but a kind of shock-therapy, which had become necessary on account of the over-intellectualisation of the religious and philosophical life of those times. Just as the Buddha was a revolutionary against the narrow dogmatism of the privileged priestly class, so the Siddhas were revolutionaries against the self-complacency of a sheltered monastic existence, that had lost all contact with the realities of life. Their language was as unconventional as were their lives, and those who took their words literally, were either misled into striving after magic powers and worldly happiness or were repelled by what appeared to them to be blasphemy.[35]

The above perfectly describes the Crowleyan method. His purpose was to administer 'shock-therapy' to Western culture and the Christian tradition in the same way the Tantrikas had once done in Asia. In this light his scandalous behaviour becomes more than just libertine indulgence; in him the sinner and the sage meet. The sexual act is, indisputably, the ultimate *creative* act. In the union of coitus, a psycho-spiritual or emotional experience escalates into physical union, then results in a materialisation of a new being. But the sexual energy, when combined with intensive creative visualisation techniques, can also result in other forms of materialisation, such as to bring money, for example. Primarily Crowley used these acts of sex magic to exalt his consciousness to the astral plane – this was not mere perversity or self-indulgence.

To distinguish his own form of sexual magical working from traditional magic, Crowley added the letter 'k' – 'Magick'. This is the eleventh letter of the alphabet, the quintessential number of magic. It was also the old Anglo-Saxon version of the word. Eleven is traditionally associated with what is called the 'Left Hand Path' or Black Magick. In *The Book of the Law* it is written: 'My number is 11, as all their numbers who are of us.' It also represented the Ancient Greek *kteis*, the concave receptacle upon which the phallic obelisk rested, and therefore a perfect sexual symbol. The letter 'k' also indicated *Khem* or Egypt, ancient home of the Gnostic magickal teachings. Eleven represented the Quliphoth, the impure and chaotic spiritual forces which the magician must overcome in Jewish mysticism, but also *khu* or magical power in Egyptian magick. As it is written in *The Book of the Law*: 'The *Khabs* is in the *Khu*, not the *Khu* in the *Khabs*.'

There are echoes of Blake in Crowley's take on the concept of chastity. As Tobias Churton observes in his recent book, Crowley meant by this the 'right-governing of our sexual natures, not fleeing from those natures through artificial abstinence'. Despite his lurid persona it is important to remember that Crowley was a serious-minded and dedicated magus. In his

---

35 Govinda, A., *Foundations of Tibetan Mysticism*, B. I., New Delhi, 1981 edn.

classic *Magick*, Crowley is at pains to emphasise the utmost importance of purification before commencing any ceremonial magical operation:

> The first task of the Magician in every ceremony is therefore to render his Circle absolutely impregnable ... The Magician must therefore take the utmost care in the matter of purification, firstly, of himself, secondly, of his instruments, thirdly, of the place of working. Ancient Magicians recommended a preliminary purification of from three days to many months. During this period of training they took the utmost pains with diet. They avoided animal food, lest the elemental spirit of the animal should get into their atmosphere. They practised sexual abstinence, lest they should be influenced in any way by the spirit of the wife ... they avoided the contamination of social intercourse, especially the conjugal kind ...

These sentiments seem incongruous, given Crowley's perverse and sordid sexual appetites, but what to a pusillanimous British press seemed the most monstrous depravity was to Crowley an exaltation of the sacred. Moreover, *The Book of the Law* was explicit in its instructions:

> I am the Snake that giveth Knowledge & Delight and bright glory, and stir the hearts of men with drunkenness. To worship me take wine and strange drugs whereof I will tell my prophet, & be drunk thereof! They shall not harm ye at all. It is a lie, this folly against self. The exposure of innocence is a lie. Be strong, o man! lust, enjoy all things of sense and rapture: fear not that any God should deny thee for this.

It is not difficult to see the attractions of such a religion for the counter-culture of the 1960s during the sexual and psychedelic revolution, when Crowley, once reviled as the 'Wickedest Man in the World', became rehabilitated as a prophet of sexual liberation. Unfortunately, this superficial portrayal is as wrong-headed as the orthodox Christian view of him as a demonic Satanist. Technically, Crowley could not be described as a Satanist because he rejected the entire Christian perspective but he was unquestionably a practitioner of Black Magick. At his Abbey of Thelema, based at Cefalu in Sicily, Crowley regularly invoked the Egyptian variant of Satan called Set or Shaitan. For orthodox Christians the differences between these god-forms seem immaterial. If the twin of Horus, Shaitan, was synonymous with Aiwass, Crowley's Holy Guardian Angel, as he claimed, then it is not false syncretism to conclude that 'the Beast' was genuinely possessed by 'Satan'. If this were indeed the case Crowley's magical operations assumed a significance few people realise. Crowley became the head of an occult organisation called the 'Ordo Templi Orientis', or OTO, almost by accident. This 'Order of Oriental Templars' possessed certain secrets of occult sexual magick which Crowley was accused of revealing in his *The Book of Lies*. Crowley rewrote the rituals of the order to bring them into line with his own Thelemic system, but he retained and refined the sex magickal elements. For him the potency and accessibility of the sexual rituals, which provided direct access to the *Yetzirah*, or plane of formation, were the master key to a potentially world-changing system.

And the world was changing. In August 1914, Europe drifted into war as though some unseen force were manipulating events. As the historian A. J. P. Taylor postulated, the exigencies of railway timetables and logistical planning, not to mention the patriotic enthusiasm of the various combatant nations, led on inexorably to the most hideous catastrophe yet experienced by mankind. To add to Crowley's already besmirched reputation, he was accused of spying for the enemy; in fact, Crowley was a double agent, working for British intelligence. He was a grudging patriot, describing himself as like 'Bulls-eye', Bill Sikes's dog in the novel *Oliver Twist* by Dickens. Bill beats the dog and starves him but he is still Bill's dog, no one else's. Crowley saw the war as 'the preliminary skirmish in a vast world-conflict' ushered in by Horus, whose nature was 'Force and Fire'. Much of Crowley's extensive international travelling and mountaineering expeditions were a convenient cover for espionage. He approached the Hon. Everard Fielding at Naval Intelligence. In his *Aleister Crowley: The Biography*, Tobias Churton quotes a letter from Fielding which strongly refutes the calumny that Crowley was a traitor:

> I can only add that my own personal very strong belief was and is that, whatever vagaries Crowley may have indulged in, which have caused him to be expelled from two countries as widely different as Italy and France, treachery to his country was not one of them.

Crowley established himself in New York, the United States was still neutral – where he masqueraded as an Irish nationalist. German intelligence had spies and agitators there who actively encouraged Irish rebellion against Britain. Crowley was well known in German intelligence as head of the OTO, originally a German order. The Austrian mystic Rudolf Steiner, a former member of the order, was famously clairvoyant. Crowley claimed that he communicated telepathically with Steiner in Berlin, feeding him false information. The Master Therion operated on a more or less autonomous basis, but soon met George Viereck, editor of a pro-German propaganda magazine called *The Fatherland*. Crowley agreed to write articles for the magazine, which he later claimed were so extremist and absurd that they actually undermined the pro-German faction in the United States.

Crowley's ultimate aim was to so alienate American popular opinion that the German propaganda effort would be perceived as ridiculous. His most useful efforts were devoted to advocating and encouraging a policy of unrestricted submarine warfare by Germany. This, he knew, must result in a tragedy which would inflame American public opinion, and so encourage the United States to join the Allied cause. On 7 May 1915, the British liner *Lusitania* was sunk off the coast of Ireland with the loss of nearly 1,200 lives, including 128 United States citizens. Although the incident did not bring the Americans into the war immediately, it galvanised popular opinion there against the Germans. Churton notes an entry in Crowley's diary, dated 2 February 1917, noting that after over two years of his dedicated work the US government had finally broken off relations with Germany, and within months the USA would enter the war on the side of the Allied powers. The freelance espionage and disinformation campaign of the Master Therion had resulted in catastrophe for the Central powers.

Once the United States joined the Allied cause the decision of the war was finely balanced, but the effective defeat of the Russian armies following the Bolshevik Revolution of 1917 evened up the score. The German and Austro-Hungarian forces now swung west, in the hope of delivering a knock-out blow to France, Italy and the now crucial British and Imperial armies before the American army could take the field. France had been 'bled white', and in 1917 its armies had mutinied on active service. The only armies which could hold the forthcoming German offensive in the west, the so-called *Kaiserschlacht*, or 'Imperial Battle', were the British and Imperial divisions which now manned over 50 per cent of the Western Front. On 21 March 1918, fifty elite German divisions smashed into the British front in an operation code-named 'St Michael'. The most titanic struggle of the war now commenced.

British and Imperial forces were pushed back or overwhelmed, but they did not disintegrate. After a week the German offensives grew weak and their supplies ran out so that they were forced to ransack captured British stores. Almost within reach of Paris, the tired German soldiers faltered, and a combined British and French counter-attack proved sufficient to drive the Germans back to their start lines. In August 1918, the British and Imperial armies smashed through the German lines and a strategy was drawn up, a sort of proto-*Blitzkrieg* called 'Plan 1919'. The mastermind of this plan, J. F. C. Fuller, author of *The Decisive Battles of the Western World*, was one of Crowley's most faithful and adoring followers. The plan for a knock-out blow using concentrations of tanks and overwhelming support from airborne assets, especially bombers, rather than conventional artillery, was later adopted by the Germans in the Second World War. The sheer ruthlessness and brutality, but also the ingenuity of this form of warfare, were telling marks of the 'New Aeon'. Had the United States government not prevented a prolongation of the war into 1919, German defeat would have been assured and complete – though many hundreds of thousands of people would have lost their lives. As it turned out, Germany agreed to an armistice, but even as it was being signed a temporarily blinded German soldier, Austrian by birth, was recovering in a military hospital – Adolf Hitler.

Another development of the 'New Aeon' was to be the emancipation of the female, and once again Crowley (or rather Aiwass) had his finger on the pulse. Tobias Churton quotes from Crowley's assessment of the consequences of this revolutionary change for the race:

> She will demand freedom to flow wherever she will, and the right to seek her pleasure. This will lead at first to sterility and the neglect of men, with blindness and narrowness, which will cause pain. The household system will break up, causing domestic inconvenience. The frustration of natural desires will lead to a deadlock. Woman's obstinacy will further estrange the sexes, and lead to evil. Sex is now seen to be a magical act – a sacrament.

Unfortunately, what a man like Crowley deemed sacramental might seem to a more sensitive soul an execrable abomination. As Francis King points out, a normal and healthy sex attraction is an ineluctable force:

> Every faith in the world imposes on the attraction the conditions of some form of marriage, and custom, which has through the ages become so inevitable as to become an instinct, imposes also the condition of privacy in its performance, and thus the Taboo governs and retrains the natural force, and the resultant tends to control of the body by the spirit. These restrictions are exceedingly various ... some form of restriction is universal ...

But this was not Crowley's credo. 'The word of sin is restriction' was his motto, and the disintegration of the traditional ethical and moral system in this regard is a telling confirmation of the 'New Aeon'. The violation of centuries-old taboos may bring temporary gratification of passions perhaps too long suppressed, but the moral entropy must itself run its destined course. In every way, our culture promotes a lack of restraint and decorum, while lionising the vulgar and the profane.

Like John Dee before him, Crowley died in penury and a combination of obscurity and notoriety. In the end the angelic and demonic phantasmagoria proved illusory. But also like Dee, Crowley had divined the spirit of his times, sensed the seismic spiritual and psychical shifts, and predicted – I believe with uncanny accuracy – the nature of times to come. Whether we approve of these developments or not, it seems only circumspect to consider the notion that new conditions have arisen. The erosion of the Christian religion in Britain is a plain fact, as even prelates concede. The apparent emancipation of women, the breakdown of the conventional nuclear family, the infantile obsessions which enthral so-called adults, the continual tendency to individualism and self-gratification (self-will), the contempt for the infirm and unfortunate, the glorification of wealth and power, all confirm the onset of a new barbaric age. *The Book of the Law* foreshadows the social Darwinism of Hitler:

Is a God to live in a dog? No! but the highest are of us. They shall rejoice, our chosen: who sorroweth is not of us. Beauty and strength, leaping laughter and delicious languor, force and fire, are of us. We have nothing with the outcast and the unfit: let them die in their misery. For they feel not. Compassion is the vice of kings: stamp down the wretched & the weak: this is the law of the strong: this is our law and the joy of the world.

Aiwass next reiterates Satan's ancient lie: 'Think not o king, upon that lie: That Thou Must Die: verily thou shalt not die, but live.' For most conventional Christians, and for anyone with an open mind, the trajectory of such thinking ends in Auschwitz. Crowley allegedly sent a copy of *The Book of the Law* to Hitler, in hopes of encouraging the Fuehrer to convert to Thelemic doctrines. Unfortunately, the Germans had their own occult notions.

Crowley's notorious reputation and his subsequent persecution ensured he was embedded in the public imagination as a pariah, comparable perhaps with the Jimmy Savile affair in more recent times. But unlike Savile, Crowley had to live from day to day with excoriating headlines which he could rarely challenge in the courts because of financial embarrassment. His quite genuine perversions and rituals of Black Magick rebounded upon him sevenfold, as the witch's catechism warned.

Crowley had founded his Abbey of Thelema at Cefalu in 1920. A steady stream of Bohemian and pseudo-occultist visitors arrived to be instructed by the Master Therion, including Raoul Loveday, a distinguished Oxford undergraduate. He died at Cefalu in 1923, after allegedly drinking cat's blood during a Black Magickal ritual. The allegations were taken to the rabid British press by his widow, Betty May, known as the 'Tiger Woman'. She was a well-known cocaine addict and it is likely that access to large quantities of the drug was one of the many attractions of the abbey for her. Other one-time friends now denounced Crowley. Nina Hamnett, the so-called 'Queen of Bohemia', stated in her autobiography that 'Crowley had a temple in Cefalu in Sicily. He was supposed to practise Black Magic there, and one day a baby was said to have disappeared mysteriously. There was also a goat there. This all pointed to Black Magic, so people said, and the inhabitants of the village were frightened of him.'

In any ordinary case these claims would have been most defamatory and libellous, but with reference to Crowley they understated the obscene reality. The villagers of Cefalu are still frightened by the ruins of Crowley's 'Abbey', from which he was eventually expelled by the fascist authorities. His pornographic murals were whitewashed over to prevent evil forces blighting the vicinity, but were exposed during the Crowleyan 'revival' of the 1960s and 1970s. By the late 1930s Crowley was a diminished, almost grotesque figure, a heroin addict, and an impotent sex-magick practitioner who was now also bankrupt thanks to failed actions for libel in the courts. Nevertheless, as he left court one day, a completely broken and despised figure, he was approached by a young woman, Diedre O'Doherty, who offered to bear the Master Therion's child. This was a kind offer for a man of such advancing years and failing health, and despite the difficulties involved in achieving an erection, eventually a son was born to the couple, Randal Gair-Crowley, dubbed 'Aleister Ataturk' by his father. Surprisingly, the relationship was both loving and enduring. Aleister Ataturk survived his infamous father.

Crowley was not quite finished. His 'finest hour' was yet to come, like another ageing gentleman who spent many a year in the wilderness – Sir Winston Churchill. There is not sufficient space in this slim volume to do justice to this maverick magus. Those who wish to study the Master Therion more seriously should peruse his own *Auto-hagiography*, his other abundant literary output, and the many hundreds of books written about him since his death on 1 December 1947. His influence on modern Western popular culture is well known, especially since he was selected by the Beatles as 'one of our favourite people' and featured on the cover of their May 1967 album *Sgt. Pepper's Lonely Hearts Club Band*. But for serious students of magic/magick, he is no mere progenitor of sex, drugs and rock 'n' roll but a profound mystic, a prophet, and a world-teacher, a British Bodhisattva. His calumniation by Christians, though understandable, and his idolisation by neo-pagans, dilettante occultists and Satanists, have all obscured his core message. He took no relish in conveying his new law, and was indeed terrified by the implications of the 'New Aeon'. *The Book of the Law* states ominously:

I am the warrior Lord of the Forties: the Eighties cower before me & are abased. I will bring you victory and joy: I will be at your arms in battle & ye shall delight to slay. Success is your proof; courage is your armour; go on, go on, in my strength; & ye shall turn not back for any!

On 1 September 1939, German tanks rolled across the Polish border as *Stuka* dive-bombers pulverised the brave but hopelessly antiquated Polish cavalry. The child Horus was about to be baptised in a sea of blood.

16

The Magical Battle of Britain

In 1871, the Rosicrucian Sir Edward Bulwer-Lytton published an anonymous novel called *The Coming Race*. In the book a mining engineer is involved in a weird accident and finds a tunnel into a previously undiscovered subterranean world. This world is populated by a superior race called the *Vril-Ya* who were once surface dwellers but were forced to live in a 'Hollow-Earth' resulting from a catastrophic flood which had destroyed the mythical Atlantis. The denizens of the underground realm have developed extraordinary superhuman physical and psychical faculties, making them resemble angelic beings. There is no sexual inequality among them – women enjoy the same rights as men, except that they may discard their sexual partner and choose another when they will. Their survival and progress derives from their distillation of a magical 'fluid' called 'Vril'. This fluid or elixir confers extraordinary salubrious powers like the *prima materia* of the alchemists. (The meat-extract drink Bovril cashed in on the cult status of the novel – Bulwer-Lytton was a bestselling author in an age when literate people still habitually read books.)

What had been a Jules Verne type fantasy soon took on another, more sinister aspect. Madame Helena Petrovna Blavatsky was a Ukrainian occultist of mixed Russian and German descent. She travelled very widely as a young woman, and claimed that she had met the 'Secret Chiefs' in a monastery in the Himalayas where she was initiated into the 'Great White Brotherhood'. She subsequently produced a body of astonishing occult literature, notably *Isis Unveiled* (1877) and *The Secret Doctrine* (1888), which laid the foundations of Theosophy, a new syncretic and mystical world religion which arose from her foundation of the Theosophical Society in 1875. Blavatsky, and later one of her followers, Rudolf Steiner, founder of the breakaway Anthroposophical Society, took Bulwer-Lytton's ideas to be occult truths. In the post-war period in Germany many occult groups and societies flourished, and the idea of a mythical race with extraordinary powers, hidden behind (or rather beneath) the scenes was an obvious psychological resort to notions of magical 'helpers' or redeemers for a proud people who felt cheated and humiliated. Organisations such as the 'Thule Society', the 'Lords of the Black Stone', the 'Black Sun Society' and the 'Vril Society' – named after Bulwer-Lytton's magical energy – all thrived in post-1918 Germany. According to Jacques Bergier and Louis Pauwels in their book *The Morning of the Magicians*, the Vril Society was already established in Germany before the war.

From these disparate groups an occult caucus formed, which underpinned the Nazi movement, and exercised an influence over the regime which extended right to the highest echelons of the evil dictatorship. The ancient Swastika symbol was used by the Vril Society who passed it on to the Nazis. They believed that the Vril-Ya really existed, and that by practising meditative exercises the Germanic peoples would transform themselves into a race of supermen. These exercises were modelled on those of the Jesuit St Ignatius of Loyola. He was a Basque, and the Nazis believed that the Basques were originally refugees from Atlantis. Bergier and Pauwels surmised that the Nazis believed these 'spiritual exercises' to be a survival of the esoteric doctrines of the Atlantean religion.

On Halloween 1895 a baby girl was born in Zagreb, Croatia. Her name was Maria Orsic, and she grew up to be one of the most stunningly beautiful women in Europe, if not the world. Maria had other unique gifts: she was a talented clairvoyant and medium. Her political sympathies were passionately pro-Nazi. She soon became the leader of the *Vril Gesellschaft* or Vril Society. But this paragon of feminine beauty had a very dark side. She claimed she had contacted beings from other galaxies or dimensions, including from a planet around the star Aldebaran in the constellation of Taurus, sixty-five light years from Earth. Some of the messages Orsic channelled were in a language later recognised as Ancient Sumerian. She also drew designs for machines resembling the *Vimanas* or flying machines of Hindu mythology. These designs were so top secret and so revolutionary that the full details have never been disclosed, but the Nazi regime may have used the designs to create 'Flying Saucers' using a revolutionary motive energy. A civilised, highly educated Christian nation had allowed itself to become deluded, one might almost say possessed – by forces which can only be described as demonic. On 1 September 1939, those evil forces were unleashed with catastrophic results for mankind.

Britain, though ill prepared for war on the material level, was more than ready for the magical fray. Violet Mary Firth, known by her magical sobriquet 'Dion Fortune', organised a magical defence strategy immediately after Britain declared war on Germany on Sunday 3 September 1939. Like Maria Orsic, Dion Fortune was a talented medium who believed herself to be in communication with 'Ascended Masters' including Jesus. The young Violet became interested in occultism because of a profoundly negative experience of 'black' magic. When she was twenty years old, Violet became the victim of an unscrupulous employer, the principal of an agricultural college in Warwickshire. This person had learned mental manipulation techniques in India, according to Janine Chapman's book (Fortune never disclosed the identity of the person in her lifetime). This person destroyed Violet's self-confidence, undermined her mental health, and finally her physical energies waned and she became seriously unwell. In her *Psychic Self-Defence*, Fortune relates how this debilitating and profoundly disturbing experience led her to study psychology. Her reading of Carl Jung's works gave her an interest in broadly 'occult' ideas, and she blossomed into one of the most influential and talented magical practitioners of her day. The occult writer Bernard Bromage described her magnetic psychical power: 'There was an odd atmosphere about her of the sybil, the prophetess, the diver into deep occult seas.' Her occult 'Community of the Inner Light', which became the 'Society of the Inner Light', mobilised its magical energies to rouse the spiritual guardians of Albion. She had been initiated into an off-shoot temple of the Hermetic Order of the Golden Dawn operated by Samuel Mathers' widow, Moina Mathers, sister of the philosopher Henri Bergson.

Like Crowley, Fortune and her close friend Charles Loveday received communications via 'inspirational mediumship' which dictated a document called *The Cosmic Doctrine* while they were living in Glastonbury, Somerset. Loveday was much older than Dion, but the magical link is no respecter of age and the pair became a powerful magical partnership. As if 'by magic', Fortune was offered a plot of land located at the foot of Glastonbury Tor, the most sacred magical site in England. Frederick Bligh Bond, an architect, had become fascinated by the Tor, which he was convinced contained secret chambers and other subterranean anomalies. He began to receive communications via a spirit medium which he claimed came from a medieval monk. These messages resulted in archaeological excavations which confirmed Bligh Bond's hunches. Glastonbury was the home of the cult of the Mother Goddess or Feminine Principle, which Fortune identified with her magical persona.

This most sacred soil in Albion, the repository of the legends of 'the Secret of the Lord', King Arthur and the Holy Grail, is a vortex for magical energies of extraordinary power, as the author can attest. Dion Fortune's small community, based sometimes in London and at others in Nissen huts below the Tor, began an ongoing cycle of creative visualisations designed to combat the malevolent magic of the Nazi regime, to defend Britain against invasion – but also, and crucially, to reconstruct a spiritually purified Albion in the post-war period. Gareth Knight's introduction to Fortune's *The Magical Battle of Britain* is the best available account of these magical operations, but the general thrust of this present chapter is that this 'magical battle' was not won in 1945, but raged long after the military struggle was over. Indeed, it is a battle which is still ongoing.

Dion Fortune was familiar with John Dee's and Edward Kelley's interest in Glastonbury, especially that it was the centre of incredible 'Earth Energies', a focus for ley lines, and that in prehistoric antiquity it had been the centre of a gigantic earthwork known as the 'Glastonbury Zodiac' which could still be discerned in the landscape for those with refined spiritual vision. Her 'Sane Occultism' as she called it was the antithesis of Crowley's approach, deeply mystical, Christian, not intimidating, structured so as to be accessible to all comers of any level of ability. She appealed to those who cared enough for their spiritual inheritance, indeed their very survival, to spare half an hour or so once a week, to practice group meditation and visualisation techniques. These were posted out in a bulletin. But Fortune and Crowley, so far apart in their magical perspectives, were both heirs of the rich British magical tradition. In her introduction to her *Quest for Dion Fortune*, Janine Chapman remarks on the similar pathways these magicians trod:

> They were contemporaries; Dion Fortune, *nee* Violet Firth, was born in 1891, Crowley in 1875. They died within a year of each other – 1946 and 1947 respectively. Both were nursed on Kabbalah and initiated in the Golden Dawn. Both sought the long-buried wine of the old gods: ancient, pure, and powerful; both called Britain home; both sought personal and racial identity in the holy places of their native land.

Dion Fortune's interests coincided with Crowley's too, in her study of Tantrik techniques, and especially her devotion to 'the primordial and elemental essence of woman – the Black Isis':

> Black Isis embodies the *sakti* (power) that destroys all that is inessential and obstructive to the soul's development. It is the power that liberates the spirit of man from the confines of limited experience. The basis of Fortune's practical work involves the bringing through into manifestation of this *sakti*, by the magically controlled interplay of sexual polarity. This is embodied in the priest, or consecrated male, and the specially chosen female. Together they enact the immemorial Rite and form a vortex in the ether, down which the tremendous energies of Black Isis rush into manifestation.[36]

Although their philosophies were so seemingly antithetical, Fortune was sufficiently interested in Crowley that she corresponded with him and visited him at Netherwood, his guesthouse in Hastings, even when she was very ill just before she died in 1946. Just over a year later Crowley died too. In the service of the 'Great Work', personal prejudices must be relinquished. At a public lecture she recognised Crowley despite never having met him before. Such encounters are common among talented occultists, but Crowley's claim that 'a secret understanding' existed by which she recognised his 'authority' over her may be dismissed. Dion Fortune was not the kind of woman to defer to anyone's authority – and knew very well how to defend herself from impure forces.

---

36 Grant, K., 'Dion Fortune', *Man, Myth and Magic*, Issue No. 36, Vol. 8, Marhall Cavendish, 1970.

In May 1940 the German army struck deep into France, routed the dispirited French army, and drove the British forces onto the beaches of Dunkirk, from which they were miraculously evacuated by sea in early June. Within weeks Britain stood alone against the most ruthless military machine in history. The 'Father' of modern witchcraft, Gerald Gardner (1884–1964) claimed that a witch coven at Highcliffe-on-Sea raised 'the Cone of Power' against the potential invasion as their ancestors had done against Napoleon, the Armada and Caligula. A sick old man exposed himself to the elements as a human sacrifice to raise the 'Cone' energy. Then the witches projected a single thought-form at Hitler's mind: 'You cannot cross the sea!' The Magical Battle of Britain was about to commence.

Of course, Britain was not really alone. Many brave Polish airmen and soldiers made their way to France, and ultimately Britain, to continue the struggle against the Nazis. A large contingent of the French army was evacuated from Dunkirk and they were absorbed into the British military for the remainder of the war, serving with distinguished gallantry. Americans, Indians, Canadians, South Africans, Australians and New Zealanders, Czechs, and even some Irish volunteers made up a large proportion of the fighter pilots who won the 'aerial' Battle of Britain. Without their valiant contribution and often their ultimate sacrifice, Britain may not have survived.

One of the refugees from Nazi-occupied France was the philosopher Simone Weil. Her parents were liberal-minded Jews, but she never subscribed to a particular religious position, though many Christians regard her as a kind of saint. She was one of the finest minds in Europe at a time when the world had lost its mind, but despite her giant intellect it was her spiritual insight which marked her out. She despised the exploitative and dehumanising machine of capitalism, and its outgrowth in difficult times, fascism, joining the anti-fascist struggle in Spain during the civil war of 1936–39. Although she hardly associated with a church, her private identification with Christ was profound beyond anything most regular communicants ever experience, a relationship of ineffable grace. In an essay entitled *A War of Religions*, written just before she died in exile in England in 1943, Weil sums up the atmosphere of this most dangerous yet also most glorious chapter in our history. She begins by describing the root cause of the sickness which has infected the collective soul:

> The method consists in delimiting a social area into which the pair of contradictories, good and evil, may not enter ... In general, throughout history this art of delimiting special areas has enabled men who did not appear to be monsters to perpetrate innumerable monstrous crimes ... A nation can do this. In antiquity both Rome and Israel were such nations. Once a Roman had divested himself in his own eyes of every quality except that of being a Roman he was emancipated from good and evil.

Indifferent to good and evil, the worshippers of a social or national cult become idolaters, devotees of what Plato called 'a great beast'. Those who no longer condemn evil seek to assure themselves of its abolition by 'torturing the weak'. The result is, literally, madness – not only on the level of the individual but of the entire social collective. But it is not only the torturers and oppressors who are afflicted, but the tortured and enslaved, 'the wretched of the earth'. Their pain and humiliation 'awakens evil within them in the form of fear and hatred. They can neither forget evil nor can they escape from it, and so they live in the best possible imitation of hell on earth.'

This woman, who died of tuberculosis in a sanatorium in southern England, refusing to eat the nourishing food she needed to stay alive on the principle that her fellow countrymen were starving, was faithful to the creed she promulgated as the only solution to the soul-sickness infecting the world – spiritual poverty. Only by the restoration of a pure spiritual elite, who would be poor in fact as well as in theory, could the population be liberated from idolatry. But unlike the medieval monastic orders, or Hermann Hesse's 'Castalia', an imagined intellectual monastic theocracy in his novel *The Glass Bead Game*, published in the year of her death, Weil's 'elite' were not to be separate or distinct from the populace, but embedded within the community and in constant contact with it. As she lay dying, her mind considered the great spiritual struggle which turned on the outcome of the Battle of Britain. The stakes had never been higher.

By the summer of 1940, Hitler's plans for an invasion, preceded by an overwhelming aerial bombing campaign to eliminate the Royal Air Force, were approaching completion in the form of Operation 'Sea Lion'. The war in the skies was indeed a heavenly war, like the ancient struggle in Zoroastrian myth:

> Anyone who had understood that this war was going to be a religious drama could have foreseen many years ago which nations would play an active role and which would be passive victims. The nations which lived without religion could be nothing but passive victims. This was the case with almost the whole of Europe. But Germany lives by idolatry. Russia lives by another idolatry and it may even be that it contains some not quite extinguished life from a rejected past. And although England is wasted by the sickness of the age she has such continuity of history and such a living tradition that some of her roots are still nourished by a past which was bathed in the light of mysticism.

Sometimes our neighbours know our business better than we know it ourselves. This remarkable tribute to the British mystical tradition soars into the heavens like a Spitfire:

There was a moment when England confronted Germany like a defenceless child in the face of a brute with a gun in each hand. In such a situation there is not much that a child can do. But if it coldly looks the brute in the eye it is certain that the brute will hesitate for a moment. And that is what happened ... The oceans of blood sacrificed by Russian soldiers have made us almost forget what happened before. And yet that moment when England stood silent and unshaken is even more worthy, by far, to be eternally remembered. That halting of the German troops at the Channel is the supernatural point in this war.

But although she died praising the nation which had given her sanctuary, she also issued a stark warning: 'If we are only saved by American money and machines we shall fall back, one way or another, into a new servitude like the one which we now suffer.'

Whatever aspersions may have been cast on Aleister Crowley's activities in the First World War, in the Second World War his allegiances were in absolutely no doubt: 'There will be no second Versailles – there will be Armageddon. The Hun must be wiped out. The Hun *will* be wiped out.' He sent a patriotic verse of his called *England, Stand Fast!* to Churchill and volunteered his propaganda expertise for 'the consideration of H.M Government'. For all his notoriety, a magus always has his uses. Tobias Churton has unearthed diary entries and other correspondence which seems to confirm that Crowley was the originator of the 'V – for Victory' propaganda campaign, designed to raise morale among the Allied populations, and also to encourage the resistance movements in occupied countries. He wrote a pamphlet entitled *Thumbs Up! A Pentagram – a Pantacle to Win the War!* The story goes that English and Welsh archers at the Battle of Agincourt in 1415 used the two-fingered salute to the French who had threatened to cut off their fingers if they were captured. But for Crowley, 'V' signified both 'victory' and 'will', or *thelema*; in Greek *gematria*, which attributes a numerical value to each letter, *thelema* adds to 93, the sacred number of the Thelemic faith.

Hitler's deputy Rudolf Hess flew to Scotland in 1941 in an abortive effort to broker a peace with potential British quislings. Crowley volunteered his services to Naval Intelligence yet again. Hess was steeped in occultism and Crowley believed he may be able to exercise a form of mind control over him. Behind the scenes the Master Therion's efforts may have been more important than has hitherto been recognised. Crowley was still the head of a number of important international magickal orders. In the United States, Jack Parsons, a rocket engineer from California, had been initiated into 'Agape Lodge' of the OTO, founded in 1935 by Wilfred Talbot Smith. Parsons pioneered the 'Jet Propulsion Laboratory' or JPL, which laid the foundations for NASA. He was also an enthusiastic practitioner of sex-magick. A pioneer of experimental liquid and solid fuel for rocket engines, he was unfortunately 'hoist by his own petard', blowing himself, his home, and a small district of

Pasadena up in 1952. This connection between the OTO and the inchoate rocket and space programmes shows that it was not just the Nazis who were prepared to resort to magic in pursuit of victory.

This little-known legacy of Thelemic influence proves that Crowley was no clownish charlatan; the new Law had made powerful converts right at the heart of the military-industrial complex, and by implication in the political complex too. But Crowley, though still mentally alert and intellectually active, was approaching his rather sad end. He retired to a country pub, the Bell Inn at Aston Clinton. It was rather difficult finding a supply of heroin sufficient for his legendary needs in such an isolated village during wartime. He eventually moved to a guesthouse called 'Netherwood' in Hastings, where he died on 1 December 1947. As he died, a great wind blew into the room and a deafening thunderclap was heard as the Master Therion's spirit departed to the gods – or perhaps to another place. Within a few years his vision of a 'New Aeon' seemed remarkably prescient – he had lived to witness the atom bomb. Despite the ignominy and the indignity of his final years, the kernel of his magical doctrine survived and prospered, whereas for his despised adversaries, the Christians, at least in Britain, the inverse has been true. In that, he would feel happily vindicated.

Britain's survival had been a kind of miracle. Operation 'Dynamo', the evacuation of Dunkirk between 26 May and 4 June 1940, rescued over 338,000 men. The weather was absolutely calm and still for the whole period, the only week of the year when the 'Little Ships', volunteers sailing their own small craft, could have made the crossing. The 'Few', less than 3,000 RAF fighter pilots who won the battle in the skies over England, were only days away from exhaustion when Hitler aborted the invasion to turn his attention towards Russia. The army had lost much of its equipment in France, and without the 'lend-lease' agreement with the USA, British forces would have been woefully ill equipped. Industry had to be completely restructured to cope with the demands of a ruthless modern war, and the army rebuilt from scratch as the U-boats waged a savage war on British shipping in the Battle of the Atlantic. Britain was often within weeks of starvation. As the German hotel guest in the 1970s BBC comedy *Fawlty Towers* wonders aloud, 'However did they win?'

Of course, the war was not won by magic alone, but required 'blood, toil, tears and sweat', as Churchill said. The 'Blitz' or aerial bombardment by the Luftwaffe, and later rocket attacks, killed 60,000 civilians. The key to victory was unity. The old Etonian socialist George Orwell, the William Cobbett of his day, wrote a small book as part of a series designed to define the political aims of the war called *The Lion and the Unicorn*. In the moment of supreme crisis, the British people knew instinctively what to do.

Just because patriotism is all but universal and not even the rich are uninfluenced by it, there can be moments when the whole nation suddenly swings together and does the same thing, like a herd of cattle facing a wolf. There was such a moment, unmistakeably, at the time of the disaster in France. After eight months of vaguely wondering what the war was about, the people suddenly knew what they had got to do: first to get the army away from Dunkirk, and secondly to prevent invasion. It was like the awakening of a giant. Quick! Danger! The Philistines be upon thee, Samson! And then the swift unanimous action – and then, alas, the prompt relapse into sleep ... But does this mean that the instinct of the English will always tell them to do the right thing? Not at all, merely that it will tell them to do the same thing. In the 1931 General Election, for instance, we all did the wrong thing in perfect unison. We were as single-minded as the Gadarene swine.

Orwell's radical patriotism, like Cobbett's in his day, recognised that the 'loyalty' of the British patriot was to a substrate of mythical values, rather than to vague and transitory institutions;

> Patriotism has nothing to do with conservatism. It is a devotion to something that is changing but is felt to be mystically the same ... To be loyal both to Chamberlain's England and to the England of tomorrow might seem an impossibility, if one did not know it to be an everyday phenomenon. Only revolution can save England, that has been obvious for years, but now the revolution has started, and it may proceed quite quickly if only we can keep Hitler out.

As one who had benefited from an elitist education at Eton himself, Orwell was quite clear that the fish rots from the head down: 'One of the dominant facts in English life during the last century has been the decay of ability in the ruling class.' Why was it that 'at every decisive moment (something) made every British statesman do the wrong thing with so unerring an instinct?' The answer, according to Orwell, was that they were ossified, decadent, senescent representatives of a hopelessly antiquated ruling class who saw the world in terms of public school 'fair-play'. The fascists, Nazis and communists, the 'Greater East Asia Co-Prosperity Sphere' of imperial Japan, were not 'gentlemen' and despised 'fair-play'. If Britain (or, as he prefers, 'England') was to survive, the cult of amateurism must give way to the exigencies of a total professionally managed war, in which the wider population at last have some investment by access to meritorious promotion.

Orwell's manifesto is not a book but a bomb, designed to shock the British population into action – like the bombs he predicted would soon fall on sleepy suburban England in his novel *Coming Up for Air*, published less than three months before the outbreak of hostilities. Orwell has gained a reputation as a kind of prophet. His dystopian *Nineteen Eighty-Four* confirms his remarkable insight into the potentials for a totalitarian surveillance state.

He was prophetic, too, in his analysis that the long-suffering people of Britain will no longer tolerate the system of elitism, patronage and privilege which colluded in the rise of fascism before the war:

> At some point you have got to deal with the man who says 'I should be no worse off under Hitler.' But what answer can you give him – that is, what answer that you can expect him to listen to – while common soldiers risk their lives for two and sixpence a day, and fat women ride about in Rolls-Royce cars, nursing pekineses? ... The working class will have to suffer terrible things. And they will suffer them, almost indefinitely, provided that they know what they are fighting for ... they will want some kind of proof that a better life is ahead for themselves and their children.

The Beveridge Report *Social Insurance and Allied Services*, which laid the foundations for a post-war welfare state, duly took note of Orwell's advice in November 1942. But what Orwell was proposing was far more radical, an 'English Revolution': 'By revolution we become more ourselves, not less. There is no question of stopping short ... Nothing ever stands still. We must add to our heritage or lose it, we must grow greater or grow less, we must go forward or backward. I believe in England, and I believe that we shall go forward.'

Eventually, after a gruelling and bloody ordeal which lasted almost six years, victory was obtained and jubilant Londoners celebrated amid a city scarred by years of air raids. The war had been won, but Britain was bankrupt and the United States of America had succeeded it as the hegemonic world power. The British Empire was abandoned, due to exigencies of cost and pressure from the USA. At this point, the 'historical' part of this book ends. It has always been my prejudice that nothing should properly be called 'history' which is within living memory, and in the author's case that chronology has almost been reached.

In general terms the story of Britain since 1945 has been that of its finding a new post-imperial role in the world. For many years Britain seemed to have chosen to act as a 'bridge' between the USA and the EU, but in 2016 narrowly voted to leave the latter bloc. More than ever, British people will need to look deep into their mythical past if they are to discover a new identity and purpose – but this may not happen. It is quite possible that the UK itself will fracture and disintegrate. Strictly speaking these matters are beyond my remit in this book, but as we reach the end of our journey, I feel it would be remiss of me to conclude without looking briefly at the 'spiritual state of the nation', as it were. This is not an enjoyable task, indeed it is obnoxious, but it is a duty on me to do it, even at the hazard of offending Christian and Pagan friends. My contention is that the spiritual condition of Britain is in an extremely poor way, and that this spiritual malaise paralyses us, as if we were victims of some spell of a malignant wizard.

Gerald Gardner, a British imperial civil servant, lived in the Far East for most of his life. He lived in Ceylon (Sri Lanka), Malaya (Malaysia) and India until his retirement in 1936. His sojourns 'east of Aden', and his natural inclinations towards the exotic religions of those regions – including Tantrik doctrines – meant that by the time he returned to his native land he was saturated in esoteric religion and philosophy, especially the cult of Kali, the destructive aspect of the Goddess. Gardner was an initiate of Crowley's OTO and knew Crowley personally for a while. He was also an acquaintance of Annie Besant, Madame Blavatsky's successor as head of the Theosophical Society. He claimed that he was introduced to a witch coven by a practitioner of 'the Craft' called 'Old Dorothy' Clutterbuck just before the outbreak of the Second World War. He took the work of the anthropologist Margaret Murray and put flesh on the bones of her theory of the underground survival of an 'Old Religion' of the 'Goddess and the Horned God'. What Gardner did was to formalise the practices of disparate occultists and to dignify them with the title of a 'religion', based primarily on goddess worship. Gardner was careful to downplay negative stereotypes of witchcraft and to emphasise a 'nature' religion based on the celebration of the eight great festivals of European Pagan antiquity.

In the aftermath of the Second World War, during which 60 million people had been slaughtered by nominally 'Christian' nations, many people were attracted to the idea of a beneficent, nature-worshipping Goddess religion – and with good reason. But was it real? The real problem with Gardner, as with Iolo Morganwg and his recreation of Druidism, is that while some of his ideas were evidentially based and intellectually robust, some others were almost certainly his own inventions, or reworked rituals taken from Crowley, whose abominable reputation still clung to occultism like a bad smell. Gardner was a sado-masochist, and his brand of witchcraft was ostentatiously sexualised. Gardner's high priestess, Doreen Valiente, was unhappy with the Thelemic element of his religion, and in 1957 she seceded from his coven. The Goddess and the Horned God had parted company, and Valiente's intuition that Gardner's exposition of witchcraft was a hotchpotch of various sources imbued with Crowleyan doctrines was correct.

Instead, Valiente turned to other native, and especially 'Celtic' influences, including the extraordinary work of the poet Robert Graves. In 1948 he published his *The White Goddess: A Historical Grammar of Poetic Myth*, which postulated the survival of a pre-Christian Goddess religion, much along the same lines as had been proposed by Margaret Murray. He became infatuated with the American poet Laura Riding, whom he believed to be his muse, a human incarnation of the Goddess. They lived and worked together in Majorca from 1929 until the outbreak of the Spanish Civil War in 1936 when they left for the USA. The relationship soon became acrimonious and hostile; the same woman who had once enchanted him reduced him to utter desolation and misery. This was the eternal price the poet must pay to the

Goddess, the only offering acceptable to her – his own life. Graves retained his adoration for Riding even when they became hopelessly estranged. During the Second World War Graves returned to Devonshire in England where, quite unexpectedly, he became obsessed with the idea of *The White Goddess*, which he wrote in a few frenetic weeks in its first draft.

Many modern scholars of the occult, including Ronald Hutton of the University of Bristol, have dismissed *The White Goddess* as the romantic whimsy of a rather sensitive and old-fashioned gentleman who was emotionally and sexually obsessed. As will become clear, there are many aspects of the pagan revival which I feel are unsatisfactory and/or fantastical, but I do not include Graves in that category. He was not a fantasist, a phoney or an intellectual 'lightweight'. Those who have felt the power of the muse or Goddess, who have experienced her grace, beauty, subtlety and mystery, *know* the reality, as one who has not felt it cannot.

Graves believed that he was able to access hidden or forgotten knowledge using a technique he called 'Analeptic Thought'. This intuitive historiography revealed a schema which, he thought, explained the origins of myth and poetry as a dramatisation of the death and resurrection of the god-king during the cycle of the solar year. Graves alleged that before the coming of the patriarchal, solar, deities the cult of the Goddess had been ubiquitous and supreme, but her usurpation had resulted in the catastrophic imposition of a culture of father-worship. As an indication of the terrible power of the solar gods, nature itself, the province of the Goddess, was to be controlled, tamed, enclosed and owned. This in turn made war between patriarchal nations inevitable, threatening the very survival of the Earth. This grim, bloody and wicked process culminated in the great wars of the twentieth century. Graves was an officer in the trenches of the Western Front during the First World War. His autobiography, *Goodbye to All That*, evokes the horror, and humour, of that war and the sense that for those who had survived the ordeal nothing could ever be the same again. Graves was convinced that the only practicable way of saving the Earth from utter ruin was to re-establish Goddess-worship as the universal religion of mankind. This, however, could not be achieved without a devastating transitional period:

> But the longer her hour is postponed, and therefore the more exhausted by man's irreligious improvidence the natural resources of the soil and sea become, the less merciful will the fivefold mask be, and the narrower the scope of action which she grants to whichever demi-god she chooses to take as her temporary consort in godhood. Let us placate her in advance.

This exhortation was based on his belief that the Goddess would assume her rightful dignity once people began to invest power in her person by worshipping her – that is, her power would grow exponentially. The power of any religion derives from the faith of its adherents. Such a proposition was, of course, very popular with witches, pagans and feminists, and although Graves should not be taken as a completely credible historical source, he was nevertheless an erudite and extremely perceptive scholar. The proof of the pudding, as they say, is in the eating, and in my opinion Graves foresaw religious developments which are only now becoming apparent. The age of the Goddess is here.

The deep longing for the Goddess felt by poets and artists needs to be balanced by the recognition that she is as mysterious, reckless, anarchic and 'bomb-happy', as my father used to say, as she is graceful, beautiful, nurturing and courageous. It is beyond my remit in this book to examine the more recent additions to the non-Christian gods and goddesses in our twenty-first-century culture, but one diaspora does stand out, because it has retained a genuine link to Goddess worship which is probably authentic. The 'gypsies' or Roma people originated in the Indian subcontinent. They arrived in Britain in the late medieval period and have been persecuted and excluded ever since. During the Tudor period it became a capital offence to *be* a gypsy. The Roma worship a form of the Goddess Kali, often represented as a variant of the Virgin Mary. They are dualists, possibly through the influence of the Bogomils, worshipping a god called *Devlah* which many non-gypsies equate with the Devil. In fact, the Roma Devil is called the *Beng*. Their history has been very similar to that of the *Marranos* or Spanish Jews, who were offered the alternatives of conversion to the Roman Catholic faith, exile or execution. The Roma chose to be practical about things, and have long professed a Christian or pseudo-Christian faith. In fact, the cult of the Goddess still lives among the Roma, and within a few miles of my house there is still a place sacred to the Goddess Kali. It is my personal belief that these traditions were absorbed by indigenous British people who lived, at least seasonally, alongside the traveller communities, and that they may have become conflated with native paganism.

It is possible that paganism is now the fastest-growing religion in the UK, but it is too disparate and institutionally weak to exert an influence proportionate to its numbers. But this is not its only weakness. Where, for me, it fails to engage with the world as it is presently configured is in its repudiation of the concept of human sinfulness. In this, it strongly resembles the Pelagian heresy which flourished here in the dying days of the Roman Empire. Gardnerian witchcraft and other varieties of 'Wicca' spread beyond Britain to its former colonies, and especially to the United States. It found allies among the counter-cultural movements which were springing up there, and among environmentalists, feminists, and of course young people fascinated by the sensual and the macabre. In this 'Age of the Child', the lesson is quickly learned that when we are being 'good' we are not usually having 'fun', and when we are having 'fun' we are not usually being 'good'. No one would be happier than the author if life were a Byronic romp in the mythical land of 'Cockaigne', where all the manifold ills of this world were somehow abolished. Now, as an older man, I find I must concur with the sage who said that life was a gradual process of 'adjustment to disillusionment'. But a religion is not just another cheap thrill. Neo-paganism and Wicca strongly promote their faiths as 'the Old Religion' but in truth, most of their rituals are products of the imagination and intuition of twentieth century magicians, poets and anthropologists. Authentic pre-Christian paganism has left traces but there is no direct historical link to modern occultism that can be validated.

This is not to say that magical/spiritual experience in itself is invalid, however. 'Theologically' paganism too often lacks intellectual rigour, and it is vulnerable to personality cults promoted by charismatic individuals for their own selfish ends, in just the same way that cults and sects have always been. Both pagans and Christians seem oblivious to the way in which their virtuous-sounding aim of promoting gentle stewardship of the Earth is vitiated by their personal complicity in the maintenance of consumer capitalism. There are very few pedestrians these days, of any faith, but the simplest way of saving the planet would be to dump the motorcar. Paganism too often displays a contemptuous and hostile attitude to monotheists, especially Christians, whose faith they often cruelly disparage based on ignorant prejudice. As Russell and Alexander say,

> Christianity was perceived as part of the establishment, so Judaeo-Christian values were deemed pernicious. Anything old had to be destroyed so that humanity could be freed to reveal its true self; its basically good nature. (This goodness of human nature, by the way, is unknown both to historians and biologists.) The radical views of the counterculture were almost identical to – and largely derived from – the movement of Romanticism in the nineteenth century, which was based on the idea of the perfectibility of human nature freed from the bonds of traditional authority. The mantra of the Romantics was that feelings trumped thoughts and that the creative and the original trumped the rational and the empirical. The 1960s ushered in a renewed Romanticism based on feelings.

Russell and Alexander sum up the thought process of many modern pagans as 'It could be; I want it to be; it is.' This is childish superstition, not magic.

And yet, for all its contradictions, its Romanticism and its dependence on rather flimsy or disputed foundations in 'history', neo-paganism is flourishing like a green sapling, whereas Christianity in the UK is in seemingly terminal decline. Church attendance has been going down for many decades now, and my impression is that the established Church of England probably has fewer 'bums on pews' on Sundays than the Roman Catholic Church. The Nonconformists tell a similar tale of woe, and although a positive-minded evangelical might retort that the 3 million or so Christians attending worship easily outnumber the combined supporters going to Saturday football matches (and with a good deal less razzmatazz), I think that to describe the UK as a 'Christian' nation would be disingenuous. I am not qualified to comment on other institutions, but the fate of the Church of England, my own native religion, is of concern to me. Its extinction seems practically inevitable – perhaps even within my own lifetime. The implications of this evaporation of Christianity are quite profound, but if I am right the parish churches will soon become desolate ruins, like their monastic predecessors. In the final chapter we will examine these implications, and possible solutions – but in a spirit of fairness let us look now at the reasons behind the apostasy.

This will be painful for many Anglicans, but we cannot 'screen our faces' from the death of God – any more than we can ignore our own mortality. The Book of Proverbs (29:18) says, 'Where there is no vision the people perish.' It is not easy to have such vision in this modern world, especially spiritual vision. Our sight is obscured, literally, by the constant bombardment of social media, the internet, television, advertising, so-called 'entertainment'. Children are dragooned into the system as toddlers, and one dreads to think of the world as it will be by the time they reach old age. The rational-scientific, neo-liberal, consumer-capitalist worldview has become a substitute 'religion'. Graves put it succinctly: 'Though the West is still nominally Christian, we have come to be governed, in practice, by the unholy triumdivate of Pluto god of wealth, Apollo god of science, and Mercury god of thieves.'

My own inkling has been that the Dissolution of the Monasteries and the Protestant Reformation marked the beginning of the apostasy we see today. For almost half a millennium the Church of England has been a sort of spiritual civil service. The social experiment of industrialism began in England, and its ravages and injustices particularly affected the new industrial working class in the filthy, squalid cities. These people felt abandoned by the Church, and often they were right. They turned instead to their own meeting houses and chapels. The Church 'turned a blind eye', too, to the slave trade during the early years of the British Empire. Because it was (and for the moment is) the established Church it was too closely intermeshed with the exploitative imperial complex to exert real moral pressure.

Until the end of the Second World War Britain was, as Orwell observed, 'the most class-ridden country under the sun'. The class interest of the Church of England was synonymous with that of the ruling elite. It resisted the extension of the franchise to working men, then women, and quoted scriptural tradition to defend this. Then there is the vexed issue of British militarism. George Bernard Shaw was right to take the Church to task over its collusion in war. In his *Common Sense About the War* he wrote:

> When a bishop at the first shot abandons the worship of Christ and rallies his flock round the altar of Mars, he may be acting patriotically, necessarily, manfully, rightly; but that does not justify him in pretending that Christ is, in effect, Mars. The straightforward course, and the one that would serve

the Church best in the long run, would be to close our professedly Christian Churches the moment war is declared by us, and reopen them only on the signing of the treaty of peace.

All this left a legacy of bad faith, and a ready supply of ammunition for those hostile to the Church. Unlike the Roman Catholics, the Anglican Church has been flexible on theological matters, so much so that it can also be readily accused of vagueness and discrepancy in what it believes. People with very little scriptural knowledge are confused by this, and conclude that if the bishops cannot agree, or are willing to trim their sails to whatever theological fashion is in vogue – what hope is there for the ordinary person? The most fatal blow of all, however, was Darwinism. This contested scientific theory – for that is all it really is – has been interpreted by the vast majority of the population as *the* 'proof' that the Bible story is no more than make-believe and myth.

So, little by little, for over a century, the role of the Church has become almost ceremonial. Its social function is to 'hatch 'em, match 'em and dispatch 'em', as they say, and to provide moral and emotional uplift to its diminishing congregations, many of whom are elderly, poorly, bereaved or afflicted. Nevertheless, these people do what they can with what meagre resources they can deploy. Those who have received kind help from 'food-banks' during the current economic crisis may ponder how much more desperate hard times would be if the churches, mosques and synagogues really did cease to exist. In addition to all this, the Church has become obsessed with internal wrangling and dispute about 'identity politics', female priests and bishops, gay rights and a host of other difficult, and admittedly important issues, which seem to me, however, to be a distraction compared to the real crisis. The disintegration of the post-war political consensus since the 1970s, the increasing poverty, racism, social exclusion and social division have all generated a host of related social problems, drug and alcohol dependence, vice, crime, and mental ill health, for example. Parish priests have to contend with these problems every day, and know full well that the political authorities have not the slightest intention of addressing them. Yet there is another, more imminent threat.

As I have said, there are reasons to believe that we are already over a century into a new Dark Age in which paganism and Satanism are resurgent. We have endured such times before. The Church is not a collection of buildings, however grand, but a body of people willing to make of themselves a living sacrifice. Such people have been resilient throughout our history, and I believe the first unease the population will feel about a secularised society will come when the Church of England fades from public life. But we are instructed to 'take no thought for the morrow' (Matthew, 6:34). The Church has been almost extinguished in this island before and spectacularly recovered. If the Bible is the living Word then Christians will be ultimately vindicated. There is much about the Church which perplexes me. I wish it were called by another name; the 'Church of Albion' would be my own preference.

Although I fully accept that it would entail the loss of such little prestige and status as it still retains, I think the Church should be disestablished. It may not lead to an increase in participation, any more than the ordination of women priests has, but like that latter reform it would be the right thing to do. But beyond this I feel the Church could do much more to address the crisis in spiritual education – a parting gift, as it were. The vast majority of the population are now hopelessly ignorant about spiritual and non-materialist belief systems in general – not just Christianity. There are educational initiatives, true, such as the 'Alpha' course and so on, but this is not the kind of thing I have in mind. Some kind of space needs to be provided, where *anyone* can discuss the meaning of their lives and learn how to think in a non-materialist way.

Like Coleridge, I suggest that we need to institute a 'national clerisy', a kind of educational NHS. It may be possible to interweave the Church with organisations like the University of the Third Age and the Workers' Educational Association to provide a template for such a project. It is an indictment of our society that we now require a 'Minister for Loneliness', but if we really do care about civic society and spiritual 'well-being' such initiatives may be a start. This is my 'vision', for what it is worth – I know it cannot come to fruition without some sort of mystical or magical transformation, but 'magic' is now the stuff of *Harry Potter*. With such cynical forces ranged against progress, where can we find help and hope in this desolating, dispiriting time? Perhaps we need to pay a visit to yet another declining institution – the traditional British pub.

17

'Final Participation'

Lo! We have heard in old days of the wisdom of the cunning-minded Inklings; how those wise ones sat together in their deliberations, skilfully reciting learning and song-craft, earnestly meditating. That was true joy!

J. R. R. Tolkien in a parody of *Beowulf*

The Eagle and Child pub, known as the 'Bird and Baby' to many generations of Oxford undergraduates, stands on St Giles' in Oxford, a well-loved 'watering-hole' for students and academic staff alike. Before it was refurbished in the early 1960s it had a private room for small meetings called the 'Rabbit Room'. This tiny closet became, in effect, an oratory, where on most Tuesdays a group of mystical Christian literary gentlemen met to 'deliberate' over a mug of ale and a pipe – the 'Inklings'. In this cramped scullery the world was changed. The original 'Inklings' group was founded as a student literary society in 1931. Two outstanding literary giants were early members: J. R. R. Tolkien and C. S. Lewis, with Lewis eventually becoming 'Master of Ceremonies' at his rooms in Magdalen College.

The meetings were really no more than an intimate gathering of friends with similar intellectual inclinations. 'Warnie' Warren Lewis, older brother of the famous C. S., was invariably there, as was Tolkien. The academic Hugo Dyson and Dr R. E. Havard attended when they could. The poet Charles Williams joined the group later, but perhaps the most extraordinary mind in this 'egregor' was that of a man less well known outside specialist philosophical circles: Owen Barfield, the 'first and last Inkling'. Although he could not always attend the meetings in person because he was busy running the family legal firm in London, Barfield's participation was crucial. The four key members – Tolkien, Lewis, Williams and Barfield – were, in combination, much more than just a literary club; they were a 'group-mind' whose theological and philosophical speculations were focused on the shadowy lands at the borders of mysticism and magic.

Tolkien and Lewis are so well known that a cursory overview of them will suffice here. Williams we have encountered earlier on in this story, so I propose to look a little more closely at him. But the majority of this chapter will be devoted to an introduction to the revolutionary ideas of Barfield, which I believe may prove at least part of the answer to the spiritual crisis of our age, a sublime explication of mystical thought. I am fully conscious that I can only express these ideas according to my own rather dim lights, and trust that the reader will forgive me for this somewhat stumbling summary. In short, I urge anyone with a real interest in these matters to go and read Barfield's extraordinary books and essays, for the sooner his philosophy is more widely known, the nearer to the 'Kingdom of Heaven' we will all be.

Of the four core members Tolkien is the most famous, perhaps, but this was not always so. The foundation of the Inklings long-preceded the heady days of the 1960s when American university campus graffiti boasted slogans like 'J. R. R. Tolkien is Hobbit-forming'. He was born on 3 January 1892 in Bloemfontein, South Africa. His father, Arthur, was a bank-manager there but his baby son's health was poor. Arthur sent his wife and sons to England in hopes of being eventually transferred there himself, but on 15 February 1896 he died of a haemorrhage brought on by rheumatic fever. His widow, Mabel, was faced with the prospect of bringing up two young boys in extremely straitened circumstances in Birmingham, a sprawling, tough industrial city in the Midlands. Not a propitious start, then, for this literary genius, but it was in this seemingly unlikely setting that the seeds of *The Hobbit*, *The Lord of the Rings* and *The Silmarillion* were sown. In fact, Tolkien's childhood in Birmingham was crucial to the development of his later concept of 'sub-creation'.

To be clear, this was *not* some kind of imaginative compensation or psychological refuge from the industrial wilderness. Birmingham was not the great metropolis then which it has now become. Only a few miles outside the city, quite near the border with the rural county of Worcestershire, Mabel managed to rent a small cottage at Sarehole, near a centuries-old corn mill, now managed by Birmingham City Museum. What are now suburbs like Hall Green, Acocks Green and Moseley were then country villages. To the south was Worcestershire, with its woods and hills, the Lickey Hills, Clent and in the distance the blue-grey massif of the Malvern Hills, the old kingdom of the *Hwicce*. To the west there were other weird places, like Kinver and Drakelow, where people still lived in 'Rock Houses' cut into the sandstone like the Hobbits.

Tolkien was proud to describe himself as 'a Birmingham man' but he was also a man of the 'Green Borderlands' who seemed to absorb the soul of Mercia by some sort of osmosis, or 'Analeptic Thought'. He received an excellent education at King Edward's and St Philip's schools in Birmingham, served in the trenches during the First World War, and remained a devout Roman Catholic for the rest of his life. He had always been clubbable and fond of the fraternity of a close group of trusted friends, but his was a generation where many such friendships were tragically cut short by the war. This was part of the emotional backdrop of the 'Inklings' and, indeed of *The Lord of the Rings* trilogy – the attempt to find meaning in the seemingly irredeemable destruction of 'fellowship'. These men were not just meeting for their own amusement, but for their departed comrades-in-arms. Tolkien's trilogy was not an allegory, or anything of that kind, but an invented or 'feigned' history. His legendary perfectionism required him to draw up detailed maps of imaginary realms and to invent complex and coherent languages spoken by the inhabitants of his 'sub-creation'.

Tolkien first met Clive Staples (known as 'Jack') Lewis in 1926. They soon became firm friends despite Lewis being an atheist. Gradually Tolkien's Christian faith impressed Jack to the extent that he began to seriously consider conversion. On 19 September 1931, Lewis went for an evening walk with Tolkien and Hugo Dyson, a member of the Inklings. They strolled along Addison's Walk in the grounds of Magdalen College by the River Cherwell. Lewis disclosed his essential distrust in the power of myth. In his biography of Tolkien, Humphrey Carpenter describes this epic encounter, the moment Jack's eyes were opened. Lewis says:

> But myths are lies, even though lies breathed through silver ... No, said Tolkien, they are not ... And, indicating the great trees of Magdalen Grove as their branches bent in the wind, he struck out a different line of argument ... You call a tree a tree ... and you think nothing more of the word. But it is not a 'tree' until someone gave it that name. You call a star a star, and it is just a ball of matter moving on a mathematical course. But that is merely how you see it. By so naming things and describing them you are only inventing your own terms about them. And just as speech is invention about objects and ideas, so myth is an invention about truth.[37]

For Tolkien myth was a 'splintered fragment of the true light' which has come from God. When we cease to make myths we no longer aspire to the state of prelapsarian bliss which is our rightful inheritance as men. Lewis began to dimly apprehend the notion that for Tolkien and Dyson, Christianity was a 'true myth'. The conversation went on until dawn, and soon afterwards Lewis became a practising Christian – one of the most distinguished theologians of the century. But to Tolkien's chagrin, Jack did not choose Roman Catholicism. He became an Anglican. Their friendship was undiminished, but privately Tolkien was disappointed.

Tolkien began the process of envisioning a species of fairy Otherworld during his boyhood in Birmingham. The 'Two Towers' of Gondor in his trilogy were based on a water tower and a folly built in the eighteenth century

---

37 Carpenter, H., *J. R. R. Tolkien: A Biography*, Allen & Unwin, London, 1977.

by a man named John Perrott in Edgbaston, and there are a host of other examples of the young Tolkien mythologising local landmarks. Tolkien said he felt compelled to study 'the nature of faerie: the Perilous Realm itself, and the air that blows in that country'. In *Romantic Religion*, the author observes that this is 'exactly what cannot be defined or accurately described, only perceived':

> Faerie may be roughly translated as Magic, but not the vulgar magic of the magician; it is rather magic 'of a particular mood and power' ... and it does not have an end in itself but in its operations. Among these operations are 'the satisfaction of certain primordial human desires' such as the desire 'to hold communion with other living things'.

Tolkien 'surveys the depths of time', and times 'old beyond measure', for fairy stories: 'Open a door on Other Time, and if we pass through, though only for a moment, we stand outside our own time, outside Time itself, maybe.' The idea of a magic which does not 'have an end in itself but in its operations' is significant, because such magic is exempt from the curse of merely 'material' production – it is essentially 'spiritual'. These so-called 'fairy stories', then, operate at the level of fantasies which offer what Tolkien called Recovery, Escape, and Consolation. For him the joy of the 'happy ending', what he called 'eucatastrophe', 'has the very taste of primary truth'.

Like Tolkien, C. S. Lewis was bereaved of a parent in early childhood, in this case his mother. He was born in Belfast in 1898. He was aware of a strange 'longing', or *Sehnsucht*, before he was six years old, something similar to the Welsh *Hiraeth*; the Lewis family originated in Wales, men 'who had not much of the talent for happiness'. It was as well, because

> there came a night when I was ill and crying with both headache and toothache and distressed because my mother did not come to me. That was because she was ill too; and what was odd was that there were several doctors in her room, and voices, and comings and goings all over the house and doors shutting and opening. It seemed to last for hours. And then my father, in tears, came into my room and began to try to convey to my terrified mind things it had never conceived before. It was in fact cancer and followed the usual course; an operation (they operated in the patient's house in those days), an apparent convalescence, a return of the disease, increasing pain, and death. My father never fully recovered from this loss.[38]

Following this blow, Lewis gradually became aware, despite his grief, of something he called 'joy', which he defined as 'an unsatisfied desire which is itself more desirable than any other satisfaction'. Although he had abandoned

---

38 Lewis, C. S., *Surprised by Joy*, Collins, London, 1990.

his Anglican faith, he knew that somehow this 'joy' had to do with an object utterly outside himself, which inspired within him a feeling of religious awe. At Oxford, Lewis met the man he called his 'Second Friend':

> But the Second Friend is the man who disagrees with you about everything. He is not so much the alter ego as the anti-self. Of course he shares your interests; otherwise he would not be your friend at all. But he has approached them all at a different angle. He has read all the right books but has got the wrong thing out of every one. It is as if he spoke your language but mispronounced it. How can he be so nearly right and yet, just not right? He is as fascinating (and infuriating) as a woman. When you set out to correct his heresies, you find that he forsooth has decided to correct yours!

This fascinating and complicated young man was Owen Barfield. The two became lifelong friends. As Blake said in his *Marriage of Heaven and Hell*, 'opposition is true friendship'. It was not long before the friendship was tested:

> It was then that a really dreadful thing (dreadful for me) happened. First Harwood (still without changing his expression) and then Barfield, embraced the doctrines of Steiner and became Anthroposophists. I was hideously shocked. Everything that I had laboured so hard to expel from my own life seemed to have flared up and met me in my best friends ... And so I came to learn (so far as I have ever learned) what Steiner thought; my horror turned into disgust and resentment. For here, apparently, were all the abominations; none more abominable than those which had once attracted me. Here were gods, spirits, after-life and pre-existence; initiates, occult knowledge, meditation. 'Why – damn it – it's medieval,' I exclaimed.

Lewis thought his friends had fallen under the spell of 'that ravenous salt lust for the occult'. What caused this spasm of dread was the reputation of Anthroposophy and its founder, Rudolf Steiner, rather than the reality. Steiner was the Swedenborg of the twentieth century, in the sense that he began his main work in occultism relatively late in life, but then produced an abundant and all-embracing spiritual or religious system. Steiner's followers claim that the 'Master', as Barfield called him, was self-initiated by means of a process of spiritual development using occult exercises and visualisations. But allegations have persisted that Steiner was heir to deep Rosicrucian and Templar traditions. In Appendix E of his *Modern Ritual Magic: The Rise of Western Occultism*, Francis King produces a letter from a German occultist – admittedly written anonymously – which purports to confirm Steiner's connections to German Temples, and in particular the OTO:

> Steiner joined the occult-masonic rite led by Klein and Hartmann in 1902. At first they treated him with great reserve, for they thought him as

not genuine but an academic striving for fame by writing about masons ... Later they decided that was not so and initiated him into the Brothers of Light and the Rosicrucian Illuminati who were real occultists and not the revolutionary and political Illuminati of Weishaupt. In 1905 Steiner was chartered to have a lodge of the Eastern Templars (OTO). Steiner sometimes called his lodge 'Secret Masonry' for the first three degrees were the same almost as those of ordinary masons. He worked with Reuss until 1914 but their world-picture-philosophy was not the same for Steiner did not use the physical sex but only the stored-up Kundalini serpent sex (the white sex magic). So his high degrees saw the symbols in a different way.

King's source states that 'the Templars did not like Steiner because he came under astral influence hostile to Germany and thus made von Moltke lose the big invasion battle in France. Steiner did not use masonic rites after 1917.' What was Lewis, so recently returned to the faith of the Templars' historic adversary, the Church, to make of all this?

King's so-called 'revelations' about Steiner, derived from an anonymous source, need to be taken in context. King also revealed the 'secrets' of the OTO in 1973, and was immediately challenged and discredited by Grady McMurtry, who assumed control of the OTO in the USA in 1971. For Lewis, many of these ideas, more or less Gnostic, were the severest challenge to the foundation of his new-found faith. His affection for Barfield and his conviction of his ultimately noble intentions overcame his gut fears about Anthroposophy:

> There is a difficulty and (to me) a re-assuring Germanic dullness about it which would soon deter those who were looking for thrills. Nor have I ever seen that it had a deleterious effect on the character of those who embraced it; I have once known it to have a very good one ... I say this not because I ever came within a hundred miles of accepting the thing myself, but in common fairness, and also as tardy amends for the many hard, unjust and bitter things I once said about it to my friends. For Barfield's conversion to Anthroposophy marked the beginning of the Great War between him and me. It was never, thank God, a quarrel, though it could have become one in a moment if he had used to me anything like the violence I allowed myself to him.

Such a tolerant and humble approach from a man regarded as a sort of Anglican saint inclines me to give Steiner's philosophy the benefit of the doubt. For Lewis the real battle was not with esoteric magical ideas, but with a hegemonic scientific rationalism. For Christians who are chary about dialogue with Theosophy, Anthroposophy or paganism, I find their reluctance surprising in view of their often insouciant attitude to a consumer-capitalism which is devastating the planet and bears comparison with Black Magick. It is true that there are Anglicans who have already grasped the nettle, such as the poet Malcolm Guite, an Anglican priest who writes and lectures widely on the Inklings and Romantic philosophy, but much more needs to be done (at least in the UK – the USA is a different case) to raise the profile of the Inklings as a philosophical as well as a literary group. This is the irony – the Inklings *could* be characterised as 'pale, male' and if not 'stale' then somewhat 'fogeyish' and elitist. In fact, these comrades were explorers of 'inner space', passionately devoted to radically differing points of view but united in a desperate effort to 'make all wrong things right', to make of the human catastrophe an 'eucatastrophe' as Tolkien called it – but by what means?

Lewis agreed with Hulme's assessment of the Romantic movement as 'spilt religion': 'And I agree that he who has religion ought not to spill it. But does it follow that he who finds it spilled should avert his eyes? How if there is a man to whom those bright drops on the floor are the beginning of a trail which … will lead him to the cup itself?' One of the key concepts Barfield took from his study of Steiner was that of the evolution of consciousness. In his series of debates and correspondences with Barfield during what they jokingly called 'the Great War', Lewis increasingly accepted this idea, which he applied to his theological exegetics. After his epiphany in Addison's Walk, Lewis became fascinated by myths and myth-making. Truth, he believed, had slowly developed out of the mythical ultimately unfolding in historical 'fact'. Thus the Incarnation of Christ was the fulfilment in history of the pagan myths. Christ is for him, as Reilly says, 'the end and fulfilment of all previous symbols and prefigurations'. But can one love God as a 'true myth'? In his classic *The Four Loves*, Lewis sounds like the anonymous author of *The Cloud of Unknowing*:

> God knows, not I, whether I have ever tasted this love. Perhaps I have only imagined the tasting … Perhaps, for many of us, all experience merely defines… the shape of that gap where love of God ought to be. It is not enough. It is something. If we cannot 'practice the presence of God', it is something to practice the absence of God, to become increasingly aware of our unawareness till we feel like men who should stand beside a great cataract and hear no noise, or like a man in a story who looks in a mirror and finds no face there, or a man in a dream who stretches out his hand to visible objects and gets no sensation of touch. To know that one is dreaming is to be no longer perfectly asleep. But for news of the fully waking world you must go to my betters.[39]

One of the messages of this 'transcendental Christianity' is that formalism, dogmatism and ritual are limitations which 'mutilate and distort the

---

39 Lewis, C. S., *The Four Loves*, Bles, London, 1960.

I AM WHO AM. In order to know God we must love Him; there is no discursive way.' But how does one express such a love, and how can one put it into human terms? This was the dilemma the poet Charles Williams, the third member of our group, set out to resolve.

Charles Williams did have magical connections. He was a member of Arthur Edward Waite's 'Fellowship of the Rosy Cross' (FRC), whose parent order was the Golden Dawn. Many of his friends, and indeed those who only met him briefly, were impressed by the strange aura of sanctity he exuded. Like Lewis he promulgated a transcendental Christianity. Lewis was influenced in his concept of transcendentalism by Barfield, who in turn had taken his ideas from Steiner and ultimately the creative imagination of Coleridge, whereas for Williams the 'Holy Grail' was a union of the intellect and the imagination in a mood of romantic-religious exaltation. He expressed this exaltation in Trinitarian terms – the FRC was a Christian mystical order. Accordingly, he proposed three key concepts which he believed lay 'behind all things', expressing man's unity with God and the divine unity with man; 'co-inherence, substitution and exchange'.

These are extremely complex ideas, but their practical effects operated right on the border of mysticism and magic – very similar to Barfield's, in fact. Like his friends Tolkien and Lewis, Williams had known hardship in his childhood. His father Walter was a journalist who wrote poetry, and his uncle, J. Charles Wall, was a noted scholar and author of the classic demonology *Devils*, so there were literary, scholastic and poetic influences on him from an early age. Unfortunately, his father gradually went blind and lost regular employment. Lack of funds prevented Williams from taking up the offer of a place at University College London, so this intellectual giant never took a degree. But Charles was simply too brilliant to fail. In 1908 he got a job as a proofreader for the Oxford University Press, one of the most prestigious publishers in Britain. His talents were immediately recognised, and he was soon promoted to editor. His most noteworthy achievement was to edit the first English translation of the Danish philosopher Soren Kierkegaard.

Williams wrote novels in a contemporary setting, but his main creative work was his poetic output. A devout Anglican, Williams corresponded with Evelyn Underhill, a member of the Golden Dawn. His own mysticism developed as he wrote a cycle of Arthurian poetry which, though difficult, displayed touches of genius, published as *Taliessin through Logres* and *The Region of the Summer Stars*. Other poems on the Arthurian theme were published after his death. His concept, recalling William Blake and his 'Giant Albion', is of a gigantic human image comprising all the provinces of the Roman Empire. The province of Britain, what he calls 'Logres', is the heart and soul of the Empire. Taliessin, a bard based on the original Taliesin, is charged with a mission to restore *Logres* to its exemplary spiritual condition so that it can become a fitting home for the Holy Grail. These poems, and his novels, became popular and received critical acclaim.

Dressed in shabby suits and continually smoking cigarettes, Williams was an unlikely academic, but his sheer charm and charisma soon captivated all who met him – especially members of the opposite sex. In 1939, at the outbreak of the Second World War, the Oxford University Press was decanted from London to Oxford, and Williams was forced to relocate there. Williams detested the move, but one consequence of the relocation was that Williams was now free to join the Inklings. Lewis and Barfield were keen that he should join, Tolkien less so. There was an element of jealousy, because Williams' pervasive charm and wide-ranging philosophy came to exert an influence over Lewis which somewhat overshadowed Tolkien. Tolkien was a little suspicious of Williams, perhaps because of his membership of the FRC, just as Lewis had been concerned about Barfield's Anthroposophical pursuits – he referred to Williams as having a countenance which seemed 'half-angel, half-monkey'. But during what were to be the last years of his life, Williams, a man without any university degree, gave lectures at the Oxford School of Divinity which astonished the faculty. On Tuesdays, at the 'Bird and Baby', Williams became a regular contributor to the meetings of the Inklings. His study of the poet Dante convinced him that the key to a loving relationship with God was prefigured in the experience of romantic love – an explicitly religious romanticism.

Williams was very influenced by his association with A. E. Waite, and especially his book *The Secret Doctrine in Israel*, a study of the mystical Judaic *Zohar*, a commentary on the Torah and Cabbalistic system. This system guides initiates along the spiritual pathways and experiences which lead to 'the end of correction', the sublime state of ultimate spiritual consciousness. Waite designed a deck of Tarot cards which are still widely used today; his were the designs I was introduced to as a boy. The Golden Dawn system of magic encouraged neophytes to study these cards, especially the 'major arcana' or 'Trumps', and to contemplate their deeper meanings. In his novels Williams uses fictional characters to convey his familiarity with this mystical meditation. By using techniques he summarised as 'co-inherence, substitution and exchange', Williams believed it was literally possible to bear the pain, despair and suffering of another human being, as an analogue of Christ's sacrifice for Mankind.

Those who are familiar with the cinematic production of *Shadowlands*, written by William Nicholson, will know the story of how C. S. Lewis married the American poet Joy Davidman. Her tragic death from cancer, evoking as it did all the terrible memories of his mother's death from the same disease, and the tale of how this 'marriage of convenience' between two people so extraordinarily different became a profound spiritual love is a very moving one. In the depths of his despair, when his wife was in excruciating agony, Lewis used the techniques he learned from Williams to relieve her pain. The author Nevill Coghill said that Lewis told him how the process of substitution and exchange gave Joy a blessed respite; 'You mean that her pain left her, and that you felt it for her in your own body?' and Lewis replied, 'Yes, in my legs. It was crippling. But it relieved hers.' Not only is this a demonstration that the Inklings were familiar with practical magic, rather than just theoretical, but it points towards a more profound conclusion. For it is just this selfless love – in the state of being in romantic love there can really *be* no 'self' – the lovers have become 'co-inherent', which stands as an exact analogue of 'Transcendental Christianity'. R. J. Reilly wrote,

> The nature of the Fall, then, may be described as man's loss of vision ... It follows, then, that the Redemption must consist of some way or ways of restoring the original accuracy of knowledge.

There are two possible 'ways' of doing this. The 'Negative Way' is that of the mystics, like Lady Julian of Norwich or the author of *The Cloud of Unknowing*. It is the way of rejection of the world, of images, so that direct communion with the divine is achieved. But there is another way, the 'Affirmative Way', an acceptance of the fallen state of the world, and even what *seems* evil in it, because for Williams evil cannot have a positive existence in itself, it is warped good, or 'good misperceived'. Like the troubadours of the medieval period, Williams saw the potency of romantic love as a means by which he could 'restore the original accuracy of knowledge'. In its most refined and pure form *fin amor* the one enthralled by love sees the world as it truly is – infinite, co-inherent, transfigured by beatitude beyond words. The illusion of evil evaporates, and there is only ineffable bliss. When Dante meets his beloved Beatrice in the street he is so utterly transfixed that 'if anyone had asked me a question I should have been able to answer only "Love"'. Beatrice is no longer merely a pretty young girl, but has become an incarnation of the divine unity, the ultimate validation of the greater Incarnation. In these precious moments, the Fall is reversed.

Through the experience of romantic love, Williams believed the lovers were 'ingodded'. But love of this kind is often all too brief. Like Christ, Beatrice departs, but she has left an indelible mark on Dante's soul, such that he is no longer capable of a return to the commonplace, everyday world. Though the beloved has gone, in our desolation we must learn to behave as if they were still with us. And for Williams, in a sense they are, for time to him was 'a mode of perception', what Barfield called 'chronological snobbery'. Williams theologised the romantic experience. The gift of love is a sign of God's grace, but also an experience, however temporary – and no matter how bitter the desolation of parting may be – of seeing the world, as it were, through the eyes of God. Tolkien, Lewis and Williams, all three communicant Christians, conveyed these neo-romantic ideas through their abundant and successful literature. Barfield was a prolific author too, but above all he was a thinker, a profound philosopher whose analysis of our modes of experiencing and 'thinking about thinking' promises liberation from crass materialism and a restoration of meaning for a world paralysed by meaninglessness.

In his collection of short stories titled *Dubliners*, James Joyce identified two key motifs of modern urban culture he called 'paralysis' and 'epiphany'. Our stultifying, banal culture has the effect of anaesthetising the human actors, inoculating them against 'meaning', but in each of the fifteen stories a moment arrives when, suddenly, like Ezekiel, they see the great wheels of the universe turning behind the pathetic props of this earthly drama – epiphany. The sudden introjection of meaning into meaninglessness is often violent, overwhelming and tragic. Too often in this modern world, our only genuine human experiences are vouchsafed us through such traumatic revelations. Barfield believed that these moments of meaningful perception were not strictly personal experiences, but extra-personal or transpersonal. He became an ardent student of Steiner while he was a student at Oxford, as we have seen. The reason why I believe Barfield's philosophy is very apposite for the study of history today lies in the unique way in which he developed Steiner's theories. He defined Anthroposophy thus: 'The concept of man's development of *self-consciousness as a process in time* – with all that this implies.' This theory of the 'evolution of consciousness', derived from Steiner, will, I hope, shed some light on my purposes in writing this book.

Charles Darwin proposed an evolutionary theory which was predicated on the idea of a gradual organisation and increasing specialisation of species, by processes of material adaptation. These processes, he averred, reached their apogee in human consciousness. Barfield rejected this view; Darwin had looked at evolution from the wrong end of the telescope. Mind did not arise from matter, but matter from mind. It was 'a descent, an involution of the Spirit into the Material, which it, the Spirit, organises and transforms, and through which it acquires a new intensity, a new level of self-awareness'. Barfield was a philologist, and his special interest was in the historical development of language. He believed that he could demonstrate, through the history of linguistic change, that spirit or mind or 'cosmic consciousness' preceded matter – the Bible conveys a literal truth when it says 'In the beginning was the Word'. What he called 'unindividuated meaning' must gradually develop on a trajectory – a historical trajectory – of evolution into an individuated personal consciousness.

But this development involved a profound sacrifice, for human beings became cut off from the natural and phenomenal world, no longer experiencing themselves as part of it. In ancient times this had not been so, and earlier cultures had experienced what he called 'original participation', the perceiver and the perceived, the subject and the object were not separated. His *History in English Words* was Barfield's attempt to reveal the 'secrets hidden in language', and to trace the way in which words conveyed different meanings over time. Language provided a proof of the evolution of consciousness in history. In his

Poetic Diction, Barfield poses the question of why certain word groupings evoke a reaction in the aesthetic imagination, the moment when one's spine tingles and the hairs rise on the back of the neck. He uses as an example the power of a poet such as Coleridge to infuse our imaginations with new meaning:

> Coleridge's point of view has already been cited. His novel use of the word *imagination* – distinguishing it from *fancy* – is another example of the introduction of fresh meaning into the English language. Similarly, a careful study of Shakespeare reveals him as a probable author of a great part of the modern meanings of several words which are practically key-terms to whole areas of typical modern thought – especially those parts of it which are peculiarly the discovery of English thinkers. He was, for example, as far as is known to the compilers of the Oxford Dictionary the first person to use *function* of a physical organ, and the first person to use *inherit*, not of property, but of moral and physical qualities.[40]

Barfield's thesis is that history is a transformational process, a 'vast age-long metamorphosis from the kind of outlook which we loosely describe as "mythological" to the kind which we may describe equally loosely as "intellectual thought"'. He thought that the 'Aryan' or Indo-European peoples whose language supplied the template for modern European languages, including English, had a different kind of consciousness to our own, revealed in words like *diary* and *diurnal*. These derive from a Latin root word, *dies*, and before that we find the Sanskrit *Dyaus Pitar*, the Celtic *Dis Pater* and the Greek *Zeus*, the father of the gods. The Anglo-Saxon *Tiw* or *Tiu*, from whom we name Tuesday, is the English version. Originally this word meant both *God* and *sky*, thus the word *divine*.

But as consciousness evolved, and a distinction was made between the figurative and the literal, a process Barfield called 'internalisation' of meaning began, in which phenomena were no longer experienced as things in themselves, but as in some sense a partial creation of the perceiver. Man was now conscious of himself as a separate entity. Now, people need not have such acute fear of the terrible power of nature or the wrath of the gods. The transformation to an 'intellectual' as opposed to a mythological consciousness undermined the authority of both priest and magus alike. Such vestiges of 'original participation' as survived, perhaps among the rural underclass, gypsies or maverick geniuses like John Clare, were crushed by the processes of the Protestant Reformation and the Industrial Revolution. The spirit of the Reformation was the doctrine of 'the inwardness of all true grace'.

The centre of gravity of consciousness was moving steadily *inward* into the *self*. Barfield notes that it is precisely at the time of the Reformation that words begin to be hyphenated with the word: self-will, self-conceit,

---

40 Barfield, O., *Poetic Diction: A Study in Meaning*, Barfield Press, Oxford, 2010 edn.

self-confidence, for example. Corresponding to this new consciousness of the self and its potentialities and freedoms came a decline in the belief in the spiritual value of the outer world. Sundered from his environment, having 'fled from nature', as Steiner put it, modern man subsists, as Reilly says, 'in a 'world drained of its immanent life by the very evolution (of consciousness) which enabled them (the Romantic poets) to perceive its deadness'. For Barfield the Romantic movement was a turning point because poets and visionaries like Blake and Coleridge saw the crucial need to reanimate and revitalise the world, to safeguard and honour Nature by what Barfield calls 'the power of creating from within forms which themselves become a part of Nature – "Forms," as Shelley put it, "more real than living man / Nurslings of immortality".

For Barfield', in the Romantic movement the wheel had turned full circle. They were co-creators of, participants in nature, just as the ancients had been, but instead of this being an unconscious process, poets such as Coleridge and Wordsworth did this *consciously*. From this, Barfield drew radical conclusions. The possibility arises that by use of the creative imagination, we can become active and creative participants in the reconstruction of the world. For the rest of his long life, Barfield wrestled with the means by which we could 'finally participate', which is to say that 'we must look for the spirits, the Goddess Natura, not on the farther side of appearances, but within ourselves'. The crucifixion of the age of materialism has given us the means by which we may be resurrected, not as before, as unconscious 'original' participants, without a 'self' or an 'identity' as we understand those terms, but as conscious individuals in a co-inherent matrix. His philosophical speculations on these matters mark him out as one of the greatest thinkers of the twentieth century, whose genius must surely be highly regarded by posterity.

Barfield was constrained in his intellectual work by his commitments with the family solicitors' firm between 1934 and 1959. He was also a family man, with two children of his own and an adopted daughter, Lucy, for whom C. S. Lewis wrote his *The Lion, the Witch and the Wardrobe*. Despite this, he kept up a regular correspondence and friendship with the other Inklings throughout, and he continued to publish a succession of remarkable books. He was a lifelong Anthroposophist, probably the ablest exponent of Steiner's ideas in the English-speaking world. G. B. Tennyson said of him, 'Barfield is to Steiner as Steiner is to Goethe.' This gives some idea of his status in the philosophical world.

The culmination of these philosophical speculations came with his book *Saving the Appearances: A Study in Idolatry*. Basically this is a 3,000-year history of the evolution of human consciousness. Barfield begins by analysing the nature of 'reality' itself. The key to the book is the concept of *participation*, that we are involved in actively creating the 'things' we experience as 'there' in the world. Is a rainbow, for instance, *really* 'there'?

Barfield says that it is an outcome of the sunshine, the raindrops and the vision of the percipient. It appears and disappears according to the presence or absence of these three factors. It seems 'real' enough, because another person standing beside me can see it too, what he calls a 'collective representation'. Science says that even a seemingly solid thing such as a tree is actually made up of invisible particles called atoms, protons and electrons. We construct the image of the tree, and the rainbow, as 'representations' in our consciousness. But there are also 'personal representations' which are just as 'real' but subjective.

As a former psychiatric social worker, my workload often consisted of making judgements about such dilemmas. My view now is that the conditioning factors are a combination of the environment (nature), and the 'history' of the 'client' (nurture). If my consciousness and that of another person or persons coincide, then we all experience the same image or thing. We do this by a process Barfield called 'figuration':

> On the assumption that the world whose existence is independent of our sensation and perception consists solely of 'particles', two operations are necessary (and whether they are successive or simultaneous is of no consequence), in order to produce the familiar world we know. First, the sense-organs must be related to the particles in such a way as to give rise to sensations; and secondly, those mere sensations must be combined and constructed by the percipient mind into the recognizable and nameable objects we call 'things'. It is this work of construction which will here be called figuration.[41]

In ancient times people were conscious of an 'extra-sensory link' between the percipient and the representations or phenomena they experienced. We gradually lost this faculty, which explains why the depictions of an Anglo-Saxon *scop* when he recounted the tale of the monstrous Grendel in *Beowulf* never found an incredulous audience. The hearers all *knew* that the stinking fens and marshes were the abodes of dragons, drakes, wyverns and *wurms*; the monster for them was 'real', a collective representation. An analogy is that of ghosts. Some people 'see' ghosts, while others do not. Sometimes ghosts appear to more than one person, sometimes not. Perhaps a solution to this mystery may lie in a deeper understanding of this process of 'figuration'?

The decline in original participation, and the correlative increase in self-consciousness, leads to what Barfield calls in his subtitle 'Idolatry', or the 'granting of objective existence to our collective representations'. It is strikingly evident in modern consumer fetishism. But as we move towards final participation, and recover the faculties lost to us when we replaced our

---

41 Barfield, O., *Saving the Appearances: A Study in Idolatry*, Wesleyan, 1988 edn.

'root soul' (the example Barfield gives is the behaviour of a flock of geese, or starlings) with an individuated self-consciousness, our minds will evolve, and as we re-establish our unconscious unity with the representations *consciously* it may be possible to 'direct evolution' according to our will.

What is proposed sounds suspiciously similar to magic. I say this not in a condemnatory sense, because the alternative to 'final participation' or a step-change in our consciousness seems so desperately bleak for the human species, animal life and the planetary ecosystem. Empiricism and science have degenerated into 'a sort of idiocy', as Barfield put it, in which 'fewer and fewer representations will be collective, and more and more will be private, with the result that there will be in the end no means of communication between one intelligence and another'. But as with all magic, the potential to use it for malign purposes is ever-present. If we are evolving to a stage where we can direct and manipulate representations, what kind of representations will we choose? This all depends on what we want to do with the creative imagination. If the output of the media is any guide, the answer is not especially appealing. The answer to this dilemma, at least for Barfield, lies in accepting creative imaginative power as a divine gift, not to be sullied by filth and trash:

> The final participation which is being thrust upon them is exercised with the profoundest sense of responsibility, with the deepest thankfulness and piety towards the world as it was originally given to them in original participation, and with a full understanding of the momentous process of history, as it brings about the emergence of one from the other.

Barfield is explicit that the only moral foundation on which he thinks final participation can be built is Christianity. Christ had incarnated to 'make possible in the course of time the transition from original to final participation'; in Christ we participate finally the Spirit we once participated originally. Our creative imagination is inspired, it can take us across the threshold of normal, everyday consciousness into the 'Land of Promise', or the 'Kingdom of Heaven'. But beyond that threshold lurk many kinds of beings, entities, spirits, angels and demons, like those encountered by Edward Kelley and John Dee, William Blake and Aleister Crowley. Barfield goes so far as to suggest that as our imaginations develop, we will come to experience ideas as 'beings'. What Barfield says about the 'magic' of poetry in his *Poetic Diction* might equally stand as a fitting summary of the operations of the magical or spiritual consciousness:

> If I pass a coil of wire between the poles of a magnet, I generate in it an electrical current – but I only do so while the coil is positively moving across the lines of force. I may leave the coil at rest between the two poles and in such a position that it is thoroughly permeated by the magnetic field; but

in that case no current will flow along the conductor. Current only flows when I am actually bringing the coil in or taking it away again. So it is with the poetic mood, which, like the dreams to which it has so often been compared, is kindled by the passage from one plane of consciousness to another. It lives during that moment of transition and then dies, and if it is to be repeated, some means must be found of renewing the transition itself.

For thousands of years, the tried and tested means for 'renewing the transition' was the resort to magical operations. Of the four men briefly introduced in this final chapter, Barfield stands out for me because of his future-orientation, and also because of the potential for final participation to restore authentic meaning to the spiritual practices of both pagans and Christians. Barfield has much to say to all travellers on the spiritual path; those, Reilly says,

> ... afraid to be God, to those glad to be God, and to the uncertain ones like Lewis ... His argument for a polar relationship between God and man suggests at once the awful closeness of God and man but also the fact that they are not one being. It retains God's transcendence while at the same time stressing His immanence, and thus His approachability by means of the imagination.

These are profound and difficult speculations, and to go much further with them would require more space than I am permitted here – and would be beyond my wit to convey with the subtlety they deserve. The 'first and last Inkling' died on 14 December 1997. He predicted, I am tempted to say 'prophesied', that his ideas would not be sufficiently understood until fifty years had elapsed after his death. In my view, the Inklings, though all respectable Christians, could also be described as mystics, even magi. Their astonishing achievements, both individually and collectively, give hope that the age of magic has not yet ended.

Epilogue

In the foregoing pages I have attempted, however haltingly, to outline a sporadic influence of magic, and a more or less continual influence of mythology, 'heretical' thought and aboriginal 'dreaming' consciousness which I believe has operated for well over 5,000 years and underlies the spiritual inheritance of Britain. I think I set out my stall fairly explicitly in the introduction that this is not a 'real' history book. It comprises a magpie's nest of cultural and literary studies, theology, anthropology, folklore and, most pernicious of all, personal testimony and reminiscence. Yet, for all its rough efforts and its many failings, I am satisfied that it is *a* magical history of Britain, in the only terms that this can have any proper meaning. On the day of its completion, *She* whose grace initiates such projects appeared to me, and with that, I must rest content. It has been written for the 'benefit' of just two people who, unless magical forces of supreme sublimity operate in the universe, will never read it, and if they could, would be unlikely to understand it. Nevertheless, in the spirit of books of this type, I have included a subcutaneous body of encrypted lore meant only for them.

We must learn to live in constant hope of magical transfiguration. Beyond that it is merely a romantic whimsy, but senescent gentlemen, like ailing civilisations, may perhaps be excused such indulgences. And yet despite all, I say that this *is* a history of a sort, and in a tradition which not only preceded that of the established academies but also informed their earliest researches. I do not apologise for the fact that it is in the tradition of Gildas' 'complaining book' or the work of his later interlocutor, Bede. The prejudice of believing that foolish, greedy and wicked actions will result in unworthy, dishonourable and damaging outcomes is one I share with my historical betters.

I have said that my intuition is that there once existed a caste of indigenous contemplatives who deliberately withdrew to the banks of the great rivers to meditate upon history and destiny, like Layamon, for example. I have come to believe, though this may be my own fancy, that there was a larger purpose to these activities than the strictly literary output. Originally 'history' was not an academic exercise, but a form of the storyteller's art – it was a *craeft*, as the Anglo-Saxons put it, not a 'discipline' or a 'science'. Even before such modern developments, there was always the issue of *whose* history was 'true' or dominant – and as we know so well, history is written by the winners. The discovery of the Staffordshire Hoard in 2009 was the single event which most inspired me to write about history and mythology. The mainspring for this was, I think, regional resentment – the sense that 'Mercia' was an almost magical, ethereal realm, mystified out of existence by a media and an establishment which simply did not *want* to know. The following book, really a development of the first, was an attempt to reveal another hidden substratum of British history – the gradual occupation of the 'Celtic' lands, many of which were once in what is now England. It was as if I were stripping back the land, excoriating it, to reveal ever deeper meaning. Finally, I found there was no lower layer, only the level I always yearned for – the magical underworld of my earliest ancestors.

Not long before my mother died I had a strange dream. The year before, some friends and I had visited Knowth Passage Tomb in Ireland, the oldest megalithic monument in Europe. In my dream, I entered a labyrinth of winding tunnels within just such a mound. But these chambers, spiralling downwards, were composed of thousands upon thousands of human skulls. As I descended, guided by a mysterious presence ahead, I became aware that each one of these myriad skulls was an ancestor. At the heart of the mound, and to my surprise, was an enclosure open to the daylight, within which was a primitive sanctuary. I noticed it had been raining heavily. There was some kind of committee, guarded by armed warriors, who were 'painted people' like the Maori people of New Zealand. But they brandished spears with *iron* spearheads, and wore *iron* helmets; a signifier, I think, that I was to know that they were folk from the time when that metal became ubiquitous.

I awoke, but it had been a disturbing experience, and I went for a morning walk. I took breakfast in a local pub and looked in one of the supplements to a Sunday newspaper. The centrefold was a photograph of an excavated tomb complex in either Central or South America – walls of human skulls, winding downwards, grinning, row upon row. I dismissed the dream at the time as a conflation of disparate aspects of my imagination. But just at the conclusion of this book, I saw an article about 'Cheddar Man', a 10,000-year-old ancestor. DNA research shows that the skeleton discovered was of a black man, with blue eyes and curly black hair – very much like the people I saw years before in my dream. I thought the people looked 'Polynesian', but the reconstruction of 'Cheddar Man' seemed more like a 'Native American'. Whatever the details, Cheddar Man seems to have been black, or at least swarthy. The reconstructed ancestor was exactly what I saw in my dream – except there was no body-painting.

Epilogue

My earliest conception of a spiritual philosophy was inculcated in childhood. One side of my father's family came from Welsh origins, near Llandovery in the Brecon Beacons, once the tiny realm of *Brycheiniog*. A considerable number of Welsh miners and mining engineers were enlisted by the Earl of Dudley and relocated to the South Staffordshire coalfield to sink the deepest mineshafts in England. My father's theory, which he got from my great-uncle, was that among these men, deep cultural traditions, some of them more or less magical and quasi-masonic, had been retained within a select group. This Celtic inheritance was especially emphasised, not in a spirit of nationalistic pride or any notion of superiority, but because it was the repository of our religious, historical and mythological traditions. One of the central tenets of this 'faith', as W. Y. Evans-Wentz called it, was that

> the material substance comprising the body of man is merely a means of expression for life, a conductor for an unknown force which exhibits volition and individual consciousness; just as material substance in a condition called inanimate is a conductor for another unknown force called electricity. Destroy the human body, and there is no manifestation of its life force; destroy a wire, and there is no manifestation of electric light; the human body seems to be merely incidental in the history of the individual consciousness, as a wire is incidental to electric light.

The question, then, is, 'Can the consciousness continue to exist in an unmanifested state when the human body is cold and motionless in death?' The answer my parents and great-uncle gave was an unqualified 'Yes'. To incredulous observers, spiritual experiences often seem implausible, unaccountable, frightening and mysterious. Such emotions muddy the waters, because all the supernatural experiences, strange as they are, are in a way no stranger than our so-called normal perceptions and experiences.

My parents believed in other paranormal phenomena, particularly telepathy, clairvoyance, pre-cognition ('prophesy') and telekinesis. I wish to make clear that they were not vulgar pagans, 'witches' or anything of the kind. They were in every respect ordinary, personable and reasonably respectable. My mother's family inherited a sort of folksy paganism, which I expect had its roots in the customs of the 'tribe of witches'. She was from 'Bella in the Wych-Elm' country. I think there was an influence, perhaps originating with the Roma, of Goddess veneration also, but primarily my mother was interested in spiritual mediumship. My father's influences were almost entirely 'Celtic', and practically indistinguishable from the 'Cult of the Dead' described in chapter 3. Accordingly, my parents more or less abandoned the Christian faith, though they never denounced or disparaged it. There was much in it of value, my father thought, and it was considerably better than the hated alternative – a soulless materialism. My parents despised the modern world, especially the motorcar, but all technology was suspicious so far as they were concerned – they were Luddites, and proud of it.

A large group of our family lived in close proximity, in fact almost 'on top' of each other. In the main house, a dilapidated old building with a large plot of land attached full of rotting old cars and pianos (my grandmother was a music teacher), lived my paternal grandmother and grandfather. My aunt lived with them, but was soon to be married, so a bungalow was under construction beside the main house where she and her intended husband were to live. Three cottages were attached, so old, ruinous and dilapidated – not to say unhealthy; I nearly died of lung disease there – that few people would have endured the conditions by the mid-twentieth century. We lived in the first cottage, next to us lived my great-uncle, and in the last cottage an elderly spinster lived out her last years. There was an atmosphere, I should say, of extreme tension and hostility between my parents and my grandmother and aunt. My grandfather tried to be as even-handed as he could, as did my great-uncle, but in effect it was a feud over inheritance, rather like something out of a Dickens novel. My grandmother was Christian, the church organist in fact, and depended upon a respectable reputation for her business. She was appalled by my father's abandonment of the faith, and her fondest wish was that I should be baptised and eventually confirmed in the Church of England – both of which aims she secured. So this was the scene for the drama which was about to unfold; it is time we journeyed, one last time, into faerie.

We were not alone in our house. Indeed, all the cottages and the main house, but especially the land at the rear of the buildings, were haunted. Only this last Christmas I met some of my cousins for lunch. Over half a century later, my cousin vividly remembered how she had seen a 'man in old-fashioned clothes' standing on the stairs, a costume which – and she only discovered this many years later – was consistent with the Elizabethan period. 'The man', as I knew him, was often around, usually in broad daylight. He seemed to emerge from the wood behind some ruined old pigsties. When my great-uncle was watering his beans one day, and I was imitating him with a toy watering can, I saw the man and pointed him out. My uncle said not to 'mind' him, and I could see he had seen him as plainly as I. Another time I was being set astride a pony by some girls at the local stables when I saw the man walking along the hedgerow into the fields. I pointed to him, but they seemed perplexed. They *couldn't* see him.

My grandparents knew what was happening, but for reasons of their own pretended otherwise, except on one night when there was a disturbance in the area next to the bungalow that was being built. My father was called, who went out to confront possible burglars armed with a heavy fire-poker. The odd events (poltergeist-type, with windows smashed, bricks thrown, etc.) went on for hours, but no one could be discovered. Winter came, and on a frosty morning with the plough soil iron-hard I went into the wood, only to see the man walking along the hedgerow again. I ran after him and yelled out,

'What's your name?' A reply came as an immediate thought in my own head: 'Jack Frost'. The man turned and walked through a gap in the hedge. When I reached the spot he was nowhere to be seen on the other side, and only open fields stretched beyond. He had quite vanished, and as I gawped through the gap, the thought came: 'If I pass through that gap – *I* will disappear!' I always told my parents and uncle about these encounters, but I was advised not to discuss the matter outside this small group, and was especially forbidden to tell the only other child in the area, a girl somewhat older than myself. It would 'frighten her', they said.

In fact *I* was 'frightened', because odd things began to happen in the house. Someone seemed to suddenly sit on my parents' bed one night as they were sleeping, so heavy that the bedstead literally sank beneath the weight. My mother rushed to comfort me many times during the night, because due to my lung disease I only slept fitfully and was continually coughing. Consequently, I was often awake and became aware of a person moving towards me in the dark. This was genuinely distressing, and finally one evening my parents explained how they made sense of these intrusions. I should *never* have any fear of the spirits, they said. They meant no harm, but they were attached to this place, and could not leave it. There was nowhere else for them to go, no other 'space'. Their problem was that they were trapped somehow, and these events were a 'cry for help'. They wanted us to notice their plight, that was all. If we could communicate with them, perhaps we could find out what it was that had caused them to become 'stuck'.

There were many other such discussions, sometimes with my uncle present; he often came in by the fire on his way back from the pit. There was a sure protection against evil spirits which I learned. I cannot disclose the details, but it amounted to 'auto-hypnosis by means of a symbol'. Now, even when I was alone, I had only to concentrate in this way and my parents would immediately know I was troubled by a spirit. I was reassured by this, and as spring came and my breathing improved, some sort of normality seemed to have been restored, until one day, when I was quite alone in the house, something very strange happened.

I knew that the man was in the house. I could not yet see him but sensed he was about to come through the door from the washhouse into the room I was in. Suddenly there was a loud noise. A black shape was attacking me, croaking at me – hitting me. I ran to the corner of the room and dived beneath my mother's fur coat. I tried to scream but could not. I tried to remember my symbol but could not. The terror of terrors was that the *magic* had failed – and I blacked out. But when I came round, my mother was there, and my father and uncle. It had only been a 'poor old Jackdaw' which had fallen down the chimney and become trapped in the room with me! All was well – except that I was not. I had gone into some kind of catatonic trance state for a while. I thought I had been gone for days, not an hour, to 'another country'.

The other country was as real as this, and there had been an 'Indian' lady there, who could 'talk without speaking'. I became ravenously hungry; my uncle chuckled as I wolfed down egg and chips. His chuckling reminded me of the little men I had seen in the other land – the *archetypal* 'fair folk', who had pointed and laughed at my distress when I first awoke there. But quite soon I became distressed, and I wanted desperately to go back – because I had made a terrible mistake! I became absolutely inconsolable, constantly crying, finally refusing to eat. I was told some years ago that I probably had an untreated traumatic stress disorder of some kind. This term cannot possibly convey the nature of the experience I had. It was, I now know, a journey into the Celtic Otherworld.

The small humanoid creatures, very similar to gnomes (I had never seen a garden gnome, and when I first did I was immediately reminded of the experience; nor had I seen any Disney animations), all wearing pointed caps, led me through sylvan glades beside crystal-clear streams and waterfalls – the first waterfalls I ever saw, in fact. There were caves and tunnels. There was no speaking, but the little fellows were always chuckling and laughing, and I was the object of their amusement – which seemed so inappropriate, considering my intense distress. Time had ceased to have any real meaning, and this was somehow soothing. I felt hungry, and the pangs of hunger reminded me of my mother. Where was she? The small fellows only ridiculed me even more and I became very angry. There was a little house in the distance which I hoped might be our cottage. I realised, though, that it could not be, because the door was a different colour – it was red, ours was green. The little fellows led me in, and there, enthroned, was the most beautiful lady in all creation. I knew that she was the mother of all mothers, the 'Queen of Heaven'.

She looked reproachfully at the gnome-like fellows, but they seemed unconcerned. I described her as an 'Indian' lady, because the only people from abroad I had yet seen were the recent immigrants from India and Pakistan. I think what I meant was that she was from a darker race than ours. Her hair was raven black, and her eyes a deep brown, slightly Asiatic, with a remarkable penetrative quality. I should say now that she was like the depictions I have seen of Egyptian goddesses. I was transfixed, and although I knew I had intruded and she was preoccupied, I also knew she could get me home. She was all-powerful, with command over all things *material*. She never spoke to me but I heard her words in my own head. She reached out her hands to me, and I sank into her embrace. She wore rich furs, sable or ermine; I was probably unconsciously aware of my mother's fur coat.

She would grant me one wish – anything I desired – before she sent me home. I *knew* that anything she promised me would be fulfilled. I told her what it was I desired – a toy, but it was no ordinary toy. It was a toy I had *imagined*, a toy which not only did not exist but, unless magic was real, could not exist. My uncle eventually teased out of me what it was. For some months my parents asked in every toy shop in the area if such a toy could be found, only to be greeted with condescending smiles from shop assistants. Nothing of the kind existed, unfortunately. But finally, a young girl overheard my mother asking about it in another shop, she said that actually such a toy *did* exist. I think it was so specialised that it had to be ordered from a store in either Birmingham or London, I forget which. I was delighted to discover it under my bed one night. I no longer have it – but like so much that is gone, I wish I did.

My uncle died of a brain haemorrhage not long afterwards. I discovered him slumped in his chair one morning. The 'death rattle' was sounding in his throat. I froze, and in that moment my consciousness and his merged somehow. I turned on my heels and ran for my father and found him shaving. I told him my uncle was making 'snoring noises' and was dying. My father dismissed this as an old man dozing in his chair; he was due to retire from the colliery any day. But when we returned there was an ambulance, and old Annie, his neighbour, was stooping over a mattress they had set him on to get him outside. I knew then that our lives were never going to be the same again. My grandmother now had total control of the properties, and so we had no alternative but to move; my health was the issue which concerned the authorities, and we moved a few miles away, to a new housing development in a small, tight-knit village.

From the start we were unsettled there. My father was very unhappy, and despite all mod-cons and central heating, my mother disliked the house. My illness actually deteriorated, and in our first winter there I had a traumatic accident which almost resulted in having my right leg amputated. I was off school for much of the time, but fortunately I was a voracious reader from a very early age. My grandmother visited weekly, and always brought gifts of lavishly illustrated books – invariably about mythology or history or both. Although I was hopelessly behind in other respects, in this rather narrow field I became quite an advanced student. As my father became more and more miserable, my mother's health, which was always quite fragile, began to suffer. She became painfully thin and was in agony from a duodenal ulcer which she feared may burst at any time. She became very interested in spiritual mediumship at this point, and befriended a lady named Mrs H. who had similar predilections.

My father had given up smoking, and he forbade my mother to smoke also. He was very authoritarian. My mother used her friendship with Mrs H. as an excuse to smoke cigarettes, which she continued to do until they killed her. I know one of her objectives was to try to contact the spirit of my late great-uncle, but I was never involved on those occasions. I would often accompany my mother, and so was aware that she was smoking, which I strongly disapproved of. Mrs H. was quite an accomplished hypnotist. She claimed Romany blood and spoke with a pronounced West Country burr. She managed to convince me to swear an oath that I would not tell my father about the smoking – or he may forbid the visits. To this I agreed, and was rewarded with delicious cakes. These meetings were really just a kind of feminine comradeship; tea, cakes, occultism and cigarettes on a rainy afternoon. But soon I became involved in the seances and various other activities – a bit like Arthur Dee had done hundreds of years before. Planchettes and Ouija boards were the main method for contacting the spirits. Tarot cards were used, I recall, and there were many books and magazines about astrology. I developed a talent for the mediumship, but I was always aware of the potential for trickery.

One thing I do recall vividly. A frequent contact was the spirit of a man my mother had worked with a few years before when she was a chambermaid in a hotel. The man was the chef there, and claimed that he was descended from the 'Witches of Pendle' in Lancashire. He was definitely psychic. One day he told the chambermaids to go anywhere they wished, have a cigarette, and hold a conversation. He could not leave the kitchen and was observed. They did as he asked, and held a silly conversation on an obscure matter – which he repeated word for word when they returned. He drank and smoked a lot, and unfortunately died of heart failure quite young. He 'came through' often, but only if I was there. Mrs H. convinced my mother that I had inherited some kind of psychic power, and I was not discouraged from experimenting, in fact rather the opposite.

Mrs H. eventually moved to be nearer relatives. For my mother this was the last straw. She 'psyched herself up' one morning to resolve all our problems. In the space of a morning she found herself a new job working at a local mansion. The employer had a cottage to rent, very old-fashioned, which was difficult to let because of its extremely isolated location in a sinister wood, and also because the place was notoriously haunted. But the rent was very low, and would be fixed during the terms of her employment. It was the perfect place for us. The only problem was the evil reputation. It was, and probably still is, spooky, and I was now ten years old, with an active imagination. My parents' attitude was the same as ever. If there were spirits we must face them out.

The history behind it all was of a foul murder which had been perpetrated there. In December 1812, a household servant in Ombersley overheard a conversation that at a certain time a gentleman was to withdraw a large sum in banknotes and other valuables from a bank in Stourbridge. The murderer, William Howe, arranged to be away on that day, and travelled to Stourbridge where he observed Squire Benjamin Robins leave the bank. He then lurked in Fir-Tree Lane, as it was then known, out on the bleak Whittington Heath. Soon Robins appeared walking home through the wood. Howe accosted him, and then produced a pistol and shot him. He made away with his ill-gotten gains, leaving Robins for dead, but incredibly he was still alive – with a pistol ball lodged in his spine. He crawled home in the snow, to the hall where my mother was later employed. Sometime afterwards he died, but he gave a vague account of the attack.

Howe was eventually apprehended by the 'Bow Street Runners'. He was tried at Stafford Assizes and sentenced to death by hanging. But there was a final twist. As an example to others, Howe's body was to be returned to the scene of the crime and hung in chains on a gibbet there. This was either the last, or the penultimate use of the gibbet in England. Large crowds came to see the body set up beside the road. Not long afterwards stories began to be told about 'Gibbet Wood', as it became known. They were not pleasant to hear, but my parents took the view that we should learn all there was to know about the incident, confront the issue, and learn to live with it. In our first winter there, the disturbances began.

It was a Sunday evening. We had just watched London Weekend Television's *Upstairs, Downstairs*, I recall, and had gone to bed when there was a furious pounding at the back door right below my bedroom window. It was so loud that it alerted my parents across the landing and my father came into my room, opened the window and challenged whoever it was to show themselves in pretty profane language. There was no one there, and when he searched outside there was no one to be seen. These incidents became regular, usually when my mother and I were alone in the house at night, and went on for over a year. My father's work meant he never got in much before 10 p.m., often later. There was never anyone there when we opened the door. The only viable escape route was into a sand quarry behind the house, but there was no cover there and no tracks were ever discovered. There were very odd characters around, and I had my suspicions about one person, but it was uncanny how they always managed to escape. Eventually a guard dog was found, and from then on the incidents ceased, which inclines me to think it must have been a mortal fiend. In fact, as my father always taught, it was mortal humanity which gave most cause for concern.

A problem, relatively minor, was that the wood was a magnet for cranks, courting couples, witch covens and thrill seekers, all of whom I would encounter on my nocturnal walks home. I became very adept at concealment because I had to outwit the local gamekeeper who made us walk the long way round instead of through the haunted part, the quickest way. From what I could observe of these people they seemed merely silly, rather than dangerous. One evening I came across a group of teenagers who were *really* scared. One girl was hysterical and babbled something about seeing a 'demon'. They were not drunk or otherwise intoxicated, and the place where they saw the apparition was very near the haunted part of the wood. There were countless spooky tales of Howe's dread form stalking the place.

In all our time there, almost a quarter of a century, I only once experienced something terrifying, which I cannot explain. In fact we grew very used to the place, and spent our happiest days there. But the point I am trying to make is that such an upbringing was slightly unusual, and as I grew older I did resent this. The sinister atmosphere cast a kind of 'spell', which was almost palpable. I began to intuit that the key to this very peculiar atmosphere was that it long preceded the events of December 1812. The heath nearby is a boundary between two ancient British tribes, a 'ghost fence', with many ancient burial mounds. The practice of excarnation, leaving corpses to rot in the open, was particularly associated with the 'Cult of the Dead'. In short, there were entities and spirits already haunting the place which I think were misidentified as Howe. In a sense, the everyday world outside seemed somehow vapid and unreal – but I was young and wanted to be 'normal' in a commonplace 'reality'. But one thing I had learned; there was a type of psychical 'refraction' involved, a natural outgrowth of an ancestral culture.

My adolescence was very difficult indeed, and I was certainly socially maladjusted and increasingly delinquent. Much trouble soon followed. I decided that the only way to answer my conflicted spiritual issues was to see what worked experimentally, as it were. Even when my interests became quite dangerous, my parents, though they were very concerned, never interfered. As I babbled about various exotic and complex foreign cults they tolerated my rather grandiose speculations, but I always had the feeling that they thought it in *bad taste* to discuss these matters, just in the same way that it was 'bad form' to discuss conventional religion. It was clear to me that they completely accepted the notion of an incarnated god-man. This was almost *de rigueur* for their private philosophy. The difference was that they saw the potential for this in every human, and indeed animal or vegetable life form. In short, even the last 'Muggletonians' could not have been more adrift from exegetic convention of all forms than I was.

It was a revelation to discover that there were *other* people who also experienced magical phenomena. This opened up the exciting prospect of group work, and over the years I have had the privilege of meeting many fascinating characters. But these experiments, though they brought illumination and comradeship, sometimes ended in catastrophe. In magic, everything has its price. Following one too many of these traumatic incidents, I decided to walk away from the 'Magic Theatre'. As Hesse said in his *Steppenwolf*, it is 'not for everyone'.

But every ten or twelve years or so an intrusion of the magical consciousness supervenes, which usually comes quite out of the blue. I can no more escape my magical history than my country can. A motto of the alchemical art is *Solve et Coagula*. *Solve* is the analysis or breaking down of constituent elements, *Coagula* is their synthesis into new elements. The spirit of our age has been *Solve*. But we are 'divided for love's sake, for the chance of union'. As Tolkien's wizard Gandalf says, 'He that breaks a thing to find out what it is has left the path of wisdom.' I regret to say that, like Coleridge's 'Ancient Mariner', I have often been guilty of this. I have 'shot the albatross', left the path of wisdom, but the sad truth is that we all do it. Perhaps the wisdom path can be found again, the route to the magic land so long prophesied, if only we can summon the will? The doing will be desperate, but we must make the attempt. It is a noble and magical tradition we inherit, a capacity to invent, create, to 'make greater' like the magi of antiquity. This astonishing innovation and industry did not come about by accident, it was a unique product of Britain and its magical and mythical history. We may perhaps concur with the Rosicrucian Kenneth Mackenzie:

> Let us then honour such men who seek, with devotion and humility, to harmonise the two sides of the great veil of Isis, which no man has, in mortal life, ever been able to lift. Dimly, under the fringe, scintillations of the life beyond may be seen, and the rapt vision of the seer ... may perhaps be gifted enough to behold the outlines of the glory which burns for ever in the presence of the Ancient of Days.

Select Bibliography

Annales Cambriae

Ashe, G., *The Quest for Arthur's Britain*, Pall Mall, London, 1968

Bagshawe, R. W., *Roman Roads*, Aylesbury, 1979

Barfield, O., 'Imagination and Inspiration' in Hopper, S. R., and Muller, D. L., *Interpretation: The Poetry of Meaning*, New York, 1967

Barfield, O., *History in English Words*, London, 1926

Barfield, O. *Poetic Diction: A Study in Meaning*, Barfield Press, Oxford, 2010 edn

Barfield, O., *Saving the Appearances: A Study in Idolatry*, London, 1957

Bates, B., *The Real Middle-Earth: Magic and Mystery in the Dark Ages*, Sidgwick & Jackson, London, 2002

Bede, *The Ecclesiastical History of the English People*

Berresford-Ellis, P., *A Brief History of the Druids*, Robinson, London, 1994

Beowulf

Bergier, J. & L. Pauwels, *The Morning of the Magicians*, Paris, 1960

Blake, W., *Milton*, 1804

Blake, W., *Poetical Sketches*, 1783

Bulwer-Lytton, E., *The Coming Race*, London, 1871

Caesar, J., *War Commentaries of Caesar*, Amereon, 1989

Caesar, J., *Gallic Wars* Book Six

Campbell, T., *The Three Sorrows of Irish Storytelling*, Ogham, Dublin, 1986

Canu Heledd

Capp, B., in McGregor, J. F. & B. Reay (eds), *Radical Religion in the English Revolution*, Oxford, 1986

Carpenter, H., *J. R. R. Tolkien: A Biography*, Allen & Unwin, London, 1977

Charles-Edwards, T., *Wales and the Britons 350–650*, Oxford, 2012

Chapman, J., *Quest for Dion Fortune*, Weiser, York Beach, 1993

Chatwin, B., *The Songlines*, Random House, London, 2012

Chatwin, B., *Under the Sun*, Vintage, London, 2011

Chitham, E., *The Black Country*, Longman, London, 1972

Churton, T., *Aleister Crowley: The Biography*, Watkins, London, 2011

Cohn, N., *Warrant for Genocide*, Serif, London, 2005

Collins, A. *The Cygnus Mystery*, London, 2006

Crowley, A., *Magick: In Theory and Practice*, Guild, London, 1986

Crowley, A., *The Book of the Law*, 1904

Crowley, A., *The Book of Thoth*, Weiser, York Beach, 1988

Cunliffe, B., *The Extraordinary Voyage of Pytheas the Greek*, Walker & Co., London, 2002

Davies, R. R., *The Age of Conquest: Wales 1063-1415*, Oxford, 1987

Dee, J., *Britanici Imperii Limites*, 1576

Dio, C., *History*, Loeb, 1972 edn

Dixon, J. J., *Goddess and Grail: The Battle for King Arthur's Promised Land*, McFarland, 2017

Dudley, D., *Metallum Martis*, 1665

Evans-Wentz, W. Y., *The Fairy-Faith in Celtic Countries*, Henry Frowde, London, 1911

Fastidius, *De Vita Christiana*

Fortune, D., *Psychic Self-Defence*, 1930

Fortune, D., *The Magical Battle of Britain*, Golden Gate, Bradford-on-Avon, 1993

Frazer, J. G., *The Golden Bough: A Study in Magic and Religion*, Dover, 2003 edn

Fromm, E., *The Fear of Freedom*, Routledge, London, 1995 edn

Geoffrey of Monmouth, *Historia Regum Britanniae*, 1136

Gibbon, A., *The Mystery of Jack of Kent and the Fate of Owain Glyndwr*, The History Press, Stroud, 2004

Gildas, *De Excidio et Conquestu Britanniae*

Govinda, A., *Foundations of Tibetan Mysticism*, B. I., New Delhi, 1981

Grant, K., 'Dion Fortune' in *Man, Myth and Magic*, Marshall Cavendish, 1970

Graves, R., *The White Goddess: A Historical Grammar of Poetic Myth*, Faber & Faber, London, 1961

Guest, C. (ed.), *Mabinogion*, 1906

Heath, R. & J. Michell, *The Measure of Albion: The Lost Science of Prehistoric Britain*, Bluestone, St Dogmael's, 2004

Hesse, H., *Steppenwolf*, 1927

Higgins, G., *The Celtic Druids*, 1829

Higgs, C., *Dud Dudley and Abraham Darby: Forging New Links*, Black Country Society, 2012

Hopkins, M., *The Discovery of Witches*, 1647

Holmes, R., *Coleridge*, Oxford, 1982

Houseman, A. E., *A Shropshire Lad*, 1896

Hughes, T. & F. Godwin, *Remains of Elmet*, Faber & Faber, 1979

Joyce, J., *Dubliners*, 1914

King, F., *Modern Ritual Magic: The Rise of Western Occultism*, Prism, Bridport, 1989

Knight, C., *Blood Relations – Menstruation and the Origins of Human Culture*, Yale, 1991

Kramer, H. & J. Sprenger, *Malleus Maleficarum*, Speyer, 1486

Layamon & F. Madden (trans.), *Brut*, London, 1847

Levi, E., *Dogme et Rituel de la Haute Magic*, Paris, 1854

Lewis, C. S., *The Four Loves*, London, 1960

Lewis, C. S., *Surprised by Joy*, London, 1990

Lhuyd, E., *Archaeologica Britannica*, 1707

Malory, T., *Morte d'Arthur*, London, 1485

Markale, J., *Women of the Celts*, Inner Traditions, 1986

Markale, J., *The Celts: Uncovering the Mythic and Historic Origins of Western Culture*, Inner Traditions, Rochester, 1993

Markham, C., *Pytheas the Discoverer of Britain*, London, 1893

Martin, F. W., *The Life of John Clare*, Macmillan, London, 1964 edn

Mathers, S. L. M. & A. Crowley (eds), *The Goetia: The Lesser Key of Solomon the King*, RedWheel/Weiser, Newburyport, 1996 edn

McLynn, F., *King Richard, King John and the Wars of Conquest*, Vintage, London, 2007

Moffat, A., *The Sea Kingdoms: The History of Celtic Britain and Ireland*, Birlinn, Edinburgh, 2008

Morganwg, I., *The Druid's Prayer*

Morris, J., *The Age of Arthur: A History of the British Isles 350–650*, London, 1973

Nankivell, J., *Saint Wilfred*, SPCK, London, 2002

Nennius, *Historia Brittonum*

O'Donaghue, J., *Anam Cara: Spiritual Wisdom from the Celtic World*, Bantam, London, 1997

Orwell, G., *The Lion and the Unicorn*, Secker & Warburg, London, 1941

Piggott, S., *The Druids*, Edinburgh, 1968

Poulton-Smith, A., *Ley Lines Across the Midlands*, The History Press, Stroud, 2009

Raine, K., *William Blake*, Thames & Hudson, London, 1970

Rawson, P., *Tantra: The Indian Cult of Ecstasy*, Thames & Hudson, London, 1979

Reilly, R. J., *Romantic Religion*, University of Georgia, Athens, 1971

Robb, G., *The Ancient Paths: Discovering the Lost Map of Celtic Europe*, Picador, London, 2013

Rousseau, J. J., *The Social Contract*, 1762

Russell, M. & S. Laycock, *UnRoman Britain: Exposing the Great Myth of Britannia*, The History Press, Stroud, 2010

Russell, J. B. & B. Alexander, *A New History of Witchcraft, Sorcerers, Heretics and Pagans*, Thames & Hudson, London, 2007

Shaw, G. B., *Common Sense About the War*, 1914

Sims-Williams, P., *Religion and Literature in Western England 600–800*, Cambridge, 2005

Southcott, J., *The Strange Effects of Faith*, 1801

Stenton, F. M., *Anglo-Saxon England*, Oxford, 1970

Tacitus, P. C., *Agricola*, c. AD 80

The Anglo-Saxon Chronicle

The Black Book of Carmarthen

The Cloud of Unknowing

Thompson, E. P., *The Making of the English Working Class*, Gollancz, London, 1963

Thompson, E. P., *Witness Against the Beast*, Cambridge, 1993

Underhill, E., *Mysticism: The Nature and Development of Spiritual Consciousness*, Oxford, 1999 edn

Waddell, J., *The Prehistoric Archaeology of Ireland*, Wicklow, 2000

Wall, J. C., *Devils*, 1904

Waite, A. E., *The Secret Doctrine in Israel*, 1913

Watkins, A., *The Old Straight Track*, 1976 edn

Weil, S., *A War of Religions*, 1943

Welch, M., *Anglo-Saxon England*, Batsford, London, 1992

White, M., *Isaac Newton: The Last Sorcerer*, Fourth Estate, London, 1997

William of Malmesbury, *Gesta Regum Anglorum*, 1125

Woolley, B., *The Queen's Conjuror: The Science and Magic of Doctor Dee*, HarperCollins, London, 2001

Yates, F., *The Occult Philosophy in the Elizabethan Age*, Routledge, London, 1979

Yeates, S. J., *The Tribe of Witches: The Religion of the Dobunni and Hwicce*, Oxbow, Oxford, 2008

Zosimus, *Historia Nova*

Acknowledgements

I wish to express my thanks to the many kind people who assisted me during the difficult time when I was writing up the book, and especially to John and Judy Gibbons, without whose generosity the project would not have been completed. Thanks to Nigel Parker for permission to use photographs, the Gardener family, Edwin Llowarch, and many others too numerous to mention. I am grateful to the British Library for permission to use copyright material in the book. Individual photographers are credited alongside the captions. Every effort has been made to seek permission for copyright material. However, if I have inadvertently used copyright material without permission/ acknowledgement I apologise and will make the necessary correction at the first opportunity.

Index